Putting a Song on Top of It

The poet is put to death . . . because he wants to make language perceive what it doesn't want to say, provide it with its matter independently of the sign, and free it from denotation. For it is this *eminently parodic* gesture that changes the system.

—**Julia Kristeva,** *Desire in Language*

And all these problems of *identity*, as we so foolishly say nowadays. —**Jacques Derrida,** *Monolingualism of the Other, or, the Prosthesis of Origin*

Expression and

Identity on the

San Carlos Apache

Reservation

Putting a

Song

on Top of It

David W. Samuels

The University of Arizona Press   *Tucson*

The University of Arizona Press

© 2004 The Arizona Board of Regents

LIBRARY OF CONGRESS CATALOGING-IN-PUBLICATION DATA

Samuels, David William, 1957–

Putting a song on top of it : expression and identity on the San Carlos
Apache Reservation / David W. Samuels.

p. cm.

Includes bibliographical references and index.

ISBN-13: 978-0-8165-2379-5 (cloth : alk. paper)—ISBN-10: 0-8165-2379-7
ISBN-13: 978-0-8165-2601-7 (pbk. : alk. paper)—ISBN-10: 0-8165-2601-x

1. Apache Indians—Arizona—San Carlos Indian Reservation—Songs and
music. 2. Apache Indians—Arizona—San Carlos Indian Reservation—
Social life and customs. 3. Country music—Arizona—San Carlos Indian
Reservation. 4. Popular music—Arizona—San Carlos Indian Reservation.
5. San Carlos Indian Reservation (Ariz.)—Social life and customs. I. Title.

E99.A6S28 2004

305.897'25079154—dc22

2004017986

Publication of this book is made possible in part by the proceeds of a
permanent endowment created with the assistance of a Challenge Grant
from the National Endowment for the Humanities, a federal agency.

Manufactured in the United States of America on acid-free, archival-
quality paper containing a minimum of 50% post-consumer waste and
processed chlorine free.

11   10   09   08   07   06   6   5   4   3   2

To the women who raised me:

Edith, Agatha, Gloria, Era, and Esther

And to the musicians whose silenced voices

sing throughout these pages:

Ross Jr., J. B., and Big Bell

Contents

Illustrations

Prologue

This book is about real people and their real lives. They are not typological representatives of "a culture." Many of the people in this book gave me permission to use their real names because, some of them said, it would have felt less real to read about people whose names were unrecognizable. And the fact is that real people have changes in their real lives. When I took the next-to-last draft to the San Carlos Apache Reservation during the summer of 2003, it was clear to a number of the people featured in it that some water had gone under the bridge since I had begun the writing and rewriting that had led to that point.

Writing preserves—even writing that shuns the "ethnographic present" and all its false rhetoric of timelessness. Yet I feel as though I need to make clear at the outset that people's lives change. Over the years of writing and rewriting, some of the people represented in this book have died. Others have become born again. People have gotten married, divorced, remarried, graduated from school, raised families. In fact, some people gave me permission to use their names in the book precisely because they want readers to know that lives *can* change. The events depicted in this book took place between 1994 and 1999, mostly between 1994 and 1996.

Putting a Song on Top of It

The blues is an art of ambiguity, an assertion of the irrepressibly human over all circumstances, whether created by others or by one's own human failing. —**Ralph Ellison,** *Shadow and Act*

Introduction

The Problem with Identity

Marshall had been asking me for some time if I had ever been to Top of the World. I thought I had—there's a place called Top of the World near the reservation, in the higher mountains west of Miami. But Marshall was talking about another place, to the south. So one day, after a trip to Globe to get his kids some ice cream, Marshall, his wife, their two youngest children, and I turned south and drove up into the Pinals. As we rose higher in elevation, Marshall pointed out the things you could see. On a clear day, he said, you can see Tucson. As we drove into the pines, the air became cooler, a breeze kicked up, and everyone's mood brightened. Suddenly Marshall launched into a performance. It was his Old Apache Man, a character whose presence was marked in his voice—by an increased volume, exaggerated nasality, and high-pitched tonality. Marshall shouted:

hééééla!	héla!
dat'éhé nadaaghaa dą'!	when we used to wander all over!
nadaalzhee dą'!	when we used to hunt!
Indian nshlįį dą'!	when I used to be an Indian!

Everyone laughed, and his wife said, "*Used* to be an Indian? What are you *now*?" And Marshall, a wry smile creasing his face, said, "Now I'm just a civilized *nnee*." (Please refer to the "San Carlos Apache Pronunciation Guide" and the "Transcription Guide.")

Marshall's character in this episode is clearly performing some kind of Apache identity. But what kind? Filled with unexpected shifts and twists, it is difficult to pin down. The exchange between Marshall and his wife involved code-switching between Apache and English, to be sure. But it also involved cunning reversals and almost willful undermining of expectations. Rather than uniformly using Apache language to point to an Apache identity, Marshall switched to the English word *Indian* in order to complete his image of the old man reminiscing about the old days. But that wasn't the end of it. When Marshall's wife pointed out the confounding anomaly of his first code-switch, Marshall responded with another, using the Apache word for people/Apaches/Indians, *nnee*, in his English response about the way things are now.

In Marshall's performance, nobody gets off scot-free, least of all the anthropologist who wants to link Apache identity to things identifiably Apache. The multiple layers of the performance uncovered complications in the naturalized or expected relationships between cultural expressions and their possible associations. Marshall productively used simultaneity and ambiguity to create signs of identity that pointed in multiple directions at once. In the tautness of his joking frame, he made manifest the clash of languages and expressions that churn within the history of the San Carlos Apache Reservation. In short, Marshall's performance, like so many others I witnessed in the communities of the reservation, presents us with a complicated and ambiguous image of contemporary Apache "identity."[1]

Why this should be so—why these ambiguous images are meaningful and how they are produced, circulated, and interpreted—is the subject of this book. How are recognizable identities fashioned out of ambiguous and contradictory experience? And how are they recognized? I address these questions through an exploration of contemporary expressive practices on the reservation. Living at the crossroads of a number of local discourses about culture, heritage, and identity—popular culture and tradition, Apache and non-Apache, technologically mediated and face-to-face, modern and historical, realistic and nostalgic—these expressions open up questions about how the material ambiguity of experience produces performances of identity filled with as many questions as statements. Do these expressions of identity resolve the contradictions of everyday experience on the reservation or, rather, highlight them for public scrutiny and response?

Anthropologists and other scholars investigating the question of contemporary cultural expression and identity must grapple with the ongoing effects of globalism and colonialism in the heterogeneous but interconnected "global cultural ecumene" (Foster 1991). Anthropologists have made important contributions to rethinking social life in ways that avoid the pitfalls of flattening culture into bounded units faced with either/or choices about "traditionalists" versus "progressives" or "maintenance" versus "change" (often glossed as "loss" or "disintegration"). The produced nature of culture—the creative negotiation of personal and social identities within shifting fields of social power, history, and imagination—has led to the envisioning of cultures as open-ended, constantly being made and remade, worked and reworked. Within that context, the relationships between cultures and identities are not fixed. Rather, identities are emergent, produced out of the practices and expressive forms of everyday life. Traditions are not simply handed along from one generation to the next. Part of their enduring power comes from the possibility for their strategic reinvention in order to speak strongly in new social and political contexts.[2] The Native American[3] powwow is a prime example of this, as is the emergence of new forms of Navajo weaving and Pueblo pottery within the capitalist contexts of trading posts and tourism. Indeed, for a number of Native American communities, the very question of group membership or even of group recognition can be the stakes in the cultural politics of negotiating the interpretation of symbolic practices.[4]

A bright thread running through these various ways of reposition-

ing the question of culture and identity is the issue of indexicality—
how particular expressions come to point to their cultural associations.
For decades, the equal-but-separate philosophy of twentieth-century
Americanist relativism solved the riddle of cultural expression and
identity through the graces of a transparent approach to indexicality.
One could find a diagnostic of "a" culture in that culture's expressions. Navajos spoke/speak Navajo, Cree spoke/speak Cree. Iroquois
lived/live in longhouses, Pequots in wigwams, Navajos in hogans, Hopi
in pueblos, and Cheyenne in teepees. Western Apaches wore/wear
moccasins with upturned toes. Eastern woodland beadwork was/is
floral and representational in nature, Plains beadwork more geometri-
cal and abstract.

The difficulty here is not that these diagnostics are "wrong," but
that their emphasis on a particular kind of continuity makes them
clumsy tools for exploring contemporary expressions of cultural identity. As symbols become moored to new docks, anthropologists often
find themselves cast in the role of the harbor patrol. Analogy continues
to be the most comfortable mode of analysis—expression A is to culture A as expression B is to culture B. Confronted with, say, a Native
American representative, sitting on a sofa in a ranch-style stucco house,
wearing a designer outfit, television to one side, crucifix on the wall,
speaking in English about how important it is to her to be traditional,
anxiety overtakes culture, disintegrating analysis into a fretful struggle
over contamination and what is really real.

This anxiety is often reduced through the discovery of or desire for
continuity. James Clifford (1988), in his essay about Mashpee Native
identity, is certainly not alone in admitting to confusion and disappointment when faced with American Indians who don't wear the right uniform. In our attempts to understand the contamination by explaining it,
we have consistently drawn on a continuing debt to philology (Samuels
1999). Metaphors of chronology, biology, and grammar also continue
to offer us powerful tools for discussing the proper organization of elements that allow meaningful information to be communicated and ex-
tracted from cultural expressions.

But if we are to understand, for example, how such popular musicians as Merle Haggard, Bob Marley, the Eagles, Led Zeppelin, Slayer,
or ZZ Top can become the raw materials for the expression of Apache
identity, we need an approach to indexicality that admits the ambiguous nature of the pointing gesture. To put this another way: a multiplicity of cultural practices circulate in the contemporary reservation

community and are enacted on a daily basis. Each of these practices indexes, in some way, the social history of the community. Some can be
traced to what one might still want to call "Apache tradition." Others
cannot because they have been institutionally imposed in the wake of
the cultural, linguistic, religious, economic, and educational ideologies
and policies of various military and governmental bureaucracies over
the past centuries. The attitude of transparent indexicality locates expressions of Apache identity in the former: those forms that can be
identified as Apache in "origin." I have no doubt about the importance
of this relationship. And an explanation of why this goes here whereas
that goes there and why some things do not fit is certainly a productive
project.[5] Yet some non-Apache forms—basketball or Angus Young guitar solos, for instance—are also sites for the play of deeply felt expressions of Apache identity. These forms also index the social history of the
community and thus help people express the complex layers produced
out of centuries of cultural expropriation, resistance, accommodation,
negotiation, maintenance, and shift. If the deep and affective meaningfulness of such popular cultural forms as hard country, album rock, and
reggae presents a problematic representation of Apache identity, it is
in part because our sense of indexicality has made us sensitive to the
anomalies rather than to the histories. At the same time, we don't like
being in the position of Dorothy standing at a fork in the yellow-brick
road, being told by the Scarecrow, "Of course, people do go both ways!"
Our sense of cultural interpretation has made us resistant to ambiguity.[6]

What are the quintessential indexical markers of a "culture"? Language? Religion? Custom? People on the San Carlos Reservation hold
a wide range of opinions about the importance of these things, not to
mention a range of practices. The evangelical Miracle Church in the
Chinatown section of Peridot takes a dim view of traditional Apache
religion. But even traditionalists told me that if I wanted to hear eloquent Apache spoken, I needed to go to Chinatown on Sunday and
hear Pastor Harris preach. One of the people responsible for me during
my stay on the reservation was Jeanette Cassa, the leader of the Elders
Cultural Advisory Council. In our first meeting, when I was explaining the broad outlines of my project, Mrs. Cassa was taken with the
"everyday life" aspect of it. It was difficult, she told me, to explain to
people that "culture" didn't just mean "traditional religion." You see
these women walking down the street, she explained, and they're wear-
ing camp dresses and speaking to each other in Apache and eating frybread and beans, but they say, "I'm not interested in Apache culture be-

cause I'm a Christian." Then again, are camp dresses and frybread and beans themselves traditional? Or are they the produced result of contact with Spanish and Mexican colonists? The location of cultural identities is not fully addressed by resorting to notions of everyday practice, either. High school students who don't speak a word of Apache nevertheless think of Apache as their language and consider English, the language they use every day, to be in truth someone else's.

There is no denying the moral authority of tradition on the reservation. But traditional practices are not isolated from the sociopolitical context of material and ideological domination in which they are performed. The problem of contemporary cultural identity is not solved by separating the one from the other in order to make sense of it. In that vein, I echo Ben Rampton's observation that "it would be helpful if code-switching research relaxed its commitment to discovering coherence and systematicity in code-switching, and attended more closely to incongruity and contradiction" (1998:290)—that is, if researchers would note the things that infect the purity of choices between various means of making a statement. Part of the affecting power of Marshall's performance related earlier stems from the ways in which it simultaneously does and does not make sense. Combining some of Antonio Gramsci's (1971) insights about "contradictory consciousness" with Mikhail Bakhtin's (1981, 1984) notion of the "double-voiced utterance," we can investigate identities that are "ambivalent and multifaceted" (Moyer 1998: 216), as ambiguous and contradictory as the disparate discourse forms used in expressing them.

Following this line of thought, my argument in the present work is that culture, in its contemporary manifestations on the reservation, takes on the nature of a pun—the structure of a sign that points in multiple directions at once. I find this analogy preferable to "code-switching" for a number of reasons. First, it makes full use of the indexical ambiguity, the simultaneity of the pointing gestures, at the heart of contemporary cultural identities on the reservation. The idea of punning brings out the "anomaly, incongruity, and contradiction" (Rampton 1998:306) that code-switching research sometimes sidesteps. Second, it avoids the metaphor of *code* as well as the overtones of lexicon and sound-meaning relationships perhaps unavoidably carried by that term. The figure of the pun thus opens up some possibilities for making links between everyday conversation and artful, poetic performances, or between "language as such" (Benjamin 1996) and other forms of cultural expression. I do not claim that the analogy of culture-as-pun is unproblematic or even less problematic than others that I could have chosen, but I do find it more productive for the issue at hand.

In *Philosophy of Nonsense* (1994), Jean-Jacques Lecercle proposes a continuum of poetic figures, with tautology at one end and metaphor at the other. In the former, identities are presented as differences. A tautology is a construction in which an identity is patently obvious but presented as though it were a distinction—Lecercle uses as an example the French nursery rhyme about Monsieur de la Palisse, "who is famous for having remained alive till the day he died" (1994:64). Metaphors, at the other end of the spectrum, reverse this relationship: they assert an identity between things that at a basic referential level are different. "What is so attractive in tautology," Lecercle writes, "is that it is necessarily true. What is so dangerous about metaphor is that it is always obviously false" (1994:64).

Puns, in Lecercle's rendering, are located somewhere in the middle. They open the possibility for proliferation of meaning, but they are not open the way metaphors are. "True metaphor is never entirely decidable, it offers a multiplicity of potential meanings, between which I cannot always choose" (1994:66). Puns exist in the sonic, embodied materiality of utterances and point to something obvious about language—the fact of homophony, that one sound image can refer to multiple concepts. This may be one reason they are considered a "low" form of humor. They potentially undermine the ideology of languages as rational systems of reference. The figure of the pun, I argue, also bears political weight, in part because of its marginalized relations to metaphor as a poetic figure. In addition, however, Apaches who speak English, love U2, and insist that they are not forgetting who they are may find it important to point out this "obvious" fact. That the same sign can point toward multiple meanings creates important openings for crafting personal and cultural identities.

These questions about the complexity and ambiguity of indexical relations raise related questions about rethinking issues of cultural continuity. Surely, one justification for saying that cultural expressions index (point to) their respective cultures is carried by the argument that there is continuity: that Western Apaches wear moccasins with upturned toes because their parents, grandparents, great-grandparents, and on down the line also wore moccasins with upturned toes. And, conversely—it sounds more circular than it is—the intergenerational continuity of the practice is what attaches it indexically to Apacheness. In other words, a practice is indexical of a culture precisely because it is also an icon: an instance of a form that is substantially the same as other instances of that form stretching back in time. The sense of iconicity between discrete instances of an expression—"the sway of pattern," as B. L. Whorf put it (1956:261)—naturalizes its indexical relations with a culture.

The appeal to continuity thus makes an important argument about history. My interest, then, in the ambiguity of indexical relationships might be taken by some as an assertion that symbolic material nowadays just floats haphazardly across the reservation. Without continuity, don't the moorings just slip away? I argue that they do not—but the question is, Does the indexicality always trump the history, or might the relationship be more open and creative? The task at hand, then, is not to dispense with the idea of indexical grounding, but to trace out the complex ways in which contemporary cultural expressions are grounded.

I take, as one starting point, the central tenet of Greg Urban's discourse-centered approach: "that culture is localized in concrete, publicly accessible signs, the most important of which are actually occurring instances of discourse" (1991:1), and that the analysis of cultural phenomena begins with the detailed examination of these concrete discourse instances. I am less convinced than Urban, perhaps, that continuity is to be located in the empirical form of the discourse instances. His more recent work on the circulation of culture (Urban 2001) is resonant here, for the movement of popular culture forms on the reservation are clearly an example of what he calls "metaculture." At the same time, "cultural continuity" on the reservation is not found only in formal parallelism—especially in what Urban calls "macroparallelism" (1991:79–104). Indeed, such an approach may be untenable in the massively disrupted and commodified context of the San Carlos Reservation.

That is not to deny for a moment that cultural forms have histories. But the San Carlos Apache Reservation also has a history. In the wake of that history, it is not necessarily the case that a sense of identity will always find its most powerful links to the material continuity of discourse forms. The task I set out for myself, then, is to find ways of writing about contemporary expressions of identity that take seriously the desire to assert continuity in the wake of cultural genocide, but without surrendering the possibility of other styles of cultural identification.[7] It is on the figure of the pun, rather than on that of socially circulating repetition, that I stake my analysis. The pun marks the material ambiguity, contradiction, and paradox of the reservation community rather than its continuity. Or, at the very least, it marks an ambiguous, contradictory, and paradoxical kind of continuity. In deliberately opening a single utterance onto multiple interpretive possibilities, punning invites us to engage the creativity of culture—as something that is always part of the production of everyday life in the community. It is not necessarily the case that an expressive form need remain consistent for its indexical properties to remain effective. Nor does the consistency of a form ensure the consistency of its indexical relations. The sense that the relation between a sign and its object is one of iconic similarity is, in the end, cultural.

Rather than an empirical continuity of material form, what counts as iconic in many cases on the San Carlos Reservation is the continuity of the *feeling* evoked by expressive forms. Cultural continuity is represented in the affective response to certain discourse forms, even if those forms themselves lack the kind of material continuity of "serious imitation" (Haring 1992) that anthropologists usually associate with cultural continuity. I refer to this continuity of feeling interchangeably as "feelingful iconicity" or "iconicity of feeling." The "feelingful" part is an attempt to gather together a wide variety of noncognitive responses to cultural expression that help to create for San Carlos Apaches a deeply felt sense of attachment to the social history of the community. The phrase is also linked to the notion of "feeling for form," both in Edward Sapir's quasi-gestalt sense of a culturally naturalized feeling of rightness about the relationship between elements and in Franz Boas's sense of an emotional attachment to aesthetic forms. It is not, then, that contemporary cultural expressions are ungrounded, but that those groundings are always a matter of historical and cultural negotiation and compromise. Sketching out some of that history of negotiation is one of my goals in this work.

If cultural expressions of contemporary identities on the reservation are produced out of the layering of contradictory and ambiguously situated elements, then it should not necessarily come as a surprise to find that those expressions take advantage of particular discourse forms and genres that highlight these "figures of discontinuity" (Sommer 1999:x). My approach to contemporary performances of identity in linguistic as well as in other expressive domains thus places questions of ambiguity at the center of the interpretive issues at stake.

The history of scholarship about language and other forms of cultural expression in the Western intellectual tradition is haunted by the problem of ambiguity and indeterminacy. The idea that language is most properly a system for the communication of rational thought can be found in Aristotle's refutation of the Sophists.[8] Theories of language in the Western tradition suffer the consequences of the "irreducibility thesis" (Hanks 1996), the claim that there must be an irreducible difference that distinguishes "language" from other forms of communication and expression (a claim usually placed on the shoulders of referentiality). But even if such an irreducible difference exists, that difference alone cannot purchase for language the status of a self-contained system. For one thing, language seeps deeply into many other areas of human social life, including everyday conversations, social studies classes, rooting for the home team, songs, ceremonies, and so forth. How can the "language" be extricated from the social forms in which it is embedded? Moreover, extricating "reference" from the other qualities that language communicates is also done only with great difficulty—if not with self-delusion. "When we look closely at language," writes Geoffrey Galt Harpham in his discussion of Wittgenstein's famous statement that to imagine a language is to imagine a way of life, "we see not simplicity but a warren of interlaced elements, codes, and levels, and mysterious horizons beyond which it cannot venture. . . . Imagining a language would . . . summon forth not clean linguistic facts . . . but the vast debris of the world" (2002:2–3).

A focus on "language" in this reductive sense of its power to refer has regrettably often meant that questions of ambiguity are placed at the margins of the area under consideration. The central questions have more often inquired about how cognitive understanding occurs—how it is that I can write about "central" and "marginal" questions and you can follow my meaning. Ambiguity is certainly recognized as a feature of natural languages (e.g., Kooij 1971), but the recognition is often limited to special cases—particular kinds of sentences, particular genres of discourse. Or it is discussed in terms of how people reduce the potential for ambiguity so that they can get on with the business of clear communication.

There is no denying that the default mode of everyday linguistic interaction is one in which people usually attempt to reduce the potential ambiguity of their utterances. And yet, although pragmatics may dictate that we choose to ignore ambiguity in observing the social amenities of getting on with life—the person who sees double entendre at every turn is not necessarily the most popular character in the car pool—we also know that the potential for it is always there. "The paradox of language is that first, the term is used to designate both the system and what lies outside it and, second, that this is not a terminological mistake . . . but a necessary situation, for the two sides of language (the systematic and the subversive) are inseparable" (Lecercle 1985:70). We can also find this inseparability in Noam Chomsky's early work, which stresses the ability to recognize immediately that a sentence is ambiguous and why, as one of the central features of "linguistic competence."

Even the founder of the systematic logic of structural relations, Ferdinand de Saussure, was haunted by the double life of language. At the same time that he was teaching the courses in Geneva that bequeathed to us the notion of a rational linguistic system composed of arbitrary, unmotivated relationships between acoustic images and the concepts they denote, he was also exploring a theory that the epic poems of the ancient world were organized by patterns of hidden anagrams within the poems, naming the gods for whom the poems were composed (Gadet 1989; Lecercle 1985; Starobinski 1979). The specter of ambiguity has given rise to a number of differing proposals about what form of linguistic practice might be the key form leading to a fuller understanding of language and communication in general—everyday interaction, formal logic, scientific discourse, or poetry, to name just a few possibilities.

In part because of the thesis that places the ability to refer at the pinnacle of what defines language, it has perhaps always been easier to accept ambiguity as an important part of what artists do.[9] And indeed, as my focus is on artful performance, part of my point is that these performances gain at least a portion of their affective power precisely from the way they combine clarity and cloudiness. For example, my Apache teacher, Phillip, enjoyed telling me the story of when he was in high school and his class was taken to Phoenix to visit a museum, where they saw a painting that depicted a breechcloth-clad Indian locked in mortal hand-to-hand combat with a uniformed cavalryman. "I know why he painted that scene," the Apache students said. "Because right after that the Indian took that knife and killed that soldier!" It is difficult to see the ambiguity of the painting as located somewhere around the edges of its meaning. The drama of the painting is not at its margins, but right at its center, in the frozen, indeterminate instant depicted in the artist's rendition of the two antagonists. And it is all the more difficult to separate the "ambiguity" from the "art."

The larger point here is that ambiguity is not lurking somewhere at the margins of rational categorization, but is intertwined with it. In certain contexts and in certain discourse forms, the knowledge of the ever-present potential for ambiguity becomes a productive resource, and people take hold of that ambiguity in meaningful ways. With the term *ambiguity*, then, I don't mean to imply in any sense an unfathomability that defies critical analysis, but an important means for organizing discourse. That is, the defiance that I mean to identify is a cultural and political practice of refusal—refusal to make discourses and contexts coincide too predictably, refusal to surrender to the unspoken codes of coherence. Speech play, paraphrase, reported speech, and other everyday practices that saturate communication and interaction on the San Carlos Reservation set ambiguity, vagueness, and indeterminacy in play.[10] None of this argument denies that distinct communities have different ways of organizing, categorizing, and structuring the world of experience, sometimes radically so. But if we set ambiguity to the side and assume that coherence and system are the (almost biological) imperatives—that what human beings desire most of all is resolution and order in the cosmos—then, I would argue, we will be poorly positioned to understand the culturally and historically situated forms of identity production on the San Carlos Reservation.[11]

The establishment of coherence as the thing to be discovered by anthropology dictates certain agendas and approaches and designates some communities and some issues more worthy of study than others.[12] A few scholars familiar with the Southwest with whom I have spoken about my work have wondered what an anthropologist could possibly find of interest in a community as "corrupted" as San Carlos.[13] Indeed, the communities of the San Carlos Reservation have been seen as somewhat anthropologically undesirable because both "factionalism" among a too-high number of competing groups and a too-close proximity to dominant off-reservation communities have made the Apache culture on the reservation, perhaps especially in San Carlos itself, appear degenerate and incoherent to researchers.[14]

These characteristics are precisely the things that make the issue of identity on the San Carlos Reservation important to understand, however. I am not saying social or symbolic life on the reservation is incoherent. The question is, How do things cohere? How can we begin to make sense of the fact that the expressive lives of people in the reservation's communities involve more than the maintenance or disappearance of traditional cultural forms? One of the major tasks in a materialist anthropology of modernity, I believe, is to consider what the ethnography of negotiation might look like. From the standpoint of the ethnographer, I think one aspect involves attending to things as they are played out in real time by real individual participants, who bring together various contradictory and ambivalent positions in their attempts to represent themselves.

This book, therefore, is about social life negotiated in the malleable spaces of the categories that dominant ideologies would like to represent as being precise, encompassing, and complete. It is about expressions that respond to, complicate, and undermine the naturalized orders of dominant histories and cultures. It is about cultural expressions that expose with pinpoint accuracy the multiple themes and implications lying beneath the meanings and intentions of expressions. It is about a social life of signs in which signs are increasingly difficult to pin down and know because they are always humming with the trace overtones of other meanings, other implications, other usages. In a classic statement about the relationship between ordinary language and poetry, Edward Sapir wrote, "were a language ever completely 'grammatical,' it would be a perfect engine of conceptual expression. Unfortunately, or luckily, no language is tyrannically consistent. All grammars leak" (1921:38). For me, this statement opens up the question, Is it the grammar or the leakiness that is the source and distinguishing characteristic of cultural identities?[15]

The material contained in this book comes from seventeen months of ethnographic research in the communities of San Carlos, Peridot, and Bylas on the San Carlos Reservation. That research concentrated on contemporary symbolic practices in those communities—most predominantly at the meeting point of language and music in the way that popular culture forms were created, circulated, represented, and interpreted. Although my fieldwork brought me to numerous sites for the performance of identity on the reservation, the greatest portion of it was spent in rehearsal, performance, and conversation with the Pacers, also known as the Country Pacers, the most popular—in some ways the only—local country-rock band on the San Carlos Reservation at the time of my fieldwork.

Recent work in linguistic anthropology has seen "an abandonment of the assumption that language should be one's [the researcher's] only or main preoccupation" (Duranti 2003:332). This abandonment has meant, in part, a new focus on global questions of power, inequality, and ideology. It has also allowed linguistic anthropologists to reinitiate an expansive embrace of modes of communication and expression beyond the strictly (and artificially delineated, as we have seen) "linguistic."

Prominent among these expansions has been a focus on the relationship between language and music.[16] The relationship is sometimes figured metaphorically or as an analogy. Ingrid Monson (1996) uses the term *conversation* as a way of describing the activity of jazz musicians (as do many of the musicians themselves). R. Keith Sawyer (2001), conversely, uses "jazz improvisation" as a way of comparatively describing the activity of creating a conversation. Similarly, Theo Van Leeuwen (1999) compares conversational turn taking to musical antiphony, and Jennifer Coates describes the conversations between women friends that she studied as "jam sessions" (1996:1). Bakhtin's musical metaphor of "polyphony" in novelistic discourse has produced major shifts in the way linguistic anthropologists consider the relationship between culture, language, and voice. Joan Pujolar (2001), for example, draws on Bakhtinian insights in emphasizing the role of the "tune of the voice" in the creation of the many characters embodied by his bilingual Spanish/Catalan consultants.

Other scholars have articulated the importance of the music of language. Deborah Tannen (1989) alludes to the resonance between these two modes of expression when she characterizes repetition as one of the "musical" aspects of language. Paul Friedrich has argued that the musicality of language is one of the master tropes of poetry (the other being myth): "The musical imagination underlies all poetry as conventionally defined, where it plays an implicit or potential counterpoint to the rhythm and beat of conversation" (1986:37). The realm of poetry—

"poetic diction," as Owen Barfield (1973) called it—has long been perceived as one in which sound is prominently displayed as a resource for the creation of culturally transmittable meaningful experience (Fabb 1997; S. Stewart 2002).

The flexible borderline between language and music—or, perhaps more accurately, between speech and song—is another area of intermodal overlap. Steven Feld's exploration of the cultural and sensorial meanings of the (re)sounding world (Feld 1974, 1990a; Feld and Fox 1994; Feld et al. 2004; Keil and Feld 1994) has been a sustained voice demonstrating what can be revealed by attending to the overlapping aural practices of speech and song. Leanne Hinton has argued strongly about the ways in which the overlapping areas between speech and song make available powerful resources for the forging of community and identity (Hinton 1980, 1984, 1994:39–43, 145–51). Work on the practice of ritual lament—sung-texted weeping—has allowed researchers to blend insights gained from both linguistic and musical modalities of expression to produce rich ethnographies that emphasize the complex, embodied, and participatory means by which cultural histories, genres, and identities, especially gender, are performed (Briggs 1992; Feld 1990b; Graham 1986; Hill 1990; Seremetakis 1991; Tolbert 1994; Urban 1988; Wilce 2002). Finally, in part through the influence of cultural studies, a number of cultural and linguistic anthropologists have focused on musical practices to provide important insights into the social practices of which they write (Briggs 1993; Diehl 2002; Mahon 2000; Meintjes 2003; Rampton 1995). As Rampton writes in arguing for the inclusion of expressive domains beyond the linguistic, "Conversation is important, but it is not the only thing that people listen to" (1998:311).

Attending to the area of the sonic world in which speech and song overlap helps us to avoid what John Ellis (1993) calls one of the "default" commonsense theories about language—namely, that language is distinct from all other symbolic modes because it can refer to objects in the world. This "language refers/music does not" trap is one that Steven Feld ([1984] 1994a) warns against in his discussion of speech about music, and one that Martin Stokes falls into in the introduction to his edited collection *Ethnicity, Identity, and Music* (1994). There, Stokes argues that music is an "out of the ordinary" experience, different and more complicated than other forms of communication, expression, and identity production. He casts his claim in a Foucauldian mold, basing his argument about music's out-of-the-ordinary complexity on its involvement with pleasure: "It is perhaps this that distinguishes the kinds of ethnicity discussed in this volume from the 'everyday' practices of boundary construction and maintenance with which much social anthropological writing on ethnicity is concerned" (1994:13).

I think Stokes is right about music, but his argument for music's distinctiveness trades on a dichotomy whereby music is about pleasure, whereas language is about rationality and reference. Although there are obvious differences between musical and linguistic expression, with lexical reference being perhaps one of them, the pleasure/rationality, body/mind dichotomy is false. As the examples of speech play and cross-language punning in the present work attest—such as Marshall's code-switch with which I began—language is as much about pleasure as any other form of human expression. Similarly, a distinction wherein "language" is about the mind but, say, "gesture" is about the body ignores the presence of the body in the voice when speaking. When we make these dichotomies the central distinctions between language and other expressive modes, we frame language in a number of nonproductive ways, sometimes in spite of our better intentions—as logical, precise, referential, rational. By centering this work at the meeting places of language and music, where speech becomes song and sense becomes sound, I hope to move into an area of cultural expression through which we may consider the layered sociability of embodied vocal performance and participation. Singing heightens the aural and visceral presence of the body in language. Thus marked, the embodied and emplaced sociability of language in the act of singing may achieve temporary dominance over referential sense. In its poetic aspect, sung vocalization reveals the taken-for-granted textuality of everyday speech.

As in other verbal art, song reveals the fundamental tension in all language use between the context-bound materiality of the utterance and the abstracting textuality of syntactic, semantic, and interactional structure, and it establishes a zone of experiment and contemplation. That is, to paraphrase musicologist Victor Zuckerkandl (1956), music may not tell us anything about cultural identity that we could not learn by studying language alone, but it may illuminate things that would otherwise remain in the shadows without it (see also Feld and Fox 1994; Feld et al. 2004).

Therefore, one reason for concentrating on the nexus of speech and song is to help us rethink the primacy of language as the model for semiotic expression and communication. When we use language as the model of models, we inevitably trap ourselves into constructing analogical relationships of the type, "X is *like* a language, except . . ." Music is *like* a language (because it appears to have something akin to syntax), except it is nonreferential. Painting is *like* a language (because— at least up to a certain period in history—it is representational), except it is not as precise.[17] These analogical constructs fail on a number of counts. First, they credit to language a precision that it perhaps has when one is thinking of music or painting, but that it never has when one is actually thinking of language. Second, they presuppose that language is the keystone symbolic system, through which all others will be best understood. Third, they reduce the concept of "language" to a bare-bones syntactic and referential transcribability, reserving to "art" the realm of expression and emotion. Fourth, they explain music and painting about as well as the artistry of filmmaking is explained in the statement "movies are like books (because they have narrative structure of some sort), except you don't read them on a printed page." The analogy refuses to grapple with the particular materiality of song, of graphic (non)representation, and, ultimately, of speech.[18]

If we loosen this hierarchy between language and other forms of expression, we can begin to tune into the embodied, participatory, performed dimensions of language. If we allow our knowledge of music's syntactic and referential openness, for example, to influence our thinking about language, we might come to different conclusions about just how we might characterize the relationships between different forms of cultural expression—including language. I want to argue strongly that the insights of linguistic anthropology extend outward to offer a means of relating linguistic interactions to other modalities of cultural expression (see, for example, Basso and Feld 1997; Elkins 1998; Harris 1996; Mendoza-Denton 1996). Turning to other, more overtly "artistic" modes of expression, however, again implies a turn to the productive resources of ambiguity. As Roy Harris notes, "in the realm of art it begins to seem somewhat less convincing to insist that the world is the same for all observers" (1996:130). But the difference is not that music is "ambiguous" where language is "clear"; rather, it is that musical expression unmasks an ambiguity that lives in all cultural symbolic action. Opening up to these potentials of ambiguity would further address the difficulty of transparent indexicality that I discussed earlier and, like Rampton's critique of "coherence," might inoculate researchers from a world in which expressive varieties transparently index contexts or social positions.

A final argument for taking seriously the interlayering of speech and song relates back to the idea, introduced earlier, that contemporary cultural expression on the San Carlos Reservation takes the form of a pun. Music is capable of presenting, and of allowing its beholders to perceive, multiple syntactic structures — in a sense, multiple utterances — simultaneously. This capability is distinct from the possibility of multiple interpretations that can be given to a single utterance. To be sure, a loosening of grammatical clarity that enables multiple interpretations is a benchmark of poetic diction in general, at least in English.[19] In contrast to literary ambiguity, however — even the undecidability of metaphor — musical ambiguity goes beyond the capacity for single utterances to be understood in more than one sense.

Of course, that kind of multiple interpretation occurs all the time in musical experiences. Indeed, such multiplicity is a necessary part of San Carlos Apache cultural expression because, in the case of popular music, a reinterpretation is implied at the outset. One night I was standing with Donnie Ray and Pat, the two other guitar players in the Pacers. Lynrd Skynyrd's live recording *One More from the Road* was playing on the cassette player in my truck. A song opened with a steady, quarter-note *bum-bum-bum* of the bass drum. Over that beat, Donnie Ray began improvising a traditional-style Apache song.

So, on the one hand, we hear the multiple interpretability of that drumbeat. On the other hand, however, we hear that Donnie Ray could sing a traditional Apache song while a Lynrd Skynyrd song was being played at the same time — that both musical utterances were perceivable in simultaneity. This potential for literally multivocal utterances is a distinguishing characteristic of musical expression, a characteristic that relates strongly to the simultaneity of the kind of layered, punning, expressive practices that I introduced earlier. This is different from code-switching. Mark Slobin (1992), for instance, has borrowed the concept of linguistic code-switching in discussing popular-music arrangements that shift between a more "mainstream" sound and a more highly marked "ethnic" arrangement of the same song. Certainly this type of code-switching goes on, and not only between mainstream and ethnic versions — for example, in Los Fabulosos Cadillacs' ska-tinged version of the Beatles' "Strawberry Fields Forever." But code-switching implies that codes are alternatives and that one code might be more appropriate than another. In contrast, music's ability to capture worldviews simultaneously, rather than in alternation, constitutes its unique expressive magic—a distinction that Slobin also notes. A musical arrangement and performance can simultaneously present different syntactic versions of the same idea, or even different ideas, interweaving them without switching between them.

For example, comedian Drew Lacapa, in a performance as emcee at an event in San Carlos, improvised hilarious lyrics to the typical, Hollywood-inspired, Atlanta Braves tomahawk-chop "Indian" melody, which he sang:

We   are   In - di - an   guys,   we're   gon   -   na   kick __   your   butts!

The lyrics are welded onto the melody, shaped by and predicated on its pentatonic melodic contours and its metrical stress patterns. And listeners experience the paradoxical simultaneity of sung melody and lexical text. Song thus becomes one of the most notable cultural sites for playing out the ambiguities and contradictions of contemporary expressive life on the reservation, in its capacity for layering disparate elements found among the expressive resources in the global marketplace.[20] In the case of the San Carlos Reservation, I believe that music highlights issues of ambiguity and ambivalence in a way that particularly rewards its exploration and thus helps reinforce my argument that ambiguity is closer to the core of meaning than one might think.

In sum, ambiguity is crucial to an understanding of the creativity of cultural expression. In his classic work on poetic ambiguity, William Empson wrote that "the machinations of ambiguity are among the very roots of poetry" ([1930] 1953:3). And the phenomenologist Maurice Merleau-Ponty places the possibility of subjectivity itself within, not outside, the context of irreducible paradox and ambiguity. For him, the essence of human social life is found in a "tolerance for the incomplete" (1964:51).

Affirming the importance of ambiguity does not demonize coherence any more than marginalizing ambiguity ever excised ambiguity from communicative and expressive practices. We should consider the ways in which coherence and ambiguity slip around each other in the embodied creation of cultural meanings. On the San Carlos Reservation, the production of cultural identities often depends on moments of performance that are at once coherent and ambiguous—interpretable precisely for the way they arrest the decidability of the layered presentation of expressive forms. Ambiguity no more means anarchy than coherence means strict formal regimentation. Ambiguity is not incoherence. The point is that they exist together, caught in each other's orbits. Homophony and metaphor exist in all languages, alongside and perhaps in tension with the strictly referential aspects that are often mistaken for the whole. In Lecercle's terms, a language that were only coherent might consist of only tautologies.

Instead, cultural identities emerge and are expressed out of the everyday experience of negotiating the tensions between coherence and ambiguity. If we pay attention only to the coherence, we will miss crucial aspects of how the contemporary feeling of being Apache is powerful for people on the reservation. The artful work of creating representations of San Carlos Apacheness involves playing with the possibility of being coherent and confusing simultaneously—of saying yes, no, and maybe all at once. The overlapping areas between music and language open the potential for this improvisatory play, allowing people on the reservation to layer social histories, personal biographies, languages, and Hollywood stereotypes into multifaceted reworkings of the possible locations of and relationships between culture, history, and identity.

For a year and a half, from August 1994 until March 1996, I lived in a trailer in the Seven Mile Wash district of San Carlos, at the foot of the road that leads up the hill to Airport '79. The trailer belonged to my Apache teacher's brother and sat on land that belonged to my Apache teacher's family, not far from the house where he had grown up. The trailer was basically inadequate; made of aluminum and uninsulated, it retained cold in the winter and amplified heat in the summer. A large hole in the roof ensured that monsoon season would always be an adventure, and I spent much time, effort, and money in purchasing and tying down the tarps that I, in my innocence, depended upon to protect me from the coming deluge, but that, after baking in the sun for weeks, were never strong enough to do the job.[21]

Sticking it out in that trailer (to which now, of course—héla!—I retain a nostalgic attachment) made my work easier. Every so often my landlord would stop by to see how I was doing—and to laugh at me. "I thought by now you'd have found a nice apartment in Globe," he would chide. White people—Bureau Americans, for of course not all of the bearers of white cultural practice are white people—lived in Globe. Some Indian Health Service (IHS) doctors and nurses and some school-teachers lived in apartments provided for them on the reservation. But many teachers, government workers, even the Bureau of Indian Affairs (BIA) superintendent lived in Globe, so they never had to put up with the electricity going out for hours when it rained. The Apache Gold Casino, out on the reservation line, must be on the electrical lines from Globe, or maybe it has its own emergency generators because it was never shut down by the rain. I sometimes think that staying put in San Carlos was the one thing I did that gave me any kind of credibility in the community.

I was given permission to do research in San Carlos and Bylas by a unanimous vote of the tribal council, with three conditions. First, I was asked not to do research into traditional religious beliefs. Second, I was asked to share any financial profits that might arise from publications issuing from the research. Third, I was asked to work with the tribal History Program and the Elders Cultural Advisory Council and with the local school district, to which I have made long-term commitments. The first request, especially, has influenced what I have written in these pages. There is a great deal to be said about the continuing presence and affecting power of Apache traditions in the community. It should be clear to the reader, for example, that the kinds of punning practices I explore in this book can be carried out best by people who are flu-ent Apache speakers. Everything I write about takes place in a context of palpable and devastating culture loss, and nothing I have written should be taken as meaning that this loss is unimportant.

In the course of my work, I myself added two more conditions. At one point, I was at the home of a high school student, speaking to her and her mother (an aunt was also present and chipped in with her own stories and responses) to get their informed consent to my interviewing the student. At one point in our conversation, the girl's mother went into a back room of the house and returned holding a book about San Carlos. She turned to a photograph in the book, a picture of a group of kids horsing around in someone's front yard in the early 1960s. "You see that picture?" she said, handing the book to me. "That's me," she said, pointing to one of the young girls in the photograph. "He didn't ask me if he could put my picture in there!" She took the book back and turned to another page, with a story about a girl and her relationships with her paternal kin. "That's me," she said. "*I* said that. He didn't ask me if he could put that story in there!" For this and other reasons, I decided that it was necessary to circulate drafts of my writings, so that the people I wrote about would be able to negotiate their presence as characters in my story. I also decided to do this because I have had friendships and associations with people in Bylas and San Carlos dating back to when I was fifteen years old. I mention this history not because I think that lengthy association makes me more sensitive or respectful, or that it lends me any authority, but because the association often made it difficult for me to maintain the newly minted guise of the professional researcher. This tension finds its way into my writing as well. I never quite resolve the narrative voices of the academic researcher and the long-time visitor into a seamless whole. The voices interrupt and intrude on each other, but in the end I welcome the intrusions. (I believe I have almost exactly the same relationship with the voices of my academic mentors.) I sometimes allow the textures of my consultants' speech to overcome my own. At times, I ignore the prescriptive amenities of the scholar's register—for example, the use of "such as" rather than "like" to introduce examples or the rule that says don't use contractions—for which I thank a patient and understanding copy editor. At other times, I am at pains to separate my voice from the voices of the people who helped me to understand everyday contemporary expressive life on the reservation. This is especially true when my sense is that someone has trusted me to tell her or his story, but it also occurs when there are multiple voices addressing the same topic of contemplation. After decades of sharing experiences and stories with people in San Carlos and Bylas, however, I cannot always extricate myself from entanglements in order to speak in my own pure voice. In this book about the problem of voice and identity, my own voice and identity are themselves sometimes up for grabs. Because this book began its life as doctoral research, I'm afraid the academic voice wins out, especially in this introduction. But perhaps there's hope for me yet.

Keeping both my long-term friendships with people on the reservation and this high school student's mother's words in mind, I was certain that despite my best efforts to be responsible with the material I wrote down and taped, people may have let slip things that they would not necessarily want to see in print. So I have written more or less in view of the people with whom I work on the reservation. Although I did not grant editorial approval in general, everyone in this book has seen every word that I have written about her or him, to the extent that it was possible, and the final result has been cocrafted.

A second decision I made was to do my best to leave religion and tribal politics out of the book, for two reasons. First, I decided that there was no good reason to pry into people's nontraditional beliefs if I was leaving traditional beliefs alone. This is not to say that religion goes unmentioned in the book—it is a crucial aspect of the arguments about "culture" in the reservation's communities. But I do not delve deeply into an analysis of the practitioners' theological beliefs or the symbolism of their religious practices. Second, although politics in its broadest sense is at the core of the book—the politics of identity, the politics of culture, the relationship between politics and poetics, and so forth—the book is not a forum for the airing of dirty laundry.

At times, I should admit, I was not the most objective observer of life on the reservation. For instance, there is my story about the Grand Opening of the Bashas' supermarket franchise in San Carlos. A man had been hired to sing a traditional Apache song as part of the opening ceremony. As he sang, a second man, perhaps a bit too obviously inebriated, wended his way through the audience to the podium, stood behind and to the right of the hired singer, and joined in. A few seconds later tribal police came and escorted the second man away. This incident has always stood out in my mind as a crystallized image of changing ideologies and aesthetics in San Carlos, not only because of the official show of security forces, but because of the tensions highlighted between the aesthetic choices that are possible in one context and those that are dictated in another. The second man was seen as a security risk, when in most situations community participation in the singing of traditional music is expected. As McAllester has noted of the groups performing healing ceremonies in Cibecue, the Western Apache community on the Fort Apache Reservation directly north of the San Carlos Reservation, "the larger the better . . . all who know the chant even partly join in. There are drummers, dancers and many on-lookers. The whole community, men, women, children and dogs are present, all participating, if only being there" (1960:469–70).

When I tell this story, I say that I asked people about this incident. Probably what I did was more like saying, "Can you believe what happened at the opening?" Although this question mimicked enough people I overheard at the event that I am confident it was an attitude others actually held, I am sure that in this case, at least, I did not do my level best to be objective about the situation. In the realm of participant observation, I leaned heavily toward the participation side. This tendency was somewhat unavoidable because the bulk of the work I was doing for the research involved hanging out, rehearsing, and performing with the Pacers, and with Boe Titla, a singer-songwriter in Bylas. It was difficult to write field notes and play the guitar at the same time. Many of my research notes consist of key words jotted down between songs during rehearsals and performances, notes that I used as cue sheets to go along with the audiotapes I was making.

I can probably get away with not telling many things, but I probably can't get away without telling about how I first met Marshall.

As I mentioned, I have been visiting friends on the San Carlos Reservation since my sophomore year of high school, when I was fifteen. A number of years ago—probably in the late 1970s—I was visiting with friends in San Carlos. One of them wanted to visit his girlfriend, who was staying at the East Fork Mission School in Whiteriver, so I agreed to drive him up there. While there, in addition to being given a souvenir ashtray from the Apache Flame Restaurant in Whiteriver (shaped like an arrowhead, with the slogan "Built By The People, For The People" printed on it), I was given a copy of the East Fork school newspaper. It was called the *Broken Arrow*, named for the 1956 Western film starring Jimmy Stewart as Tom Jeffords and Jeff Chandler as Cochise.

One of the things that the school newspaper carried was articles about various students at the school, especially new students, and their various likes and dislikes. On page 2 of the paper, I found a piece introducing some of the new girls to the rest of the students (I have removed the students' names from the article):

> Next, is [name given here] a nice, sweet, charming gal. She likes to fool around and laugh a lot. Her favorite T.V. show is Emergency. She loves to play sports like basketball and softball. Her favorite song is "Ain't that a Shame." Her favorite singer is the one and only Mr. Marshall Bylas, also known as Mr. Handsome.
>
> Our next freshman is [name given here] a nice, cute, pretty, incredulous, and understanding girl. She's such a special gal, who loves to joke around. Her favorite song is "Bring it on home to me." She also has another favorite song called "We Should Be Together" which is sung to her by the one and

only "[Marshall] Bylas." She loves to [play] all kinds of sports. Her favorite
t.v. show is Starsky and Hutch.

And on page 10 of the same paper was this little item:

> The first senior for this month [name given here] doesn't have any nick-
> name. She lives at Canyon Day, with her 3 brothers, 5 sisters, 1 father and 1
> mother, 2 ducks and a dog named Gidda-up. Her favorite class is Phy. Ed,
> and she said her favorite teacher is Mr. Zimmermann. Her favorite song is
> "The Blackberry Hill" and her favorite singer is Marshall Bylas.

Fast-forward about ten years, to around 1988 or 1989. I was visiting
in Bylas, and as I walked toward Jimmy's house, I saw a skinny guy
slouching on a wire milk crate, with a cowboy hat pulled down over
his face and an acoustic guitar in his hands. Ants and Farlan came up
to me and said I should jam out with him, so they went to my car and
pulled my guitar out for me. I sat down next to this stranger and joined
in on the country songs he was playing. The only distinct memory I have
of what we played that afternoon is Charlie Daniels's "Long Haired
Country Boy." I remember it because on the last chorus, where Charlie
Daniels sings, "if you don't like the way I'm living, you better leave this
long-haired country boy alone," this guy sang, "you better leave this
long-haired Bylas Indian country boy alone," and everyone laughed in
approving recognition of the localizing twist.

When we had played a few songs, he looked over at me from under
the brim of his hat and said, "Hey, bro, what's your name?"

"Squirrel," I said, using the name I had become accustomed to in Bylas. "You?"

"Marshall," he said. Then, putting on the exaggerated intonation contours of a rodeo announcer's voice, he said, "Marshall Bylas."

"Marshall *Bylas*?" I said. "You didn't happen to go to East Fork, did
you?" He looked at me quizzically, wondering how I might have known
that, if maybe we'd met back then or maybe I worked for the FBI or
what. Finally, with a laugh, he said, "Yeah." I told him the story of how
I'd read about him in the newspaper all those years ago, and now here
we'd stumbled across each other in the place I always visited. I don't
think he believed me. But it's true.

In any case, that chance meeting sparked a friendship. Marshall was
the bass player and lead singer in the Pacers, and from then on, when-

ever I visited the reservation, if the Pacers were playing, I would be invited to join in and jam out with them. That is one of the ways this project has emerged from my long-term relationships with people in the community and one of the ways in which I became exposed to contemporary popular music as a means for the performance and circulation of Apache identities.

The Pacers had been around forever — or at least since the 1970s. During the time I was living in Seven Mile, they were Marshall on bass, Pat Margo on lead guitar, Donnie Ray Dosela on rhythm guitar, and either Kane Miller or Darryl Dude on drums, depending on who was available. Darryl's older brother Kenny had started the band when he was in high school. My own position in the band was complicated. This is not to say that everyone else's was simple, but I can speak about my own position a little more clearly, and it impacts the nature of the dynamics of my most prominent site of research and interaction. To put it bluntly, I think my presence in the band caused tension between Pat and the other band members. On occasion, I asked the others about this, and they insisted that it wasn't me, that it was other things, for example that Pat didn't own his own guitar. When Pat went out on fires one summer during my stay, he came back with a few thousand dollars and bought himself a car, a bright yellow Camaro Z-28. The fact that he hadn't bought a guitar baffled and annoyed the other band members, especially when the Z-28 broke down a couple of weeks later, and every time we went to Pat's home, we were greeted by that bright yellow symbol of . . . something. As time went on, it seemed that Pat grew further and further away from the rest of the band, and I couldn't help feeling responsible, even though everyone told me that these other things were to blame. And in fact, Pat never seemed to have a problem with me personally. We hung out together and jammed out together. He taught me country licks on the guitar, and I never felt any animosity. But to the other band members, Pat felt obligated to defend himself, to compare himself to me, to say he was better — which he was — to fight for his rightful place. So try as I might to tell myself that whatever was going on was about things that went on long before I arrived, I still can't get around the idea that my arrival triggered something.

I had two difficulties. The fact is that Pat was a far better guitarist than I. Far better. No comparison better. I'm OK, but Pat can just do things with his hands that I can't. Also, my position with the band was not based solely on my ability to play the guitar. What I brought to the band, besides whatever musical skill I might have had, was a skin color that lent the Pacers a certain legitimacy with the bar owners off the reservation. My presence in the band let those people know that we were "reliable" and "responsible," that we would show up on time for the job and not get too drunk during it. At the end of my fieldwork, I stopped by one of the bars to hang with some friends, and when the owner heard I was going back to Texas, he said, "Well, I guess I won't be able to hire those guys anymore." He did end up hiring them again, but what he said is interesting nonetheless. Mine was a skin color associated with a "knowledge" that is assumed to be the cultural property of Bureau Americans: business sense, money management, and organizational skill. If they only knew.

Another thing the Pacers felt I might have brought to the band was an ability to "open doors" for them. In lieu of payment for interviews and such, the band asked me instead to help them make a cassette tape. "I've been in nine or ten bands in my lifetime," Marshall said, "and I don't have nothing to show for it." When we were getting ready to go to Tucson to record what turned into the Pacers' cassette *Better Late Than Never*, I suggested that everyone should be involved, including Pat, and the other band members agreed. So Marshall, Pat, and I drove to Tucson one day to overdub lead guitar parts, where, despite not having picked up a guitar in a while and despite some studio nerves, he played me under the table. Finally, I think, the other members of the Pacers liked the fact that I had traveled a long distance specifically to spend time with the band, so they treated me like a special guest. We never talked about it, as I said, but I think Pat was frustrated by all the attention I got when it was clear that he was by far the better guitar player.

During the course of my stay, my days were varied and basically organized around my consultants' availability. I spent most of my time in San Carlos. I had originally intended to split my time evenly between San Carlos and Bylas, but San Carlos was where most of the action was—the Pacers were there, my Apache teacher was there, my best translators were there, my rickety old trailer was there, the tribal offices were there, as were the assigned liaisons with the Elders Cultural Advisory Council and the tribal History Office. My friends in Bylas didn't think I belonged there in Airport '79, and I didn't spend enough time with them when I had the chance, which has made me heartily sorry. But the pull of activities in San Carlos kept me from being in Bylas as much as I would have liked.

My time was split among four basic activities, most of which involved the fine art of "hanging out with Indians" (Darnell 1991:269):

1. Hanging out with my friends fairly informally, taking notes sometimes, other times waiting until I'd returned home to write down as much as I could remember. I did the latter especially when I was practicing or playing with the band, and my hands and mind were otherwise occupied. During rehearsals or performances, I would try to jot down key words to trigger my memory later on — which sometimes actually worked.

2. Visiting my friends in a more formal way, with tape recorder running and notebook out. At the beginning of my stay, I asked permission to turn on the tape recorder every time I wanted to use it. I was soon advised that asking would mean that I would never get permission to tape anything. A colleague advised me that I needed to be able to turn the tape recorder on when I thought it was important, making it clear that people either could tell me to turn it off or could turn it off themselves. It eventually became easier to run tape, especially when people were teaching me Apache. But the tape recorder often put a significant damper on the proceedings. I explained as best I could that I wanted to run the tape so that when I wrote my book, I would have people's actual words and would not simply be putting things into my own words.[22]

3. Conducting more formal "interview" sessions. These sessions included open-ended discussions with musicians and others who had stories to tell. They also included some discussions that will eventually become part of an oral history archive on the reservation.

4. Conducting more formal transcription and translation sessions with my closest consultants. These sessions sometimes involved playing a taped conversation for a third party or doing a feedback interview, in which a tape would be played back for one or more of the participants.

A few words about names and about beer. With the band members' permission, I present the Pacers by their real names, for two reasons. First, it would be impossible for me to protect their identities from other people on the reservation — everyone knows who I was hanging out with and who the only band on the reservation was at that time. Second, the band members are proud of what they do and want people to know who they are. The same is true of other musicians represented in the book — Boe Titla, Velazquez and Anson Sneezy, the late Big Bell Goseyun, and so forth. These men were and are joyful about their accomplishments, and I have used their names, with their permission, because they want people to know that they were in those bands. I have also called Phillip Goode, my Apache teacher, by his real name, again because it would be silly to think that I could make him anonymous to the rest of the community. Having spoken with these musicians, though, I felt it seemed arbitrary to stop there. Because of what that high school girl's mother had said to me, I did my best to track down all the people whose words are in this book and to show them the developing manuscript. Over a period of about four years, I traveled to San Carlos with multiple drafts and revisions of the manuscript, distributed copies to people, showed passages to them, read passages out loud to groups of consultants and their families, took note of people's responses and edited the manuscript accordingly. Some did not want their names to appear in the book. Others did. Some even insisted that I do so. If I could not relocate the person, I have changed the name — with one exception. In my discussion of the history of the Band Era on the San Carlos Reservation, if a person whose name appears was still living, I did my best to locate her or (usually) him. I have kept those names intact, in part for the sake of making a record of the history of the reservation community at that time.

I also decided not to exclude from the book the fact that some drinking went on during my fieldwork. I understand that by doing so I run the risk of reinforcing a long-combated history of stereotypical representations of Indians and alcohol. The fact is, however, I conducted my fieldwork playing with a band that performed in public at bars and at parties. It would be silly for me to pretend that everyone in these contexts was drinking fruit juice and herbal tea. Instead of hiding this aspect of my field experience, I decided to include it as it was included for me: as a matter-of-fact aspect of everyday life in San Carlos and Bylas. Alcohol abuse is an issue on the reservation, both in terms of that portion of the population that drinks to excess and in terms of the kinds of ugly stereotypes that circulate about drunken Indians. Unavoidable covert arguments about race and class lurk in these discussions; when teachers, doctors, or missionaries talk about the problems of drinking, they often do so in the white middle-class terms of job prospects and upward mobility. But the argument is never easy to typify. Some of my closest friends are alcoholics, others never take a drink, others work for the substance abuse prevention program in San Carlos, still others used to do a little bootlegging on the side. I do not want to romanti-

cize people by pretending that they live problem-free lives in the unfettered natural beauty of their ancestral lands. At the same time, I do
not want to romanticize people's suffering by employing a linguistic
register meant to manipulate sympathy from the reader. Nor do I want
to ignore the physical, familial, and social destruction that alcohol has
caused for many of my friends. It is a difficult subject to represent on
the page, and I do not know that I have succeeded in defusing all the
mines that lie beneath that landscape.

Acknowledgments

One of the most pleasurably complicated things in my life is that some
of the people of San Carlos, Bylas, and Peridot have trusted me with
their stories. I can never repay my debt to the people of the San Carlos
Apache Reservation who have accepted me into their homes and lives
for years and who have enabled me to write this book. There is an unavoidable autobiographical dimension to this work. I have been visiting
and corresponding with friends in San Carlos and Bylas since the summer between my sophomore and junior years in high school, when I
first went to the reservation as part of a summer "youth helping youth"
project. When I first went there, I had no idea I would wind up in graduate school. And when I wound up in graduate school, I had no idea that
I would wind up working with my friends in San Carlos and Bylas.

 The people who remember our little group from that first summer
remember us as "hippies" and "VISTA workers" (see Basso 1979). We
were neither, and I don't remember doing much of anything. We lived
in one of the Quonset huts out at the old Manpower Development Center going out toward Cutter on the old road to San Carlos. I remember helping kids build soapbox derby cars for a soapbox derby that
ran down the road leading up the hill to the Forestry Service airstrip.
And I remember that a few of us put together a trip to Disneyland for
about forty kids and that we stayed at the Riverside Indian School in
California.

 For whatever reason, I got along with people. Friends began invit-
ing me to their houses for lunch of frybread and beans or *tamalecho*.[23]
In Bylas, I was given a nickname, "Squirrel." No one knows why. The
two brothers who gave me the name are long gone, died before they
got out of high school, electrocuted along with two older men in an un-
speakable freak accident when a TV antenna they were helping to put

up got tangled up in a high-voltage power line. Years later I was told the stories—how their fingertips were black and burst from the jolt of electrical power; how contorted their bodies were, lying on ground that was damp from recent rain; how one of them lived long enough to whisper something incomprehensible to his cousin, who happened to be the first to stumble across the scene.

At Bylas, we worked at the old Community Hall. Every day we would pile into the bed of a pickup truck and drive there from the Skill Center. At noon, the adults in charge would kick all the Apache kids out so that the white kids could eat lunch. Pretty soon I would sneak out and get the grand tour of Bylas from my friends, walking down to the Gila River across Mrs. Alice Chinne's Cookies, looking for rattlesnakes to bombard with rocks. In San Carlos, someone taught me how to ride a motorcycle, but the group leaders put a stop to that.

Over the years after this first trip, I exchanged letters and phone calls with my friends, and I visited when I could, during vacations from school or jobs in New York. People invited me out to participate in family members' weddings and in traditional Sunrise Dances— for which I was often commandeered to be the official photographer. Around the late 1980s, when people I knew were asked "Who's that white guy?" they started to say in reply, "That's my son from New York, my grandson from New York, my cousin from New York, my brother from New York."

So in many ways a number of people in this book are people I might say I grew up with—although this is not literally true—people with whom I have long-standing, intimate relationships forged through shared experiences both joyful and tragic.[24] I don't say all this to bolster my authority by claiming to be "adopted by the tribe." I haven't been. I have been accepted as a quasi–family member by a small group of people. While that acceptance has afforded me "access to the max," as one woman put it to me, it has also added burdens of responsibility. People have trusted me to do the right thing with their stories, and for that trust I am in immense debt. To the Duane and Moses families and to the Goode family, especially, my thanks.

Others to whom I owe my thanks: the Pacers—Marshall Bylas, Darryl Dude, Pat Margo, Kane Miller, and Donnie Ray Dosela—as well as Boe Titla and Phillip Goode, who was my Apache teacher for ten years and who has been sorely missed in the years since he's been gone by everyone whose life he touched. Other people in the community to whom

I owe thanks are members of the Antonio, Bead, Belvado, Boni, Bullis, Burdette, Cadmus, Cassa, Cassadore, Chatlin, Cracium, Dewey, Dillon, Dosela, Dude, Goseyun, Grant, Haozous, Hinton, Hudson, Hunter, Johnson, Juan, Kenton, Kitcheyan, Lorenzo, Machukay, McIntosh, Miller, Nash, Noline, Phillips, Polk, Preston, Reede, Sneezy, Stanley, Steele, Titla, Thorne, Victor, and Wesley families. I think that's everyone.

My mentors at the University of Texas—Steven Feld, Pauline Turner Strong, Katie Stewart, Deborah Kapchan, Kathleen Higgins, and Tony Woodbury—were my large, dependable, and inspiring committee when this book was a dissertation. Keith Basso also joined the committee from New Mexico and has read my work with great generosity and unfailingly precise critique. Steve Feld was a model mentor. My work simply would not be the same if not for his teaching, insights, and support. Polly Strong stepped into the breach when Steve left Austin. She read and commented on every word of every draft I passed her way. As time goes on and I see things from the mentor's side, I have less and less idea of how she managed to do that. Ginger Farrer was an early and continued source of level-headed advice. Jeremy Beckett's year in Austin left an indelible impression on my thinking. Calla Jacobson, Andrew Causey, Susan Lepselter, Aaron Fox, Tom Porcello, Louise Meintjes, Stephanie Brown, Chantal Tetreault, and David Henderson had a hand in helping me make this manuscript. Without Louise's help, the book might have been called *Self-Titled First Release*.

My colleagues in the anthropology department at the University of Massachusetts and in the Five Colleges have supported my efforts both emotionally and financially. Jackie Urla, Bob Paynter, and Enoch Page deserve special mention for their part in helping me finish and let go of the manuscript, and Janet Rifkin made its completion possible. Debbora Battaglia's kindness and advice has been precious. Don Brenneis read and generously commented on the manuscript in various stages, and Norma Mendoza-Denton has helped me clarify my positions immeasurably. The students in my undergraduate and graduate seminars patiently allowed me to clarify my jumbled thoughts in real time. Marge Bruchac, Gabriel de la Luz Rodriguez, Tilman Lanz, Carla Hammar, Lisa Modenos, Rafi Crockett, Kaila Kuban, and Jian Ge gave me valuable feedback that has greatly improved the presentation.

In Globe, Donna Anderson, Bill Haak, and Paul Machula helped me clarify the sections of the book that deal with the relationship between the city and the reservation. They generously offered this assistance even though the picture of Globe from across the reservation line isn't necessarily the picture they themselves would paint of their hometown.

Parts of this book were written during a postdoctoral semester at the American Indian Studies Center at the University of California, Los Angeles. My thanks to Duane Champagne, Paul Kroskrity, Candy Goodwin, Tara Browner, Alessandro Duranti, and Leila Monaghan for discussions and support. Other parts were completed during a Mellon postdoctoral year in the Penn Humanities Forum at the University of Pennsylvania. My thanks to Wendy Steiner, Daniel Baraz, John Zeimbekis, Rebecca Zorach, Julian Yates, Richard Eldridge, Ann Norton, Robert Vitalis, Greg Urban, Asif Agha, Ghautam Ghosh, and Alex Rehding for their engaged and critical discussions of the work and their bolstering of my waning confidence.

The fieldwork for this project was supported by grants from the National Science Foundation, the Wenner-Gren Foundation, and the Jacobs Fund.

Finally, I thank my parents, Hershel and Edith Samuels, who inadvertently set me on this path, as well as my brothers and sisters, Karen, Paul, Judie, and Alex, who knew that I should be following it a few years before I realized it myself.

It's enough to have it in pieces. It's enough to have heard it once and then never again all the way through but just in fragments. Like a spring which never comes. But you see a few flowers burst open. And a black cloud move down a grassy slope. A robin. Long, fine legs in a pair of shorts. The sun hot on your face if you lie down out of the wind. The fits and starts and rhythms and phrases from the spring-not-coming which is the source of all springs that do come. —**John Edgar Wideman,** "Across the Wide Missouri"

1

A Sense of the Past

Dominic, Catherine, and I were visiting around the kitchen table in the finished part of the house they were building in Beverly Hills. For years, they had lived in Mormon Hill, but recently they had decided to move onto family land south of the highway. The new homes going up there were much more isolated than the ones in the town of San Carlos— some people referred to life in Beverly Hills as "living like Navajos." It took me a few tries to find my way around the unmarked dirt roads to their front door. I hoped the trip was worth it. Dominic and Catherine were extremely busy people, and often when I would stop by and knock on their door, there would be no answer—especially after they moved out and I didn't know about it.

But today luck was with me, and the three of us got a chance to catch up with each other and reminisce. Sharp-witted with a keenly developed sense of irony, Dominic and Catherine were always opening my eyes whenever I saw them. Fluent in both English and Apache, Dominic is greatly concerned over the loss of the Apache language in the community. When he hears Apache children speaking English, he sometimes says, loud enough for them to hear him, "Who are those white people talking over there?"[1] He spoke in bemused tones about his recent attempt to tell a joke in Apache to some young people, only to face their blank stares when he reached the punch line. Catherine told us about her days in boarding school and how the teachers instructed the children to "dream in English," as that would be the proof that they had learned the language sufficiently well.

Dominic recalled the time when Sluggo recruited him to play with Sluggo's band, the Valiants. "Now, Sluggo was a guy you would enjoy every day," he said. Because of his polio, Sluggo didn't stand on stage. "There was a certain chair that he would bring up and sit in," Dominic said. Dominic didn't feel very musical, but as a teenager he used to help the band load up and set up their equipment. Then one day, he said, "Sluggo talked me into playing tambourine and cowbell, triangle. He said, 'When I make a face at you I want you to stand. I want you to move around, too!' he said. 'Don't just stand there like wooden Indians!' he said." Everyone around the table laughed at the joke, and Dominic recalled the Santana songs that Sluggo sang.

The conversation turned to the na'íees that he and Catherine had recently attended. Na'í'ees is the traditional "coming of age" or puberty ceremony held for girls on the reservation. In English, it is often referred to as a "Sunrise Dance." Raised in the Mormon church, Dominic and Catherine had turned more toward tradition on growing into adulthood and attended a number of ceremonies. This one had been for a relative, though, so they had lived in a brush arbor in the girl's camp for the weekend of the ceremony.

"It was just beautiful," Catherine said. "The weather was perfect, not too hot." When you go to as many Sunrise Dances as they do, you learn how to distinguish one from another—who danced well, who sang well, who had good food, who had the luck of good weather. Dominic talked about an experience he had one night at the dance. The festivities were over for the day, and, tired, he was relaxing in the veranda, dozing off. As he listened to the gentle breeze whispering through the leaves of the arbor, a very light rain began to fall, the sound of water on brush. And the thought that ran through his mind was, "Wow, this is what it was like back then."

Dominic's response to this brief moment in the afterglow of the ceremony's strenuous activities gives us a sense of how expression works on the San Carlos Reservation to mold experience and identity. Expressivity reveals the recoverable past to people in the affective response to aesthetic experience. The past is a major avenue of aesthetic pleasure on the reservation. The backward look, through space and time, is an important and desired aesthetic effect. All sorts of expressive endeavors are judged to be particularly successful if this transcendence of the bounds of the present and transportation to the past occur. By linking aesthetic pleasure to an imagined sense of the historical past, expression makes the past available to people on the reservation in their imaginative and feelingful responses to cultural expression. This sense of the recoverability of the past pervades both concrete instances of expression in the community and people's responses to it: Dominic's affective interjection of surprise ("wow"), followed by the deictic pointing to the past ("*this* is what it was like back then").

The sense of history on the reservation isn't necessarily about chronology. Thinking about the past isn't strictly a matter of thinking about things that no longer exist. This sense of the recoverability of the past pervades expression and the response to expression in the community. *This is what it was like back then.* This is what it was like: not the modal— not "this is what I think it might or must have been like"—but the declarative. And "back then": not a chronological period forever closed off by the passage of time into the present, but an open, enigmatic, feelingful place to which one can go if given the proper invitation. As we shall see, the invitation need not be engraved on an old or traditional card.

This recoverability of the past and the recoverability of that past in contemporary expression make history an ambiguous and enigmatic domain. San Carlos historical imagination stands in contrast to the mainstream sort of schoolbook sense of history in which one often finds mention of Apaches. In a deservedly well-known formulation about nationalism, Benedict Anderson wrote, "Communities are to be distinguished, not by their falsity/genuineness, but by the style in which they are imagined" (1991:15). San Carlos imagines its community in a style that calls the past into continual presence. My purpose here is to trace out some of the more telling and pervasive effects of this style of imagining.

What do I mean by claiming that people's sense of the past on the San Carlos Reservation is not chronological? I don't mean that people on the reservation prefer cyclical time to linear time, as Eliade's (1954) famous dichotomy might have it. Nor do I mean that people in San Carlos and Bylas can't tell the difference between the past and the present. Even less do I mean that they never produce or are unable to produce narratives contrasting the way things were with the way things are. What I am referring to is a pervasive set toward the past and toward narrating the past. That attitude denies "the code of chronology," as Lévi-Strauss (1966) puts it, or "the hysteria of causality," as Baudrillard's (1990) more evocative formulation would have it. It denies that the ultimate interpretive meaningfulness found in the typified Western historical narrative—the relationship between history and chronology—is in fact the most meaningful way to narrate the past.

The sense of the past on the reservation is perhaps best understood by first contrasting it to the general, layman's history that makes dates and chronological order equivalent with knowledge and understanding. The roads of Indian country are filled with commemorative markers, placed by the government and other entities at important historical sites located along our modern American highways. On Arizona's Route 80, near Douglas, one such marker memorializes Geronimo's final surrender to General Nelson Miles:

Geronimo's Surrender

Near here, Geronimo, last Apache chieftain
and Nachite with their followers,
surrendered, on September 6, 1886, to
General Nelson A. Miles, U.S. Army.
Lieutenant Chas. B. Gatewood with Kieta
and Martine, Apache scouts, risked their
lives to enter the camp of the hostiles
to present terms of surrender offered to
them by General Miles.

After two days, Gatewood received the
consent of Geronimo and Nachite to surrender.

The surrender of Geronimo in Skeleton
Canyon, on that historic day, forever
ended Indian warfare in the United States.

Erected A.D. 1934
City of Douglas
With Federal C.W.A. funds

"And so the story ends, we're told," as the song says. In the world
of highway markers, place marks the finality of the past. The markers mark precisely those things that used to be there, but are there no
longer. The marker performs a commemorative duty, showing the place
where things "forever ended." The event is markable, but unrecoverable. The highway roadside sign tells a story of things that happened
in the past. Something else used to go on here—there was a mill, there
was a battle, there was a fort, there was a celebration. But it is over and
done with. Something that happened "on September 6, 1886," changed
everything from that day all the way up to this one.

The highway marker thus becomes one piece of a naturalized chronology—and conversely, one way that chronology is naturalized as the
proper unmarked form for historical narrative to take. The past, in this
sense, is a string of these markable but unrecoverable events. This sense
of the past lends itself easily to the kind of waxing-and-waning chronological histories into which the Apaches are often incorporated. In those
narratives, the Apaches were preceded in the Southwest by the Salado
pueblo dwellers, whose abandonment of their towns may have been
hastened by drought or by raids from encroaching Apaches. The as-
cendant Apaches were, in turn, superseded by the Spanish, Mexican,
and finally American settlers who brought Western civilization to the
desert.

Uncomplicated and vaguely Darwinian in scope, this story of conflict and resolution presents chronology as justification. The inevitable
march of time out of the past and into the future means that all things
shall pass—or that someone might be gaining on you. In the larger narrative alluded to in this marker's text, "Apache history" effectively ends
in 1886, with Geronimo's surrender (and deportation to Florida). That
stroke "forever ended Indian warfare in the United States," making possible the economic development of the Southwest. And, indeed, the
classic scholarly histories of the Apaches end just there. Terrell's *Apache
Chronicle* ends on September 8, 1886, with Geronimo boarding the train
in Bowie "under heavy guard" (1972:385) and with the irony of the

Fourth Cavalry band playing "Auld Lang Syne" as the train pulled out of the station. Lockwood's *The Apache Indians* (1938) includes as a sort of afterword a final chapter on fifty years of reservation times. Both Thrapp's *The Conquest of Apacheria* (1967) and Ogle's *Federal Control of the Western Apaches, 1848–1886* (1970) cover the military engagement between the U.S. Army and the Apaches, Ogle's title making it clear precisely where the cutoff between Apache history and some other, later history, exists.[2]

Richard Handler has justly criticized anthropologists for naturalizing the authoritative reality (natural realism) of Western scholarly histories:

> Social-scientific writing often doubly presupposes this authoritative constitution of reality by taking historical scholarship for granted as background, to be used as a prelude to some variety of synchronic sociological analysis. That strategy obliterates any sense of history as a story or construct. Relegated to the background, history can be presented as facts. The existence of such facts in turn proves the existence of the "thing" the facts are about. Thus to begin an ethnographic narrative with historical background becomes a powerful rhetorical device for establishing the reality of the object of one's study. (1985:179–80)

In how many ethnographies does the ethnographer's insight and empathy end where the community's "history" begins?[3] The history of a community cannot unthinkingly be cast into a Western-style model of how to tell that history. If the past exists as both narrated events and narrative events, then locally meaningful ways of producing narratives must enter into the account. Locally meaningful literary tropes and the everyday symbolic practices of narrators must enter into the analysis of a cultural style of attachment to and imagining of the past.

What happens when we remove chronology as the dominant organizing model for talk about the past? In that case, the history of the reservation becomes more ambiguous, and ambiguity becomes a resource for expressing history. Unlike the clearly marked highway, the landscape vibrates with contingency. As you drive east from Phoenix up into the Pinals, through the jackknife switchbacks that lift you up off the floor of the Valley of the Sun, it is easy to get this sense of a past that refuses to recede. History becomes a series of layerings and juxta-positions—ruins etched into the land, hewn out of the rocks. As you drive east up into the mountains, leaving Superior behind, look into the valley below to your right. Down on the canyon floor is a nar-rower ribbon of concrete, snaking into the mountains at other and more precarious angles. The old highway, which was built in the 1920s to replace the poorly graded dirt roads—mostly mud during Arizona's "monsoon season"—that preceded it. Beginning in the 1920s and con-tinuing for half a century afterward, the federal and Arizona state gov-ernments embarked on numerous road construction and improvement projects. These roads not only eased travel from place to place in Ari-zona but also gave birth to one of the most successful travel and history magazines in twentieth-century publishing, *Arizona Highways*, which is also one of the premier showcases for southwestern Native American culture and art. Highway construction also offered the Lutheran mis-sionaries scattered around the Apache reservations an incessantly easy metaphor for conversion, one that linked modernization and progress to moral uprightness: "I can shut my eyes and see two roads very simi-lar to the old and new Cedar Creek roads. . . . The one who invites you to travel the old crooked road is none other than its builder, Satan himself who delights in wrecks and pain and sorrow and despair" (Guenther 1939:149).[4]

The old highway ribbons up to an old tunnel, the Claypool Tunnel, which disappears into the craggy rocks below. The new highway leads up to the Queen Creek Tunnel, completed in 1952. Observant drivers, looking to the right again, will see on the other side of the Queen Creek Tunnel the old highway below and, looking up across the canyon, will spy an even older road clinging to the scraggly rocks above. An old mule or wagon trail, or an even older Apache footpath—or both, no-body is really certain.[5]

Part of the contingency of the topography is performed in the place-names that mark it. Non-Apaches have memorialized the Apache pres-ence in all the places—towns and cities, streets and businesses—that are called "Apache" or named for prominent Apaches such as Geronimo. As one friend's mother commented, searching for her favorite oldies station on the car radio as we drove down to Phoenix to visit her son, "They took all this land from us and then they named everything after us." Apache Junction. Apache Avenue. Apache Boulevard. Apache Dry Cleaning. Apache Whirlwind Staircases. Cochise Contracting. Apache

Dental Lab. The names sense some kind of historical presence in the landscape—to be sure, even in the very rocks, such as the glassy, grape-size globules of obsidian known to local rock hounds as "Apache tears." But they do so in a way that memorializes something that is supposedly no longer there. Apache tears are found around the town of Superior, which sits at the western foot of the Pinals, below the sheer face of "Apache Leap." This is where, the legend has it, a group of Apache warriors jumped to their deaths rather than be taken captive by the U.S. Army. When their wives and daughters came to collect their broken and mangled bodies, the legend continues, the women's tears hardened into stone upon hitting the ground, becoming the black stones called "Apache tears." The legend of Apache tears, then, does what many narratives of its kind do: it relegates the Apaches to a romantic past, romanticizing the "waning" of the Apaches' dominion over the Southwest by showing their noble stubbornness in defeat by the U.S. Army—their raging against the tide of the present, modern world, their insistence on traveling that older, crooked highway.

The use of "Apache," "Geronimo," or "Cochise" in a place-name isn't the only way that non-Apaches memorialize the chronological history of the region. Sometimes the Apache language is used to denote certain places. One of these places is the Salado ruin in Globe, which is called by the Apache name "Besh-Ba-Gowah," despite its having little, if anything, to do with Apaches. The name is adapted from one San Carlos Apache designation for the town of Globe itself, *beesh baa gowąh*, which means "metal among/between/around the houses" and is said by some to refer to the copper mines that have been the major industry of Globe's economy. The name, like so many Apache place-names (Basso 1996), is fairly elliptical. *Beesh* is a generic, referring to any kind of metal, so it is entirely possible that the name refers to the railroad tracks that run through the town. If members of the Globe Chamber of Commerce prefer the other explanation, well, why shouldn't they?

To people on the reservation, however, the landscape is *filled* with places known by their Apache names, even to the monolingual English speakers among them. Some of these names are entirely independent of English or Spanish place-names, designating specific places that, to non-Apaches, are just more anonymous scenery. Others, such as the Apache names for Globe, for the Triplets, for Mount Turnbull, run parallel to the place-names that denote non-Apache settlement of the area.

Still other names force the clash of languages and denotational difference into exquisite tension, through practices of speech play and cross-linguistic punning. Phillip's father, Britton Goode, in the written and oral notes that he collected before he died, said that the derivation of the name "Tucson" came from the Apache *tús si'án*, meaning "a water jug sits," or perhaps *tú nzaad*, meaning "water is far away" (Samuels 2001). A number of people say that the San Carlos Apaches are descended from the Western Apache band associated with the area, known as the *tsee k'aadn*, or "metate people." These geographical puns perform the historical and political ambiguity of the reservation community and its relationship to the clash of languages that ambiguously situate the community within the concentric circles joining it to the modern nation. These place-names shift "history" from chronology to topography. They shift a sequential series to the simultaneity of the pun by discovering sonic, phonological similarities in Apache and non-Apache topographical lexicons. The Apache names are not simple memorials, preserving the past in amber. Nor is the representation of identity or the imagination of history bound up completely in practices or ideologies associated transparently with the past. Rather, these punning place-names show one of the ways in which contemporary expressive materials are taken up to craft a poetics of political position, identity, and history on the San Carlos Reservation. The past insistently elbows its way into the present, and the present evokes a sense of the past. These cross-linguistic punning practices are resonant with Stuart Hall's important, but too often forgotten, observation that "Cultural identity . . . is a matter of 'becoming' as well as of 'being'. It belongs to the future as much as the past" (1990:225).

I have little doubt that non-Apache people living off the reservation—in Globe, Miami, Superior, and Wheatfields to the west, or in Geronimo, Fort Thomas, Pima, Thatcher, Safford, Clifton, and Morenci to the east —have experiences that mirror in some ways those of the Apache people in San Carlos, Peridot, and Bylas. After all, they, too, see the old highway and the footpath when they drive to Phoenix, and they also shop at the stores named after Geronimo. But when these experiences are mediated through the dominant forms of expression in the non-Apache community, there seems to be an almost inexorable pull of chronology. I am familiar with two histories of Globe written by local authors (*Honor*

the Past 1976; Bigando 1990), although there are more that might complicate this point. Each of the histories I have read takes a strictly chronological, "and then this is what happened next" approach. And each fash-
ions its chronology so that the Apaches are off the stage by the turn of
the twentieth century. The story of Globe is a story of ascendancy, of developing Arizona's mineral riches for the good of the community and
the nation.

But for people on the San Carlos Reservation, history isn't about or-
dering events chronologically in order to explain an outcome. Rather, it
is about topography and feeling, especially the feelingfulness of expressivity. I was told, on more than one occasion and by more than one consultant, that cultural belonging and identity aren't part of a logical order—that "being Apache is a feeling." Phillip, my Apache teacher, used
to say it in relationship to his attempts to "nativize" me. "It's like you're
a piece of chewing gum stuck to the bottom of this table," he would
say as we sat in his kitchen for my Apache lessons, "and I'm slooooowly
peeling you off."

The layering of present and past is a primary means of summoning
that deep Apache feeling. The past is ubiquitous in people's talk in the
community. As you go around the San Carlos Reservation with people,
you learn just how ubiquitous the past is. It is in the land and in the way
people talk about places. Driving people around, you learn that everyone knows something about places, and anything can trigger a story.
As one consultant put it to me, "Everything makes them think about
the past."[6] Over my stay in San Carlos, people pointed out the footpath across from the highway. They took me to the graded bed where
the railroad tracks ran to Old San Carlos before Coolidge Dam was
built. Some people know the peak from which the outlaw Apache Kid
sang his songs of loneliness for San Carlos. Many pointed out to me
the small cliff dwellings on the way up to Point of Pines and a place
where pictographs were drawn on the wall of a cave. Everyone knows
the old Military Trail leading to Fort Apache, and they know the can-
yons where old cavalrymen are buried. Phillip showed me the place that
was named because it was the last point from which Apaches enlisting
as scouts at Fort Grant could look back and see Old San Carlos. One
woman always pointed out to me where the Battle of Bloody Tanks took
place, "where we made our last stand." Marshall knew of a place where
the frame of an old covered wagon still stood and walked me back behind Moonbase to show it to me. And everyone has a story about where

the real boundary of the reservation is. The easy way in which experience, place, memory, and history slide into one another marks everyday verbal interaction in San Carlos and Bylas.

But if history is ubiquitous and pervasive in the social life and interactions of the community, it is also disjointed and fragmented. These episodes and bits of knowledge don't find their coherence by being drawn together into a chronological statement of events. History isn't about chronology. It's about feeling—the feeling of belonging in a place, of knowing that your presence in a place is justified. That feeling is cultivated in San Carlos in brief, cameo moments of aesthetic pleasure, where complex and divergent elements are superimposed and linked in transcendent instants that are often as short-lived as they are poignant. In these moments, present, past, self, other, knowledge, and feeling coalesce in a richly layered image of historical meaning. Those moments open a window onto the past, making it restorable to the present.

The expressive, feelingful, and affective presence of history doesn't mean that Apaches can't or don't talk about the past as something that has, well, passed. Basso (1996) discusses *doo aníí dą́*, "a long time ago," as a category of Western Apache narrative.[7] On the San Carlos Reservation, it is pervasive as a means of reorganizing or reframing everyday experience into more feelingful signs.

One group of stories that I heard often concerns the availability of gold "back then," when Apaches were still "Indians" and not "civilized nnee." These stories also explain, in some sense, that money is really something that white people understand. "If only we'd kept all the gold we took back then," one woman said to me, "instead of throwing it away. We'd be rich today!" Many people expressed a similar sense of chagrin at the loss of this windfall.

But many people—including some who offered the kind of response just mentioned—also believe that someone must know where all that gold went. "They threw it down the deepest holes in the mesas," one person told me. "The real old-timers knew where it was, but none of them told anybody." One time, as I was driving along the road to Soda Canyon with Marshall, he looked up at two mesas standing side by side back from the edge of the road. "A long time ago," he told me, "the old people said, 'You guys, don't worry, you're taken care of. There's gold put away for you in two hills.' I always wondered if that's the two hills they were talking about." Another time, driving by the Triplets, a friend told me that there was a gold mine back in there somewhere. Two Apaches followed an older man back into the Triplets, he told me, and they waited for him to come out with his sack of gold so that they could make him show them the mine. But he never came out. When they finally decided to look for him, they found him, back in the hills, dead, his sack of gold by his side. So they never found that mine.

The people who spoke to me generally attributed Apaches' attitudes toward gold during the nineteenth century to cultural difference. It was useless and unnecessary in a life without stores and banks and wages. I heard about a raid that took place in the saddle behind Jerusalem Mountain, on the old road from Fort Grant to Fort Apache. The Apaches got a number of sacks of gold from the people they raided. They threw the gold away and kept the sacks to carry their belongings. Someone else told me that during those times Apaches would have contests with gold coins from a raid to see who could throw a coin the farthest. One older man told me about the old wagon trail that leads from Yellowjacket through Fort Grant to Fort Huachuca. There were lots of wagons hauling money on that road, and the Apaches would attack them. They would keep the cooking outfit, but the money got dumped in the canyon. Phillip's brother, who rented me the trailer in Airport '79, also mentioned the Fort Huachuca military trail: "There's stories about gold, they attacked these soldiers and threw it over the cliffs I heard."[8]

These stories are associated with others, about the dangers of finding gold—or at least the dangers of finding gold if you're Apache. The rumors of discarded gold bring white treasure hunters out to the old trails. "They go out there looking for gold all the time," said one consultant. Another told me, "White guys from Kansas City, Missouri, want that money." But according to story after story, when Apaches find gold, it can spell trouble. One is about a woman who found gold and bought a new truck with the money, only to die in an auto accident. I heard another about four men who found a gunnysack with money and hid it. They shared it, went to Las Vegas, bought themselves a hundred head of cattle. But then one of the men's sons drowned, and another's drowned in Coolidge Dam. Or there's the story about a man who "found six bars and he sold it and now look at his health." People say gold makes you crazy—*biłnagodimaas*.

One of my older acquaintances thought the whole thing was silly. "Gold is heavy," he insisted. So it would sink into the soft ground when it rained. He estimated that it would sink about a half-inch per year, which means that over the course of a century it would have sunk more than four feet.

In other versions of the story about Apaches and gold, however, the Apaches' disregard for gold is not a mark of their lack of knowledge about its value, but rather an index of how precious they knew it was held in the estimation of whites. Throwing gold away, in these versions, is presented as defiance, an active practice of resistance to Bureau American domination. Knowing how much value the Americans placed on gold, Apaches deliberately disposed of it. Geronimo would find the deepest crevices to throw gold down. Here again, however, people also wonder if Geronimo—being no fool—perhaps held onto the gold. If so, perhaps it would be found in his least accessible hideouts. The ones only he could get to. I remember driving to Salt River Canyon once to deliver some firewood. My companion pointed up to a tear-shaped cave opening, down the sheer wall of the canyon. "You see that?" he said. "That's Geronimo's hideout. Man, I wonder what you'd find up there if you could get in?" As with the whole topic of "history," the point in these narratives is only partially to know *when* these things happened. It is at least as important, if not more so, to know *where* they happened.

This is not to say that Apaches can't or don't construct resistant versions of dominant history—counterchronologies. Nor is it to say that the way these counterchronologies push against the power of dominant forms of historiography to contain meaning are not worthy of serious consideration. They are; and people told me a number of them while I was working on the reservation. Near the end of my stay, a group of honor students from San Carlos High School went on a trip to Washington, D.C., and New York City. One of the students told me on her return that she had been shocked that there was an African American art museum in the nation's capital, but no Native American art museum. She also gleefully told me about the students' bus tour of Manhattan. One of the sights to see was Columbus Circle near Central Park, with its statue of Christopher Columbus standing on his pillar. The tour guide announced that they were approaching the statue of Columbus, who discovered America. From the back of the bus, the Apache kids started shouting: "Who *cares* about Columbus?" and "He didn't discover *us*!"

By the end of the day, the tour guide had amended her remarks to say that Columbus *supposedly* discovered America.

Here's another example. My friend Duane told me the story of the Pilgrims so that I might understand clearly his frustration at the position of "Indians" in the mainstream political economy of the United States:

> If God was to make man as one certain thing, like a white man, why then in the hell did He make him come all the way across the ocean, just to find another place to live, just to take over the land, which he had no idea what was on the land except for natives, wild, renegade natives that are gonna just kill anybody in sight who's of opposite color, you know.
>
> And then it comes out the white man was really helpless in this wilderness, that he had to have help. And there was this one certain Indian that came out to help the white man. And what does that do? It brings up a change, I mean a chain as to where the white man says, "Hey, wow, man, these guys are really easy to get by," you know? "You can tell them something and they'll just do it. Or if you can take away something they won't care because they think that they have this whole big land as freedom."
>
> And now we're under their judicial laws, which wasn't like that way back then.
>
> And then the white man had to have help from the Indians to get medicine to cure certain illnesses that the Indian knew about long time ago, centuries ago, knew where to get it, how to get it, how to make good use of a certain thing. Now that he's learned all that stuff, he comes out and says, "Hey, man," you know, "thanks a lot for helping us." You know, "Thanks a lot for doing that for us. Now, we're the top nation in the world, and you didn't even have nothing to do with it," you know? "You're just another minority like the Mexicans and the blacks."

Duane offers a terse and telling perspective on the story of empire and conquest. He gives his version of the European landing in America and European views of "wild" natives (with the use of the word *renegade*, which is often reserved for such groups as the Apaches). He retells the story of Squanto and of the help the Indians offered the English settlers of the New World.[9] But I think it's worth noting that by casting his story in a chronological mold—that is, by retelling "the same story," with a trajectory familiar to anyone who knows the legends of Plymouth Colony and the first Thanksgiving—Duane runs into a snag at the conclusion. To be sure, triumph is recast bitterly, victory is restated as dispossession, but the narrative is counterhegemonic in a classic sense, insofar as its resistances and contestations are cast within the terms set by American nationalist or cultural hegemonic and narrative forces (see Beckett 1994a).

Duane's problem with chronological narrative and endings was underscored in another story he told me.

> The only thing us young people probably know is what's been written in the history books about us, you know? There's hardly nothing written about us. It's the great Sioux nation, Cherokee nation, all those other big nations that made it big. Us guys, we were just—
>
> But I'll tell you one thing, we were the strongest, man, we were the last to give up, to the white man. We had to be chased all over this reservation. Just to be settled down. But all those other tribes, man, they gave up right away, man. As soon as the Big Chief I-Don't-Care-What-His-Name-Was, man, you know, put his thumb mark on that paper, that was it, it was time to give up. Not us, uh-uh. We got chased all over the place, and we didn't give up, man—
>
> Till we were forced to.

Here, Duane begins by distinguishing what he is saying from what is written in history books, although he phrases his complaint in terms of which indigenous groups merit inclusion in that written history at the expense of others. He interrupts this first narrative, however, to embed a second about the steadfastness of the Apache resistance—a commonly circulated trope in the community, despite Geronimo's problematic place within the history of the San Carlos community. Some people are quick to point out that although Geronimo was incarcerated at Old San Carlos for a time, he was a Chiricahua Apache with little to tie him to the Western Apache people of the San Carlos Reservation. In fact, Geronimo's surrender was achieved with the aid of scouts hired from the San Carlos agency. He was, it is true, the last Native American leader to surrender to the U.S. government, but he was not from San Carlos. Nevertheless, his ability to hold out the longest against the forces of the U.S. Army makes him an important figure to many in San Carlos, despite the supposed tenuous connections.

But Geronimo escaped the military by going into Mexico with his followers—some of their descendants are constantly rumored to be living in the Sierra Madres still. What are we to make, then, of Duane's imagining the place that the Apaches were "chased all over" in order to be "settled down" as being limited to the reservation? Even if it's just a slip of the tongue, it's certainly an interesting, if not a telling one. I do think that Duane thought of himself as narrating a different story from the one found in any elementary school history book. I take this in part from the earnest intensity with which he told the story and in part from the fact that it emerged directly, as an interruption, out of his complaints about "what's been written in the history books about us." But if I am right that Duane's initial intention was to narrate a counterhistory, the rhetorical force at the beginning of his embedded narrative is surely stripped away in the narrative's conclusion: in Duane's unwillingness to finish the story, in the deathly pause before his final sentence, "Til we were forced to." For all the difference of its perspective, Duane's story ends in the same place, with the same conclusion: the chronological ascendancy of Bureau Americans to dominance in Arizona in 1886.

And that's the basic problem of chronologies on the San Carlos Reservation: they end. And they end with the wrong side winning. But there are ways of reimagining the past other than counterchronology. One is a more radical approach that denies pride of place to chronological form at all. Rather than tell history as a chronological procession of events — causes and effects—this approach represents history on principles of simultaneity, juxtaposition, and layering rather than of sequence. Its organizing trope is place rather than time. These emplaced juxtapositions are something like being able to look out on the present and see the past, an experience that is partly in keeping with people's experiences of the world. Old things here aren't necessarily removed to make room for the new. They stick around for a while.

But there is more to it, for, as I noted earlier, non-Apaches in towns and cities off the reservation also witness and experience these layerings of old and new in the world. But the same sign, the same expressive symbol, can create different affective meanings in individuals with differing social histories and allegiances to different historically constituted social groups. In the complex "circuit of culture" (du Gay et al. 1997), the intersection of experience, representation, and identity constitutes specific cultural means of access to meanings. A single sign can generate a multitude of significances. The continued presence of the past in the material world is not simply a *thing*. It also presents people with a way of organizing their imaginative experience. The memory work involved is nicely encapsulated by a brief event that took place when an old friend of mine in Bylas moved out of her mother's house in Southside and into her own place in Home Alone, a new housing development that the tribe had built just up the hill from her old neighborhood. We were helping her move in and admiring the new house, with its stucco walls and linoleum floors. Her cousin, whom I had known since we were teenagers, was sitting at the kitchen table, looking out the window at the houses down the hill, where they had all grown up. "Man," he said. "It's like you're looking out at the past, huh." This juxtaposed layering of images is the essence of the form of historical narrative on the reservation.

This sense, that the present melts easily into a window on the past, is a common element in the traffic of symbols on the reservation. It can crop up at any time. One day I was visiting Marshall out at his mom's house by the lake. We sat out back, in the shade, while Marsh did some work on the Cutlass's engine. His brother and stepson were with us, talking about "riding the bull." I thought they were talking about bull riding, like in the rodeo, but it turned out that they were talking about sitting on a piece of cardboard and sledding down the hill behind the house.

"They call that 'riding the bull'?" I asked.

"Yeah," said Marshall. " 'Riding the wild bull.' You mean you never heard that story? Back then," he said, "some cavalry were out on patrol, regular patrol, looking for Geronimo. And they heard some kids laughing. And they looked around, and it turns out they found some Apache kids, sitting in a wooden crate, sliding down a hill. And I always wondered," he said, "where that hill was. You know that hill behind where you drive up to the Peridot dump? Into that canyon? I think that might be it."

Later that afternoon I was at an elder's house, and I told her the story that I had heard, and she called her husband out from the back room because he used to play in Peridot as a boy, riding down the hill on a cowhide. He told me exactly which hill it was—indeed, it was in the canyon going toward the dump yard.

At first, this story appears to be a simple etiological explanation of a cultural practice, so it's worth noticing that Marshall's story doesn't actually explain the origin of the game at all. Rather, it places the game within the ambiguous political, historical, and cultural contexts of the reservation community. Nor is he curious about where the game or its name came from. Rather, what he "always wondered" about was *where*: which hill, specifically, the story is about. Marshall's narrative and the older man's acceptance that Marshall's question about where the episode occurred was the right one to ask point again to the importance of the recoverable past in present places and practices. Such narratives are common enough in San Carlos, Peridot, and Bylas. People's imaginations are constantly reworking place and past. A cigarette is sometimes passed with the admonition, "nádint'ii," meaning "go look back over there," in the sense that your thoughts would be transported by the smoke. One time, when the Pacers were driving back from a gig in Mescalero, the three cars carrying the band got separated. Pat, Darryl, and I pulled over into a rest stop because Darryl thought that he had seen Marshall's car stopped at an earlier rest stop. As we sat and waited for them to catch up with us (as it turned out, Darryl was wrong, and they were way ahead of us), I said to Pat, "Where do you think they're at?" Pulling a GPC out of the pack in his pocket, he said, jokingly, "I don't know, let me see. Let me smoke on it."

At the same time, though, there are also less-joking moments, in which the walls surrounding the present melt away and the here-and-now can be transcended. As in Dominic's response in his veranda at the Sunrise Dance, the feeling embodied and encapsulated in an instantaneous moment can transport one into the past, to share that feeling with an imagined community of long-gone comrades.

The occurrences that put people in mind of how it was in the past are many and varied. One thing they seem to have in common with each other, though, is that they create the sense of history through an iconicity of feeling. That is, the persistence of a practice (in the form of tradition) is not necessarily the only key to the historical imagination. Although the feelingful sense of the past can be brought about in a setting indexically marked as traditional, neither persistence of practices that are indexically related (or relatable) to a prior lifeway nor a representation of those practices is necessary for people on the San Carlos Reservation to feel deeply connected to the past. What is needed is a meaningful juxtaposition that sets the witness momentarily free in an interpretive frame in which the present affective state is layered onto an affective state that would have occurred in the past. That is, if the person in the present could somehow exchange places with an Apache in the past, both would have the same feeling. For being Apache is a feeling, and the constancy of that feeling makes the past recoverable.

Iconicity of feeling also explains how it is possible to craft a fully Apache identity out of the clearly "not-Apache" materials of the modern world—why the sense of identity travels far beyond instances of traditional practice. One consultant told me of a time when he was sitting in his Spanish class at Globe High School in the late 1960s. He was leafing through a library book that contained old photographs of Apaches. The class was supposed to be learning a Spanish song that day. "[And I'd stopped to look at] a picture of those guys being herded toward Old San Carlos from—they were walking, Geronimo and his group, and soldiers on horseback, and then they were, you could see the dust, it was like in a wash. And I still remember how that song goes, [sings] 'cuando calienta el sol, da da da da da da,' it was a mellow song, and it gave me a melancholy feeling over me, and I *felt* for those people." This song—not a traditional Apache song by any means— allowed him to enter into the photograph he had been looking at and experience that world—not to imagine what those people felt or to understand what they felt, but to feel what they felt. Songs, and not only traditional Apache songs, turn people's minds and feelings back to those days and to hard times. As I discuss later, one twelve-year-old girl told me her sense that if Indian people back then had heard certain songs by Bob Marley, Guns 'N' Roses, and Mariah Carey, "they wouldn't have lost faith."

This juxtaposition of past and present in the representation of contemporary identity is detectable in other forms of contemporary expression. For example, the names, many in English, given to the numerous small neighborhoods and federal housing developments on the reservation place them not only geographically, but historically and ideologically as well. A number of them are derived from mainstream American popular culture in ways that underscore the irony, playfulness, and ambiguity at work in the creation of a geography of contemporary identities on the reservation.

Sections of San Carlos and Bylas are named for a physical feature of the houses there, such as the colorful stucco TWEP[10] homes of Rainbow City, the whitewashed clapboard houses of White City, or the semicircular bay windows in the brick homes of El Taco City. Moonbase, a housing development in Peridot, perhaps appeared that way to someone looking down on it from the high road to the west. Then there are the sections named for their proximity to a particular defining feature, such as Mormon Hill, near the Mormon Church; Three Tank, near the water tanks; Chinatown, named for a two-story pagoda-style home that someone built there; or Ready to Go, which sits beside a church cemetery in Bylas.[11]

Other sections of town take their names from the people who live or lived there: Hallelujah Square, so named because a number of its origi-nal residents were born-again Christians; or Land of the Giants—bor-rowed from the TV show produced by Irwin Allen—where all those tall people used to live. Or La Bumba City and Tarzan Valley, which took on the nicknames of their most prominent residents. A physical charac-teristic of the space may name it, as in Darkest Corners. Or an area may hold onto an older, no longer extant functional name, such as Farmer Station.

Then some places take on names made possible only by popular culture. By news stories: Waco, a secluded collection of wood-frame homes, some of which burned down during the spring that the Branch Davidians were battling the Bureau of Alcohol, Tobacco, and Firearms. By movies: Airport '79, where I lived, is located down a hill from the landing strip at the Forestry Service headquarters; it was also con-structed in 1979, when the movie of the same name was released. Home Alone is a housing development behind Southside, Bylas—old-time residents complain that it spoils their view of the frozen-custard peak of Ch'idishdlaazhé. When the tribe added on to the original development, that addition of course became known as the sequel, Home Alone 2. The most recent addition to this lexicon during my stay was an area of grass and trees in Seven Mile Wash, down by the San Carlos River, which is now referred to as Jurassic Park.

All these places, named or not, have stories connected with them, stories about the things that happened there. "Here's where I used to stand to hitchhike back to Globe from East Fork—East Fork, Carrizo Junction, Cibecue, Globe, then go into Pinky's Tavern and find a ride back to San Carlos." "At this switchback is where a white guy fell asleep at the wheel and drove off the road and down into the Salt River Can-yon." "Out that way is a pile of rocks; it's a place where Apaches used to meet; whenever someone passed by that place, they would put an-other rock on the pile." "You mean you never went on the old road to the dam?" "Way back in there is where they built the first housing de-velopments on the reservation." "My grandmother told me that all of what's Bylas used to be under water."

On one hand, emplacing history within the feelingful response to narra-tive and the landscape rather than in linear chronology makes the sense of the past more ambiguous and layered. On the other hand, this emplacement is, at least in some sense, in better keeping with the social relations between Apache and non-Apache people in the area around the reservation over the past 150 years. Globe, for instance, is itself an ambiguously situated community in relationship to the standard public memory of the Frontier West. This ambiguous situatedness is often erased in the chronologized narrative of the town's development. For one thing, although the area includes a number of important Arizona ranches, Globe City is a mining town—a copper-mining town at that. As important as mining has been in the economic development of the United States, it has never captured the imagination the way farming and cowboying have. Edward Buscombe (1988) estimates that for every Western film about mining, there are perhaps twenty about cowboys. Globe started as a silver camp, but at present, being a copper town, it misses out on other commonly privileged icons of the Old West: no quaint images of bearded mountain men panning the creeks and rivers here, no ghost town. Globe is a commercial center, playing the role of a hard-working, broad-shouldered community where men come home with the taste of copper in their mouths, covered from head to toe in a film of green after operating the smelter all day. Unlike the movie-set tourist sites of Arizona—Old Tucson, Tombstone, Tortilla Flat—Globe's history is somewhat marginal to the events and the images of that imagined past. Phineas Clanton, of Shootout at the OK Corral fame, owned a goat farm in Globe in the 1890s and is buried there. Butch Cassidy was rumored to have lived in Globe for about a year in 1909–10, under the alias "William T. Phillips," after supposedly escaping Bolivia.

I learned these things because some people would like to see Globe and the Pinto Valley join this mainstream history. It would mean expanded tourist dollars. Route 70 heads east out of Globe through the San Carlos Reservation and into New Mexico, terminating in the town of Lordsburg. The communities along this ribbon of blacktop have banded together to rename the route the "Old West Highway." There is a question of what along this route would attract tourists. The Apaches, icons of the untamed frontier that they are, might bring in the people, perhaps. The consultant who helped plan the cultural center on the reservation certainly thought so. But like Globe, the reservation is neither historical museum nor theme park. The Apaches are not about to don buckskins, jump on horseback, and chase cars down the highway for everyone's entertainment, as Phillip joked they might.

Despite its own marginality to the mainstream romance of frontier history, many people in Globe do attempt to chronologize the Apaches into the past when they talk or write about the history of the area. The attempt to do so, however, involves manipulating the history of the reservation boundary—a shifting and ambiguous line, but one that is crucial to making these chronologies. To make the story of the development of Arizona "work," the Apaches' place in the narrative must be clearly marked off in the waxing and waning force of its organization. That is, the Apaches may have replaced the earlier Salado pueblo dwellers— even raided them out of existence—but eventually, according to this narrative, they had to bow to the greater force of the American settlers and be satisfied with having the Salado ruin named for them. Thus, the Salado ruin, Besh-Ba-Gowah, also reinforces the naturalized narrative of Globe's history: a succession of groups have been dominant in the area—first the Salados, then the Apaches, now "us." In the stories of Globe's and Arizona's development, the Apaches are cast in the role of the willful and belligerent opponents of modernity and development, a role made separate and racial, marked by greater and more natural distinctions.

This separation occurs not only in the written histories of Arizona in general or of the Globe-Miami area in particular, but in everyday talk by people in the town as well. Every year, for example, the Globe Chamber of Commerce sponsors the Historic House and Buildings Tour, and in 1995 I took it. Globe has a number of lovely nineteenth-century homes, some with breathtaking views of the Pinals. It also includes a number of historic factory and warehouse spaces, dating back to its heyday as a center for the production of copper during America's age of electrification. Broad Street in Globe used to boast the Mirror Barber Shop, which claimed to be the oldest barbershop in Arizona.

A rotating pool of drivers was designated to take us from house to house. At the conclusion of each individual house tour, a car or van would be outside to take us to our next stop. On one of those drives, the conversation turned to Globe's ethnic groups. A passenger had noticed that one of the local restaurants served pasties, considered perhaps the quintessential item of the Cornish culinary heritage. One person talked about the hard-rock miners who had come over from Cornwall. He also told us of Mexican woodcutters and miners who had settled in the area and mentioned that people from Croatia, Serbia, and Herzegovina had settled in Globe, too, as well as many Italian stonemasons who faced the hydroelectric dams going up in the area at the turn of the century. All these people of different descent were buried together in the municipal cemetery. They all had different funeral practices—headstones or footstones, Roman or Cyrillic orthography, image or no image of the deceased. A native of Globe, this person thought that perhaps the cemetery should someday be included on the historic tour. You can see history in those cemetery grounds, he claimed. Important events, such as the influenza epidemic of 1918, were marked in the number of lives lost. There were burials extending back to 1880, he added. He recalled one from the 1880s: "Gentleman was 'killed by Apache Indians,' that's what it states on the headstone." He might have been speaking of the grave of Sheriff Glenn Reynolds, who died on November 2, 1889, and whose headstone, in addition to its quotation from the book of Job,[12] also contains the inscription: "Killed by the Apache Indians." Or perhaps he had in mind the oldest plot in the municipal cemetery: the burial site of Thomas B. Hammond, dead at the age of thirty, whose headstone proclaims that he was "Murdered by Apaches" on September 1, 1876.

This is how the chronological narrative of Globe's history eases Apaches out for separation and exclusion—except as the image of the threat of violent death, as the killers of the people buried in the town cemetery. Despite the presence of Apaches from San Carlos in the Globe community, not only as bearers of Apache cultural traditions but as workers in the development of the roads, the dams, and the mines, the reservation boundary is both a geographic location and a historical and narrative location. Crossing the reservation boundary is not really traveling through time, but if the story of Globe is the story of a succession of events that led up to the narrative resolution of the present copper-mining community, then the Apaches have to be kept to one side of those events.

Making the reservation border the marker of historical difference between "before" (the Apaches) and "after" (the Europeans and Americans) is problematic on a number of counts and papers over a more ambiguous situation than a simple chronological account of ascendancy can contain. For one thing, there is the actuality of the boundary—a literally shifting line. The border that demarcated "Apache land" was often respected in the breach. Encroaching settlers who desired the mineral deposits and farmland along the Gila River determined for themselves that "Apache land" didn't refer to any land that might happen to be developable. Arizona contains the second-richest deposits of copper in the world, after Chile, and Globe sits on land that was originally designated part of the Apache reservation. Well, it's more complicated than that. The original silver-mining camps were set up in the late 1860s. The borders of the reservation were designated in 1871. The western boundary of the reservation was drawn behind the miners, and by law they should have removed themselves from the land. But the miners simply squatted on the reservation for five years, until their petitions to have the land removed from the reservation and returned to the "public domain" was granted. Globe is certainly not the only place where this happened. The Christmas mine, to the south along the San Pedro River, was also struck on land later removed from the reservation. On the eastern border of the reservation, in Clifton-Morenci, Phelps-Dodge operates the largest open-pit copper mine in North America on land that was also once part of the Apache reservation.[13] Making the border a sign of the historic break between Apache and European dominance erases the ambiguities inherent in the land's history.

Both then and now the "need" for extraction of resources is the most common reason given for the "need" to contain the Apaches on a reservation, to hold them outside the "public domain." But as Richard Perry (1993) notes, some Apaches tried to hold the U.S. government to the idea of incorporating the Apaches into the economic flow of the nation. In meetings with government officials over annexation of the Mineral Strip in the late nineteenth century, "Mose Gila opposed the agreement and noted that 'their children, educated in Government schools, could develop these mines and sell the coal to the whites'" (Perry 1993:154). Nineteenth-century ideas of cultural evolution help explain why Bureau Americans insisted that mining was something that only white people did and that the Apaches should instead be taught to be subsistence farmers. "These coal fields, as you know," said the government spokesperson, "are utterly worthless to you; they have no timber or grass worth speaking of upon them. They are entirely valueless for agricultural purposes. Their value consists alone in what is under the ground in the shape of minerals. This coal land is worthless to you. Why? Because you can't work them. They are valuable to the white people because they understand how to utilize them" (Reynolds 1896, cited in Perry 1993:153). The Apaches did grow alfalfa and eventually became quite successful in the cattle industry. But if the idea was to turn Apaches into farmers, that doesn't explain why some of the best farmland, in the eastern portion of the reservation along the Gila River, was also returned to the "public domain," a euphemism for "non-Apaches."

A second difficulty with the chronological narrative that pushes Apaches into the region's past is that it ignores the involvement of Apaches in the social life of Globe from early in the twentieth century, if not earlier. Pastor J. F. G. Harders, for example, arrived in Globe in 1907, sent by the Wisconsin Synod of the Evangelical Lutheran Church. He went on to write two novels based loosely on his missionary experiences in Arizona (Harders 1953, 1958). As H. C. Nitz's (1939) brief memoir of Harders puts it, Harders was sent to Globe in order to pastor to the "Apaches in the dispersion." Nitz paints a picture of turn-of-the-century Globe as a multiethnic, multilingual settlement—"a modern Babel":

On its streets, swaggering cowboys rubbed shoulders with grimy copper miners, or "muckers," as they are called. Chinese truck gardeners sold their vegetables from house to house. Jews conducted clothing stores. Germans sold meats and milk. Swarthy Syrians conducted grocery stores. "Cousin Jacks" from the Cornish Coast in England descended into the hot bowels of the earth to mine the precious copper, and many of them spent their earnings in the numerous saloons, gambling dens, pool halls flanking the walls of the canyon that formed the main street of the city. English and German, Italian and Polish, Russian and Spanish, Syrian and Turkish, French and Apache, Greek and Ethiopian—these and other languages could be heard on the streets of this bustling city, justly called the "crossroads of the world." (Nitz 1939:82)[14]

Harders was sent to this polyglot community "to be missionary to the scattered bands of Apaches living at Globe, Copper Hill, Miami, Wheatfields, Roosevelt, Gisela, Clarkdale, Jerome, Ft. Huachucca, Bylas" (Nitz 1939:82). That is to say, by 1907 at least, Apaches were living in Globe, Miami, and Superior and in settlements all along the Apache Trail (Arizona State Highway 88) through Wheatfields up to Roosevelt Dam and, to the east, out past Geronimo toward Thatcher and Safford. In fact, Apaches lived in their own communities off the reservation through at least World War II, if not into the 1950s and 1960s, in areas around Globe known as Little Hollywood and Mackey's Camp. One of my neighbors in Seven Mile grew up in Superior in the 1930s, when his father was working in the copper mines there. When I asked him if they had rented their house, he said, "No, we just lived there. If you stayed there for three days now, someone would come by and say, 'Hey, you owe me rent, this is my land,' but back then nobody cared." In a sense, it is the stranglehold of private property rather than the U.S. military that finally pushed the Apaches back behind the borders of the reservation. Until quite recently, for instance, Apaches picked acorns at an area back in the crest of the Pinals, just before the road dives down the switchbacks into Superior. One elder woman told me that when she was a girl, they would get on the bus to Phoenix early in the morning and catch the return bus at the end of the day. But Apaches can't pick acorns there anymore because the area is now a community called Top of the World. No doubt, much of the land on which Apaches lived in Globe was claimed by various mining concerns, but the mines did not develop the claims, and Apaches lived there for decades after they were "confined" to the reservation.[15]

In any case, back in 1907, Pastor Harders spent some of his own savings to build a small Lutheran chapel, called the New Jerusalem Church, at the corner of Devereaux and Apache Streets in Globe. In an indication of the polyglot community he served, the chapel bell was purchased with funds donated by his Apache congregants, and his Chinese congregants had the chapel, the pastor's house, and the adjoining school wired for electricity. Globe's multiethnic heritage can also be seen in the fact that the town still boasts Serbian and Croatian burial grounds. The municipal cemetery has a Chinese section, and Buffalo Soldiers are buried in a special section as well. If Nitz's memoir of Harders is taken at face value, at least nine or ten distinct languages have disappeared from Globe's discourse community.[16] Unlike the acknowledgment of multiple ethnic groups that I heard on the house tour, however, Nitz's memorialization of Harders—not to mention the fact that Harders was sent to Globe at all—prominently includes Apaches and must make a reader question the marginalization and exclusion of Apaches from the social history of Globe.

None of the foregoing should be taken to imply that I think the way of imagining and telling history on the reservation is any more "true" than the imagining and telling of history off it. But neither do I think that the reverse is the case. Just as discourse is historically shaped and situated—molded by the power relations that allow certain topics and forms to thrive at the expense of others—so too is history discursively shaped and situated—made real and natural by the naturalized genres and tropes of its narrative forms and contents.

This persistence of the past for people on the reservation—on an ever-receding horizon, always accessible, always partially recoverable —is perhaps nowhere more eloquently encapsulated than in the image of Old San Carlos. Nothing offers a more evocative commentary on the problems with anthropology's naturalizing of a chronological representation of Apache history than the way people in San Carlos remember and talk about the drowned original agency settlement. What is now known as San Carlos was once called Rice. The elementary school in San Carlos is still called Rice Elementary School. Old San Carlos was located at the confluence of the Gila and San Carlos Rivers. It was covered over by the rising waters of San Carlos Lake, the reservoir that formed behind Coolidge Dam when it opened in 1928.

In 1962, the Arizona Highway Department commemorated Old San Carlos with a historical marker, placed in a rest area overlooking the road that goes down to the lake.

Old San Carlos

This famous old Indian agency of
the bloody Apache war days was
covered by the waters of San Carlos
Lake upon completion of Coolidge Dam
in 1928. The old Indian cemetery
was covered with a cement slab.
Buildings were moved several miles
north to a new San Carlos.

One wants to say, the government typically can't write the word *Apache* without surrounding it with the words *bloody* and *war*. What is striking in the context of the foregoing discussion, however, is the way in which the plaque marks history as something that has passed. The marker treats Old San Carlos as something already finished, its pastness finalized by something having happened in 1928 that forever covered it over with the waters of progress and modernization.

In the communities of the San Carlos Reservation, however, Old San Carlos continues to reverberate with meaning and presence. More than seventy years ago children sat on the hills and watched the waters of the Coolidge Dam reservoir creep up the cragged walls of the rocky basin.

Today those children, now respected elders, joke that the only things besides the Indians that made it out of Old San Carlos were the snakes and rodents that followed them up the hills. Old San Carlos continually returns into the consciousness of people whose parents, grandparents, and great-grandparents, if not they themselves, grew up there. This continued presence of Old San Carlos works in a figurative sense as well. People who are old enough to have grown up in Old San Carlos are accorded a great deal of respect. In contrast, blowhards and scoundrels who speak as if they have earned a level of respect that they have not are sometimes cut down to size with the comment, "He acts like he's from Old San Carlos."

In a literal sense, too, Old San Carlos is a recurring image in the consciousness and everyday experience of the reservation communities, for the old agency town was not forever and finally covered by the waters behind the dam. In fact, most summers, when the waterline of the lake gets low, the foundations of the buildings of Old San Carlos break the surface of the water. Years of drought, which have also resulted in major catastrophic forest fires in the early twenty-first century, have made the reservoir even lower. You can drive down to the old town, following a winding path of poorly marked dirt roads, and walk among the ruins of old barracks, agency buildings, the stockade, and old concrete aqueduct conduits. Looking out farther into the water, you can see the foundation of the old ration house and what looks like the skeletal structures of guard towers. One time, walking down there, friends and I found where three or four Apaches—children, we assumed—had written their names into the wet cement of the aqueducts on December 15, 1922. Old San Carlos isn't simply a place of the imagination, but a place whose material reality insistently impinges on the people's consciousness every day. As both place and concept, it refuses to recede below the chronological horizon.

One night, driving back from a gig in Bylas, the Pacers pulled off the highway to hang out for a while at the Old Rest Area on Route 70. Marshall pulled out the acoustic guitar and played Sluggo's songs. I always noticed that when Marsh was playing the acoustic guitar, he played an almost completely different repertoire of songs than what he played with the band. We hung out in the dark, no beer, just passing the guitar around, the other band members reminiscing about Sluggo. Then Marshall mentioned to me that we shouldn't stay there too long—and Pat and Darryl agreed—because in the early hours of the morning after midnight, the ghost of an old Apache woman comes out and walks the ground there.

If we were focusing on ethnographic observations of "Apache culture," a number of ethnographic works might tell us of the traditional Apachean practice of encircling grave sites with ashes in order to keep the spirits of the departed away. Ethnohistories would inform us that this practice relates to a more widespread fear of the dead among all Athabaskan-speaking groups. We would learn of the precautions taken by these Athabaskan groups to ensure that the spirits of the departed would pass onto the other side.

And yet San Carlos is a haunted place. Work crews completed the Queen Creek Tunnel on the new highway in 1952. Those crews included a number of Apaches, such as the grandfather of a friend whom I have known since I first went to San Carlos when I was in high school. My friend's mother told me that her father had worked on the tunnel and had told her this story. Every day the crews would blast and dig, tunneling into the mountain, and every morning they would come to the work site to find their previous day's efforts filled in with sand. Some people said the spirit of Geronimo didn't want the work to proceed. During a break at a meeting of an inter-Apache group to determine cooperative procedures regarding repatriation of skeletal remains and other artifacts, a woman told me that she heard a story at the Smithsonian, where they have numerous Apache remains, including fourteen skulls, five complete skeletons, and two brains. A woman who worked at the Smithsonian—this woman was not an Apache, the storyteller was quick to point out—well, she must have dozed off, and the next thing she knew, an old man was standing in front of her desk, asking to be sent home. He used the Apache pronunciation of the name "San Carlos." He said, "When are you sending us back to Sen Gaa?" At the conclusion of this story, another woman responded in kind, saying, yes, you see them now, in groups, kneeling, and they're crying. Or you'll be driving down the highway at night and see a man in nothing but a breechcloth and headband, and you'll almost hit him, but when you turn around to look, the road is empty.

How many of these stories did I hear as I went around with people on the reservation? On the old road to the Circle Seven Ranch, you may pass a pallid cowboy with fiery red eyes, driving his three friends into town in an old Model T Ford. Here, at this flat, you might encounter the old woman who carries a burlap sack slung over her shoulder. Somewhere else you'll find two women dressed in real old-style clothing, looking for the beaded jewelry that some grave robber stole from them. At that bridge over there, a school bus once went careening into the Gila River, and if you come out at just the right time of night, you might hear, briefly, the laughter of children playing. You may repeatedly see a man walking away from your house toward the road at all hours of the night. He may even come to your window and ask, in Apache, what you did with his clothes ("shidiyágé hago ándzaa?"). And if, well after dark, you were to go down to the edge of the water that buried Old San Carlos, they say that at that water's edge you would hear the old-timers singing.

Any good history begins in strangeness. The past should not be comfortable. The past should not be a familiar echo of the present, for if it is familiar why revisit it? The past should be so strange that you wonder how you and people you know and love could come from such a time. —**Richard White,** *Remembering Ahanagran: Storytelling in a Family's Past*

Quotation and History

In his landmark essays on Western Apache language and landscape, Keith Basso (1996) writes about his first attempts at learning to pronounce the names of the places he was mapping around the community of Cibecue, on the Fort Apache Reservation. Basso began his work by traveling around with two consultants from Cibecue, Charles Henry and Morley Cromwell. He writes about his difficulties wrapping his lips, teeth, and tongue around these place-names in his early attempts at saying them. After a number of failed attempts, he turned to Charles and apologized. Charles turned to Morley and scolded Basso in Western Apache: "What he's doing isn't right. It's not good. He seems to be in a hurry. Why is he in a hurry? It's disrespectful. Our ancestors made this name. They made it just as it is. They made it for a reason. They spoke it first, a long time ago. He's repeating the speech of our ancestors. He doesn't know that. Tell him he's repeating the speech of our ancestors!" (1996:15). Charles's admonishment was unsettling for Basso. Among other things, Basso explains, "never had I suspected that using Apache placenames could be heard by those who use them as repeating verbatim—actually quoting—the speech of their early ancestors" (1996:16).

Among the people I know on the San Carlos Reservation, the past and present can similarly be brought into copresence with each other through acts of quotation. The practice of repeating the speech of others saturates talk in the community, the past made audible in the mouths of the present. Speakers in present contexts re-present past speakers and their words through repeating and reporting. This aesthetic of quotation is a key social means of performing all sorts of interactions and expressions, from gossip and everyday conversation to songs and more formal genres of narrative.

The habitual use of these discursive resources can create, in certain circumstances, a deeply felt sense of resonance between those presently speaking and those who spoke in the past—what Basso calls "quoting the ancestors." But the practice is pervasive. Everyday interaction in San Carlos and Bylas is marked by a heavy reliance on report and quotation, by repetitions both within and across speaking turns, and by recontextualizations of salient utterances among groups of speakers. Talk on the San Carlos Reservation is heavily recycled. In conversation, an utterance is often crafted out of bits and pieces of preceding talk. The voices of others are consistently hearable and speakable in one's own voice. Successive speakers link their utterances together in a chain, the links of which are portions of a previous utterance. These linked chains can take a number of forms. In one, these practices of reenactment and reembodiment are a part—perhaps a substantial part—of the iconicity of feeling discussed in chapter 1. In another, this cycling of commonly held material can spin off into a joking frame, called *yati'nłke'* (throwing words), in which responsibility for the meanings of utterances resides not within any individual speaker, but between speakers, in the spaces opened up by the dense recombinations of their words.

These forms of repetition and quotation make meaning making an intensely social and cooperative process. In public meetings and wakes, repetition and report contribute to a distinctive way of reaching com-

munity consensus and agreement. At the same time, linguistic and social factors contribute to constituting these exchanges. The San Carlos
dialect of Western Apache, like other Athabaskan languages, is distinguished by the way its speakers rely on forms of repetition in the creation of discourse. For example, Dagmar Jung (2000) found repetition
to be an important resource in the shaping of Lipan Apache narratives.[1]
And according to Melissa Axelrod, "the structure of Athabaskan languages may make repetition strategies especially available to speakers"
(2000:22).[2]

In general, then, conversation in San Carlos and Bylas is filled with
the repetition and recontextualization of prior speech acts by others.
Words and phrases float from speaker to speaker, each speaker adding to the possible array of meanings that accrue to those words and
phrases. Images are built up through this social process, as successive
speakers blend their own words with those that have come before, almost literalizing Bakhtin's observation that each speaker's words are
only half her or his own. The culturally salient image of the speaking
subject on the reservation is someone who productively uses the words
of others in creating his utterances. A speaker also uses her utterances
interactively to charge conversations with possible resources for later
citation by others.[3]

In this chapter, I explore that aesthetic of quotation. For the past to
circulate and resonate in the present in San Carlos and Bylas—or in any
community, for that matter—it must be by some means representable
in the present. On the San Carlos Reservation, one common element of
those representations is the recurring instances of direct quotation and
citation of past speakers and expressions. The particular feelingful relationship to the past that many experience in San Carlos and Bylas—the
kinds of feelingful iconicities discussed in the previous chapter—are
partially constituted in the dense layering and expressive importance of
repetition. The ways in which speech forms circulate among individuals on the reservation help shape relationships not only between those
individual speakers, but between present speakers and past speakers as
well. By reanimating and reperforming the utterances of past speakers,
people in San Carlos and Bylas forge relationships that are simultaneously intersubjective and historical.

A major argument in this chapter is that this pervasive style of representing past speakers has a cumulative effect. Because present speakers
repeatedly and consistently place themselves in the role of reanimating

the voices of past speakers, they are enmeshed in social relationships not only with their present coparticipants, but with the past as well. The recoverable connection between present and past discussed in the previous chapter emerges at least in part out of everyday language use and out of the ways that historical relationships can be evoked through everyday communicative action on the reservation.

I explore the pervasiveness of these forms by examining a number of repetition and reported-speech phenomena in San Carlos and Bylas. First, I examine the direct reporting of past spoken clauses. Second, I explore the reporting of the thoughts, or inner dialogue, of others. Third, I discuss some of the ways that people make their interactions with each other poetically dense with repetition. Fourth, I explore the reporting of narratives. Finally, through a discussion of song structure and texts, I discuss the way that the embodiment of other voices can become a form of reported history.

Reported speech is a representation of one person's talk in the mouth of another. As representation, reported speech carries traces of both the originator and the reporter of the utterance. It is, in Voloshinov's classic definition, "speech within speech, utterance within utterance, and at the same time also *speech about speech, utterance about utterance*" (1973:115, emphasis in original). It is "both the representation of linguistic actions and the commentaries about these actions" (Besnier 1993:161). With good reason, the sense of verbatim faithfulness implied by the term *report* has been critiqued, and scholars have proposed alternative conceptualizations, such as "constructed dialogue" (Tannen 1989) or "modeling speech" (Errington 1998). Although I bear these legitimate correctives in mind, I use the more common term *report*.

The only manner of reporting speech in San Carlos and Bylas is direct citation. The absence of indirect reported speech is a well-attested feature of Navajo (Li 1986; Toelken and Scott 1981), as well as of other Athabaskan languages. The basic form of reported speech in Western Apache is the quoted portion followed by the third-person singular incompletive form of the verb *say*:

"X" nii
s/he says/said "X"

In all cases in San Carlos Apache, reported speech is represented as direct quotation. Like other Athabaskan languages, Western Apache lacks complementizers for embedding quoted speech, as in the English "She said that . . .":

> She said *that* the food was tasty.
> "Idán łicąh" nii.
> "The food is tasty," she said.

> I told her *to* leave him alone.
> "Doo baa nanaa da," biłdishnii.
> "Leave him alone," I said to her.[4]

Nor does Western Apache syntax include the shifts in personal pronouns in indirect speech in English that coordinate the reported clause with the reporting clause.

> ZACHARY: *You* should call *me* tonight.
> INDIRECT REPORT: Zachary said (that) *we* should call *him* tonight.

Direct and indirect reported speech in English are further distinguished, at least in the minds of some grammarians, by a required "backshift" (Comrie 1986) in grammatical tense, aspect, or mood in order to make sense:[5]

> RITA: I *will* meet you at seven o'clock.
> INDIRECT REPORT: Rita said (that) she *would* meet us at seven o'clock.

Spurred in part by the translation of Voloshinov's (1973) and Bakhtin's (1981, 1984, 1986) work on reported speech and intertextuality, the attention of anthropologists and other cultural theorists has been attracted in recent years to the twin life of reported speech as both discursive resource and metadiscursive ideology (Goffman 1981; Güldemann and von Roncador 2002; Hanks 1987; Lucy 1993; Rumsey 1990; Silverstein 1985). This literature forms a basis for much of my own thinking in this area. There are aspects of reported speech in San Carlos Apache, however, that fit only imperfectly within the body of work on this topic.

One important area of distinction concerns the range of syntactic possibilities for reporting speech. Many languages, English among them, have a number of such possibilities. One recurring theme of scholarship on reported speech has been to map out this range and to analyze the cultural and ideological weight borne by using one or another possibility in the course of a conversation. This aspect of study finds its roots, in part, in Voloshinov's interest in the development of "free indirect style" in the modern European novel.

Athabaskan languages such as Western Apache are difficult to bring under this umbrella, for they have only one syntactic means of attaching a reported instance of speech to a reporting clause—direct quotation, as I have illustrated. Languages with only a single quotative form can be difficult to fit into an approach to reported speech that emphasizes the meaning of a range of possibilities because "Quotatives, like other linguistic forms, acquire meaning in part by virtue of their value in a paradigm of alternatives in a language" (Lucy 1993:93). Although no linguistic anthropologist would argue that the singular form of reported speech in Western Apache renders it meaningless, the general approach to reported speech sometimes comes uncomfortably close to the position on "choice theory" critiqued by Roy Harris: that "when the range of choices is reduced by circumstantial factors to zero . . . then it becomes pointless to ascribe any meaning to the next move in the proceedings" (1996:37).[6]

But direct reported speech is not simply a distinctive syntactic feature of Western Apache. It is a grammatical rule, to be sure, but by the very fact of its rule-governed existence it is also a recurrent phenomenon, distributed over a wide range and number of clauses in everyday talk. The habitual use of these discourse resources makes quotation part of the linguistic "groove" (Feld [1988] 1994b) of Western Apache within the community, part of the "feeling for form" (Sapir 1921) that grammar holds out to speakers, part of a form of representation. Because direct quotation is the only way for one Apache speaker to report what a previous speaker has said, the grammatical parallelism across numerous instances of reporting has a cumulative effect of shaping the naturalized sense of the relationship between past and present. In other words, quotation—"ventriloquation," to use Bakhtin's vivid term—is a discourse-level phenomenon on the reservation.[7] The pervasive constancy of direct reporting of speech across numerous utterances helps to create imagined social relationships between present and past speakers—relationships that can stretch across historical time as well as the immediate past.

Scholarly work in reported speech has offered new, important, and productive ways of conceptualizing the relationships between speakers, audiences, addressees, coparticipants, ideologies, and the social histories of languages and discourses. In "Word, Dialogue, and the Novel" (1980), Julia Kristeva argues that within this three-dimensional space virtually all speech is reported speech: because all the words of a text or utterance have their social histories, "any text is constructed as a mosaic of quotations" (1980:66). At the same time, I would maintain that it is one thing to assert this mosaic of quotation as a theoretical perspective on language and literature and another to be socialized into a community such as the San Carlos Reservation, in which citation and repetition are placed in such high relief; in which the speech of others is so prominently and deliberately displayed in one's own speech; where so much communicative energy is spent in reenacting, reanimating, and reperforming other people's utterances—in being, in a sense, other people.

Reporting and citation start at the beginning of a conversation. In one typical greeting in Western Apache, the greeter requests quoted speech from the person greeted:

A: "Doo dagot'éé da" nnii.
   Say "Nothing is happening."
B: Doo dagot'éé da.
   Nothing is happening.

It has long been argued that direct reported speech—because it preserves the grammatical tense and aspect, as well as the pronominal person of the original utterance—implies that the reporter is in some way "performing" the original speaker (Coulmas 1986). Whatever the "accuracy" of direct quotation in reported speech, it implies a relationship of embodiment between present speakers and past speakers.[8] On the reservation, the performance qualities of direct report are undeniable. Indeed, in San Carlos and Bylas, speakers often slide into quite theatrical performances of other speakers, animating figures (Goffman 1974) rather than merely speaking another's words. In filling the gap between one's own speech and another's, the slippage between various performed first-person positions (see Urban 1987) accumulates into a style of historical representation: past speech and past speakers as things reanimated, embodied, performed in the present, not referred to deictically through third-person speech.

The centripetal force that causes one speaker to shift into the voice of another in reported speech is strong. One time at a family gathering in Seven Mile Wash, one of the older men, James, told the following story to his cousin, Mann.

1 Ííí shogheeł łá'
    one time I was riding a horse[9]
2 Hannah hik'eh Linda
    Hannah and Linda
3 Gary bisisterhíí
    Gary's sisters
4 nadazįį dą' aigee.
    as they were standing at that place
5 Ííí shogheeł łá'
    one time I was riding a horse
6 Hannah nagolni'.
    Hannah told this story
7 akú Ííí shogheeł dą' ganíí
    really, when I was riding the horse there
8 "ha'ih, hadín ląą Ííí bił hilwołíí at'éé
    "ha'ih, who in the world is that person riding the horse
9 beodzidgo?" nii niwíí
    scarily?" she said[10]
10 doo shigołsįh da wíí
    she didn't know me, you see
11 "James dáku at'íí," mił ch'inii.
    "That's James," she [Linda] said to her [Hannah][11]
12 shii doo hásht'íni da ganíí
    I really didn't want it
13 lán shanłtíni wíí Thomas
    Thomas lent it to me, you see

James's story begins to show us a little bit how the dictates of direct reported speech become a crucial aspect of the construction and circulation of embodied intersubjective relations on the reservation. Like all storytellers, he must negotiate the relationship between the (past) narrated event and the (present) narrative event. He must also manage the shifting relationship between his existence as subject of his own story ("I was riding") and object of Hannah's story ("Hannah saw me"). Similarly, he has to negotiate his position as teller ("I am speaking") and his position as reporter ("Hannah spoke"). This negotiation took some time for James to work out. He repeated the topical focus of his narrative, *I was riding a horse*, three times: in lines 1, 5, and 7. In the last instance, he placed himself in a subordinate clause (łį́į́ shogheeł *dą́'* / *when* I was riding a horse).

James's shifting of his own presence in his narrative followed his announcement that it was actually Hannah's story that he was telling and preceded his embodiment of her frightened reaction to him. Such declarations of reported speech—interrupting a story in order to reveal the story's actual originator to the audience—are a common narrative technique, especially among older speakers. Britton Goode, Phillip's father, taped a story of a large flood that hit San Carlos around 1905.[12] Goode himself used the word *naízhjool* (flood) to describe the event. But—perhaps because the event took place six years before he was born—Goode also acknowledged that others described it differently. Some called it *túyaa* (downflow), he said; others called it *ták'eh* (wash out). And as he continued his story about the 1905 flood, he let us know that it was not, in actuality, his story at all.

1 akohgo díí ła' isdzán bayánhi shił nagolni' ni' áí
   there was an old woman that told me about this
2 áí isdzán bayán shił nagolni'íí t'ah hinaa áí
   this old woman that told me this is still alive
3 áíhi áłdishnii wónkoh áí
   that's the one I'm telling you about
4 aí "ałdó' Tábąąt'iiségee gonshłį́į́ łeh ni'
   "I also lived at Cottonwood trees by the river
5 na'ilín nshłį́į́ dą́' ni'" nii go'íí koh.
   when I was a girl," she said, you see, that one
6 "dá'asts'íségo," nii ni' áí isdzánhíí
   "I was little at that time," said the woman
7 go áí shił nagolni'i áłdishnii gáníí
   so she is the one who really told me what I'm saying

Similarly, the singer and humorist Vincent Craig preceded a live performance of his popular song "Rita" (also known as "The Crazy Candy Bar Song") with a disclaimer as to who is responsible for the performance (the song has particularly thick "Navajo-accented" vocal inflections): "Remember, this song is sung with an accent, okay? And it isn't really me singing. Because I went to *kallij*, heé. And I got *edumacated*, zhǫ́" (Craig 1981).

Direct reported speech mediates the representation of self and others in language. On the one hand, quoting others distributes responsibility for an utterance across a variety of speakers. On the other hand, it also takes up another responsibility—namely, that of representing another's voice. James's announcement that he was going into a stretch of reported speech enabled him to take up Hannah's perspective of James on horseback. It also allowed him to perform Hannah's utterance fully, including its opening feminine-gendered exclamation "ha'ih!" without confusion as to who said what. Similarly, Vincent Craig's announcement of reported speech freed him to enter into a performance in which he could fully embody the voice of the character in his song.

A preference for direct reported speech is not limited to discourse in Western Apache, a fact that lends weight to the idea that it is not merely an obligatory grammatical rule, but also a way of imagining the relationships between present and past speakers. In the fall of 1994, the Elders Cultural Advisory Council called a public meeting to discuss what should be done with the skeletal remains of San Carlos Apaches in the Smithsonian Institution. The general opinion of the attendees seemed to be that—in spite of traditional beliefs that might dictate otherwise—it was more important that these people be laid to rest in their homeland. One woman got up and spoke eloquently, in both Apache and English, of her sadness at knowing that Geronimo was buried in Oklahoma. In her English portion, she spoke what she felt were Geronimo's words during his incarceration in Florida and Fort Sill, Oklahoma: "Geronimo, when he was living, said, 'The cactus misses me. The mesquites miss me.'"[13]

Direct report is also linked to another feature of discourse and interaction in San Carlos—namely, the "triadic" structure of directives (Field 2001). That is, rather than person A telling person C what to do, person A tells person B to tell person C what to do, as in this command I heard at a family gathering:

"'Akú dándaa' niłnii" biłnnii!
"'Sit there' she says to you," you say to him!

Thus, not only do speakers directly quote the previous speech of others, but they expect that their own speech will also be quoted and often ensure that this quotation occurs in three-way interactions. I return to this issue again later, but for the moment I want to go back to Basso's example. When Charles scolded Basso for his disrespect to the ancestors, he did not confront Basso directly, but rather turned to Morley and told Morley what to say to Basso ("Tell him he's repeating the speech of our ancestors!"). This triadic directive structure is maintained in English, as Margaret Field (2001) discovered in her work in Navajo day-care centers, where adults socialize children by directing them what to say to others and then expecting that the children will repeat what they have been told to say.

Not only is reported speech embedded in requests, but speakers also often simply request speech from each other as a means of socializing. These requests were certainly part of my own language socialization in the community, as people told me what I should say in various social contexts. These requests are no doubt part of child language socialization as well. Learning this practice is part of acquiring a cultural way of doing things together (Feld [1988] 1994b).[14] Ongoing conversations in San Carlos and Bylas are peppered with one person requesting that a second person say something in response to a situation and with the second person responding with the elicited utterance, as in the following two examples, recorded during a backstage break with the Pacers during which we were trying to fix the bass drum pedal (it was always breaking).[15]

PAUL: "storezhi' shiłnlyeed," nnii sáh!
       Say "Run me up to the store!"
ARTHUR: storezhi' shiłnlyeed!
       Run me up to the store!

Then later, from the same conversation, when Mike did not want to lose the screwdriver we were using:

MIKE: "doowha ch'a'okees da dą'" nnii.
       Say "Before it gets lost."
GREG: doowha ch'a'okees da dą'.
       Before it gets lost.

These requests elicit assent through repetition by creating a sort of linguistic feedback loop. The first speaker quotes the desired speech to the second, and the second then provides the desired speech by quoting it back to the first. The linguistic-expressive performance of sociability in San Carlos and Bylas thus can be said to consist of saying the same thing. But the originator of the utterance is in a sense not the person who makes the declaration, but the one who requests that the other speaker make it.

To sum up: In San Carlos and Bylas, one's own speech is constantly infected by the speech of others. Direct reported speech is not merely a grammatical necessity. It permeates the expressive life of the community, contributing to the formation of a style of intersubjectivity. Quoted speech restates past speakers' words and enables the embodied performance of various characters, both present day and historical. It is used in the making of requests, most notably in the making of requests for speech.

Autumn 1995. Driving through the dark with Kane and Donnie to another gig at Mark's Tavern in Globe. Andy, who owned Mark's with his brother Gino, lived in a house built high on a hill overlooking the McDonald's on Ash Street in Globe. People said the house was built by winos. One time I took a friend's mother to Globe so she could do some household shopping.[16] On the way back, we went to the McDonald's drive-through for lunch. As we came out, she pointed out Andy's house to me—a stuccoed ranch home with big bay windows that had a nice view of the fast-food franchises below and the Pinals beyond. She told me about a rumor of how a bar owner might save some money in home construction costs. "They say winos from the bar dug his water lines for drinks," she said. "And then they say he sealed the pipes with commodity honey instead of pipe dope! He built it so cheap!" she said. "Those winos worked for beer all day. Now they say, 'that's *our* house.' Meaning that's where all their money is."

We drove through the dark because we were late. Before we played, we usually would gather wherever the instruments were being stored —at Marshall's or his mom's or Donnie's—at around 5:30 or so. After a little hanging out and telling fish stories, we would load up and take off. We didn't want to be late because we didn't want the owners to think we were irresponsible. But sometimes things don't go exactly according to plan. So there we were, driving through the dark on this fine September Saturday evening, late for setting up at Mark's.

With the sun down, the long-distance radio could come in, and I tuned the truck's stereo to Oklahoma City, KOMA. As we talked about this and that, Booker T. and the MGs were on the air—"Green Onions."

"Hey, Sluggo used to sing that one," said Donnie.

"Really?" I said, a bit surprised because the song has no words.

"No," Donnie corrected himself. "Not that one. That song redone by

Huey Lewis?" After some discussion, we figured out that he was talking about the Wilson Pickett song "634-5789."

"Héla!" said Kane. " 'Stewart' nii."

"Yeah," Donnie agreed, "a lot of good music came out of there."

" 'Sluggo' nii."

Herman's Hermits came over the air with "Can't You Hear My Heart-beat."

"That one right there!" Donnie exclaimed. "Sluggo used to sing that."

Here, on this trip, driving down Route 70 into Globe, the worlds of personal and social history were compacted into dense moments of me-diated expressivity, charged with the vitality and life of both the ex-pressions and the people who experienced them. Responses to those moments reveal a great deal about the social life of cultural expres-sion on the reservation. Those moments and the artistic expressions that provide them are densely ambiguous because they are layered with numerous cultural, historical, and symbolic associations that col-lect and adhere to them over time and across space, crystalized layer-ings of instants and locations that Bakhtin (1981) calls "chronotopes." These associations may be hidden at the surface level of the expression, but they are detectable in nonverbal response and talk about art (see Feld [1984] 1994a). Often, on hearing "I'm Your Puppet" or "Hey Joe," Marshall would exclaim, "Héla! White Cityyú!" remembering the place where Sluggo lived, where they used to go to jam out. Kane's statement, then, that Booker T. Jones is really saying "Stewart" is hardly trivial. It's a deeply considered statement of the locally significant response to artistic experience. By making "Sluggo" and "Stewart" his verbal re-sponses to the song "Green Onions," Kane revealed the stunning im-portance of place and the turn to the past in aesthetic evaluations on the reservation.

"Stewart," you see, is Stewart Indian School, the BIA boarding school in Stewart, Nevada, where Donnie Ray went to high school. There, Sluggo, Donnie Ray, Red, Milton, and Pinky got together and formed the Valiants, which was one of the most popular and successful bands in San Carlos in the late 1960s and 1970s. "Green Onions" was a hit in 1962, "Can't You Hear My Heartbeat" in 1965, and "634-5789" in 1966.[17] The Valiants eventually broke up a number of personnel changes later, when three of the band members were drafted and sent to Vietnam in one of the early waves of troop buildups. Only two came back alive.

But Kane never went to Stewart Indian School. When he said, " 'Stewart' nii," he was giving voice to *Donnie Ray*'s inner speech, projecting himself into Donnie Ray's mind and imagining that he was speaking what Donnie would have said if Donnie had spoken what was in his own mind. Kane's statement doesn't necessarily achieve its effect because of its objective truth value—which is, of course, unknowable in any case. Rather, his statement was successful for the way it performed the intersubjectivity and empathy between himself and Donnie Ray.

The freedom to speak another's thoughts is a potentially dangerous practice. Some ceremonial practitioners shun Horse Songs because they feel that the purpose of those songs is to control the mind of another. No doubt, joking about what is going on in another person's thoughts requires a long-standing, well-worked, soft, and supple friendship so that the friends don't get offended at the teasing (Basso 1979). At the same time, however, this practice runs counter to the stereotypical image of the Native American discourse community, in which speakers are always respectful of each other's thoughts and words, and in which joking with another's words is always subject to potential dangers. The expectation that part of conversational skill involves entering the mind of another and extracting his or her inner speech to put it on exterior display in a joking frame offers an alternative and more ambiguous view of subjectivity and intersubjectivity on the San Carlos Reservation.

This deep personal relationship, whereby one speaker enters the thoughts and voices the interior monologue of another, is often marked by a tag clause, *tah nnii*. The tag was most commonly glossed for me as "you might say." People translated *tah* as meaning "maybe, possibly, could be, might"; *nnii* is the second-person singular of the verb *say*. Phillip, who also offered "you might say" as a possibility, sometimes interpreted it as "don't tell me!"—as in, "don't tell me you're going home!" But I find the "don't tell me" translation unsatisfying. For one thing, it converts direct reported speech to indirect and so loses that quality of actually giving voice to another's words. Indeed, it completely loses the quality of linguistic intersubjectivity. "Don't tell me" is often, if not in fact usually, used in English to talk about occurrences that happen in the world, not in the interior monologue of other speakers: "Don't tell me it's three o'clock already!" "Don't tell me it's raining!" In English,

utterances beginning with "Don't tell me" are often coded as "rhetorical," as in the tired routine where one person says, "Don't tell me it's
three o'clock already," and the second says, "It's three o'clock already,"
to which the first person retorts, "I asked you not to tell me that."

Neither am I completely satisfied with the "you might say" option,
despite the fact that it was the most commonly offered translation. It's
an accurate enough interpretation of the words, but "you might say" in
English carries more impersonal and, in a way, less threatening implications. These implications are in part owing to the way in which the
personal pronoun *you* merges with the impersonal pronoun *one* in sentences such as "you [one] might say that she was the most unrecognized
genius of her age."

By contrast, *tah nnii* indicates the possibility that someone might actually say something. Furthermore, some speakers were unsure whether
the Apache phrase in question was *tah nnii* at all, or whether it might not
be *tah ndįh*, which would simply combine two ways of saying "maybe."[18]
Ultimately, as with many other Apache phrases, people told me that *tah
nnii* is untranslatable. This untranslatability is manifested in its reten-
tion in English conversation as one of the more frequent lexical items
in code-switching utterances.[19] In the final analysis, then, the full implication of *tah nnii* doesn't seem to be matched by any of its English
alternatives and therefore must emerge out of its habitual use in the
expressive practices of people in the community.

Tah nnii is almost exclusively employed in a joking frame. The frame
embraces the intense sociability of expressivity in San Carlos and Bylas.
Interactional participant roles in San Carlos include a role that I might
call "interjector" or "commentator"—someone who adds into the conversation what the participants are not saying but might. The interjector role isn't necessarily filled by a third person, of course—a single
speaker may enact multiple participant roles and animate the voices of
multiple figures and footings in the course of an interactional sequence
(Goffman 1974, 1981; Hill 1995; Irvine 1996; Urban 1987). It's important
as well to keep in mind that the interjector role, if enacted by a third
party, is not the role of a meddling busybody, which would be highly
criticized behavior. Rather, the interjector adds to the rich intersubjectivity of expressive interaction on the reservation.

The habitual nature of this practice, the expectation that this kind of
joking language game will occur, made my ethnographic elicitation a
challenging experience. As one person asked me, "Does it ever bother

you that you can't have a serious conversation with anybody around here?"

One afternoon, rehearsing with the Pacers, Marshall called for one of the group's original songs, "Cry Baby." He called for it first in English, then, jokingly, in Apache: "me' ch'aich'iihéé."

"What did you say?" I asked.

"Oh, nothing," he said, now aware of himself. "It's just the name of the song."

"Yeah, but what did you say?" I asked.

"'Cry Baby.'"

"I know," I pressed. "But how did you say it?"

"Me' ch'aich'iihéé."

"Anánnii, shįh," I said. Please say it again.

"Me' ch'aich'iihéé," he repeated.

"Detaadego!" I said. Slower! "Anánnii." It was filled with glottalized affricates, and I was unsure that I had heard them all correctly. Chaich'ii? Ch'aichii?

"Me' . . . ch'ai . . . ch'ii . . . héé."

Okay. I almost had it. If Marshall would repeat it one more time at normal speed, it would become part of my vocabulary. But before I could say anything, Kane chimed in.

"'Say it *again*,' tah nnii!" he whined imploringly. Everyone laughed, hard, and then through the laughter Pat completely broke my outside researcher interview frame.

"'Strike three you're out,' tah nnii," he said, letting me know exactly how many times I had asked for the same information. There was nothing to do but go back to jamming out.

As Pat's final joke demonstrates, *tah nnii* is also a frame for the circulation and recontextualization of the catch phrases of mass media. Such popular phrases and slogans as "I've fallen and I can't get up," "I love you, man," "You can't have my Bud Light," "Is it soup yet?" and "Where's the beef?" find their way into this joking frame. One time in Southside, as we were sitting outside the house on milk crates, a woman told me with great delight about the time a relative of hers came to Bylas to preach the gospel, and then it turned out that he was only preaching for "utility money," to make enough in donations to pay his electric bill. She told the story as a bittersweet joke. Funny—but at the same time sad. In order to set herself apart from the hypocrisy of her relative's actions, she said, in a more serious tone, "Usually, I read my Bible, Scriptures, you know, daily . . ."

But her sister couldn't resist. "'Today's Chuckle,' tah nnii," she said, referring to the syndicated newspaper cartoon that runs in the *Arizona Republic*.

Later in the conversation, the second sister asked me, "Do you have a title for your book yet?"

"No," I said and started to *explain*, but of course I didn't realize that I was just being used as a foil.

"*Medicine Man* tah nnii!" she said with a loud laugh, proclaiming the title of the then-current movie starring Sean Connery and Lorraine Bracco.

The use of *tah nnii* doesn't necessarily indicate an act of mind reading, as Kane's voicing of Donnie Ray's thoughts had. It isn't always necessary that the words spoken be thought of as the actual words that an actual participant in a conversation would or should speak for himself or herself. Sometimes it's simply an utterance that might be spoken by someone in a similar situation or just something that strikes the speaker as funny. I have heard a speaker at a public meeting blow into the microphone and say "tah nnii" as a way of warming up his audience. Another time, during an evening filled with jokes in Moonbase, one young man kept the already-roaring group in stitches by imitating a snorty, milk-through-the-nose sort of laugh and saying "tah nnii." The frame makes the social process of meaning making tangible by allowing participants to inhabit multiple roles and to participate from multiple perspectives in a conversation. Expressivity in San Carlos and Bylas emerges in this realm of possibility. Participants are constantly filling the gap between what is said and what is meant, filling it with what might be said, shining lights down the roads not taken, and underscoring the instability of—and the unstable relationship between—signification and personal or cultural identity in the community.

Successive utterances in this game don't replace those that came before them, but rather adhere to them in an additive verbal construction of the world. The making of meaning becomes a social process of adding on, filling in, densifying, making successive utterances adhere to what has come before. The practice wrests control over meaning from any particular individual speaking subject by exploding and making publicly accessible the entire range of expressive possibilities—saying, in effect, "These, too, have potential."[20]

Of course, it isn't necessary to use a grammatical tag or a verb of saying in order to place the words of one person into the mouth of another. Speakers may evoke the presence of other characters simply by performing another person's speaking style. This is especially true when a person in the community is known for a highly individual laugh, a distinctively high voice, an emblematic phrase, or some other identifiable feature of vocal performance. (At one point, my friends detected that I often said, quite defensively, "So?" when they teased me—which, of course, became additional fodder for teasing.)

In everyday interaction on the reservation, a speaker often lifts a portion out of a previous utterance and recontextualizes it within a successive utterance. When this reshaping is successful, the words almost fly around from speaker to speaker, as jokes build on jokes, puns on puns, meanings upon meanings, until what emerges is extremely complex and luminously layered, a product for which no speaker can claim ultimate responsibility.[21] This is a practice that some people referred to as *yati' nłke'*, a term glossed for me as both "kicking words" and "throwing words"—the verb stem, *-ke'*, might best be associated with an English concept such as "scattering." This form of verbal art is more likely to occur at gatherings where people are comfortable with each other, in social contexts where inhibitions drop away in the course of a conversation.

Here is an example. The Pacers had just finished playing up on Mormon Hill. After the gig, we picked up some quarts and then cruised over to the old house. At the house, we rolled down the windows of my truck, put a tape in the stereo, and gathered around the bed. Having been given permission to tape the conversation, I placed the microphone in the bed of the truck to try and pick up all the speakers. The talk ranged around a number of topics—how well Kane had played the drums, what happened when one of the amps blew a fuse, why we didn't play certain songs, whether we saw someone's neighbors, who was dancing in a funny way, why someone from Texas would want to learn Apache. The transcription picks up at a point where Mary was accused of really dancing away to "La Bamba" when the band played it. She admitted it, then said that they don't dance like that in Whiteriver. She tagged her sentence with an evidential particle, *go'íí*, which she pronounced in an imitation of the fast-speech contraction common to Whiteriver, *wǫ́ǫ́*.[22]

1	MARY:	Whiteriver zhinéé doo ai k'ehgo goz'ąądа wǫ́ǫ́ Whiteriver side it's not that way wǫ́ǫ́.
2	MIKE:	goz'ąąąądа wǫ́ǫ́ǫ́ǫ́ Not that way wǫ́ǫ́ǫ́ǫ́.
3	ALEX:	Bik'ehgoihinán yáá nadaiziidii wǫ́ǫ́ They work for God wǫ́ǫ́.
4	MIKE:	Bik'ehgoihinán yáá nadai*zii*dii wǫ́ǫ́ They work for God wǫ́ǫ́.
5	MARY:	doo baa ch'idlóh da wǫ́ǫ́, da hago shįh at'éé zhǫ́ ágádaołnii yúgo. You shouldn't laugh about them wǫ́ǫ́, it's really somehow if you say that.[23]
6	GRANT:	"ts'inádiskos" nnii "Whiteriveryú" Say "I think back to Whiteriver."
7	BRETT:	Migózįįd, migózįįd! She's found out, she's found out!
8	MIKE:	k'ad miłgongaa yúgo "Akú shił nłbąąs" niłnii wiláh Pretty soon if she's buzzed out watch her say "Drive me up there" to you.
9	MARY:	lúlá Way over there.
10	ALEX:	lúúúúyúlá Waaaaaay over there.
11	MIKE:	hey. doo bii nat'íni da wíí, Peabo godisanii wǫ́ǫ́ Hey. It wasn't him that did it; it was Peabo that started it wǫ́ǫ́.
12	ALEX:	Peabo godisanii wǫ́ǫ́. Peabo mik'enniigo nłt'éé wǫ́ǫ́ It was Peabo that started it wǫ́ǫ́. You should be mad at Peabo wǫ́ǫ́.

This stretch of conversation is clearly filled with repetitions. If we take Mary's opening line as a jumping-off point for what followed, then there are eleven subsequent speaking turns, seven of which contain some repeated material. This is most noticeable in the recurrence of the evidential *wǫǫ́*, which appears a total of seven times, in six of the eleven utterances. Three of the eleven utterances — in lines 2, 4, and 10 — are composed exclusively of repeated lexical material. Of these utterances, two are instances of intensification, reflexively focusing the participants' attention on a particularly salient portion of the preceding utterance. The first is Mike's repetition in line 2. He used part of the final clause of Mary's prior statement, taking up her sonic representation of Whiteriver and getting the ball rolling by broadly overperforming the evidential particle. The second occurred in line 10, in which Alex performed two standard Western Apache word games. One was that he combined the deictic particle *lúlá* with the Apache lip-pointing gesture, thus exaggeratedly fronting his vowels. The other was that he overperformed the semantic relationship between vowel length in deictics and physical distance in time and space — the difference between saying "a long time ago" and "a looooong time ago."

In this example, repetition indicates what we might call "metapragmatic assent" — agreement as to a shared idea that this is a proper way to talk about talk. It also creates coherence between turns, sociability between speakers, and interpretability of the exchange. The evidential particle is thrown from person to person, each participant playing with what he or she has been given by previous speakers before passing it off to the next participant. The productive success of Mike's initial repetition, however, also indicates the close relationships felt between the participants. Response is by no means assured. It isn't simply a question of the appropriateness of the textual material being offered into play. Response is also shaped by the context, including the setting and the participants. The absence of a response can be interpreted as a comment on the speaker's relationship to the addressee rather than as a comment on the speaker's words themselves.

In the fall of 1994, the Pacers played at Marshall's mom's house at the lake for a birthday celebration. Because of its proximity to the lake store, the sound of the band often attracted visitors looking for a party. On break because, once again, the bass drum pedal had broken, the band members and some others were gathered behind the shade, talking, joking around, and fixing the equipment. Chris, who was hanging out backstage with the band, watched as Darryl cut a strip of leather with a Bowie knife. As Darryl worked, Chris offered his advice on how best to repair the broken pedal. In line 4, Darryl had slipped with the knife, which prompted Chris to try to throw some words around.

1 "beer bik'eh" ádishnii!
  "Pour beer on it," that's what I said!

2 díntsood áwą
  So it can stretch.

3 yeééééeee
  Heeeeey.
  [Darryl's knife slips, cutting the leather.]

4 kú, kú, baa gonyaa t'ązhį' kehéé!
  Here, here, be careful back off hey!

5 míchį' nadigęęs
  He's cutting his nose off.

6 níchį' dadįhgo síndaa doleeł iskąą abįdá'
  You'll be sitting with your nose cut off tomorrow morning.

7 níchi'ła' zhį' hishgizh da' coffee indląągo síndaa doleeł
  Part of your nose is/will be cut off while you're sitting drinking
    coffee.

Three times—in lines 5, 6, and 7—Chris attempted to get the ball rolling. But he suffered topic failure each time. He ended up offering a number of possible ways of thinking about the sight of Darryl with his nose cut off, none of which elicited response from anyone. He was throwing words around with himself. Chris's failure was underscored by the conversation going on beside him, which was replete with words being picked up and thrown back by various participants. A few minutes later in the break, Darryl asked Marshall when the band was going to eat:

1 DARRYL: daos'aa da'idąą
           When are we eating?

2 MARSHALL: [laughing] Ah, *shit* man, k'eda ąął, ąął no'ne daiskoo!
             [laughing] Ah, shit, man, it's already
                finished, they already took the food away!

3 MCGARRETT: gusé ch'inadis'ąą
             They threw it to the dogs over there.

4 DONNIE: gusé bibid nayideeł kóh
         The dog is carrying his belly around.

5 MARSHALL: bitł'age
           Underneath

6   crumbles hijaad aigee.
          there'll be a pile of crumbs.

7 MCGARRETT: gusé bibid daayiłnad
             They'll be licking the dog's belly.

8 DONNIE: hee, naadiłch'id wiláh, guitar nayił'íį

> Hey, watch, they'll be scratching themselves
> like they're playing guitars.

Here the exchange is intense and features the kind of verbal and pre-fixal repetition Axelrod noted. In contrast to Chris's earlier attempt, Marshall, McGarrett, and Donnie Ray cooperatively transformed Darryl's innocent question into a site for cooperative speech play. Each speaker fashioned his own successive image of what it meant that the food had been thrown to the dogs and how the band was going to eat now that the food was gone. Turn taking was important. No speaker offered more than one image in a row. Each speaker threw out his idea and waited for someone to respond before throwing out another. The order of turns was regimented. The session was capped by Donnie's uncanny comparison between the way a dog scratches its belly with its hind leg and the way a human strums a guitar.

I originally thought that Chris's failure to generate the kind of inter-subjective responses inspired by Darryl's hunger had something to do with his social relationship to the band. I assumed that his failure was because he was unwelcome and was being given the cold shoulder. As it turned out, however, when I played the tape back for various band members, Chris was actually a close friend and distant cousin of Marshall's, so my original theory didn't work. A number of people speculated as to why there had been no response because on second hearing they agreed that the images were humorous. One person thought that it might be that Chris was trying to "be involved" with Darryl's work—this is the critical line over which one becomes a busybody. Even though Chris was a close friend, he wasn't a member of the band and so perhaps shouldn't have acted that way. Another guessed that no one had heard Chris's jokes; it's possible that everyone was preoccupied with fixing the equipment, but his voice is loud and clear on my tape. One person speculated that because I was the closest person to Chris, he expected that I would provide the proper response, so his failure was actually my fault. Someone else mused that Chris's jokes had been ignored because they may have seemed inappropriate. It is believed that a traditional practice by men whose wives had been adulterous was to cut off the tips of their noses. One of the more well-known photographs of an Apache woman, taken by Markey in the 1880s, purports to be an image of a woman with her "nose cut off for adultery" (Arizona Historical Society, photograph no. 3237). This consultant thought it possible that by talking about cutting noses, Chris was interpreted as broaching the subject of adultery and was feminizing Darryl in the bargain. Another person thought that perhaps what had interfered with people's responses was that Chris had addressed Darryl directly ("you'll be sitting with your nose cut off") rather than addressing someone else about Darryl ("he'll be sitting with his nose cut off"). Ultimately, though, no one could tell me the diagnostic difference that would have triggered yati' nɫke' in this case.

Talk about the Pacers brings us once again to a discussion about the links and overlaps between the spoken and the sung, the linguistic and the musical, in considering the importance of repetition and report in fashioning expressivity and identity on the reservation. The embodiment of other voices through one's own voice is not a practice limited to speech. The sense of one body enacting multiple voices is found in other vocal practices as well, and singing is one of the most prominent. I turn now to a discussion of traditional song structure on the reservation and of the evocative values of enacting figures through song. This discussion leads to an exploration of the power of direct report as it circulates through the voices in sung performances on the reservation.

I have two ends in mind here. The first, as I have said, is to further the connections between linguistic and musical expressivity. I discuss this idea in more detail at the end of this chapter. For the moment, though, I simply wish to maintain that the realm of sound—the musical dimensions of language in its vocalized performance—is a crucial site in which people craft deeply felt connections between their present lives and their sense of the Apache historical past.

The second end I have in mind, therefore, is to deepen the discussion of the relationship between feelingful iconicity and historical imagination on the reservation and to prepare the way for the discussion of musical practices that occupies the next few chapters. Song emphasizes the shifting ground of representation and identity. Perhaps this is because song moves nonsemantic modes of signification—the indexical and iconic—to the foreground of experience and interpretation. Perhaps it occurs because song is itself so cyclic and repetitive that it offers an example of the ever-changing, never quite recoverable return. In any event, song comes "to resonate deeply with the ambiguous journeying of our identity in the world" (Chambers 2000:74). It highlights the inevitability of ambiguity and incompleteness in cultural expression, coupling it with the desire for recoverability and for true intersubjective coexperiencing.

Traditional songs on the San Carlos Reservation are structured strophically. That is, they consist of two alternating and distinct parts, cycling one after the other in an A-B-A-B sequence. One basic difference between the alternating parts is that one of them tends to have a great deal of melodic movement, from high notes to low notes, whereas the other is more staid and stable melodically, generally lingering on one or two notes throughout. For example, a person does not have to be an expert sight-reader of music to know that between these two melodies the first displays a wider range of tones and greater movement between them than does the second:

In traditional San Carlos Apache song, the alternation of these two musical sections is often mirrored in the sung text, which itself alternates between two characters vocalizing the lines of the song. The alternating melodic lines are represented in the verbal text as a conversation between two characters.

The two melodies given here act as the musical embodiment of two characters—sweethearts in the midst of a breakup. One is begging the other, "Don't throw me away! Don't leave me in misery!" The other, singing the second melodic line, says, "I'll throw you against this rock and run away from you."

Yó'oshoołt'e' hela gha	Don't throw me away
Yó'oshoołt'e' hela gha	Don't throw me away
goyeeyo ashole' hela gha	Don't leave me in misery
heya ha 'eya 'e neegheya	heya ha 'eya 'e neegheya

Yó'oshoołt'e' hela gha	Don't throw me away
goyeeyo ashole' hela gha	Don't leave me in misery
heya ha 'eya 'e neegheya	heya ha 'eya 'e neegheya
"Tsee bee nidishtee adá'	"I'm going to throw you against this rock
nits'á nádishyeed"	and run away"
Yó'oshoołt'e' hela gha	Don't throw me away
goyeeyo ashole' hela gha	Don't leave me in misery
heya ha 'eya 'e neegheya	heya ha 'eya 'e neegheya
Yó'oshoołt'e' hela gha	Don't throw me away
Yó'oshoołt'e' hela gha	Don't throw me away
goyeeyo ashole' hela gha	Don't leave me in misery
heya ha 'eya 'e neegheya	heya ha 'eya 'e neegheya
Yó'oshoołt'e' hela gha	Don't throw me away
goyeeyo ashole' hela gha	Don't leave me in misery
heya ha 'eya 'e neegheya	heya ha 'eya 'e neegheya
"Tsee bee nidishtłoh adá'	"I'm going to throw you against this rock
nits'á nádishyeed"	and run away"
Yó'oshoołt'e' hela gha	Don't throw me away
goyeeyo ashole' hela gha	Don't leave me in misery
heya ha 'eya 'e neegheya	heya ha 'eya 'e neegheya

In addition to the melodic alternation, part of the poetry of the text also resides in the playful shifting of Apache handling verbs between the first and second stanzas.[24] In the first, the second lover sings "tsee bee nidish*tee*," meaning "I'm going to throw you against this rock" and using -*tee*, the verb form for handling a single live object (though one of a fairly small size—say, like a baby). In the second verse, the character sings, "tsee bee nidish*tłoh*," meaning, "I'm going to throw you into this rock," but using a handling verb stem, -*tłoh*, which is used to refer to mushy objects, such as mud or oatmeal. The song, then, in addition to embodying multiple characters, also displays the kind of humor available in the shifting ground of joking repetition seen in verbal art and speech play discussed earlier.

The embodiment of characters in sung performances can be filled with seriousness and respect as well, performing personal and social histories. We saw this earlier in the way people heard Sluggo in particular songs on the radio. We will encounter it again in the way some people respond to Boe Titla's country songs about meaningful places in and around the reservation (discussed more fully in chapter 5).

But in 1996, the Apache-language teacher at the junior high school asked me to write liner notes for a tape she had helped the Apache Culture Club make, which they were going to sell in order to raise money for the club. She gave me a copy of the tape to listen to. One of her favorite songs on it was one she titled "Geronimo's Song." Traditional Apache songs rarely bear official titles, but for the purposes of printing something on the tape — how many songs on each side and the like — the teacher felt it was important. She was wavering between "Geronimo's Song" and "Lonesome Song," for the mood of the text. She ultimately settled on the first because it was more in keeping with the thing that makes this particular song special: it is purported to have been composed by Geronimo himself during his incarceration as a prisoner of war in Florida and Oklahoma. The young woman from San Carlos High School who sang the song did so with great feeling, and it was the favorite of a number of people who heard the tape.

Geronimo's Song	Geronimo's Song
he ya ya 'ene ya yo	he ya ya 'ene ya yo
he ya ya 'ene ya yo	he ya ya 'ene ya yo
he ya ya 'ene ya yo	he ya ya 'ene ya yo
he ya ya 'ene ya yo	he ya ya 'ene ya yo
he ya ya ene yo he neegheya	he ya ya ene yo he neegheya
Dził̲ligai si'ání baa ch'ínágóyee yo	I'm lonely for White Mountain yo
he ya ya 'ene ya yo	he ya ya 'ene ya yo
he ya ya 'ene ya yo	he ya ya 'ene ya yo
he ya ya ene yo he neegheya	he ya ya ene yo he neegheya
Mexico bich'į' dadistiní baa ch'ínágóyee yo	I'm lonely for the roads to Mexico yo
he ya ya 'ene ya yo	he ya ya 'ene ya yo
he ya ya 'ene ya yo	he ya ya 'ene ya yo
he ya ya ene yo he neegheya	he ya ya ene yo he neegheya
Oklahoma bitisyú ch'íníyaa yo	I've gone past Oklahoma yo
T'ąązhį' nádisht'įįgo	As I look backward
Tú shinaadí' nadazlįigo	As water flows down from my eyes
Baa ch'ínágóyee yo	I'm lonely for it
he ya ya 'ene ya yo	he ya ya 'ene ya yo

he ya ya 'ene ya yo   he ya ya 'ene ya yo
he ya ya ene yo he neegheya   he ya ya ene yo he neegheya

Did Geronimo "really" compose and sing this song? It would certainly be interesting to know, but I'm not certain either that it's the most important question to ask of the song or that it's necessary to know the answer to this question to appreciate the song and the power it has in the singer's voice. Composed by Geronimo or not, the song creates a feeling or mood that people attribute to Geronimo. The song in its contemporary, mediated performance is thus a core example of the iconicity of feeling embedded in the direct report of another's speech or thoughts. It bridges the gaps of historical time by giving the singer the opportunity to express, in Geronimo's own words, what Geronimo was feeling more than a century ago and to communicate her feelingful mediation of Geronimo to her listeners. For this moment, the wall dividing now and then becomes transparent, and the past becomes recoverable, not through linguistic reference, but through the iconic evocation of mood. In a sense, whoever composed the song *was* Geronimo, and whoever sings the song *is* Geronimo in that the song compacts the sweep of history into this sung moment of loneliness and longing for home.

The song that puts people in the mind of how things were doesn't have to be an old traditional Apache song. In fact, of course, Geronimo's song must have been composed after 1886. Recall, for instance, the feelingful response that Phillip had when he heard the Mexican song while looking at the old photographs of Apaches in his high school Spanish class. And, as is discussed more fully in the next few chapters, popular mediated musical forms such as rock, country, and reggae play important roles in the evocation of this turn to the past. Boe Titla, to whom I return in chapter 5, often casts his English-language country songs about the Apache places around the reservation as stretches of reported speech. He introduces his song "Chiricahua Mountain," for example, by saying that Chiricahua Mountain is where the San Carlos Apaches used to live before they were forced onto the reservation. "And then they got gathered up," he said, "and moved to San Carlos, Old San Carlos. And I'm pretty sure, when they were brought to Old San Carlos, somebody there was looking back where they once lived and missed the Chiricahua Mountain. . . . And this song is about that." The song is a stretch of reported speech and reported mood, set in a contemporary musical framework, which allows listeners to be transported back to that time and that place and to feel what that person felt.

─────────

As language becomes music, as speech becomes song, questions of language as a system for the grammatical communication of semantic and referential statements about the world fall into the background. In their place, issues about language as performed vocality, as a complex indexical marker and situated evocative performance of the ambiguities of identity as it emerges in everyday expression surface.[25] The work of the imagination involved in the additive, densifying processes that contribute to a full understanding of expressive practices in San Carlos and Bylas is one way in which people on the reservation experience "the excess of language that spills over the edges of formal enclosure" (Chambers 2000:79).

One of the areas in which this spilling over occurs is, palpably, sound. Sound and repetition are important domains through which expressive practices make manifest the nature of historical imagination on the reservation. Through these practices, people in San Carlos and Bylas recognize the inherent ambiguity of semiotic systems. They recognize further that a primary source of this ambiguity in language lies in the realm of sound.[26] People on the reservation recognize that sound implicates the sensuousness and feelingfulness of iconicity and indexicality, rather than assuming that language lives completely in the realm of cognition and reference. They recognize that sonic performance is a key element of reported speech, repetition across utterances, and embodied figures in interaction. My consultants also recognized that ambiguity, sound, feelingfulness, and reported speech can be combined in order to create and circulate powerful, evocative recuperations of the past. This recovery is performed through expressive forms that create an iconicity of feeling, experienced as the recovery of historical feeling.

It is important to emphasize that I do not claim these practices to be "traditional Apache" practices or ideologies or ways of being. That this collection of expressive practices often partakes of elements found in the syntax and expressive opportunities in the Western Apache language is undeniable. But this connection by no means vouchsafes a claim that these practices are therefore ancient in their existence as forms of interpersonal expression. The desire in these forms may just as easily be one of the produced effects of contemporary life on the reservation. Powwows similarly make generous use of older forms of Native American expression but are largely contemporary in their origins, design, and meanings (Browner 2002; Lassiter 1998). The question may ultimately resist resolution in any event, so I must stop short of making grand claims about authentic Apache traditions and here simply observe that these expressive forms are part of a crucially important means of performing and circulating deeply felt senses of attachment to Apache history in the San Carlos Reservation community. I want to stop short of hyperbolic claims of traditionality also because in the next few chapters I discuss how contemporary mediated forms of popular music are an important and indispensable part of the construction and circulation of these forms of historical desire and imagining.

The first time I heard him was when I was herding sheep. I was 6-years-old at the time. I didn't know who he was but I really liked his voice. I found out his name and started learning his songs by mimicking the words. . . . I always herded sheep alone, so when I heard his songs on my father's portable radio I would jump onto a huge rock and pretend I was the one singing.

—**Rex Redhair,** a.k.a. the Navajo Elvis (qtd. in the *Navajo Times*, March 6, 1997, 1)

3 The Band Era

These days there aren't nearly as many performing bands on the San Carlos Reservation as in years and decades past. Thirty, forty, or fifty years ago, when the population of the reservation communities was less than half what it is today—beginning in the 1950s and continuing through the 1960s and into the 1970s—sometimes upward of a dozen bands were working at any given time, perhaps more. At least, that's how people remember it. In contrast, during the time that I was living in Airport '79, in 1994, 1995, and 1996, there was, for all intents and purposes, one band in San Carlos: the Pacers.[1] Understanding how that shift occurred is one of my goals in this chapter. If you want to hear someone go on forever about the good old days, ask an Apache in San

Carlos or Bylas in his or her fifties about the Rebels. Or the Cyclones. Or the Dreamers, Shakedown, the Black Point Valley Boys, the Dominoes, the Statics. All these bands played important roles as participants, mediators, mentors, and teachers in the musical practices of a particular generation.

The claim that popular musicians on the reservation express deeply sensed feelings of Apache identity is in no way meant to overlook the centuries-long history of cultural genocide, linguistic imperialism, and primitivist fantasizing of colonization. As in every generation, the communities of the San Carlos Reservation face extremely serious issues of loss of language and cultural practices under the institutional regimes of the modern bureaucratic state. Mandated statewide standardized testing in Arizona gives little incentive to the already overburdened school system to incorporate Apache-language fluency into its curriculum. The home context is increasingly English dominant as well. An entire collection of children's expressive genres has been lost to the dictates of schools and consumerism.

The decline in language proficiency, however, has not necessarily been matched by a decline in other cultural practices associated with San Carlos Apache tradition. It may be that more puberty ceremonies are held for girls now than a couple of decades ago. In fact, people say that you can see a na'í'ees ceremony almost every weekend, and one person I spoke to joked sympathetically about a girl who had to dance in the frozen weather of January. But for all the crowding on the ceremonial dance ground, forcing people to hold their daughters' ceremonies outside the proper season,[2] few of the twelve- and thirteen-year-old girls being sung over understand much of what is being sung. Ceremonial practitioners often find themselves in the position of having to explain subtle and complicated Apache theological concepts in English.[3] Even the girls' parents may have only a passing, passive fluency in Western Apache. From grandparents to grandchildren, a sickeningly precipitous drop has occurred in the ability to speak Apache. Given the ominous and urgent linguistic situation in the community, if anyone were to argue that country-western bands were simply a mark of the disintegration of indigenous culture, in certain contexts I wouldn't necessarily argue with them.

Yet in the midst of these dire circumstances of the San Carlos dialect of Western Apache, it is ironic, perhaps, that this adult generation of fully bilingual San Carlos Apaches holds such store in the ability to perform American popular music live in front of an audience. This is co-incidental, but it is not simply coincidence. Rather, it demonstrates the ways in which linguistic and musical practices are linked in the modern project of rationalizing and assimilating indigenous communities to a generalized American consumer standard. It also shows the complex negotiation of domination, resistance, and accommodation that results in the emergence of new and ambiguous expressions of identity. The "Band Era"—both its rise and its demise—is a part of this community history. The importance of the Band Era in people's imaginations is connected to this sense of the community through the passage of time. It is also linked to the piecemeal and incomplete nature of the agenda of modernization on the reservation, underscoring the irony and contradiction of the reservation as a place that is meant both to be incorporated into the American mainstream and at the same time to be held at a distance from that mainstream (White 1983). Before looking at the Band Era itself, then, I want to backtrack a bit in order to discuss the historical role of musical practices in the project of modernization and assimilation on the reservation.

Music and the cultural practices that produce, circulate, and evaluate musical sound have long been key areas of the contest over assimilation on the San Carlos Apache Reservation. Language, of course, has also been the focus of a great deal of policymaking and cultural struggle. The place of language in the project of "civilizing" and "Christianizing" America's indigenous communities has long been recognized and critiqued from a number of perspectives.[4] But as we extend our purview outward from language to other semiotic and symbolic systems in the communities of the reservation, music—especially singing—has clearly played a thematically central role in the dialogic struggle over meaning and identity on the reservation. This central theme in part grows out of the strong layering of "civilization," "Christianity," and "education" in federal policies that resulted, for example, in Christian hymnody being taught in mission schools as a means of educating and "civilizing" indigenous communities.[5]

The first Lutheran missionaries on the reservation were John Plocher and George Adascheck, who arrived in San Carlos on October 10, 1893. Francis Uplegger, the best-remembered Lutheran pastor on the reservation, arrived in 1919 and remained in the community for forty-five years before he died in 1964. His son, Alfred, had preceded him to San Carlos and remained there until his death in 1982.

In keeping with the Lutheran dictum that the Gospel be read in the vernacular language of the community, the missionaries used bilingual interpreters in the community, learned Western Apache themselves, and translated portions of Scripture and numerous hymns into Apache. Some of my consultants believed the Lutheran missionaries were able to learn the subject-object-verb construction of Apache more easily than English-speaking Americans in the community because they were Germans and thus spoke a language that allows verbs to appear in clause-final position. Some of the Lutheran pastors, such as the Upleggers in San Carlos and Paul Meyerhoff at the East Fork Mission to the north, preached in Apache. Those who did not used interpreters.

The Upleggers developed their own orthography for Apache. It is somewhat clumsy, filled with special marks such as (, /,), and /" following vowels to indicate length, tonality, and so forth. Given the missionaries' lack of formal training in linguistic transcription and analysis, however, their method was ingenious. In a 1956 interview, Francis Uplegger claimed that he developed the writing system for his own personal use because "The Apaches are learning our language in school. . . . Who would want it after I am gone?" ("152 Years" 1956:27). The Upleggers' form of Apache literacy, though, did travel more widely in the community. Francis contributed an occasional column, "As the Apache Says It," to the newsletter published by the mission, *The Apache Scout*, in which he offered Scripture translations in his personal orthography. The Upleggers also published—or had printed—a collection of Lutheran hymns translated into Apache. They compiled a dictionary of San Carlos Apache, which appears to have been a personal document that exists only in manuscript form. It is currently housed in the Huntington Library in Pasadena, California.

Although it's not my intention to write a history of the Lutheran missions on the San Carlos Reservation, the work of the Lutherans is fortuitous for two reasons that concern me here. First, the translation of Gospel and Epistle begun by the Lutherans (and continued later on by the Summer Institute of Linguistics [SIL] and the Wycliffe Bible Translators) brought questions of translation into a central place in the discussions surrounding cultural maintenance and change in the reservation communities (Arteaga 1994; Cheyfitz 1997). The practices and ideologies of Scripture translation highlighted issues of cross-linguistic indeterminacy and ambiguity in the production of cultural meaning and meaningfulness. Britton Goode, a traditional dream interpreter in his younger days, converted to Christianity sometime after World War II and joined the evangelical American Indian Church. He worked closely with Faith Hill on the Western Apache interpretation of the New Testament sponsored by SIL. "He used to say to us, 'What does it *really* mean?'" one of his daughters once told me. The question of "real" meaning behind the constructed looking glass of language and people's sense that Apache is ultimately untranslatable into English in part grow out of the community's experiences in Scripture and hymn translation.

Second, the translation of song texts from English into Apache brings us once again to an area in which questions of language and music interpenetrate each other. If part of music's power resides in its invitation to participation through instilling pleasure (Stokes 1994), part of that pleasure is linked in song to such features as rhythm, meter, and rhyme, and to the ways that these elements are linked to the semantic or referential content of the text. That is, "Where's the beef?" is not simply a question or simply a famous advertising slogan. It is also an anapest— that is, a poetic arrangement of three beats in which the first two beats are unstressed and third stressed—a poetic arrangement that is not preserved in translating the cognitive content of the phrase into Apache: "magashi bits'in hayú?" This sense of rhythm and meter may help explain why catch phrases and slogans are primary transition points for code-switching into English for bilingual speakers. In order to preserve the melodic and rhythmic architecture of a song, then, a translator may have to make compromises in the realm of referential meaning or pragmatic indexical form in order to make a text scan and fit its prearranged musical mold.

The Lutheran missionaries taught people to sing hymns in Apache, both in church and in school, reading the Upleggers' devised orthography. Many of my consultants had vivid memories of Alfred Uplegger, the son, teaching people how to read Apache in church; others thought that a number of his hymn translations, written in large letters on oak tag for the congregation to see, were still to be found in the basement of Grace Lutheran Church in San Carlos.

Teaching the people of San Carlos to sing his translated hymns, Pastor Uplegger was accompanied on the piano by his sister, Dorothea. She gave piano lessons in the community, and one of my consultants,

Edmund Hunter Jr., took some. He was born in 1918 in Claypool, moving to Old San Carlos as a young boy. By the time I met him, he was a sprightly septuagenarian—the first time we met was on the roof of his house, where he was climbing around, repairing his swamp cooler for the summer—with a consistently bemused twinkle in his cataract-fogged eyes. He remembered playing a piece in a school program when he was in the seventh or eighth grade. "I don't even know what note I was playing," he said with amusement. "I just memorized the key —which key to push—and I learned on that, that's the only thing I knew. I couldn't read music." He said he "wasn't too eager or ambitious about it" because the other boys made fun of him, laughing and jeering, "ch'ekii zhą́ bah adzaahii ánł'įį"—that's only for girls to play. He involved his wife in his joking performance. He turned to her and said, "What grade was I in when I made my, what do you call it," and they couldn't think of the word *debut*, and they made jokes about how he "could have sounded like Liberace" if only he'd kept up with it.

But hymn singing and classical piano were only a small part of the Bureau American musical practices to which people in San Carlos were introduced in the early part of the twentieth century. Edmund also remembered that when he was in the seventh grade, one of his buddies got a "box guitar" (local vernacular for an acoustic, as opposed to an electric, instrument) through a mail-order catalog. "He told me there was instructions for it, and I was going through it, reading it, and so I started fooling around with it, so I ordered me a guitar myself, and both of us, uh, tried to learn how but were never too successful." Edmund remembered learning the G chord and the C, the easy ones. "And the F is kinda hard, like that," he said, mimicking the bar you need to make with your index finger across all six strings to play the chord. "And then when you move it up, way up this way, it's kinda hard. Blew my brains," he said with a laugh. "So I just quit." His younger brother learned the guitar pretty well, though.

I asked Edmund what songs he played when he was learning the guitar, and he sang, in a joking, swooping, whining voice, "Home, home on the range," and then, switching to the crisp, clipped rhythmic inflection of the Mexican *ranchera* style, sang "I am the rancho grande . . ."

The schools also had bands. *The Apache Scout*—the Lutheran newsletter—featured on the front page of its August 1935 edition a photograph of "the Whiteriver School band of about the year 1909" (Guenther 1935:421). The photograph features a twenty-two-member band—brass, woodwind, and percussion. Although the author refrained from giving the names of the band members, "because I thought it would be more interesting to each reader to try to 'place' each face himself" (Guenther 1935:421), he did note that one band member, sitting on the far left of the photograph, was "Fleming Lavender, the leader who could play almost any instrument including the violin. Once he had toured the United States with an Indian band. Their schedule took them to Pabst Park in Milwaukee. Here Pastor Harders, ever on the look-out for Apaches, made his acquaintance and took him home to be his guest for the day" (1935:421–22). One result of these school bands was that a number of San Carlos Apaches developed an undying love for John Phillip Sousa. They were mostly of an earlier generation — the sixty-five-year-old parents or grandparents of the people I know best — but many people told me about a relative or two who loved Sousa marches.

Another example of the way new music and musical practices infiltrated the reservation communities is through school songs and anthems. Francis Uplegger's collection of hymns — *Red Man and White Man in Harmony: Songs in Apache and English* — contains as its first item a song called "Apacheland," set to the melody composed by Fredrik Pacius in 1848 for the Finnish national anthem.[6] Marshall also remembered and sang for me a song he was taught at the East Fork Lutheran School when he was a student there. Based on a pseudo-Indian two-note melody of an open fifth, the text is "Eaaaast Fork, Eaaaast Fork, our best, hadeya, hadeya."

These various mixtures and representations of musical practice — Lutheran hymns in Apache, English-language German-Scandinavian anthems about "sun-kissed Apacheland," boys' bands playing Sousa military marches, English-language school songs set to "Indian" melodies and incorporating "Indian" vocables, cowboy songs and Mexican songs played on guitars bought mail order out of the Sears catalog, highbrow piano lessons and recitals — give a sense of the range of means by which musical expression was used as an important part of the contact between the San Carlos Apaches and the governmental, educational, and religious institutions and individuals who were trying to "civilize" them at the beginning of the twentieth century. That this process was inevitably incomplete and contested is noted, I think, in Edmund Hunter's joke that he could have been another Liberace had he continued his piano studies — a joke about social class that unmasks the pretense that "piano lessons" would inculcate the proper cultural capital by socializing the student into a particular race-based and class-based practice. Edmund's distinction between the piano and guitar also reveals the layers of class and gender ideologies associated with various musical sounds and practices.[7]

At the same time, the musical training and materials that educators and missionaries introduced into the community have brought competing ideologies of performance and the interpersonal coordination necessary to achieve a good performance into contact with each other. At one Pacers rehearsal, an older man with whom Marshall had played a number of years earlier spoke during a break about how music had to be "perfect." Drawing on such European composers as Johann Sebastian Bach, he spoke about how each instrument or each voice or each individual piece of a work of music has to fit together perfectly with the other elements in the piece. It has to come in at just the right time, no early or late entrances. It has to be perfect.

"What about the singing down there at the ceremony?" I asked, referring to the na'í'ees taking place at Beaver Spring that weekend.

"That's different," he said emphatically, and Kane agreed. I tried to get the man to say more, but he just maintained his emphatic stance that the ceremony was different from the kind of perfection required by music.

The first half of the twentieth century also brought media technologies—the radio and the phonograph—to the San Carlos Reservation, as it did to other communities around the world. These various arrivals have unique features. For instance, although Bell's patent for the telephone was granted in 1876, a full twenty years before Tesla's patent for the radio, telephones were uncommon on the reservation until the late 1990s, when the tribe bought the rights to wire the community from Southwestern Bell.[8] For this and other reasons, it's important to resist the assumption that the introduction and circulation of these modern American technological innovations is automatically linked to "progress" and "modernization." Rather, I would like to turn to questions of the impact these innovations had on senses of the voice, of memory, and, again, of history.

Michael Carroll refers to the incorporation of telephones, phonographs, radio, and moving pictures into the everyday lives of modern Americans as the "naturalized uncanny" (2000:37). One distinctive feature shared by these inventions is the disembodiment of the voice from its original resonating chamber, the mouth, throat, and body of the speaker. The otherworldliness of the experience of hearing such a dis-embodied voice is captured by one Californian who tried a telephone in 1897 at a public demonstration of the new contraption and reported that he "could hear the voice very clearly although the speaker was a long distance from me. It was like a voice from another world" (qtd. in Fischer 1992:62, cited in Carroll 2000:36).

The disembodied voice from the phonograph was explicitly charged with the sense of memory and history; it "suggested to many listeners an entirely new sense of what the memory of voice might from now on mean" (Kreilkamp 1997:215). As a glowing review of the new device noted in 1877, "whoever has spoken or whoever may speak into the mouthpiece of the phonograph . . . has the assurance that his speech may be reproduced audibly in his own tones long after he himself has turned to dust. The possibility is simply startling. . . . [O]ur great grand-children or posterity centuries hence [will] hear us as plainly as if we were present. Speech has become, as it were, immortal" (qtd. in Kreil-kamp 1997:215–16).

These associations between technologically mediated mimetic voices and the re-creation of the past dovetail in interesting ways with the commonly circulating notions about the expressive importance of his-tory in the reservation community and with the value placed on the reembodiment of past voices as the most telling way that the past is ex-pressively recuperated. The preservationist capability of magnetic tape makes modern recording not simply a sign of technological progress, but simultaneously a technology of memory, a means to preserve and directly revoice the past.

People in San Carlos and Bylas listen to the radio like SETI astronomers monitoring their arrays of radar dishes, actively searching the airwaves for significant signs of extraterrestrial life, not only tuning in but also reaching out, attempting to send decipherable messages of their own out into the beyond. One friend described people's listening practices at the house behind the tribal hospital, where he grew up. He set the scene for me in detail:

> That little wooden house, and then you got that wash there, and then that hill, the graveyard? And right, there's that old dirt road that comes out

the side, towards the power house? As you get to the top there's that one tower there.

Then he talked about people walking up that dirt road to the top of that hill with their transistor radios because they could get better reception up there. "And people used to walk up there, and, with their little Japanese thing? Tune it." He started laughing as he described the state of these radios.

> I mean some of these box, music, were taped, and soldered, and wired, and threaded, they were, you know the plastic they threw away already, and they, wrapped everything you could think of, and it seemed like it was a contest between who, who was more inventive, and creative, and who could hold the most transistors together and get the loudest sound? And out of *nothing*, boy, they were getting some loud sounds!

Vel Sneezy, whose band the Statics recorded a single in the mid-1960s that is still played and sung in the community, also talked about the radio. His story underscores not only the importance of radios, but also the reach of the imagination as the listener is transported to the places from which the long-distance AM signals originate. Vel told me his version of a recurring story in San Carlos and Bylas, about the importance of KOMA, the rock-and-roll station in Oklahoma City. That station was—and is—reachable only at night, when AM signals can travel. It was a beacon of the good sound to that generation in the reservation community.[9]

> I was probably about ten years old, when I picked up a radio that was thrown out by my parents. They said that it wasn't working, so they threw it out. And I went to the dump yard, and I decided to sneak it back to the house and work on it. And so, I was working on it, and I was lucky to connect some wires together, and I got the radio going. And the first song I heard was "Lonely Teardrops." And then afterwards "What Am I Living For," and "CC Rider," it was KOMA, that station from Oklahoma, we got it through there, and I had it picking that station up. It was at nighttime and that, was the only time I could work on it, 'cause during the daytime I was out playing with the kids. But at nighttime I occupied myself, by experimenting on different things, and that radio was something which I kinda snuck in. It was white. And then after I fixed it I got the paint and painted it blue.

People bonding with their radios, bonding to each other through their radios, through the intimate and public practice of searching for a clear signal of the good sound, hanging out on FM Hill, as one place in Bylas where the signal comes in particularly powerfully is known. I don't know if Jackie Wilson's "Lonely Teardrops" was really the first song that Vel heard over that radio. But in telling the story that way, he performed an act that was repeated for me in numerous other contexts: narrativizing his life to the dramatic soundtrack accompaniment of the radio, the record player, and the jukebox. The sentence "And the first song that came on was . . ." was a recurring narrative marker in numerous life histories and personal experience narratives I was told.

The evocative power of radio and records can't be explained away by merely accounting for its force of assimilation as such. The social intensity of the search for good songs made the radio an important contributor to contemporary expression and identity in the reservation communities. It contributed new symbolic meaning to the landscape. I have already mentioned FM Hill in Bylas, the mesa behind the old railroad underpass near Ready to Go, where people liked to spend time because of the strong reception there. The airwaves also map a microgeography of specialized knowledge about the reservation. One time when I was driving a friend home, he made sure to point out to me the briefest stretch of road, about twenty feet of blacktop, where you could really hear 96.1 clearly from Tucson. The songs, too, contributed imagery and metaphor to the landscape. A rickety wooden shack on the way up to elk-hunting country is called "Heartbreak Hotel." The steps that lead up the side of the hill below the Mormon Church has been known as "Stairway to Heaven" for as long as I can remember. An old munitions storage area—a hillside cave with a heavy iron gate across it—is known as "Jailhouse Rock."

In those days on the reservation, a hundred miles from the cities of Phoenix or Tucson, technology limited the number of radio stations that came in on the airwaves. The nighttime availability of AM radio took on added importance. High school kids would walk the railroad tracks at night, tuning the radio to different stations. Donnie Ray told me about his nights climbing a hill near his home in Chinatown. He remembered sitting up on the bluff, drinking some beer with his friends, tuning the radio to Globe, to Winkelman, to Denver—they didn't care; rock and roll, country, Mexican—it didn't matter; they were just looking for a good song. One woman recalled walking the tracks at night, a stack of worn-out 45s in her hand, tagging along with her older sisters and their friends, who carried radios and portable, battery-operated record players purchased from Cody James Electronics in Globe.

Big Bell Goseyun was the lead singer for the Dominoes, a well-known band in Bylas during the Band Era. The first time I met Big Bell, his buddies told me all about those days and how important that band had been. They urged Big Bell to sing a song, as if to prove that their enthusiastic praise for his talents wasn't simply a fabrication. Big Bell obliged them, launching into "Tutti Frutti." He sang bits and pieces of "Come and Go with Me," "Whispering Pine," and "Long Tall Sally." Then, when he was done, he altered his tone of voice and announced, "This is K-O-M-A, coming to you at 1230 on your radio dial"—imitating a radio DJ, imagining himself as the voice on the air. The radio doesn't turn people into automatons who just sit back passively and listen. Tuning into Oklahoma City as you sit on top of a hill, reaching out for a sampling of the good sound, also helps you imagine yourself on the radio—that people in Oklahoma City or El Paso or Chihuahua might twist the dial and end up listening to *you*.[10]

Donnie Ray remembered that sometimes he would go to a friend's house in Chinatown, where his friend's older sister had one of those big console furniture stereos. "We listened to Elvis quite a bit," he said. A new record would come out on the radio, and she would get it as soon as she could. Donnie and his friends would sit there and listen to the new records over and over, asking her to replay them again and again. Donnie remembered Chubby Checker and said, "Elvis was pretty famous with us then." Later on the older sister named one of her sons Elvis.

The 1950s was a unique period in the history of the reservation community. The San Carlos cattle industry, based on whiteface Herefords, was in its heyday. In 1954, the San Carlos School District signed an Intergovernmental Agreement with Globe, by which they agreed not to build a high school on the reservation and instead to bus students into the Globe School District from the fifth grade on. It was a modernizing time. Britton Goode helped the tribal council bring indoor plumbing and toilets into the homes in San Carlos (although in Bylas people lived without indoor plumbing well into the 1980s). Nobody knew then what they know now: that the generations of children schooled in Globe would stop speaking Apache; that the locally operated Tribal Trading Enterprise would go out of business, eventually to be replaced by a Bashas' supermarket franchise.[11] It was a hard time as well, during which families were taken off the reservation and sent to Los Angeles, Dallas, or elsewhere as part of the federal government's misguided relocation program. It was a "progressive" time, filled with changes and government-sponsored resource development reports.

One of the best known of these studies was the report prepared by the Stanford Research Institute (1955). Undertaken with the assistance of noted anthropologist Edward H. Spicer (1906–83), the report is filled with photographs and captions that worry, in a distinctly gendered way, the relationship between progress and tradition in the community. Women in traditional camp dresses were photographed pushing shopping carts around the Trading Enterprise, which, according to the caption, had "the look of any metropolitan community market. The store is well stocked and provides a wide variety of goods encouraging some dietary experimentation" (1955:14). Another photograph depicted a group of young women talking outside the tribal office, with the caption, "Contrasts in dress, but not in the friendly and even dispositions of the young women of the community, can be observed during informal conversational gatherings in front of Tribal Headquarters during sunny afternoons" (1955:21).

The frontispiece of the report shows a photograph of tribal chairman Jess J. Stevens, along with a portion of a speech he delivered at the Western Area Development Conference in San Francisco in November 1954. Stevens emphasized economic development: "We, the Apache leaders, are trying to train our people to help themselves. We realize the old days of the Indians are gone. However bitter we may have been and despite whatever bitterness there might be about the past, we sincerely want to progress and improve and be able to take our place in the mainstream of American life as citizens. But we insist that this must begin with development of our own resources, both human and natural, right in our own reservation" (1955:vi). "That was when they were reeeeally trying to assimilate us," said one friend, telling me about the Elvis Presley movies that would be shown every week at the gym as entertainment to give the kids something to do.

The various media technologies discussed earlier marked this particular period in distinctive ways. Time after time, in conversations or more formal interviews, people talked about the impact that the radio and records had on their formative musical experiences. "That's how I started, with just the records," or "we started with records," or "listen to the radio, play after it," or "we just start playing after, you know, we'd listen to records." "Playing after" is a metaphorically extended English interpretation of an Apache lexical concept, *bikee anashdah*, "I follow in his/her footsteps." Lamphere (1977) uses the cognate concept "to run after them" in discussing Navajo modes of cooperation. In San Carlos Apache, the concept implies not only doing things jointly, but also having a certain sense of desire: the phrase *bikee nadah* is used to talk about courting, one person chasing after another romantically.

To say that people in the reservation communities have active, embodied responses to mediated musical experience is not meant to discount the importance of live performance in the community. As someone reminded the audience when the Pacers were playing at a wedding reception, "This ain't no MTV, VH1, this is *live!*" [12] Mediated and live performances are not derivative of each other. Their relationship is symbiotic. The rise of rock bands in San Carlos and Bylas during the 1950s and 1960s was predicated on this sort of active participatory experience of the radio and records, and on the way the play of imagination mobilized local identities as a response to the flow of musical expressions in the community. The constant traffic in radio signals and in 45s and LPs from Richard's Music in Safford and from Cody James Electronics in Globe or through mail order contributed to the formation of these expressive forms. Marshall's mother used to buy records by the Fenders, one of the original Navajo country bands, through the mail. Marshall said that as a young boy he thought his mother might be having an affair with a Navajo because she sent so many letters up that way. But she explained it to him.

Vel Sneezy told me about how the Statics had begun: "My brother Baxter, Charlie Stevens, Brian Bunney,[13] Jackie Patten, Ronnie Patten, Rhyne Nash, these people used to get together and just, kind of horse around, by playing guitar and pretending like they are rock stars." As Vel recalled it, those guys never really did anything with their music, until one day he suggested to them that they put on a dance. So they put on a free dance at the Rice gym. Vel said he just watched from the sidelines—at that time he didn't know how to play guitar—until his brother called to him and said, "Why don't you come up here and sing that song by Chuck Willis?" So Vel came out and sang "What Am I Living For?"

and "did real good, all the kids they, instead of dancing they stood there and watched, because I was only eleven years old at that time." The crowd demanded more, so he thought of other songs that he knew— "Be Bop a Lula," "Whole Lotta Shakin' Going On," "You Win Again," "Your Cheating Heart," "Since I Met You Baby." He said, "And so I was singing those songs, and some of the words I didn't really know, and I just, made it up, as I was singing. No one knew the difference." Boe Titla, a singer-songwriter from Bylas, also commented on the audience-stopping power of a little kid playing rock and roll when he spoke to me about his days as a youngster in a surf band called the Little Visitors.

Rock and roll was, no doubt about it, a way to be progressive and contemporary at that time. But it was also a way to participate in the community and to craft attachments to people and experiences on the reservation. Consider the story of Theodore Kindelay, better known as Sluggo. Sluggo passed away in the mid-1980s, but he is still remembered by those who heard him as the best rock singer the reservation ever produced. Sluggo sounded like Rod Stewart, said one. Sluggo sounded like Smokey Robinson, another said. Pat, the Pacers' lead guitarist, told me that Sluggo had the right voice for every type of song. Someone compared him to the impressionist Rich Little. To this day, when one of the songs he was known for comes on the radio—say, "Slip Away," "Sail Away," "I'm Your Puppet," or "Love Potion Number Nine"—people remember him.[14] Sluggo influenced two generations of popular musicians in the community; all the members of the Pacers were in a band with Sluggo at one time or another. "He taught all of us," Kane told me. Vel Sneezy, who loved to tell me how great the Statics had been, remembered Sluggo fondly and said of him, "Now there's a guy who could've made it" if only things had been a little different.

Sluggo was Phillip's wife's brother, so I heard much about him from his family members. His favorite name was "Aloysius"—he liked that it didn't sound the way it looked. Sluggo had a difficult life. As if being born in Bylas wasn't hard enough. He contracted polio as a child and at various times lived with different foster families. He eventually returned to the reservation, where he became an important member of the community because he sang rock and roll like nobody else. He eventually went to broadcasting school and had some jobs as a radio announcer. But he became chronically ill in his early thirties and died young, although he maintained a joking, positive attitude to the very last.

Before Sluggo died, he tape-recorded at least a portion of his life story. His family allowed me to make a copy of one of those cassettes, which covered the period from around 1956, when he was sent to the Franciscan St. John's Indian School in Laveen, Arizona, through 1965, when he went to the BIA boarding school in Stewart, Nevada, where he formed the Valiants with Donnie Ray, Pinky, and Red. In the early 1960s, Sluggo returned to Bylas and was reunited with his family after many years' absence. Initially uncomfortable because he didn't speak Apache and didn't know anyone, by the end of that summer he felt part of the community and decided not to return to St. John's. He spoke of the part that rock and roll played in that experience:

> But that summer was a whole change in my life. First starting out, my cousin Carl had a band known as the Cyclones. Every evening they would practice at Andrew Juan's house, and we the peons would stand around outside smoking cigarettes, checking out the music. That went on most every evening. The songs they usually played I learned by listening to them were "Mathilda," "Just Because," "Breaking Up Is Hard to Do," and "Hello, Josephine." That's how my singing began.

Later that summer Sluggo was "discovered" when he jumped into a Cyclones rehearsal. In keeping with Vel Sneezy's story about stumbling into his notoriety as a very young boy, just on the serendipity of being asked to sing, Sluggo treated the first episode of his rising reputation matter-of-factly:

> One afternoon, cousin Carl and Andrew were practicing up on a couple of chords, that [sic] they were taking out their Silvertone amps and Silvertone guitars. We hung around them until I asked them, "Do you want me to sing 'Breaking Up Is Hard to Do' for you?"
> "Do you know it?" they asked.
> I said, "Sure!"

When Vel Sneezy made his singing debut at the dance in Rice gym in San Carlos, the band that night was just guitars. "No drums, no bass," he said. Having drums was a rarity. Anson Sneezy, Vel's brother and also a member of the Statics, told me about kids using boxes for drums and wire coat hangers hung on the back of a kitchen chair for cymbals. Kane, too, told me about banging on boxes as a child, using bamboo stalks as drumsticks, accompanying his cousin on such songs as the Seeds' "Pushing Too Hard."

The arrival of bass guitars into the musical community was a highly marked event, offering the players the addition of bottom tonalities to the musical texture. Both Vel and Anson Sneezy mentioned it to me, as did Boe Titla. Sluggo discussed it in his taped autobiography as well, saying,

> Another big moment for the band was when we first purchased a bass. Here's another cat that's a good friend of mine, his name's Austin Titla, by the time he had been sitting in on some of our music at dances, so he was asked to play the bass. We did real good.

So Vel's very first performance was with guitars only. Later on, he said, they might have had a lone, borrowed snare drum to keep the beat. Still, Vel said, with their imaginations working that night at the Rice gym, people had "the feelings of a rock star being there."

Those first performances got Velasquez's wheels turning. "Well, these guys that got me up on the stage," said Vel, "that was just a one-night thing for them and they just split and they went their own separate ways." But now he started talking to his school friends. There was Ronnie Patten, Walter Talkalai, Harry Patterson, whose nickname was "Front Line," and Willie McIntosh. They would get together and play. Willie remembered that at the time he owned what he called "a junk guitar" that had only three or four of the six strings. Willie said,

> Velazquez came along, during the summer, school out, you see, so he dropped by after summer school, and he asked me, "Hey, let's form some band." And that evening, they used to have the café down in San Carlos, we went down, we talked about it, "Hey let's go for it man, I'm not doing anything this summer, I need some books for next coming class." So, "Okay."[15]

The four boys would sit up on top of the hill behind Vel's house in Gilson Wash, in the area now known as Tarzan Valley — "nothing but Mesquite trees," said Willie, "it's *hot*, too, in the summer." They would sit there, practicing songs and, as Vel put it, "daydreaming about how one of these days I'm gonna be a rock star."

Recollections of these band days prompt memories of the way San Carlos used to look, the way life used to be in those days—re-creations on kitchen tables with coffee mugs, salt and pepper shakers, saucers, cans of El Pato, and hand gestures that place things in relationship to one another. Airport '79 was nothing but trees back then. This was when the Southern Pacific Railroad still ran the Gila Tomahawk, which made a stop at the depot in San Carlos, now long gone, and "high-class" women would get off the train for a rest and take a stroll down to the Tiffany store, also long gone, for a cold drink.[16] And there was the café down there, too, where Vel and Willie had made their plans to form a band. The café is gone now, too. But it had a jukebox. According to Willie, the first song they ever played on that jukebox was Bill Haley's "Rock around the Clock." And the girls used to come by there in their long poodle skirts.

> WILLIE: I still can see it. It's a bridge right here, okay? That's the wash. I used to live right here. Railroad right here. This is the mesa right here, okay? This is the railroad right here. The bridge. This is the cattle office right here, this is the BIA office, this is Bashas', and you keep going through, this is the post office, the Catholic church, the BIA right here. And that road used to go through, stop right here, cement. And there used to be a school, it still is, they changed everything, that school, and this middle building they used to have the old pictures about San Carlos Apaches. Now it's the Rice School, I don't know where they put the old pictures at. So they knocked this one off. So they made a road all the way through to Burdette Hall, right here. I don't know why. Anyway.
>
> DAVE: That's the Lutheran Church there?
>
> WILLIE: Yeah, Lutheran church here. This is the hospital. Used to be a high school. Everything used to be football players, the whole thing was a football field . . .

At the same time, other bands were springing up on the reservation. In San Carlos, there was Sluggo's band the Valiants as well as the Strato-tones, the Rebels, and the Dreamers; out in Bylas, there were the Domi-noes and the Cyclones. According to Vel, there was a man who saw the success of these bands and realized that there was potential money to be made, "that there was money involved in bands. So he bought all the equipment. I mean he was a rich guy," Vel said, "and he bought all the equipment. I mean, you know, top-notch equipment. Fender, amplifier, microphones, the best of the best, you know, just, he bought all the stuff." And then, according to Vel, the man convinced Walter and Harry to leave Vel, Willie, and Ronnie behind and to play for him instead.

It seems appropriate here to make a few comments about the role equipment plays in gaining a reputation as a band, a topic I expand on in chapter 7. In his taped autobiography, Sluggo mentioned the Cyclones "taking out their Silvertone amps and Silvertone guitars." Silvertone was a line of musical instruments and home audio equipment carried by Sears. By alluding to this brand, Sluggo placed the Cyclones in a distinct light, as a band that has less money and is more homegrown than a band that plays Fender and Gibson guitars through Fender or Marshall amplifiers. The most famous Silvertone model had the amp in the guitar case. You could just stand your case up, plug the guitar in, and be ready to go. But if you wanted to sound your best or enhance your reputation, a Silvertone guitar probably wouldn't do.

What managers offered to a number of musicians was access to better equipment. A manager would buy name-brand guitars, bass, drums, amplifiers, microphones, and other equipment and then find boys to play and sing in return for a percentage of the money earned. Years later, when I arrived to approach the question, the relationship between players and managers was hard to decipher. I was introduced to a couple of managers, neither of whom was willing to speak to me about their involvement in the Band Era on the reservation. "I was just helping the boys out," one said, as though he had sponsored a little league team. But it's more complicated than that. I didn't meet a single musician from those days who enjoyed playing for a manager. It was a compromise that they made, perhaps because they couldn't afford their own equipment. A number of musicians from those days had bitter memories of working for managers, and some claimed that their former managers had photographs and tape-recordings of them from their glory days, but that they wouldn't let the musicians have access to any of it.

In any event, with the departure of Walter and Harry, the group was shorthanded. Willie had a cousin, Wilson Boni, called Mitch. "Now he was good," said Vel. "That Wilson Boni was so good with guitar, you know, he missed his calling." Willie remembered things a little differently. He put Mitch in the band from the start, recalling that on the evening when he spoke to Vel at the café about forming a band, he had suggested, "Okay, I know one guy who can play guitar, Wilson Boni." After his meeting with Vel, Willie said, he went to his cousin's house to ask him to join in. Willie also remembers Charlie Stevens being involved from the start, whereas Vel remembers Charlie coming back to replace Walter or Harry. However it happened, though, Mitch could really play, and Charlie could play Duane Eddy tunes like "Rebel Rouser" and "40 Miles of Bad Road."[17] So this group got together, and, according to Willie, they would play every day, all evening, and into the night.

Everyone I spoke to agreed that it was Mitch who came up with the name "the Statics." Vel said that every time a new band member came or went, they would think about changing the name of the group. They would sit down to talk about it. They would consider going back to one of the former names, like the Midnighters, the Rebel Rousers, or the Coppertones. At one point, Willie wanted to name the band the Poor Boys. And then, everyone agreed, Mitch said, "Well, what about the Statics?" And everyone thought it was great, so they said, "Okay, let's go for it." I find it appropriate and telling that the name they settled upon—the name people remember them by and under which they recorded their single for Canyon Records—is also a word that describes noise on the radio, the crackling interference you hear through your radio speaker when there's electrical disturbance, energy in the surrounding atmosphere.

Vel's father was a judge in the tribal court, as was his brother Anson for a time later on. Because of that, Willie was surprised that his father let the kids make so much noise, but he never bothered them. "We bang, we bang, we bang, till ten o'clock," he said, "then we go home, you know, then start thinking about it, 'What's the next day, what's the music [that] will come out?'" Day after day of listening to records and playing, it was inevitable, said Willie, that someone would eventually come to rehearsal and say, as Velazquez said one day, "I got a new song"—that the music that came out would be talking back to the music that came in. The song was "My Little Girl."

You can't find the single anywhere anymore. Vel thought there were probably some squirreled away in the back of the Tribal Store when it was taken over by the Bashas' franchise. But who knows if they survived and where they ended up if they did. Bulldog had dubbed a copy of the A side, "My Little Girl," onto cassette years ago, to play on his "Indian Trails" radio program on KJAA. Although you can still hear "My

Little Girl" on Apache radio, you never hear Anson's flip side, "I Need Your Love." I heard it once, when Darryl played it on the guitar. The record was made in 1966. Thirty-odd years later, although the vinyl has all but disappeared, "My Little Girl" still circulates in the community. Anson plays with his sons and nephews, who have a band called the Sneezy Boyz. Sometimes Vel, even while he was tribal vice chairman, has joined them on stage to sing. When Vel ran for tribal chairman as a write-in candidate a number of years ago, some women jokingly promised to vote for him "if you'll sing that song for me."

Given their father's position as a tribal court judge, it's not surprising that the Sneezy family was one of the more prominent families on the reservation. In fact, a number of prominent families lived in Gilson Wash at that time, and in discussing the band's success it's difficult to discount the role played by the relative social stature of the people involved with the Statics. Although Charlie Stevens, who knew all those Duane Eddy licks, was no longer in the band by this time, he was the son of tribal council chairman Jess Stevens, whose 1954 speech to the Western Area Development Conference in San Francisco I quoted earlier.

Nor is it terribly surprising that Judge Sneezy would have been "a very good friend" of Philip Cassadore, another prominent Gilson Wash resident and perhaps the most well-known singer of traditional Apache songs at that time. Cassadore made a number of recordings of social songs and ceremonial songs for Canyon Records and in part through this notoriety had a weekly radio program on KIKO in Globe every Sunday afternoon. Cassadore was a somewhat controversial figure during his life—some people, perhaps inevitably, accused him of "selling his culture." But Vel had nothing but fond things to say about him:

> Philip Cassadore was not a person of, that has a jealous attitude, animosity toward anyone. I knew Philip as a person, that wanted to help other tribal members to succeed, in whatever they wanted to do. If he could be helpful in helping them he was there. And he was a very smart man. He worked very closely with people, the white society, to make them understand what Indians are. He did not go out there to promote the negative part of the tribe, he promoted the positive, what potential the Apache people had.

With Philip Cassadore's support, the Statics began appearing live on KIKO radio in Globe, where Cassadore did his weekly Apache-language radio program. They performed live at the station about every other month, exposure that garnered them jobs off the reservation, playing for weddings and parties in Globe and Miami. Most important, though, in 1966 Cassadore got them in the door at Canyon Records to make a record. By that time, with various members having come and gone, the group was made up solely of four Sneezy brothers: Velazquez, Anson, Fergus Jr., and Ricardo playing the drums.

There's no way of knowing just how many copies of "My Little Girl" were sold, but it's clear that the song was a huge hit for San Carlos and Bylas. It's still played on the radio today; people still request it from the original singers; and when the Sneezy Boyz play it in their own live performances, it still pulls people out onto the dance floor.

The Statics were the most successful band of their day, perhaps at least in part because they were the best positioned. The events that led to their recording of "My Little Girl" are indelibly marked with the cultural capital enjoyed by the Sneezy family since at least World War II, before Fergus Sr. was a tribal judge, but was a guard at Coolidge Dam. Not every band is so fortunate as to have a tribal judge and a tribal chairman in its corner.

But there were other bands. They came and went, some playing locally at house parties or in Burdette Hall in San Carlos or Stanley Hall in Bylas. Some became popular enough to play larger venues off the reservation. Big Bell's Dominoes played regularly at the Old Armory and the Little Maverick in Safford. The Pacers struggled for decades, first under Darryl's older brother Kenny, who started the band, then with Darryl, Marshall, and Pat after Kenny moved on to other things. The band, despite its skills, was never more than a local phenomenon. They never made a single for Canyon Records. One of the things that led to the Pacers' decision to make a tape during my fieldwork was Marshall's feeling, which he expressed repeatedly, that "I've been in about ten bands in my life and don't have nothing to show for it." There are untold reasons for this, of course, some of which must be laid at the feet of the band members themselves. But the point is that the Statics' story is easy to find—its protagonists included a number of very prominent people in the community, some of whom are happy to talk about their days in the band. The Statics' story also ends more happily than do many others—with a single that has a mythic reputation today and with a second generation of Sneezy Boyz becoming successful musicians in the community. But that doesn't mean other stories can't be found or shouldn't be told. After all, there is no such thing as a band era with only one band.

The members of the Pacers told similar stories about their active and engaged responses to mediated music and about imagining themselves as the voice coming through the speaker. Darryl said that when he was getting started with Pat and Marshall, they would play "every music that comes out on the radio." They would gather at someone's house and listen together, sit to the radio or to records, teaching each other the songs they heard. They all were at Globe High School at the time. Marshall didn't go to East Fork Mission School until later, when he got into trouble for fighting with a Mexican boy. ("He told me Apaches all stink, so I told him Mexicans all smell like tortilla chips, and it just went on from there.")

Darryl, Marshall, and Pat would get together to play guitar and learn new songs. They started by listening to records, "those little records, you know, the 45 records," or sometimes albums. Darryl was mostly into the Fenders and country-western music, whereas Marshall was listening more to the Ventures and surf music. Darryl said, "While he's playing the Ventures music, while, here I'd be sitting to the Fenders' music. In other words, the Ventures music we add on so [unclear] it's just going." The three of them had a desire to play "everything"—the genre categories of the music industry didn't concern them. Everyone in the Pacers remembers when the album *Play Guitar with the Ventures* came out because it taught them how to play the music. Marshall remembered it as coming with a companion book. But Darryl thought it was the record jacket or inside dust sleeve that said "play a C chord" or "play a D chord." So they would sit to it and listen—surf music, country, rock and roll, California boys like the Ventures, Navajo boys like the Fenders—listen and practice.

Pat exhibited early on the perfectionist streak in his musicianship. He was usually the one who figured new things out, who would go home to his house and come out a week later having solved the problem— knowing all the notes of a lead, then going to the other two and saying, "We got to rehearse." Darryl said, "He's the one that'll, you know, tell us go this, do, change the chord, all that stuff."

At one point, Pat bought a book of Creedence Clearwater Revival songs. "He'd look at the book, listen to the music, then he's the one that started, in the '70s, he's the one that stayed home in his house, he'd never go anywhere, he'd just listen to it, he learned all their chords and everything." Pat's musicianship stunned everyone in the band. Said Marshall, "In those days, Pat would just pick up anything from records. He was always listening and coming out with the newest stuff."

Darryl played drums with the Pacers, but he started with the guitar at an earlier point. His uncle had a band in Haskell Indian Junior College (now Haskell Indian Nations University) in Lawrence, Kansas, called Dude and the Fireballs. When Darryl was eleven years old, he saw his uncle playing guitar. "I just stared at him," he said. "I just listened to him and he looked at me and said, 'You want to learn it?'" At first, Darryl was "puzzled" about what to do. His uncle said, "Hey, you want to learn it, you know, I'll teach you." Darryl said he didn't really care at that time—as a young boy he was more interested in running around, hunting, and fishing. "At first I said, 'Naaaah.'" But as time went on, he became more interested, and his uncle taught him how to play a C chord and a G chord, and Darryl got to like it.

> Next thing you know, I asked my mom, I said "Can you buy me a guitar?" First they laughed at me, you know. I told them "Yeah, yeah, I really want a guitar." They said, "Who, who's gonna teach you?" So I said, "My uncle's gonna teach me." So they bought me a guitar and I started playing. Next thing you know, I took that guitar up to his house and he tuned it up for me, next thing you know he had his guitar and I played after him and he told me he'd teach me, I'd have to sit with him like three or four hours. That's how I got started.

Darryl's story of his first band with Marshall and Pat has many features in common with the ones told earlier. For instance, he touched on the unique instrumentation of that group: "That time, we had no bass player. Only had, I think it was three guitars, because nobody knew how to play drums you know, just this one little kid, he just messed around with drums."

The Pacers as I knew them had joined together in the early 1970s. As other bands began to break up or fall by the wayside when the members moved onto other interests or away from the reservation or got married—marriage is a notorious band killer in San Carlos, unless the new spouse is involved with the band in some way—the Pacers, bolstered by Marshall's whiskey voice and Pat's guitar playing, remained popular and continued to perform. But being the lone surviving band also made things more difficult. With only one band in town, people in the community began looking elsewhere when they sought entertainment for big events. More successful bands, with better equipment to play on and records put out by Canyon, were imported to perform at larger, more important events. Bands such as Apache Spirit from Whiteriver and Common People from Tuba City were often brought in during my stay in San Carlos, much to the Pacers' chagrin.

Two other social shifts impacted the local band scene in San Carlos during the 1970s. First, the early 1970s had seen a shift in the place of Indians in the American national imagination. The American Indian Movement (AIM) takeover of Alcatraz Island and the standoff at Wounded Knee brought contemporary social issues to the nightly news. Marlon Brando refused the Oscar for Best Actor for *The Godfather* to protest Hollywood's cinematic depictions of Native Americans.

These events were perhaps the best known at the time, but changes in other areas of cultural expression also revealed shifting representations of Native Americans in the media. In 1971, Paul Revere and the Raiders had their only number one hit, "Indian Reservation (The Lament of the Cherokee Reservation Indian)"—which, ironically, was a cover version of a three-year-old record by British singer Don Fardon. The early 1970s also saw the rise of Native American rock bands on a more national level. Redbone, a Native American band from California, had two top-forty hits in 1972 and 1974. Also in 1972, Tom Bee's rock group XIT released its ground-breaking first album *Plight of the Redman*. For a local band of teenagers such as the Pacers, this release was inspiring, but at the same time it signaled a shift in the professionalization of Native American contemporary music. The shift—emphasizing top-of-the-line equipment, management representation, national distribution networks, professional recording studio time (*Plight of the Redman* was recorded at Motown's Hitsville studio in Detroit), and pop music sensibility—was one with which a local band of teenagers such as the Pacers was not quite prepared to compete. Keeping pace now meant coming to grips with the new ways in which forms of American Indian consciousness had been annexed by the popular American mainstream. Ironically, despite the fact that Indian singers and guitar players were hearing more Indians on the radio, the growing technological divide between the sound that they heard on the radio and the sound that they could imagine producing themselves made it harder for them to imagine themselves as Big Bell did, as the voice coming over the airwaves.

This technological divide was made materially, visually, and sonically manifest by the second shift affecting the Band Era in the 1970s, a shift that altered the sense of live performance in the community: the shift from bands to turntables as the source of musical sound.

Well, OK: disco.

Disco turned the tables on live bands because the goal was no longer to produce a live performance, even one that was more or less faithful to a recorded original, but simply to play the record. Oh, there had been record hops and sock hops in the 1950s. But this was different. The technology and capital involved in the production of the original recording made it harder for a local band to perform; not too many were going around with string sections and horn sections and women choruses back then. From the perspective of someone putting on an event, the question was, Why hire a live band to play when you can have the "original artists"? The Pacers kept up, learning such songs as Wild Cherry's 1976 hit "Play That Funky Music White Boy" (Pat always wanted to change it to "Red Boy" for the Pacers' performances). The band members were certainly more interested in the harder edge of rock and country music than in the smooth, 126-beats-per-minute sheen of disco. But by all accounts, it wasn't so much the musical sound that ended the Band Era as it was the shifting audiences for different mediating technologies, as people became less interested in live bands and more interested in hiring dance deejays. Darryl said, "The music stopped when we were playing because it was, it was '70, what, '78, '70, something like that, '77, because the people went to disco, or, stereo music, what do you call it, you know, record player music."

Fernando Machukay, who was the recreation director for the tribe in the early 1970s, put it more clearly. The style of music changed across the country, he said.

> Okay for example. Rice school, for their prom and stuff, hired somebody from Phoenix, and they got these tape machines. And you set up all that and there's no guitars, no drums, and for a long time schools, Rice school was bringing that in, and maybe even Fort Thomas, and people didn't know what a lead guitar was.

He offered up a puzzled laugh. Then he talked about the arrival of boom boxes, so now, "you know, there's a live band wherever you walk, you know?" Finally he described one scene from those days that he found particularly horrifying:

> They had um, a deejay from uh, Phoenix. And they brought these smoke machines even, you know, and it, well you know where that cafeteria is, Rice School, that patio? That whole place would just smoke up. And people were dancing in there, it was some kind of a, smoke, light show. And then in the winter they had it inside, *in* the cafeteria and it was the same thing, nothing but music, turntables and stuff.

Changing tastes and the increasing difficulty with which the technical sophistication of high-end recordings could be reached drove many bands out of business and apparently put a damper on the formation of new bands. I know a number of people on the reservation who play instruments and sing, but none of them has put a band together.

But perhaps to go so far as to call live band performances a "dying culture" would be to make the same mistake that American anthropologists have always made when writing about Native Americans. During the 1980s, with the deaths of Philip Cassadore, Murphy Cassa, and Chester Buck, the state of ceremonial singing in San Carlos, Peridot, and Bylas also fell into decline. Families holding ceremonies for their daughters had to bring in ceremonial practitioners and singers from Whiteriver and Cibecue. And the ceremonies themselves were few and far between. But the last decade of the twentieth century was a time of resurgence, as more people held ceremonies and new singers became known on the reservation. Now, during the summer, as I mentioned at the beginning of this chapter, multiple ceremonies are sometimes performed in a single weekend at various dance grounds around the communities of the reservation. Similarly, it's important not to close the book on the Band Era. There may still be bands. As I mentioned earlier, the Sneezy Boyz have continued the family legacy set down by the Statics. But as I explore in chapter 7, these new bands will have both the opportunity and the obligation to produce musical sounds that extend beyond the local communities of San Carlos, Peridot, and Bylas, which earlier bands did not. The question may not be so much whether these performers will be local favorites, as whether their local meanings will be qualitatively distinct from the local meanings of the Statics, the Dreamers, the Cyclones, the Pacers, the Valiants, the Coppertones, the Inkcasts, Universal Joint, the Black Point Valley Boys, the Dominoes, the Royal Chiefs, the Little Drummer Boys, Rock of Ages . . .

Oh, the songs! Indian blues bellowed at the highest volumes. We called them "49s," those cross-cultural songs that combined Indian lyrics and rhythms with country-and-western and blues melodies. It seemed that every Indian knew all the lyrics to every Hank Williams song ever recorded. Hank was our Jesus, Patsy Cline was our Virgin Mary, and Freddy Fender, George Jones, Conway Twitty, Loretta Lynn, Tammy Wynette, Charley Pride, Ronnie Milsap, Tanya Tucker, Marty Robbins, Johnny Horton, Donna Fargo, and Charlie Rich were our disciples. —**Sherman Alexie,** "The Toughest Indian in the World"

4

Earmarks of Past and Place

I had arrived at Marshall's early—which means on time, which means white man's time—for the rehearsal. When I got there, he and Pat had the tools out and looked to be tearing the old house down. One wall of the house frame stood bare. Old one-by-sixes were strewn about the yard. The back door was off its hinges, leaning against the side of the house. Pat was busy with a couple of boards across a sawhorse.

"What's up?" I asked.

"Oh, we're just fixing this door up," Marshall said. "It's gonna be gettin' cold soon."

Pat was pulling the old nails out of the old boards, so I picked up a second claw hammer and began doing the same. Tap the nail out by hitting the point, grab it with the claw, yank it out, drop it on the ground. Tap, grab, yank, drop. Tap, grab, yank, drop. Tap, grab, yank—

"*Hey*, Indian!" Marshall said with a laugh, using one of his favorite nicknames for me. "Don't throw those away, we're gonna use 'em!" That's when I noticed the plastic bucket of rusted nails, curved and bent at odd angles, that Pat had been filling. I collected my nails from the ground and threw them in the bottom of the bucket. Marshall asked me to start straightening them out.

The old house was just that. Marshall's mom lived in a new, stucco, ranch-style home out by the lake at Soda Canyon. The old house stood in Peridot, and it had been built by Marshall's dad many years earlier. It was perched on a small hill on the south side of the road leading into San Carlos. The front door faced east. Another, leading to a rehearsal room that Marshall had set up in the back of the house, faced north. We were working on that door and the north side of the house. To the northeast side of the house was a long ramada, a shade of *t'iis* greens supported by railroad ties for posts. The shade stood to the right and behind you as you walked in the east door, to the right and in front of you as you walked out the north door. This was where Marshall worked on engines. "Shade Tree Mechanic," he called it. The path up the small hill to the house approached from the north and circled counterclockwise around it, behind the west side of the house and winding up the gentle slope, bringing you to the eastern door, facing the shade directly. The back of the house used to be a screened-in porch before Marshall rebuilt it into a rehearsal room. During my stay in San Carlos, that is where the band practiced when we needed to practice indoors.[1] The sound of the band often attracted spectators, and rehearsals had the habit of breaking down into parties and jam sessions.[2] The back room was often crowded with friends and relatives, leaning against the walls or standing outside the window, keeping us supplied with beer, making requests, joking around, commenting on a solo, suggesting new songs we should learn. The room had a single, bare light bulb hanging from the center of the ceiling, but at one point Marshall strung the entire length and width of the ceiling with Christmas lights, deep red and blue lights that flashed six different ways and included a box that beeped Christmas carols when you turned it on. Then, during the winter months, Marshall would schedule Christmas or New Year's or birthday parties at the old house, and the room would be stuffed with people jamming out to the live sound of the Pacers.

During those winter months, filling the room to the brim with people was the only way to keep it warm. The back of the house, at least, had been built without any insulation at all, so what we were doing on this particular day, Marshall, Pat, and I, was resetting the wallboards, tightening up the gaps between them to keep as much wind and weather out as possible. At the same time, we would reframe the door and reset the hinges to tighten the fit. Marshall and Pat joked with each other in Apache while we worked, and I tried to follow along. We got the boards nailed onto the outside of the house and the one-by-fours for the doorframe set. We went inside to measure the inside wall, then back out to mark the plywood and cut it down to size. Marshall and Pat laid the board across the sawhorses. Marshall pulled out a tape measure, and he and I stretched it across the board.

"How's that," Marshall said. "Dabik'eh, néh?"

"Mmmm," Pat said, looking at the tape, "I think maybe, a couple more lines."

"Kehéé," Marsh said, "couple more *lines*."

Pat laughed. "Couple more lines. Hey Squirrel—I think it needs a couple more *lines*."

"I don't get it," I said.

"You mean you never heard that one?" said Marshall. "There's this guy, you know, he don't know how to read a tape measure, like, he don't say 'one-eighth,' 'one-sixteenth,' like that. He just says, 'A couple more lines.'"

We finished tightening up the wall and door. "Al*right*!" said Marshall. "*There* you go."

Work done, we kicked back in the yard, sitting on wire milk crates, cracking open a few cold ones. Pat nodded down the hill, pointing with his lips.

"Ań kúdi' higaał."

Darryl came walking slowly up the hill to Marshall's house. To his everlasting credit and my everlasting gratitude, Darryl insisted that I learn to deal with hearing and speaking Apache if I were going to hang out with the band, but this was quite early in my stay, so I followed very little of what the three of them talked about when he got there. Darryl cut a piece of leather to fix his bass drum pedal. Donnie wasn't around —he'd come over after he got off from driving—so we set up the equipment, tuned up, and started without him. We ran through the band's usual standards—"Time," one of Marshall's originals; "Indian Cowboy," the popular Apache Spirit song; "Where Am I Gonna Live When I Get Home," "Long Haired Country Boy," "Walk Softly on This Heart of Mine," "Cadillac Style." Pat threw in a few that he sang—"Squeezebox" and "Poor Side of Town." Finally, Donnie showed up from his job driving the school bus. He took his guitar out and plugged in, and the four of us—Pat, me, Marshall, and Darryl—helped him tune up.

The band all together now, we got back to the run-through after a bit more joking in Apache: "Better Man," "Apache Girl," "Born on the Bayou," "Cry Baby," "Achy Breaky Heart," which Donnie sang. He sang it because his middle name was Ray. The original version of the song, a number one hit, was recorded by Billy Ray Cyrus. In one of those San Carlos language games that link the global and the local by finding tangents within tangents, people passing Donnie at the store or the post office started calling him "Donnie Ray Cyrus." Similarly, knowing that my name was David and that I came from Texas, in the early 1990s some people in San Carlos started calling me "David Koresh."[3] So we didn't play the song because we liked it—band members were just as likely to make fun of it in rehearsal as to play it straight. We played it because Donnie's middle name was Ray; it was one way for the local band to reach out to the global world of mediated representation.

Then, out of the blue, amidst the constant Apache patter between songs, Pat launched into the following riff:

We were playing "Apache"![4] I had never played it before in my life, but I had heard it enough times to fake my way through the rhythm part while Pat played the lead. The whole thing had come from nowhere, dropping in and interrupting the rehearsal for a short, sudden visit.[5] Everyone sort of leaped onto the moment and went along for the ride, following as Pat riffed through the song's spiraling paces: the open-chord bends, the pizzicato sixteenth notes. Pat returned to the introductory figure and started to fade out, just like the record. The rest of the band followed him, quieting down to near nothingness before stopping. Everyone expressed their pleasure at the moment—in English, in Apache.

Then, from his perch atop his twenty-watt Crate amplifier, Donnie put two fingers in a V behind his head, for feathers, and with a laugh shouted the Apache exclamation for sweet revenge: "Hahááí!"

In this chapter, I explore the threads that connect musical experience with biographical experience. I discuss how such everyday experiences as living in an old trailer or an old uninsulated house, keeping your guitar tuned, or getting your guitar out of hock blend into experiences that are rich with personal or social history. I want to show how people constantly reconstruct their lives using the rusted and bent nails of previous experience, creating "structures of feeling" (Williams 1977) that are always falling apart and never really quite keeping the wind out.

I am especially interested here in how mass-marketed and massmediated popular musical forms gain these kinds of deeply felt indexical layerings and connections. I approach my subject matter in this way in order to open up a discussion of how problematic is the concept that we sometimes so unproblematically call "identity." The question of why San Carlos Apaches like rock and roll or country or reggae or any other popular musical form is not mysterious. But it often strikes people as facetious if I say, "Because they grew up with it." Jimmy used to play pool with me at Curley's, always seeming to let me come close enough to lose by one shot. One night, on the way home from Curley's, I asked him, "How'd you get so good?"

"Shit," he said. "I grew up in the bar."

At the same time, though, that answer *is* facetious because it doesn't explain what "growing up with it" can mean in the specific contexts of various communities and individuals. So in this chapter I discuss what having "grown up with it" produces in San Carlos. I want to show how such popular performers as Merle Haggard, Creedence Clearwater Revival, Bob Marley, and others become part of the fabric of San Carlos Apache historical consciousness and imagination. I approach the topic in this way because identity on the San Carlos Reservation is not maintained simply through the construction of ethnic boundaries. It is also maintained through the ambiguous flow of popular expressive forms across those boundaries, and how and why these forms might be interpreted as a critical part of the formation of how it feels to be from the reservation.

_____

In the spring of 1995, Marshall's mom set up a pop stand at the dance ground at Beaver Springs, making some extra money selling popovers and beans, pop, and chips during a Sunrise Ceremony. It was Saturday afternoon, and Marshall, Kane, Chuck Taylor, and I were down there, hanging out with a couple of guys from Cibecue who had come down to help sing during the ceremony. The ceremony would continue that evening, and the Pacers would be playing at Mark's in Globe. But now was down time, and we were just standing around the truck under a cottonwood tree, sharing an acoustic guitar and good feelings. Marshall was proud of his light touch on the guitar. "I don't bang away at it like some other guys do," he said. He credited a music teacher at the East Fork Lutheran Mission School for teaching him to play with subtlety. Another thing about Marshall's solo guitar playing was that he played a different set of songs when he picked up the acoustic—lots of Pink Floyd and Merle Haggard—than he did when he was playing bass with the Pacers. That, plus the fact that the jokes were flying fast and furious, made me decide to record the events of the afternoon. Turning on the recorder, of course, ran the risk of causing the events I wanted to record to cease—people don't joke around quite so much with a microphone staring them in the face. This would in turn put extra pressure on Marshall to entertain, to keep the jokes moving when everyone else was nervous. Out of respect for his dislike of the recording situation, I often took five with the microphone and just tried to absorb as much as I could. It could be frustrating—on two separate occasions, when Marshall asked me to leave the tape recorder at home, I missed taping performances by MacArthur Williams, who composes rockabilly-style songs with Apache lyrics. At the second one, Mac also rapped in Apache. When he was done, he came over to me and said, "I guess I did something that made your hair even curlier!" But this particular afternoon was too good to pass up recording.

As I turned on the recorder, Marshall was in the middle of singing "Sweet Dream Woman," when he noticed the microphone. "*Sweeeeeet, dreeeeeeam*—testing, one, two, three, testing!" The rest of the group erupted in laughter. To try to alleviate what I felt must have been tension, I asked, "How do you say 'testing' in Apache?"

"I don't know," Marshall said, pointing to one of the guys from Cibecue, "you gotta ask that guy over there."

"Bigozįį," said the one he had pointed to, even before Marsh was done speaking.

Marsh cracked up. "Bigozįį, one, two three," he said with a laugh. *Bigozįį* literally means "let's find out about it," but pragmatically it's fighting words—*nigozįį* means let's find out about *you*. "Go homego nigozįį wįį," you would say to an adversary at Globe High School: "When we go home (on the way home), we'll find out about you." The idea that "testing" and "finding out" and "challenging" can be simultaneously implicated by speaking Apache into a microphone had the entire group laughing.

Kane tried it another way, with a code-switching pun. "Ch'es ts'in," he said, finding a phonological similarity between the English word *testing* and the Apache term for a soup bone. But it appears that *bigozįį* was the solution of choice here, its superiority sealed when one of the guys from Cibecue put the whole thing into Apache: "Dała'a, nakih, tą̄ągi, bigozįį bigozįį!" (One, two, three, testing testing!).

All of us roared with laughter, and then first Kane and then the two men from Cibecue repeated it, "dała'a, nakih, tą̄ągi, bigozįį," trying it out for themselves and affirming its rightness for the situation.

Then Chuck Taylor wanted Marshall to play "Silver Wings," but Marshall said, "No way." C. T. persisted with other suggestions. " 'Infatuation,' " he said, requesting the Rod Stewart song from 1984. "Seventies." But Marshall had something else in mind. Turning to the two from up north, he said: "Ts'ínátsíkeesgo láá Cibecueyú áshłe' " (I'm gonna make you guys reminisce way up there to Cibecue).

Marshall's fingers caressed the guitar strings, and the song he sang was Johnny Horton's "Whispering Pines":

> See that squirrel up in a tree
> Slowly walking by
> Is it the loneliness in me
> That makes me wanta cry

Marsh sang the song with a bit of oral-formulaic composition: the second line of the verse is not in the original, and the second couplet comes from a different verse than the verse begun in the first line. But the rhythm works out, and the rhyme scans.

Everyone listened attentively. The song was one they all remembered from their days at the East Fork Lutheran Mission School in Whiteriver, when they used to gather in someone's room with a stereo and listen to the Navajo Sundowners, the Fenders, and the Zuni Midnighters playing country music. It was one of the songs that Big Bell had sung for me when we met at his house in Bylas. Then, at the end, Marshall hit us with the punch line: "Whispering pines, send my baby back to me in, uh, Beaver Spring." When Marshall brought the song home, literally and figuratively, by tagging the last line with the place where we were standing and listening to him, the group again erupted in gales of laughter. The mass-mediated song, performed in a face-to-face setting, accumulated evocative and indexical meanings by being linked to personal biography and history as well as to local place.

On San Carlos Apache Veterans' Day 1995, the Pacers got a gig playing for the tribal Cattle Association outside its office building after the big parade. We spent the afternoon and evening switching off, five songs at a time, with an all-veteran *conjunto* chicken-scratch band from Sacaton, a punk band from San Carlos, and a man from Sells who sang country songs to a karaoke accompaniment. As we played, I noticed Big Bell dancing across the parking lot. He rocked and jittered to the beat, shimmying and shaking to the bottom-heavy pulse laid down by Little Drummer Boy. Someone once told me that Kane plays "'Hawaii Five-O' style," and as Kane thundered through yet another roll around the tom-toms, Big Bell seemed to quiver with every note, allowing the sound to possess him.

With a voice like Aaron Neville, Big Bell was the backbone of the Dominoes, from Bylas, an important group during the Band Era. Big Bell's cousin Ernie Lee had passed away a year earlier, and his family had made sure that the obituary in the *San Carlos Apache Moccasin* included the information that he had "played guitar and sang" for the Dominoes (January 3, 1995, 2). Many people who were not there at the time would probably be surprised to learn that Big Bell had been a mainstay of the Band Era on the reservation, but those who were there remember it.

People in the crowd shouted for "Mathilda," as they had all afternoon, as they did every time the Pacers played. Most of the band members had grown tired of the song, as you might expect they would after playing it by request three times a night every time we performed publicly. Marshall once described to me his attitude toward the song: "Well, they want to hear 'Mathilda,' so I figure let 'em choke on 'Mathilda' if it makes them happy." I had developed an intellectual curiosity about this thirty-five-year-old minor hit, however, and wondered how and why it had retained so much evocative power in the reservation community. So a few months earlier Marshall had decided both to take advantage of my interest and to allay the band's boredom by having me sing the song even though I didn't know more than half the words. "Don't worry," he said. "No one really knows the words." So once again, on Veterans' Day in 1995, we launched into "Mathilda." And suddenly, standing a couple of yards away from me, was Big Bell, facing me with his arms outstretched, his back arched, a look of beatific release on his upturned face, singing along, leaning into every note with all his heart. *He* knew all the words.

I am still gripped by our coperformance. He felt the song so thoroughly. As I sang, watching him sing along, I saw that "Mathilda" possessed him fully, as he possessed it. The distinction between my musical, yet certainly distanced response to "Mathilda" and Big Bell's feelingful, deeply embodied response forced me to rethink the place of popular cultural forms in the constitution of personal and ethnic identities on the reservation. I had begun my fieldwork thinking that I would investigate the formal hybridization of "dominant" and "resistant" forms of cultural expression, showing how people on the reservation take one from column (code) A and one from column (code) B and put them together to make interesting and artful aesthetic objects.

This no doubt does go on. Some people make beadwork that features images of Mickey Mouse or Bob Marley. Others make songs that combine popular elements with traditional Western Apache elements. But shortly into my stay, I was at the house of one of my consultants, a well-known if somewhat controversial ceremonial singer. When I got to his house, he was working on his truck, changing out the spark plugs. I grabbed an extra socket wrench to help out. As we worked under the hood, we talked about this and that, mostly about how intractably his old truck had been acting lately.

"Yeah," he said matter-of-factly, "you got to be a full-time Indian."

Then, after a pause, he added, "You can't be a full-time Indian unless you got car trouble."

Car trouble. One night at Marshall's, when I was ready to head back up to Airport '79, we discovered that one of my tires had a slow leak and was almost flat. I wasn't driving anywhere in my truck that night. Marshall said I should just drive the Cutlass home and come back the next day, when we would get the tire repaired. We walked over to the car, which was on the east side of the house facing the shade. Marshall gave me the keys, and I got in.

"Now, the transmission takes a minute to kick in," he said, "so put your foot on the brake and shift into drive and wait until it clicks."

I started it up, put my foot on the brake, and put the car into drive. After a minute or so, I heard a *chunk* as the transmission engaged.

And the Cutlass started rolling slowly toward the shade.

"Hey, man, put your foot on the brake," Marshall said.

"My foot *is* on the brake!" I shouted back.

Slowly moving toward the shade, my mind spun. If I can't stop the Cutlass, it's going to go straight down the hill into Marshall's neighbors' yard. And the Cutlass isn't stopping.

Then I got an idea. I headed toward the shade. As I passed through the support posts, I cut the wheels to the left as hard as I could, making a ninety-degree turn around the near-left post.

As I passed by the post, I reached out to grab it with both arms in an attempt to stop the runaway vehicle.

I missed.

Now the Cutlass wasn't going to go down the hill, but it was heading directly for my truck. Everyone who had been standing around the bed of my truck now scattered to the four winds. Suddenly Marshall's wife ran up to the window of the Cutlass.

"*Pump* the *brake, pump* the *brake, pump* the *brake!*" she called out to me.

I picked my foot up off the brake pedal and stepped on it again and again. The Cutlass ground to a halt in front of my truck, with inches to spare. (I have to make it sound like a suspense movie, don't I?)

Marshall walked up to the car, laughing. "I told you to put your foot on the brake," he said to me. I just stared at him. This was my first experience behind the wheel of an Indian car. And this tale of culture shock is the only incident that the people who were there *insisted* that I include in this book. It's indelibly etched into our memories.

Like that story, like Big Bell's performance of "Mathilda," the ceremonial singer's offhand comment, linking indigenous identity to an intimate relationship with one of the quintessential technological artifacts of modernity and colonization, stuck with me. In other situations, of course, this same medicine man has said that being a "full-time Indian" would mean giving up automobiles entirely, speaking your native language, hunting for your food in the mountains instead of at the supermarket, making your own clothes instead of pushing a shopping cart around Wal-Mart. But his comment that day stayed with me. As time went on, I realized that he had not said that being a full-time Indian would mean hanging an eagle feather, a baby moccasin, a safety-pin headdress, a dream-catcher, or a beaded something from your rearview mirror. Of course, people do these things all the time. They add bumper stickers, special license plates and license plate frames, and rearview mirror ornaments that index an "Indian" identity. But he was saying that you do not need to *add* anything to your vehicle in order to "Indianize" it. What you need is an engagement with the object that embodies your personal and community historical relationships to it.

Similarly, Apaches were not "being Apache" or "expressing identity" only when they added identifiably traditional or Apache elements to a popular song form. Rather, they were doing those things when they listened to the radio or to tapes and CDs as well.

That is to say, the study of identity and hybridity has perhaps focused too closely on the construction and production of new forms and not enough on styles of consumption. The insight that ethnicity doesn't consist of a closed set of distinctive features but rather is constantly reconstituted and reenacted in performance has been extraordinarily valuable, but it comes with a price. That price is a too-close focus on the practices involved in the construction and reconstructing of new forms, at the expense of a closer look at active practices of absorption through which creative materials circulate in a community.

Listening is one such practice. During my stay on the reservation, I realized that people in San Carlos and Bylas have deep and affective responses to contemporary music that linked certain songs to people and places, to personal and community histories. These responses and links aren't necessarily dependant on the addition of a "more Indian" element to the songs. "Full-time Indians" are just that: Indian not only when singing traditional songs or dancing at powwows or praying in their indigenous language, but also when driving in their cars, eating at McDonald's, or listening to the radio. Listening to Pink Floyd, AC/DC,

Bob Marley, Eric Clapton, Merle Haggard, the Eagles, or Santana with my friends and hearing them talk about and respond to these artists' recordings, I gained a different sense of what the connections between popular culture and local identities might be. Those connections are only partially attainable through binary local-global or inside-outside models or through models of hybrid cultural construction that emphasize the philological roots of the elements of an expression. Watching Big Bell's joyous possession of and by "Mathilda," I was forced to wonder: Who was I to say that this was somebody else's music?

The answer to that question is only partially arrived at by placing the original mass-mediated song at the center. "Mathilda," for instance, was originally recorded by a New Orleans–based group called Cookie and the Cupcakes. The song was a minor hit, rising as high as number forty-eight on the Billboard charts in 1959. Despite this somewhat limited status, the song, one of the anthems of "swamp pop" (Bernard 1996), was intensely influential through an area extending westward from the Gulf of Mexico, the Gulfport–Beaumont–Port Arthur area, through Texas and across the lower Southwest. Over the years, it has been remade by Roosevelt Nettles, the Fabulous Thunderbirds, and Freddy Fender.

Although an approach that stresses the sanctity of the original instance and then demonstrates global-local contact and relationships can tell us where the song came from and how it arrived at its final destination, it can't tell us how the song became meaningful to people on the reservation. The question isn't "Where does it come from?" but "How do things become part of a community?" How is material that obviously and arguably comes from "the outside"—such as Jorgen Ingmann's "Apache," Johnny Horton's "Whispering Pines," and Cookie and the Cupcakes' "Mathilda"—woven into the fabric of everyday life on the reservation, taking on deeply contextualized symbolic meanings?

One reason that these philological models lose some of the texture of the local situation is that they treat the mass-marketed version of an item of popular culture as a sort of final text, without attending to the forms of *inter*mediation that help account for the item's powerful resonance in the community. It is not simply "Mathilda," but more complexly it is Big Bell singing "Mathilda" that helps to explain the song's social life in the community and opens up the artifact to compound layers of indexical richness and history. The groups that played during the Band Era were intermediators, making popular music that was locally meaningful and resonant within the community. Time after time in my fieldwork, when I would hear a song with which I was unfamiliar, I would ask, "Who did that song?" And the answer would often be, not "Merle Haggard" or "Waylon Jennings" or "Eric Clapton," but "the Fenders," "the Navajo Sundowners," "the Zuni Midnighters," "Apache Spirit."

The intermediation of popular musical forms in the community is one way that songs become layered with local resonances. When people remember the hit songs they grew up with, they don't necessarily remember them as the songs heard on greatest hits collections. They remember them as performed by local singers in local contexts. These intermediating performances are one means by which mass-mediated popular music becomes locally resonant. The "Apache" element that is "added" is the fact that the songs are performed by people who have social relationships with others in the community, who in turn find the songs saturated with their experienced histories of circulation in the community. This isn't to say that people on the reservation are unaware of more commercially marketed versions of these songs. They know where the songs come from. But it may be just as likely that someone will hear, say, a George Jones country song on the radio and think of a local person, as that someone will hear a local person sing that song and think of George Jones.

This connection was brought home to me, sadly, when one of my oldest friends in Bylas died in 1992. Ross Dosela, known affectionately as "Junior," was a highly regarded country singer. He had a very minor career off the reservation. He made one record, which never went anywhere. His family still keeps dubbed cassettes of it circulating among themselves. To promote the record, he appeared on a very small-time Hollywood talk show. His family also keep dubbed videocassette copies of his television performance. Every time I went to Bylas, if Uncle June was there, we would sit down and play music. The last time I saw him, a friend from Texas and I drove him from Bylas to his sister's house in Moonbase. We had a lively discussion about the controversial telescopes being built on Mount Graham. The next morning—three days before Christmas—his brother-in-law came by where I was staying to tell me he was gone. A year later, when I was back in Bylas with my guitar in hand, people asked me to play "some of Ross's songs." They didn't mean songs that he had written. The intermediary performances of popular songs expose people to various possible ways of having locally meaningful relationships with them, even though the songs are from "the outside." This is one of the ways popular music becomes Apache.

So it's not surprising that "Mathilda" has become an artifact of so-cial memory in the community, resonant and saturated with the ex-periences and knowledge of the people who have heard it and sung it through the years. Sluggo learned it from the Cyclones, and Mar-shall learned it from Sluggo. The song, like so many, acts as a memory box, not only for people, but for places as well. One way of express-ing that sense of connection was to verbalize the association. "Héla! Sluggo used to sing that." Or as Marshall often exclaimed, "Héla! White Cityyú," remembering the neighborhood in San Carlos where Sluggo lived and where they used to jam out together when they all were in Sluggo's band. Another expression that often came out of Marshall's mouth was, "Héla! Alchesay Hallyú," invoking memories of days at East Fork Lutheran Mission, playing for dances on the stage at old Alchesay Hall in Whiteriver.

One reaction to these memory practices might be to say, "But this is how everyone responds to 'oldies.'" The questionable universal truth of this assertion notwithstanding, I would argue against it on a number of grounds. First, this issue is not about genre. Martin Stokes writes, "Musicians in many parts of the world have a magpie attitude towards genres, picked up, transformed and reinterpreted in their own terms" (1994:16). Although Stokes's focus is on the practices of performing musicians in producing sonic identities, his point about the looseness of genre definitions extends to issues of consumption and listening in San Carlos. Music-industry generic categories, such as "rock" or "coun-try," are complicated by the musical practices of people on the reserva-tion. This is, perhaps, truer of an earlier generation, those teenagers who would actively search the gap-filled airwaves for radio signals. Boe Titla told me that when he was in high school, KATO-AM in Safford began playing country music for thirty minutes every afternoon after school. But before KATO had its thirty minutes of country, people in Bylas used to tune their radios to Willcox for rock. And at night, when the sun went down and the Heaviside layer appeared, they could tune in to Okla-homa City, Denver, Los Angeles, pirate stations from Chihuahua, "just looking for good music," said Boe.[6] Genre didn't matter to them. Those early bands started out playing what they listened to: a mixture of Mexi-can, surf, rock and roll, and country. The term *eclectic* doesn't quite do it justice. As Darryl pointed out in describing the Pacers' history and influences, when Marshall was getting into the Ventures, Darryl had started listening to the Fenders, the country group from up Navajo way. And Kane had begun banging on boxes with bamboo stalks to help his cousin sing mid-1960s psychedelic rock. All these influences mix together. Similarly, when the people in the community listened to music, although they certainly displayed preferences, I never witnessed the kind of taste disputes or generational divisions that appears to be the stock-in-trade of music industry marketing departments.

But the question about oldies and nostalgia is misdirected in a second sense. The point isn't that "old" songs evoke these feelings for the past in listeners, but that nontraditional, non-Apache songs evoke in listeners these feelings for the Apache past. Early in my fieldwork, I was in Southside, hanging out with Jimmy and Giant—who, I only found out later, is also known as "the Philosopher." We sat behind the house where Jimmy grew up, cracking open some cold ones and listening to Giant's Gary Moore tape on Jimmy's boom box. We talked about this and that. At one point, though, Giant turned to me and asked, "Hey, how come you write down everything that everyone else says but you never write down anything that we say?"

I explained that because the people of Southside had been my friends, my family, since I was in the ninth grade, I didn't want suddenly to turn them into research subjects.

"What, don't you think we have any important things to tell you?"

I was flustered.

"Go to your truck, get your notebook and your pen, and come back here. I have things I want to tell you," Giant instructed me. I did as I was told. I came back, settled back onto the wire milk crate I used as a chair, and opened my steno pad. As Gary Moore's electric blues guitar wailed in the background, Giant began telling me what he thought it was like to be Apache, to feel that you *are* still Apache, in spite of all the changes you see around you. At one point, he said something that I didn't understand, and I asked for clarification.

"Well," he said, "put it in the spirit of Geronimo."

That didn't really help me. "The spirit of Geronimo," I repeated. "What does *that* mean?"

Giant—aptly named—spread his wingspan to its fullest extent. "To be *free*," he said. "Free."

"'Un*civ*ilized,'" Jimmy chimed in.

"To be *free*," Giant repeated again. Then he folded his body into the tightly wound position of someone playing the guitar high on the strings. "To listen to some bad-ass fuckin' *blues*, man!" So, as it turns out, Gary Moore plays Apache music, too. Later in the conversation, Giant told me that if he were living back then, "I would raid. I would. Just to let them know that I exist." He paused for a moment. "I'd need my tunes, though."

We thus return to talk about the past as a primary aesthetic response in San Carlos and Bylas. But the backward look through space and time —marked by the interjection "Héla!"—is not, or is not simply, a nostalgic yearning for the past. Rather, it marks the rediscovery of something that one thought had been lost forever, the recoverability of the past. In its insistence that the past is recoverable, it is in a sense antinostalgic, indicating that recoverability is mediated through the affective response to expressive forms. One ceremonial singer I know told me how he had made his father-in-law cry. Not intentionally, but when he sang a certain song on one occasion, it brought tears to the elder man's eyes because he had thought that the song had disappeared when Chester Buck had passed away. The man then went around telling his friends, "shila'azh knows that song."

But this sense of reexperiencing the Apache past through the iconicity of feeling engendered by expressivity runs both deeper and broader than thinking of it as a response that links "traditional Apache music" to "Apache traditional culture and history." A good song is one that allows listeners to imagine the way things used to be. A traditional song can do that, certainly, but so can a rock and roll song, a country song, a reggae song. Most Apache adults on the reservation seem to have a collection of old 45s and cassette tapes, and many compile them into personal collections that they carry around, ready to play on any available car stereo. These songs remind them of other times and places, of friends and relatives long gone, of days at the Lutheran Mission School in East Fork or at the BIA boarding schools at Stewart or Riverside, of days at Old San Carlos before the dam was built, of the outlaw Apache Kid and his loneliness for San Carlos, of Geronimo and his loneliness for the desert. Feelingful iconicity dissolves the wall separating the present from the past, and memory easily becomes historical imagination. It travels on a strong current, and the past is downstream, so that remembering the 1950s flows easily into remembering the 1850s. I would raid. But I'd need my tunes.

Old songs—"oldies"—do this well, of course, because they are en-
crusted with the kinds of histories and experiences that are easily
brought to mind on rehearing them. But it's not the age of the song that
gives it this transportative power. Rather, it is the feelingful responses
the song evokes in a listener. A new song, such as Mariah Carey's
"Hero" or Guns 'N' Roses' "November Rain," can evoke these feelings
as well. Mediation plays an important role here in its capacity for repetition. This is part of what I meant in the last chapter by saying that mediation is a technology of memory. The recurrence of a song played on
the radio or on the jukebox at Curley's, on a boom box or by a band at
a party, allows a building up and layering of experiences and feelings.
These experiences and feelings are recoverable by being linked to the
repeatability of the mediated expression. Repetition brings these feelings—linked to past experiences, places, and people—back into the ap-
prehension of the listener, so that what once was is again: "Héla! Uncle
June." "Héla! Tú daskaayú!" This layering of people, places, events, and
music is the thickening of experience, the knowledge of what it means
and how it feels to be from San Carlos. This thickening becomes historical consciousness, for more accurate than saying that music triggers
memory is to say that music triggers the imagination through the evocation of mood. The feelingful layering of indexicality and iconicity brings
listeners to the sense that they share that feeling with the past. "Wow,
this is what it was like back then," Dominic said as he lay in his veranda
the evening after the ceremony. Meaning: "If I exchanged places with
someone from 'back then,' we both would be having the same feeling
that I'm having now." One Bob Marley song, "Johnny Was," always reminded Phillip of Old San Carlos, drowned under the waters of the lake
twenty or more years before he was born. "Never been there, never saw
it, never lived there," he said. Yet and still, the song put him in mind of
those days and of hard times.

The importance of Bob Marley in all this brings the question of language and music to the surface again. I once formulated a theory about
Bob Marley's place in the community—namely, that he couched his
political messages in the terms of biblical quotation and apocalyptic
vision. And, to be sure, many people who spoke with me felt that Bob
Marley was important because he sang about the struggle of oppressed
people, especially their struggle against the government. But when I
asked Phillip about it, he thought this theory was the silliest thing he'd
ever heard. "Man, he sings with that Jamaican accent," he said. "We

can't understand half the things he says!" When I pressed him on the point, he said, "It's the beat." Then he said, "You know how some white people are into the Indian beat? Well, some Indians are into the reggae beat." Similarly, I once asked Donnie Ray the question that many academics so often ask me: Why do Apaches like rock and roll, anyway? Donnie was thoughtful for a moment and then said, "I may as well ask you why you like the Crown Dancers."

This connection between mass-mediated popular music and the sense of local social history is bound up in performance as well as in recordings. It is also intimately linked to the practices of code-layering and translational ambiguity that I discussed earlier. Bilingual members of the community are constantly translating the lyrics of songs into Apache. "Tú łid bika', kǫ yaa yúne' " was Marshall's version of "Smoke on the water, fire in the sky." Phillip used to translate entire songs in real time as they played on the radio or on tape. I remember one time as we drove around San Carlos, we had one of Boy's favorites, the Neville Brothers' *Family Groove*, in my truck's cassette player. The final song on the tape is called "Maori Chant," and on it the brothers juxtapose their a cappella vocal arrangement of the Christian hymn "How Great Thou Art" onto a Maori chant. The first time we listened to the tape, Phillip exclaimed, "Oh, it's 'How Great Thou Art'!" and began singing along in Apache, in the version his father had translated. So there I was, with Phillip singing along in Apache to the Neville Brothers singing along in English to the Maori singing in, well, Maori. Global village, indeed.

Another practice localizes mass-distributed songs by replacing text with more locally salient places and characters. In singing the last verse of the Creedence Clearwater Revival song "Proud Mary," Ross used to replace the word *river* with *Bylas*, his hometown, whenever he sang the lines "If you come down to the river" and "People on the river are happy to give." Similarly, I heard the Sneezy Boyz sing "Bylas" instead of "Dallas" in George Strait's "Does Fort Worth Ever Cross Your Mind?" Marshall used to sing "You can go to Seven Mile" instead of "You can go to Paris, France," in the first line of McBride and the Ride's "Every Step of the Way." In the first line of Sammy Kershaw's "Cadillac Style," "Well I ain't Burt Reynolds and I ain't Tom Selleck," Marshall would replace the names of those stars with those of whoever happened to be around when he was singing. These replacements sometimes maintained the flow of the original text and sometimes disrupted it. As I mentioned earlier, the very first time I met Marshall, he extended the last line of "Long Haired Country Boy" from "You better leave this long-haired country boy alone" to "You better leave this long-haired Bylas Indian country boy alone," an addition of four syllables that broke up the audience in part because of the way it broke up the rhythm of the line.

The Pacers sometimes used to hang out in Seven Mile after a gig, at some close friends' old house up the street from T. C. Alley, the dirt road that runs behind the Full Gospel Church, where a bunch of Seven Mile pachucos known as the Top Cats used to hang out in the days before there were streetlights. Wherever the band played, when we were done and the instruments were packed into the backs of our trucks and cars, we would choose a place to converge and unwind. Drop the instruments off, maybe a quick trip to Globe, and then back to someone's house. Often we would just hang out at the old house or behind Darryl's if we dropped the instruments off there. One time, we went to the Apache Gold Casino and spent our money in the "G. A."—the nickel slots—till the sun came up. Sometimes, especially when we had played outside San Carlos at Mark's or Curley's or at a party in Bylas, we would just gather at a roadside rest area, out under the stars. At all of these gatherings, Pat or Marshall would usually keep the entertainment going by playing songs and jokes on the acoustic guitar that always seemed to be around. Sometimes they would make me play something. Every once in a while, Kane or Darryl, who played guitar in addition to being drummers, would play a song or two.

This night we were in Seven Mile. Like many people on the reservation, our host, Flash Gordon, owned a prodigious collection of oldies, and they played on the stereo in the background as we joked and partied—"Peppermint Twist," "Try Me," "Mathilda," "Lover's Question," "Stay," "Seems Like a Mighty Long Time," "At the Hop," "C. C. Rider," "Just Because," "Lonely Weekend," "The Great Pretender," "I Hear You Knockin'," "Only You," "Rock and Roll Part 2," "What Am I Living For," "Bring It On Home to Me," "Angel Baby," "Will You Love Me Tomorrow," "Raining in My Heart," "Shake, Rattle, and Roll," "This Should Go On Forever," "Cry Baby," "Casual Look," "It Tears Me Up," "When a Man Loves a Woman," "Let It Be Me," "Someday We'll Be Together," "Since I Fell For You," "You Beat Me to the Punch," "I Cried a Tear," "Stagger Lee," "La Bamba." Sometimes a song would provoke a response from one or more individuals, moving the music into the foreground by making it a topic of conversation. When "Seems Like a Mighty Long Time" came on the tape, people shouted for a slow song, and Pat, who had the acoustic guitar, joked and played, deliberately cracking his voice, punning in Apache on the English lyrics.

Pat launched into MacArthur Williams's "Sober Up Song." Mac's song is a Buddy Holly–inflected rockabilly number with Apache lyrics. He wrote it and recorded it in the late 1980s, and it circulates around the reservation as a community favorite. The lyrics of the song as Mac wrote them recount the travels of two friends who go from place to place buying drinks, the singer's companion always getting angry about something with little reason. In the chorus, the singer tells his friend to go home and sleep it off. But, like many favorite songs, the "Sober Up Song" is also a site for speech play, oral-formulaic composition, and double entendre. The first time Phillip introduced me to MacArthur, MacArthur told us about hearing some new joking lyrics to his song in Whiteriver, about picking up food stamps at the post office.

There are, in a sense, two drinking "problems" on the reservation. The first has to do with that portion of the population that has an actual problem with the extent of their habitual alcohol consumption. The second problem is that the association of Apaches and alcohol consumption is entirely naturalized by people off the reservation and to a certain extent on it as well. "When they look at us, all they see is a tilted bottle," Phillip once said to me. As a result, all Apaches are in a sense engulfed in a conversation about the use and abuse of alcohol. Sometimes it's presented as an argument about religious morality, which may simply mean a debate between people who don't drink and people who don't go to church. But the argument is never easy to typify. Some born-again Christians have told me that there should be a bar on the reservation and that people should be given the opportunity to make up their own minds.[7] At the same time, drinking may be recognized, in talk, as a problem by those who do it. Many drinkers emulate in the first person what doctors and evangelists have told them in the second ("you need to stop"). Furthermore, although not necessarily quitting themselves, they will often encourage a relative who has decided not to drink anymore. I once made the mistake of wondering out loud when a friend of mine was going to backslide again, and his brother scolded me severely for not giving him credit for trying (and thus indirectly scolding me for engaging in dangerous linguistic practices). When Phillip had problems, many drinkers continued to call him "Pastor" and encouraged him to stop and return to his church to preach.

Furthermore, until recently, with the opening of the Apache Gold Casino and the convenience store next door, the only place to buy alcohol legally on the reservation was at the lake store in Soda Canyon, fifteen miles from San Carlos. All the alcohol was sold at stores and bars in Globe. As an economic activity, selling drinks to Indians was a profitable way for some non-Indians to make a living. (With the opening of Apache Gold, the two Indian bars at the edge of Globe, Mark's and Pinky's, have closed.) As a percentage of the population, the incidence of alcoholism in San Carlos may be no higher than in any rural area in Arizona. More bars in Globe cater to whites than to Indians, and you're at least as likely to see a white person buying a twelve-pack of Bud and some cigarettes at the convenience store as you are to see an Apache. And certainly non-Indians in Globe or Thatcher are arrested on PI and DUI charges. Still, despite any and all evidence to the contrary, the stereotypical image of the drunken Indian is as powerful as ever.

On this particular evening, whether or not what followed was connected to Pat's earlier rendition of MacArthur Williams's character at the mercy of drinking buddies, the next song he sang was an old Mel Tillis tune, made locally famous by the Fenders, called "Wine." As you might tell from the title, it has something to do with drinking. The song is actually part of the commonplace discussions about drinking that go on in the reservation community. People often used the opening line of the song's chorus, "Pretty red wine, pretty red wine," as a means of deriding the dominant culture of sales and advertising that makes alcohol so enticing.

But Pat's performance of "Wine" also opened up areas of contention and ambiguity, as the people at Flash Gordon's party sequentially toyed with the dominant stereotype in order to undermine its pretense of completeness. They didn't challenge the stereotype by placing a more authentic (and sober) representation of indigenous identity in opposition to it. Rather, the performers in sequence exposed the hypocrisy of the stereotype's vain attempt at iconically associating a given practice with a single and bounded cultural or ethnic group.

In succession, Pat, Flash, and Marshall created a chain of what Goffman has termed "Mockeries and say-fors," a subset of his larger category of "Figures" (1974:534). The characteristic example of someone performing a figure is the work of actors, who speak not for themselves but rather possess the ability to become a variety of characters who will be accepted as *not* the actor.[8] Actors who "play themselves" are thought to lack some requisite skill at acting. "Mockeries and say-fors," in contrast, seem to be intentionally left incomplete. "He [the performer] puts words and gestures in another's mouth. However, serious impersonation is not involved, since no effort is made to take anyone in. . . . At the center is the process of projecting an image of someone not oneself while preventing viewers from forgetting even for a moment that an alien animator is a work. Neither the animator nor the figure he projects are thus allowed to hold the stage, allowed a full hold on the imagination of the viewers" (1974:534–35). By layering together the performed and the performers' voices, mockeries and say-fors are inherently ambivalent. In the case here, this ambivalence in turn emphasized the ambivalent root of the song's affective meaning in the sequence of joking performances. Pat, Flash Gordon, and Marshall traded performed figures that moved stepwise along a continuum from reference and sense to vocality and sound. Each performance of "Wine" in the chain centered on nuances of vocal production rather than on referential lexical content, but each moved progressively further from reference.

Pat began with a performance that was perhaps most closely tied to the expected implications of the song's referential subject matter. He laid a thick, ridiculously exaggerated, and overperformed imitation of a slurred affect onto his singing voice. He made himself sound like the soused stork in a Warner Brothers cartoon, who slurs his words and accidentally delivers a baby mouse to the cat family while "How Dry I Am" plays on a blatty trombone in the background. Pat told me later that his performance was simply responding to the implication of the song's lyrics, that "it's about this guy who lost his house, you know, lost his wife 'cause he was drunk all the time."

Flash Gordon joined in with Pat as he sang the last line. His performance, however, responded not simply to the song's lyrics, but to its genre. The last line of the chorus concludes, "'cause of drinkin' that wine." On the last two words of the line, Flash altered the sound of his voice, layering an overperformed "redneck," hillbilly, country-western pronunciation on top of Pat's continuing overperformance of inebriation. He accomplished this layering through a manipulation of the placement of vowels in his mouth, by moving them far to the back of his vocal cavity and by swooping heavily up to the proper note from about a fourth below.[9] He placed the song squarely in the country genre, linking that genre to a chain of symbolic connections that attach the song and genre to a sensed cultural group, and finally linking that cultural group to a particular way of forming words in the mouth.

Taken in combination, the two performances presented a complex and somewhat unresolvable contrast. If it's tempting to say that Pat subverted the stereotype of the drunk by exaggerating it and performing it to the fullest, Flash's response doesn't afford us the luxury of that interpretation. Flash's response—a joking imitation of the "Whiteman" (Basso 1979)—places a figure at a very different point. His vocal intonation places the brunt of the song squarely at the feet of "white people," at least of a certain class, region, or background. The "authorial unmasking" (Bakhtin 1984) of both the song and of Pat's initial performance, causes an identity crisis—a crisis for those who want expressive culture to be unproblematically and transparently about singular "identity." The sonic combination of the two performances brought the ambiguous layers of "yes," "no," and "maybe" to people's ears simultaneously. All three answers to the question of identity could be found in the song and in people's pleasure in the song.

At Flash's rendition, everyone laughed, and Pat stopped playing. Then, people started calling for Marshall, who had just walked in and was standing at the door, to sing it. On the first line of the song, instead of "Pretty red wine," Marshall sang a capping performance of vocables. In a nasal, strident, whiny, high-pitched voice he sang, "ræ ræ ræ ræ æ æ æ" to the song's melody. All tone of voice with no words attached. It was a joking figure he did often. When I asked him about it, he said, "Oh, that's the Fenders." Another crucial aspect of Marshall's performance, then, is that it found its power not in the song itself, but in the multiply mediated experience of the song in the community—in the intermediation of mass-produced products through more local performers such as the Fenders. The Fenders are the reason that Pat, Flash, and Marshall all knew "Wine" to begin with; they had recorded it on one of their cassettes (*The Fenders on Steel*). By underscoring the social history of the song in the community, Marshall's figure also challenged the naturalized notion of the song's culture of origin, complicating the relationship between where the song comes from and why the song is important. This challenge again underscores the dilemma of philological approaches to understanding local expressivity in San Carlos. Because you can't be a full-time Indian if you don't got car trouble.

These figures and say-fors are reminiscent of the jokes in Basso's *Portraits of "the Whiteman"*, but I shouldn't leave off in this chapter with the idea that people in San Carlos are "being Apache" only when they play and joke with these expressions. Without a doubt, playing and joking are important means of reworking local identities in distinction to the stereotypical Apache identities forced onto the community by the outside, on the one hand, and to assimilated identities, on the other. But joking with this material is not the only way to undermine its dominant meaning. People in San Carlos are also "being Apache" when they take and perform these expressions seriously. It's important to keep in mind, then, not only Flash Gordon's joking performance of "Wine," but also his lengthy collection of songs playing in the background and his pleasure in putting those songs together on a cassette and playing them for the party. Mass-mediated popular music is important not only because it's susceptible to humorous subversion, but because it's part of the architecture of social memory and historical consciousness in the community.

As discussed in the following chapter, memory is a central node that links these songs to history, feeling, and place. Here again, mediation is a technology of memory, playing an important role in the constitution of historical consciousness through its capacity for endless repetition. The technology opens the possibility for the true re-creation of past utterances. The thickening of experience through repetition also flows easily into historical consciousness because a song can open a door onto "back then." The response to expressivity releases the affected listener from the constraints of temporality. A good song doesn't lead people in San Carlos and Bylas only to those memories bounded by the release date of the record. It makes the social act of reminiscing extend beyond a nostalgia for a personal past to a deeply felt sense of historical connectedness. Thus, not only traditional Apache songs or rainfall at a ceremony, but also a "kick-ass blues" number by Stevie Ray Vaughn or Gary Moore opens the possibility for people to claim that they feel *now* as *they* felt back *then*—an enigmatic, open place to which one can go if given the proper invitation.

One way of thinking about how contemporary songs connect place, feeling, and the past is to consider the blending of poetic elements that come together to create the feelingful experience of place and song in San Carlos and Bylas. Paul Friedrich (1991) has broken the field of poetic tropes into five subsegments, which he calls "macrotropes." Songs in San Carlos and Bylas gain their power to transport their listeners, I would say, by highlighting the way that what Friedrich refers to as "image tropes" and "modal tropes" "interact with each other, reinforce each other, and feed into each other to create insight, ambiguity and richness of meaning" (1991:19 n. 3). If musical expression is saturated in the same rich ambiguity as poetic language, then that ambiguity is central to the way in which musical expression helps people create meaningful identities.

For Keith Basso, Western Apache place-names are something like quintessential image tropes—the figures of speech that create "images that 'stand for themselves,'" that evoke a particularly vivid feeling (Friedrich 1991:27–30).[10] According to Basso, the descriptive precision of Western Apache place-names is such that hearing them transports the listener's mind immediately to the place mentioned. Phillip Goode told me that his father said that in the old days men with power could speak those names and be physically transported to those places. "Like a laser beam," he said (see Samuels 2001).

The feelingfulness of these connections is highlighted in the way that people respond not simply to the lyrics of a song, but to the mood it evokes—the people who recognize the melancholy in Boe Titla's George Jones–influenced melodies; the people who perked up and moved onto the dance floor when the Pacers would launch into "Born on the Bayou" or who shouted out loud when Kane would play the opening tom-tom beats of "Hang On Sloopy"; Big Bell, who danced and sang "Mathilda." These people are responding to the mood evoked by the melodic, rhythmic, harmonic, timbral elements of these songs and performances. People may be reminded of places, people, and events either because a singer makes explicit reference to them in a song or because the layered connections that have built up over hearing the song multiple times are evoked by hearing it again. These modal tropes become almost tattooed onto the image tropes with which they appear. Hearing a song opens a pathway that can transport the listener to other places and other times.

This link between songs, feelings, memory, and history was brought

home for me one morning in Bylas. Bob and I had just rescued his guitar from the pawnshop, and we were at a friend's house, jamming out
a little bit. One of the other men there asked if he could play Bob's guitar, and Bob let him. The man picked it up and held it, not sure what
song he wanted to play. People started shouting out the names of songs:
"Hotel California," "Wish You Were Here," "Born on the Bayou." Suddenly he lit on it and played an E chord, followed by a G and an A. To the
B, up to the D, and back down again. It was the introduction to Eddie
Floyd's "Knock on Wood," and people shouted as they recognized it
and he sang:

> I don't want to lose
> This good thing
> That I got
> 'Cause if I do
> I'll surely
> Surely lose a lot . . .

'Cause there was something that told Indian people
in the '70s that, Creedence Clearwater was sending us
some kind of subliminal message saying that
everything's gonna be alright. —**Drew Lacapa,**
A One Night Stand in Paradise

5 Boe Titla's Idiosyncratic Authenticity

Boe Titla and I sat in a booth at the Super Wok in Safford, Arizona. He was telling me how he had lost a gig to play during a pageant. He was supposed to have provided part of the entertainment while the pageant contestants prepared backstage for different portions of the evening's events. At the last minute, however, he heard that the students running the pageant had decided not to engage his services. "I don't know," he mused. "I guess, they want someone who *does* Apache culture."

Boe composes and performs country songs, with lyrics in English, about places and events in and around the San Carlos Apache Reservation that many of the people in the community feel are important.

Because his country songs are so steeped in feelings for the historical past, he calls them ballads and refers to himself as an "Apache ballad singer and writer." Boe has recorded a handful of self-produced cassette tapes. He performs at festivals, rodeos, cowboy poetry gatherings, and various events around Indian country.

Boe's songs and performances situate him ambiguously for people both on and off the reservation. He told me what he had heard that the students had said about him: "Boe Titla? *He* don't do Apache historical music!" And it's true—Boe's songs aren't "Apache historical music," not in the sense that there's anything in the language of their lyrics or in their musical notes and arrangements linked to traditional Apache expressive practices. For many people on the reservation, however, Boe's songs about Mount Turnbull, Point of Pines, Chiricahua Mountain, and the old cattle roundup at Cutter are evocative miniature portraits, moving them to tears as well as to personal and historical memory. Just what kind of "cultural performances" (Singer 1972) are these? Are they "genuine" or "authentic" expressions of cultural identity? If so, then what do we mean by "Apache culture"? And if not—if Boe Titla doesn't do Apache culture—then what is he doing, and why do so many people on the reservation find it so moving? These are some of the questions I address in this chapter.

Boe was born in the Black Point section of Bylas on October 25, 1951. The story of his musical apprenticeship and career mirrors a number of those discussed in previous chapters. Like Velazquez Sneezy, he began performing at a very early age, and his first performance stopped dancers in their tracks. Like Sluggo, he got his start when he was hanging out at a rehearsal of the Cyclones. In fact, it's because of the Cyclones that Boe began to learn the guitar in the first place.

When he was about ten years old, Boe started learning the guitar from a neighbor and relative, Emanuel Moses. Emanuel was the Cyclones' lead singer and had been coming over to teach Boe's older brother Davison. But Boe picked it up, too, through watching and listening. So Boe and Davison would "bang on a box guitar every now and then," learning chords and songs. At that time, Boe said, the Cyclones used to practice over at Andrew Juan's house, outside in the yard, and people ("we the peons," as Sluggo said) would come stand around and listen to them practicing.

Like Sluggo, too, Boe was "discovered" when he jumped into a Cyclones rehearsal. One day, while the band was on a break, Boe said, "I just grabbed an electric guitar and just banged on it."

When Andrew Juan saw the eleven-year-old Boe playing the guitar, he asked him, "Do you know how to play lead?"[1]

> I said, "What's a lead?" I didn't know what all the names were then. I just knew the chords. I said, "No, what's a lead?" And he asked me, "Is that all you know, just that?" I said, "Yeah, that's all." So at that time, that's all he heard. Then I went home. I guess something went through his mind, and then he had a brother, George Juan, little boy, oh, about eight or nine years old, no, about six, something like that anyway. And I guess he thought, "I should put these kids together as a group, to play."

So Andrew Juan put a band together with Boe, Davison, a third boy on guitar, and little six-year-old George Juan, Andrew's brother, playing drums. These were the days of no bass guitars. Even having drums in a band was a rare occurrence then.

Like many little kids on the reservation at that time, thanks to *Play Guitar with the Ventures*, Boe's band started out playing surf music—hits such as the Routers' "Let's Go," the Surfaris' "Wipe Out," the Ventures' "Walk Don't Run," and the Champs' "Tequila." The boys practiced until Andrew Juan felt they were ready to play in public, and then he decided to use them at a dance. The Cyclones scheduled a dance in the old Community Hall below the Assembly of God Church in Bylas, and they had these young boys, now known as the Little Visitors, warm up for them. Like Vel, Boe remembered that people stopped dancing and just stood and stared when the Little Visitors played their set:

> Everybody was kinda surprised, you know, little kids playing instruments, and a lot of kids was just standing around us, looking at us. Looootta little kids, bunch of little kids was looking at us. Then we ran off about six songs, instrumental music, and then, later, the Cyclones came in and they did their stuff.

After that first performance, other people in the community began to get involved. Instruments, amplifiers, and other equipment could be hard to come by for poor people in those days, especially kids. If you couldn't afford your own instruments or weren't lucky enough to stumble across them at the dump, as Velazquez said he had done, there was the option of working for a manager, one of the adults in the community who owned guitars, drums, amplifiers, PA systems and provided this equipment to bands, or who provided transportation or were otherwise involved with helping out bands and band members.[2] One of these men, from San Carlos, was involved with the Cyclones and heard about the Little Visitors. So one day Boe was told to go over to Andrew Juan's house, and when he arrived, "they wrote down our size. Shirts, pants, shoes, everything. Size." A week later the manager brought over the Little Visitors' uniform: a red-and-white sweater with a shawl collar and a zipper up the front, "white shirt, necktie, belt, dress pants, shoes, everything," Boe said. "The whole works."

The Little Visitors played a few more times—at the pool hall in Bylas again and at the Rice School gym in San Carlos—and then the band fell apart. Boe and Davison kept banging away at the guitar, though. Then sometime during their high school days, KATO in Safford started to play country music for thirty minutes every weekday after school from 4:00 to 4:30. Like many people in Bylas at that time, Boe's family didn't have electricity. Although Graham County Electric Cooperative began wiring some homes in the late 1950s, many families went without for another twenty years. When I first met Boe in 1994, he ran his electricity off a gas-powered generator behind his house—the utility company had never built any lines up the hill. But, electricity or no, Boe's family owned a battery-operated transistor radio, and every afternoon Boe and his high school buddies would tune into KATO. At night, of course, like many others, Boe would tune into KOMA, listening to rock music from Oklahoma over the clear channel. And friends and relatives with portable record players and boxes of 45s created a constant traffic in the latest hits purchased from Richard's Music in Safford. From KATO in the afternoons, Boe started picking up Merle Haggard's "Branded Man" and "The Fugitive," Buck Owens, and George Jones, especially that "Open Pit Mine" song that George Jones sang about Morenci, Arizona, the copper town tucked below the boundary of the northeast corner of the reservation.

The listening practices of teenagers on the reservation at that time complicated the clarity of music-industry categories such as "rock" or "country" by largely disregarding them. People would just search the airwaves for a good song; it didn't really matter what kind or from where—Safford, Willcox, Denver, Oklahoma City, pirate stations from Chihuahua—"just looking for good music," said Boe. The inherent ambiguity of the musical forms entering the marketplace is revealed in Boe's discovery of the Byrds, whose 1966 hit "Turn, Turn, Turn" is often cast in the hyphenated category of "folk rock":

> See, on the radio, we used to tune it where there was music. We didn't know if there was country or rock, we used to tune it around where there's good music coming out. So, we notice that there's country music. . . . But at that time, we were teenagers and we didn't know the difference between country music and rock music. All we saw was just the music. A song. And we couldn't really, you know we were young. And we thought, "That's just a song." We didn't look at it like there's two separate things, there's a rock music and country, we didn't know that. All we know is a good song. So we start learning then. So, as we go along we're beginning to notice the difference. Like, country has violin and steel guitar and kinda like a sad music like? And the other side was rock. So we had the Byrds album at that time that our manager bought for us. They almost sound like country, too. And that's how we kinda got you know, "What, this must be country. They *sound* country." You know, because, they didn't play kinda like a hard music, like, but they, in the middle. So, that's how we began to notice the music. The songs.

When Boe was in high school at Fort Thomas, the Little Visitors' former manager started making little visits again. He bought Boe and his brother a portable phonograph and some 45s, and he kept trying to get them back to the music again. He would come by and take them to Safford and buy them boots and pants, and then they would go visit the record shop and the music store and buy some more records. Then from there, he started bringing his instruments and equipment over, and he would ask, "Do you think you can use those other two boys over there and start something going?" So finally they told him, "Okay." Within a couple of months, the four Little Visitors were together again, practicing country music now. Boe and his brother Davison played guitars, and the third guitarist now played the bass. Davison was supposed to be the lead singer, too, but Boe said, "Somehow, he couldn't play lead guitar and sing at the same time, so he told me to sing while he plays the lead for me. So that's when I kinda got pushed to sing more." The trips to the record shop in Safford became more intentional, the boys asking the store clerk for the songs they had heard on the radio and directing their manager to buy them so that they could go home and practice and learn them.

The Chaparrals, as they began calling themselves, played a mix of rock and country music, plus a few instrumental songs from the early days to fill in. "You know," Boe said, "just bang on it here and there, and somehow it got started again." The manager would bring his instruments out to Bylas, then take them back to San Carlos, then bring them out, take them back, "just off and on," Boe said. So it took quite a while until things got going. But finally the band went up to Whiteriver, on the Fort Apache Reservation, to play in public for the first time. According to Boe, "Everybody was country up in that area—pickup trucks, cowboys—even little kids, *everything* was cowboys."[3] From that first performance, playing country music, the Chaparrals got invited back every year for the annual Whiteriver Tribal Fair and Rodeo.

The Chaparrals enjoyed some success. They played for dances and private parties in Bylas. They were invited to play at senior proms for Fort Thomas High School, some years playing at the school and then rushing back to Bylas to play at a graduation dance at someone's house the same night.[4] They were invited to San Carlos, Whiteriver, Cibecue. They were invited to play at the Elks Club in Safford and at the Graham County Fair.

They continued to play in and around the reservation, eventually changing their name to the Black Point Valley Boys. Under that name, they became one of the mainstays during the latter part of the Band Era on the reservation. They stuck together until Davison went into the service and was shipped off to Vietnam after his high school graduation; then things slacked off again. Boe still kept at the guitar, but the band didn't really play; only every once in a while, when his brother would come home on leave, they used to play a little. Eventually, George Juan, the drummer, got married, and Boe got married, and all of them started to go their own way.

When Davison came back from the service, though, two things happened. First, this was when Boe began to get involved in the rodeo. At the time, he was unemployed, with not much of anything going on.

> So I said, "Well, what can I do?" So, "I think I'm gonna become a roper or get involved in the rodeo or something. . . . I might as well become something." So I went over to my neighbor, I told him: "Can I buy your horse?"

I said. "Yeah." He was two years old, then. So I just ride around, rode around, then later, I got into a guy that was practicing at the rodeo ground, and I visited him, and he, that's how he taught me how to rope. So, let's just make the story short. So my mother saw me practicing, she bought me a calf to practice on. At Safford. So I started practicing. So my mom, I told my mom, "I think I'm ready for a rodeo." So we went to Chandler, she bought me a horse trailer, and I taught my horse everything. So that's how I got myself involved in the rodeo.

The second thing that happened was that Davison, back home from the service, started up the Black Point Valley Boys again "because he had money," Boe said. Little by little the two brothers got things going again. Because of changes in people's lives, they needed to find a new drummer and bass player to complete the band. They finally asked two brothers from the other end of town who had once had their own band. Boe knew them from when they had played high school basketball together.

This band also did well, playing in San Carlos, Bylas, and Whiteriver and at the Graham County Fair. By this time, Boe was roping and competed in a rodeo every weekend. At the same time, he had the band, and he used to haul the instruments in his horse trailer, a double with the horse on one side and the instruments on the other. Sometimes he would compete in calf roping in the afternoon and play for a dance at the rodeo that same night. The routine put a strain on Boe's family life—either he would leave his wife and daughter behind when he went to rodeo, or he would take them along to the somewhat disreputable places where a calf roper and country musician sometimes spends his time. "Seems like I'm dragging them into a dance hall," he said, "I'm dragging them into a rodeo, I'm dragging them into bars where we used to sing, in bars."

Through this self-examination, there came another break in Boe's country music career when he got involved in the Pentecostal church. "So deeply involved," he said, "where they tell you to get rid of this, get rid of that. So I got rid of my horse trailer, my rodeo, and I told my band, 'I guess this is it. I can't play in this dance anymore. Pastor told me that I can't involve two things at one time.' 'Good times and serving the Lord,' he told me, at that time. 'So you need to put your good times away and think about your own family.'"

So Boe stopped thinking about his songs and about how well he was singing and how well he was roping, and he turned his mind back to his family. Later, when he was writing songs again, one of the first that he recorded was called "Shame on Me and My Rodeo." It depicts a rodeo cowboy who falls in love but forgets about the woman when his rodeo gets in the way. "It's kinda like true," Boe said:

> You forget about everything and you get so involved in rodeo that you forget things. . . . When I was in the rodeo—I look at myself—I leave my family behind. And you know I hear cowboys talk like that: 'I don't know what happened to her. I was with her last night but, I don't know what happened to her.' You know, 'I met her there, but my rodeo just got in the way, where I forgot about her, I don't know where she's at now.' So that song, 'Shame on Me and My Rodeo,' I thought to put it that way, and maybe some cowboy might pick it up and like that music.

Boe remained deeply involved in the church for eight or ten years. Then, in the late 1980s, he received news of the Country Showdown in Safford. Unemployed at the time and with the blessing of his pastor, Boe decided to enter the contest. He got himself a box guitar and sat outside his house in Black Point, composing the songs that he would perform at the Showdown. The first two he wrote were "Mountain Turnbull," a song about the eight-thousand-foot peak that rises over the community of Bylas, and a two-step called "Can We Start All Over." Boe took these two songs to the Country Showdown in Safford and came away with second place.

After Boe returned home with the runner-up prize, a number of things started happening. First, he told his eldest brother what he had done over the weekend, and when he played "Mountain Turnbull" for his relatives, they got excited:

> So, they kind of thought, "Hey, I think you can start something for Apache. Here. There's no songs, only in Indian, songs, with the drum, there is, for Apache, but in, in English, with country music. You ought to do something like this. It's kind of a good idea," he said.

So some of Boe's family members—his brother, a cousin, a niece— came back a couple of weeks later and started to get involved in helping him rewrite the song.[5] Boe originally wrote "Mountain Turnbull" just sitting under the tree outside his house, looking at the mountain, just putting things where he thought they might fit. But once he won the prize in Safford, the project became more serious. Besides the help from his relatives, Boe began going around Bylas, visiting his elders, his mother, tribal council members, asking if they knew anything about Mount Turnbull. Boe started learning things about Mount Turnbull that he hadn't known when he wrote the original song. An elder man told him that there was a legend about something that had happened at Mount Turnbull, but the man didn't know what the legend was, and no one else with whom Boe spoke had been told the story.

> There is a mountain where I come from
> And it holds a lot of memories
> It sure holds a lot of memories for the valley
> And they say there's a legend that's never been told

The first time I heard this song, on Boe's tape, it struck me that the typical move after such an introduction would have been to spend the rest of the song telling the legend. Boe didn't do that, though, instead passing over it to move to another thought in the next verse. So I once asked him if he ever actually heard the legend:

> Uh uh. See that's what, this elderly man was telling me about that Mount Turnbull, that things used to happen in that area. That people had a lot of things going in that area, where, that she,[6] learned from another person that there's something happened, there, but they never told. It coulda been known up to this day, but they never did but, there's some big event took place, beneath that mountain. There is. "I wish I knew!" he said. "I wish I knew what that was, but it's never been told, but there is a legend there. Nobody knows today," he said. So, that's all I add in there, if, myself, as a singer, if I knew that, I woulda included that. . . . I just wish, yeah, I wish he told me! You know, I wish he knew. That would have made it bigger. You know, it would have became popular!

Here we see one way that loss is potentially recovered in the emotional response to Boe's songs. In distinction to Keith Basso's work (1996), for example, in which the mention of a place-name brings a response to a known story behind the place-name, in this example the mention of a place-name brings a response to an *un*known story behind it.

Another thing that happened after the Country Showdown, Boe said, is that "People started coming over again."

> People began to hear [about] it out there, "I heard you wrote a Mount Turn-bull music. I heard you wrote a Mount Turnbull song." You know. [I] said, "Yeah." "I heard you almost won at Safford." You know, I don't know how it got around but it got around, and people start coming over. "How did

you do that," or "what kind of music they're talking about, do you got a tape to sell?" I said, "No." "You need to make a tape. You need to do this, you need to do that. You got a good song there. [We] think that's a *hit*, for Bylas people. 'Mountain Turnbull.'"

So Boe made a tape at his brother's suggestion, "just to see what happens": Boe and his box guitar, singing the two songs that had won him the prize at Safford. A local tribal councilman came over to Boe's house and listened to the finished tape. "He said, 'Boy that's good, that's real good.'" Everyone seemed to like the Mount Turnbull song.

Then Boe was invited to perform his songs at Stanley Hall, the big gym in Bylas. There, a small problem surfaced. Boe sat on stage, with his guitar and a microphone, and sang his song. But there was no microphone for the guitar, so only his singing voice could be heard, no chords. The same thing happened a week or so later at Fort Thomas High School, when Boe was invited to play his songs at halftime of a basketball game. "I was sitting there with box guitar and microphone and, I guess it sounded boring because only my voice went out there and they couldn't hear the guitar—that's what I heard later on."

So his cousin came around to the house again and told him, "Go to the music store and find something for your guitar, so we can start hearing guitar." Boe went over to the music store in Safford, but everything was too expensive for him. So instead of something for his guitar, Boe's family members pitched in and helped him get a Casio Tone Bank CT-395 electronic keyboard featuring an auto-accompaniment system, which allows the player to get the effect of a band playing, say, a C chord in country-western style simply by selecting an accompaniment style and tempo, and then pressing the C note on the keyboard. The purchase represented a number of compromises—between the expense of buying the kind of guitar setup Boe had been looking at and buying nothing at all, between Boe's desire to have a band and his concerns about working with musicians who might drink or might try to get involved in his personal songwriting project.[7] The keyboard thus lent itself to Boe's remaking of himself as a solo artist, a singer-songwriter, an "Apache ballad singer and writer," as he began calling himself.[8]

In that incarnation, Boe has written and sung original songs about Mount Turnbull, Point of Pines, Chiricahua Mountain, the Gila River, and other places on and around the Apache reservation that hold the memories and histories of the people. He has made a half-dozen recordings and continues to give live performances. His guitar is now amplified. During the time of my fieldwork, his daughter usually played the keyboard for him; but Boe sometimes asked me to play the keyboard because his daughter, an all-state guard for the Fort Thomas Lady Apaches who averaged twenty-six points a game in her senior year of high school, had her own life to get on with.

Not everyone on the reservation celebrates Boe's music. Some people disparage Boe, make jokes with his music, and make fun of him. For one thing, Boe sings with a full, local, Western Apache–accented English pronunciation. Although country singers in the community almost always avoid the dialectal distinctions that mark a singer as "redneck" (Feld et al. 2004), at the same time they also shun the pronunciations associated with an older, less cosmopolitan generation of Indian country singers—the sound Marshall associated with old groups like the Fenders and the Sundowners.[9] At the same time, the sonic and textural inadequacies of Boe's automatic keyboard—the fact that he doesn't have a band—create a level of musical disbelief that some listeners find difficult to suspend. My sense is that these skeptics are predominantly younger people. Whether this disbelief indicates a generational shift in tastes and responses to musical expressions, or whether in fact the kind of performance that Boe enacts is something that listeners need to "grow into" is a question that remains open at the moment. For his part, Boe is aware of this mixed opinion and seems reconciled to the idea of not being able to please everyone.

Some people, however, are brought to tears by Boe's songs and by the memories and histories they suggest, in spite of any possible flaws in their production. I told one woman with whom I worked that I was also working with Boe, and she said, "Oh, Boe Titla's Mount Turnbull song sure made my mom cry." When I asked her why, she replied, "Because she thought it was all gone, that no one cared anymore." Just as the ceremonial singer I spoke to was able to move his father-in-law to tears by singing a song that the older man thought had disappeared because no one cared, here we also find that the past is recoverable. In this case, however, it is not recovered in hearing the sound of a traditional song, but rather in the new sound and story of a country song. Another woman said:

The first time my brother heard that song about Mount Turnbull he was in Phoenix, and he just got in his car and drove for two hours, from Phoenix to the base of Mount Turnbull, and threw himself down, and cried, and prayed, and realized that this was where his grandmother brought him, and "now I can go on, because I got my strength from Mount Turnbull."

Boe, too, has heard these stories of people's intensely heartfelt responses to his music:

Even, this guy. The ranger. Told me. Before I started working for the ranger, he came up to me. "Do you have a tape that, sing about. Chiricahua Mountain." I said, "Why." He said, "I was coming up, Hilltop, down. And, uh, Globe, k'uh, KJ, played that song. Boy, it *hit* me," he said. "My *tears* start coming down. When I was *listening* to it. I could just *see* it," he said. "My *tears* start coming down. And I *cried* to it. When I came home, I told my wife, '*Boe* made another song. *Boy* that was beautiful. I *heard* it on the *radio*. And, it's something about Chiricahua Mountain. It made me cry!'"

So the lady, told my wife that "I can't believe what my husband told me that, he heard a song that made his tear come down. He didn't cry it out, he just, tears start coming down. He just kinda like visualized that he made it sound so beautiful, which was kinda, true, that, he sometimes wished, 'I wonder how it woulda been if we were still, you know, up there.'" So, you know, something like that. Things happen. . . . "If they were still there, I wonder how it woulda been." You know, "What would they name that." It was a pretty country—pines, streams, you know, everything. So I heard some of those stuff that, you know it grabs them.

What is it about Boe's songs that "grabs them"? In part, I think, the connection grows out of a tacit understanding of the way in which Boe combines the expressive elements at his disposal in composing and performing his songs. Let's return for a moment to consider those people who are not so moved by Boe's music, for, despite the deeply felt and intense responses that many people in the community have to Boe's songs, there are those who remain unconvinced. Quite aside from the questions surrounding Boe's accent or the production values of his tapes and performances, the personal and idiosyncratic nature of his creative output makes it difficult for some people, both in and out of the community, to determine just what kind of cultural identity he is performing in his songs. Let me provide two examples.

The first brings us back to the case of Boe's rejection by the students planning the pageant. According to him, they questioned whether in fact he did something that could be called "Apache historical music." I should note that the teacher who supervised the students denied this claim, saying that it was simply that Boe charged more than they could afford for his services. But Boe claimed to have heard it from someone, so although we might question whether or not issues of Boe's claims on history were in fact operating in this particular case, it seems plausible to accept the critique of his songs as one that Boe has heard before.

If this was the reason behind the students' decision, it struck Boe that to the students "Apache historical music" must have meant only one thing: traditional indigenous Apache songs. I attended the pageant, and Boe's sense of the matter is supported somewhat by the fact that instead of Boe, the students hired a young Navajo man who played traditional Navajo flute. In addition to this young man, the Rainer Family also entertained with a puppet show that included a musical lesson about naming body parts in Apache, set to the tune of "Pop Goes the Weasel." One of the gym teachers also performed, singing a couple of songs with her guitar. So it wasn't necessarily Boe's music that the students objected to, but rather the idea that he claimed to be doing something "Apache" and "historical."

Boe certainly understands the indexical relationship between flutes and tradition. A few months after this incident, he and I were rehearsing a song that he had recently written, called "Wood on Mama's Back." The song is about his days as a young boy, when he used to go out to collect firewood with his mother. Boe suggested that we might have a brief solo flute passage precede the Turtles-influenced introduction to the song, "since it's kinda historical like." We ultimately decided not to because the flute setting of the Casio keyboard was unsatisfactory to accomplish Boe's musical intention.

At the same time, the performance by the Navajo flute player, a college student, garnered a level of respect that I had difficulty imagining for Boe. During the young man's performance, small children were restless and noisy, as they had been all evening. But in the context of the performance of traditional Navajo music, the master of ceremonies was prompted to break the frame of his own evening-long performance of joking and teasing to deliver a lecture, to scold the children and appeal to their parents:

Okay, for any young person out there, I'll give you five thousand dollars if you can repeat twenty words this young man said.
Five thousand dollars.

Too late. Hííii, our kids really listen sometimes. I was always told that the reason those young people do that is because that's their special way of listening. They move back and forth, and talk to one another, converse, and everything else. And that's their way of learning sometimes. But I'm gonna ask you parents once again, to please, keep your children with you. Put 'em in front of you. Keep 'em close to you. It's disrespectful. As young as this man is, he's our elder and he's teaching us something. For the way he sings and the way he speaks, that's something to be, there's something to be appreciated by it. And I am very thankful. And in that way I would ask Mr. Benally's forgiveness of our children and my relatives and my in-laws, here, because we haven't the sense yet to listen, 'cause we don't know how to keep our children in front of us. If you have a child parent, please take 'em out in the foyer. Young people, please keep close to your moms and dads, it's important. There's things that are going on here that they want to teach you. And although I like to have a lot of fun and I tease a lot of times, there's sometimes when we need to listen, and that was one of them. When we miss it, we talk about life and life is really short that way. If we forget to listen at the right time, we're gonna miss it. For that's something that could save our life. Mr. Benally's heard a lot of things in the short amount of time that he's been alive. But those things are valu-able. Those are things that I chose not to listen to. Those are the things that I got in trouble for. And now that I'm a bit older, I listen a lot closer. He may even be younger than I am but he's still an elder because he's able to teach me. Young people, that's what he's talking to you about. And I ask you again.

Okay. Off my soap box. . . .

I'm hard-pressed to imagine a master of ceremonies taking such a long detour to chide people for making noise during one of Boe's per-formances, or reminding them about the important and valuable things that Boe is teaching them that could save lives, or referring to Boe as an "elder" in spite of his youth. Because of the musical genre of Boe's songs, they are easily categorized as merely "entertainment" by those whose expectations of a performance of "historical music" is based upon the idea that one points to tradition by sounding traditional. The extent to which this indexical pointing to tradition may be based on an iconicity of musical style and sound—a sort of homage—rather than on a rendition of the full content of a time-honored song opens some interesting ambiguities. In an ironic twist, the young traditional flute player performed a Navajo-style flute rendition of the Christian hymn "Amazing Grace." Christian hymns performed in a traditional style on the Navajo flute can contribute to respect for cultural knowledge in a way that a country song about Chiricahua Mountain can't.

To put it another way, for the students planning the pageant and for others who criticize Boe's connecting his songs to a sense of the historical, the topicality of his texts doesn't make up for the nontraditional musical form in which those texts are situated. They consider his musical style, country-western, as indexical only of a "non-Apache" form of expressivity. For another group of people, who also consider Boe's songs along this binary distinction, his choice of musical style is unproblematic, but his texts don't convey the proper symbolic representation of Apache identity.

Which brings me to the second example. Boe is often approached, when he plays at the Graham County Fair and other off-reservation events, by non-Indians who want to "help" Boe make his songs "better."

One time Boe received a letter in the mail containing a poem about Chiricahua Mountain, his song rewritten. Boe felt that this person was saying, "Change your music and sing about this. In your song. That's *really* the Apache way." But he didn't want to dismiss the poem out of hand, so he showed it to his oldest brother, who said, "'Well, we already wrote it, and this came from a white guy, and we Apache wrote it, we know what we're talking about, we know why we want to have that word in there. But that white guy doesn't know what the words are in there for. He probably just saw it in a book!' . . . So, we just left it alone." Boe was puzzled by the letter writer's presumption of editorial expertise. He said, "Some guys, they wanna, touch it, with a different, you know. They think, 'you should do it this way, should do it that way,' you know." [10]

I asked Boe what the writer wanted to change, and he said, "The whole thing!" In the entire new poem about Chiricahua Mountain, Boe explained, "he didn't mention anything about acorns, which I put in there, and he didn't know what we meant when the thunder, it reminds me of, you know, Chiricahua Mountain." [11] The poem that Boe received, he said, was about

a deer, like an eagle, and . . . all that *feather* stuff, you know, and he told me that I left a lot of them out, which pertains to Indians, you know, but he just thought . . . a feather represents an Indian, a deer represents an Indian, and stuff like that, he just put it all in there. You know . . . like an eagle feather. And a deer, standing on top of the mountain. Stuff like that.

Finally, Boe said that the song had already been recorded on his first tape, and he worried what people would say if he were to redo it and make a new tape of the same song.

So what *does* represent an Indian? And to whom? Those left unsatisfied by Boe's songs assume that Boe's choice of musical form—country songs with English texts—is pointing outside, toward communication with the dominant culture. If this were true, certainly it would help explain responses such as those of the people involved with the school pageant. It would also explain the attempted editorial involvements of non-Indians, for it would be more important for Boe to craft statements of Indian identity that would be readily accessible to non-Indians. Indeed, the popular Oneida singer Joanne Shenandoah has said that popular music forms are an important means of communicating *across* cultural boundaries, of helping non-Indians to understand Indians (Vennum 1992).

I think, however, that this assumption about Boe's intent is inaccurate. It's clear to me that Boe enjoys playing his music for non-Indians as well as for Indians and that he appreciates it when non-Indians enjoy his music. It's also clear to me that he recognizes that acceptance by a large non-Indian population with an interest in authentic expressions of Indian identity and with the disposable income to purchase it on tape or CD has its potential benefits. But it's unclear to me that Boe has a non-Indian audience in mind for his music. In the case of the poem about Chiricahua Mountain that Boe received in the mail, we saw that when given the opportunity to refashion his music for an audience of outsiders, Boe ultimately rejected the move and the potential advantage from it and instead elected to criticize the proffered help because of its outside origins and because of the possibly negative response from the local community were he to accept such changes.

I now want to return to that group of people who grew up mostly in San Carlos or Bylas for whom Boe's songs are "affecting presences" (Armstrong 1971), capable of producing deeply felt memories and tears. I want to explore Boe's local meanings: how he ties together place, loss, and feeling in his songs; how these symbolic connections tie into locally meaningful notions of expressivity and historical consciousness; and how it might be that Boe is able to foster these associations through the ambiguous relationship between hard country and San Carlos Apache historical imagination.

As I discussed previously, a turn to the past—a backward glance through space and time—is a highly valued feature of aesthetic experience in San Carlos and Bylas. A sense of longing connected to particular places in the landscape pervades this backward look. Apache scouts on their way to Fort Grant named a place on the old road going west from Old San Carlos "t'ązhį' nách'idit'įįhé." It means "one looks backward again," with a final enclitic that makes this action the essential nature of the place.[12] It's the place where you take that one last look back.

One of the desired effects of musical expression in San Carlos, then, is to transport the listener backward, into other times and other places. This transportation involves setting up an iconicity of feeling between the mood evoked by the song being sung in the present and the feeling the listener imagines that Apaches living in the past would have had. The sense of feelingful iconicity can be brought about, certainly, by hearing an old traditional Apache song, but that is not the only way because the traditional song is not the only kind of song that evokes an affective response a listener can indexically connect to the feelings of others. What is called for is not an old song, but a meaningful juxtaposition of song, feeling, place, and past. Part of the meaningfulness of the juxtaposition is its open-endedness and ambiguity, but it's important to note that the elements of this style do not simply float haphazardly into one another. Rather, the point of the juxtaposition is that its poles are grounded indexically in the sense of history of the people who craft these relationships. Boe Titla's songs combine and juxtapose elements of musical style, linguistic text, and vocal timbre to create feelingful social memory.

In the fall of 1994, before I got to know Boe, I went to see him perform at the Salado ruin in Globe, Besh-Ba-Gowah, in a Native American "harvest festival." At that performance, he introduced his song "Chiricahua Mountain"—the song that made the game ranger cry and that one of his white fans tried to rewrite for him—by referring directly to this iconic relationship of emotional affect between present and past linked by the song. He told the audience that Chiricahua Mountain was where Apache people once lived, including Cochise and Geronimo. "And then they got gathered up," he said, "and moved to San Carlos,

Old San Carlos. And I'm pretty sure, when they were brought to Old San Carlos, somebody there was looking back where they once lived and missed the Chiricahua Mountain. And this song is about that."

But, in a sense, the song isn't "about that" at all, at least not in the sense that the text of the song is "about" the people who were moved to Old San Carlos. Instead, the song is an extended reminiscence of the mountain, a longing for a place that, like Old San Carlos, is both present and absent, both near and distant. Like "Geronimo's Song" discussed in chapter 2, it's an extended portion of reported speech. The character singing the song isn't necessarily Boe himself but could be any Apache in any place or time:

> Chiricahua Mountain
> Oh I miss you Chiricahua Mountain
> I belong to you
> I watch you now and then
> It breaks my heart to see
>
> Chiricahua Mountain
> Sometimes I wonder how's the acorn doing
> Does the cloud still visit you
> Sometime I hear the thunder
> Reminds me of you

The song opens a way for listeners imaginatively to connect the feeling the song evokes in them with the feeling of being in other times and places. As Boe sings in his earlier song about Mount Turnbull, "it sure holds a lot of memories for the valley." In an interview, he drew rich connections between important places and the deep feeling of connection that those places give people. The feelingful connection is not just to the place, but more meaningfully to history because the assumption is that what you feel about the place now is the same as what people felt about the place then:

> There's a story—not a story, but—in the old days, that was kinda like their great grandfather, looking out for them. Like, the tallest mountain or a, big mountain, that's all they used to—even in Bible days, you know, mountains were important to them. Mount Sinai, Mount of Olives where Jesus used to be, you know there's lotta mountains being mentioned in the Bible.
>
> So, in these days, the same way. That we look up to the tallest mountain, they used to look at it as their great grandfather, been looking out

after them. When they leave that town, they used to pray to Mount Turnbull, "Shichoo," that's what they used to call it, "Shichoo. I'm going on a
trip. Shigadín'ii," you know, "look after me. You're the tallest kinda like
the tallest person like, that watch after me. Let me come back safe to you."
So, the song is really true, what I sang that, wherever you go when you
see the tip of Mount Turnbull it makes you proud. When we go to Point
of Pine, we stayed for the whole summer, during cowboys. When we're
leaving back down, when we get to Barlow Pass, they say, "Hey, lookit
there's the tip of Mount Turnbull! Look at that, just look at that, that's
where we're going!" It makes them happy. For some reason. You know
they think, "there's Bylas." That's their home town, that's why they're saying that there's the tip of Mount Turnbull. Then they kind of say that, "Hey.
I'll see you later." They talk to that mountain like that. You know, "I'll see
you later, when we'll get there pretty soon." It makes them kinda like relieved, when they see there's Mount Turnbull, that's where Bylas is. Everywhere you go, even in Willcox, like, when you're driving through the free-
way: "Is that Mount Turnbull?" You know, people start saying, "Which one
is Mount Turnbull?" "Is that Mount Turnbull?" "That's where my home is.
That's where . . . ," you know, it makes them feel good. So in the old days,
when they leave, they used to look for the tip of Mount Turnbull. When
they see it, it makes them proud. It makes them relieved that they can still
see the Turnbull. Shichoo, you know, they're saying that you're still watching me. You still can see me. I still can see you. But I'll be back, don't go
anywhere. You know, I'll be back. That's how they used to pray, to them.
As they travel, there's not only Mount Turnbull. There's Mount Graham,
when they travel, they used to pray to the mountain like. You know, kinda
like a protection like. It's not, they're not praying to that, they're not praying to that for as a God, that's just some kinda like a, what they call, just
like the Bible. You know, there's a God, yes, we all know, but sometimes
people depend on the Bible, they put [it] under their head to have a good
dream, so, the mountain is kinda like a symbol, like.

 So that's how they used to look at it, you know. For that reason, they
say, it gets lonely, lonesome when you're away from you know your home,
you always look for some kind of tallest thing, when you leave from your
home. Like maybe yourself, when you come from Texas, you probably
have something there that can picture you and you could visualize that.
In your mind, probably your home, something that you want to see that
you used to know. That's just kinda like that.

These connections are deeply felt, but at the same time they are tenuous,
for they are steeped in the sense of loss and change that accompanies
the knowledge that the legend of Mount Turnbull has never been told.

Boe uses the sense of heartache in country music so that people can continue to feel these deep but ambiguous attachments to Apache places. "A person came up to me one time," Boe said, "and told me, 'Boe, why do you do kinda like sad songs, why do you sing sad songs, Boe?'" Boe's explanation took him back to his high school days, when he and his friends gathered around the radio at Black Point every afternoon to listen to their thirty minutes of country music: "After school, all we used to hear is George Jones. You know, he was a top star, then. Him, and Merle Haggard, and stuff like that. So, in that, we picked up George Jones. He made a song about Morenci.[13] So they kind of grabbed that, how he made it sound." Other George Jones songs, like "She Thinks I Still Care" and "I'll Share My World with You," also had great influence on Boe:

> So, that kind of grabbed me, and I thought, "Hey. I'll do it that way." And then, it kinda soaked in, real deeper that I began to like those types of music, George Jones style. And as we grow older, that's all we used to buy. George Jones tapes, George Jones records, George Jones, we grew up with it. So, now, after we got older, you know, it's there. Because, I grew up with it, and I love that kind of style. George Jones music style.

In another conversation with me, Boe clarified that when he had said, "I thought, 'Hey. I'll do it that way,'" what he meant was that it just came out that way without thinking. "And today," he said, "it's still kinda still there. I'm just living with it now. Whatever thing I'm gonna do, it's gonna sound like George Jones music." To Boe himself, his songs aren't necessarily sad, although he concedes that people might feel that way because a slow song is often supposed to be sad. But for Boe, it's simply that "that's the style that's still within me, because I grew up with that music, you know."

And Boe feels that George Jones–style music helps him create "the mood that I put into the song." He's not certain what exactly is the magic ingredient, but whatever it is, it enables listeners to envision people and places. A song—like a place-name—can make you see things in your mind:

> Maybe they remember somebody, if I mention Mount Turnbull maybe they remember somebody in their relation down the line. That they could

see. Like music can make somebody, you see somebody. When a song comes on, "that reminds me of somebody." You know, you see a person. So maybe the *sound* that I put in there, the *mood*, the emotion of the song, or the *speed* of the song, or the *words* that touch them, that makes them see somebody, or back those days, or something like that.

Here, it is important to avoid an analysis that casts Boe's songs as a combination of a persistent "Apache" attachment to places and place-names embedded in a contemporary musical style that is established from the "dominant" outside. This type of analysis would lure us into the same either-or trap I discussed earlier. Country music is not simply a default or anonymous bed on which Boe can place "resistant" Apache textual themes. In fact, Boe depends on his musical style to carry a large part of the symbolic weight of his sung communications. There is no doubt that Boe's texts play an important role in the affective response engendered by his songs. But we can't simply reduce the effect of Boe's songs to the effect of his texts. In the previous passage, Boe is clearly conscious of what a song does evocatively and emotionally to combine image and mood. He also is clear that the tempo or the sound or the beat of the song can be as important as its words.

Boe depends on music to get his message across to his audience. In our discussions, he suggested that he distrusts language to accomplish what a song can do for him. "In a song," he said, "it'll go a long ways. By just talking, it won't." People love music, he said. "They'd rather have some kind of action to perform than just sitting there and tell words. They get tired, they get bored just sitting there listening to a story. But in music," he said, "it grabs them."[14] For Boe, musical performance involves the audience in a way that language alone cannot. "I could have just told a story," Boe said, but "it brings out nothing, you know, you just sit there waiting and waiting and waiting, 'why don't we get to the next entertainer,' you know?" When I pressed him about the importance of music, the first thing he mentioned was music's invitation to participation—that the first response of a listener is to want to hum along with the tune. And indeed, some of the most affecting portions of Boe's songs are those wordless parts, where he hums the melody in his gently crying country-western timbre.

We can also get a sense of the additional layer that Boe finds in musical performance by comparing Boe's spoken and sung utterances. In live performances, for instance, Boe doesn't script his between-song talk to the audience. In other ways as well, it seems clear that he considers himself a singer and that speech is only a secondary conveyor of meaning in the context of his performances. A comparison of Boe's spoken and sung communication in live performance will further clarify what this means. By showing the similarities and distinctions between speech and song in Boe's performances, this comparison will also further clarify the importance that sung melody plays for Boe.

At the harvest performance at Besh-Ba-Gowah that I mentioned earlier, Boe sang his new song "Wood on Mama's Back." As he tuned his guitar and his daughter prepared the presets on the Casio keyboard, Boe talked to the audience about the song. On its own, this narrative is, perhaps, unremarkable. However, the spoken text in conjunction with the song that follows it takes on greater significance because of the ways that it and the text of the song parallel each other. These parallels allow us to ask exactly what it is that music, sung melody with guitar and keyboard accompaniment, rather than text, contributes to Boe's feelingful historical project. I have lined out Boe's monologue to show the pause structures in his speech:

1   next song I'm gonna do is about my mom
2   I wrote this song
3   my mom is very special to me and
4   she passed on not too long ago.
5   And she never heard this song
6   but
7   I put it all together how I spent my time with my mom
8   when
9   she used to use an old stove
10   where we used to go out and make some wood.
11   I still remember.
12   I used to carry a jug of water
13   and she used to carry an ax
14   in her hand.
15   and we used to go about a mile[15]
16   and spend all day
17   making wood.
18   and sometime we do about two cords of wood.
19   and she used to carry some old rags
20   and tie them together.
21   and make a rope out of it

22 because we didn't have any rope.
23 and she used to have a
24 when they pile that wood together
25 and tie that rope around the wood
26 and I used to help her
27 put it on her back
28 and carry it on back home.
29 and when we get to the highway
30 a lotta tourists stop us and took many pictures of us.[16]
31 and I still remember today.
32 it seems like
33 just not too long ago
34 but I just
35 it
36 the time goes so fast
37 that
38 I thought to write a song about it
39 and this is how it goes.

And then Boe sang the song:

I can still remember my mom
How she carried wood on her back
A load of wood on her back

Something like a journey
Away from home all day long
I thought was fun for me
For something she didn't plan to do

When we come near highway
The tourists look and took some pictures
I hold me jug of water
While mama hold an ax in her hand

Yes I can still remember my mom
How she carried wood on her back
A load of wood on her back

The weather just didn't matter
I guess the love she had for me
We never owned a truck
But she never did complain

> Yes I can still remember my mom
> How she carried wood on her back
> A load of wood on her back.

Significant parallelisms and overlaps can be seen between Boe's spoken introduction and the song itself. In his introduction, Boe repeated the alliteration "my mom" three times (in lines 1, 3, and 7), twice in line-final position. He repeated the phrase "I still remember," which forms part of the opening line of the chorus to the song, in the spoken introduction (lines 11 and 31). That phrase also appears once in line-final position—Boe set it off in its own line the first time he said it. The key word *wood* occurs five times in Boe's introductory comments, in lines 10, 17, 18, 24, and 25. It appears four times in line-final position. Key words and phrases of his musical text are thus also found in his introduction, sometimes exactly as they are found in the song ("my mom," "still remember"). Of the ten instances, seven are heavily marked off by a strongly coordinated concurrence of clause-phrase, breath-phrase, and pause-phrase boundaries.

In his introduction, Boe also told the story of tourists taking pictures of him and his mother (Is it significant that he told this story at a tourist event?) in words almost identical to those in the song. In his introduction, he said,

> And when we get to the highway
> a lotta tourists stop us and took many pictures of us.

In the song, he sang,

> When we come near highway
> The tourists look and took some pictures
> I hold me jug of water
> While mama hold an ax in her hand

The second two lines of this verse have parallels in Boe's spoken introduction as well. In lines 12–14, he said

> I used to carry a jug of water
> and she used to carry an ax
> in her hand.

It is not simply the narrative content that is parallel. At least part of the pause structure in Boe's spoken introduction is duplicated in the rhythmic and metrical structure of his song:

So the line break after the word *ax* is found in both Boe's spoken and sung performances.

Yet the spoken and sung texts also exhibit significant differences. In the context of a song, Boe's text becomes a great deal more elliptical and vague in its presentation, as the referential aspect of his words gives way to their rhythmic and sonic possibilities. The text of the chorus corresponds significantly with the spoken introduction, but the melodic and rhythmic contours of the song draw greater attention to the alliteration of "remember my mom" and the repetition of the phrase "wood on her back" draws attention to the alternation of back and front vowels.

Referential and grammatical sense also begin to fall away in the lyric text of the sung version, making it more evocative, ambiguous, and indeterminate rather than sensible, propositional, and referential. For example, the line "For something she didn't plan to do" might refer back to the previous line, meaning that Boe's mother didn't plan the trips as a way for him to have fun. But the listener must make this connection through reflection. Because the grammatical function of "for" in *"for* something she didn't plan to do" is more open than in the previous line, "I thought was fun *for* me," the semantic and syntactic moorings become a bit undone. Similarly, in the last verse, the line "I guess the love she had for me," although interpretable, stands as a sentence fragment: "I guess the love she had for me" *what*?

As with the textual presentation in "Mountain Turnbull," with its missing legend and its elliptical verses, the strictly linguistic text of "Wood on Mama's Back" is filled with fragmented images, ellipsis, topics raised and then dropped without being referred to again. This approach is in part in keeping with the parameters of poetry, in which the semantic clarity interpretable from syntax can recede into the background.[17] But it is also in keeping with the fragmented expressive means of representing history in the communities of the San Carlos Reservation. What holds the pieces of Boe's evocative imagery together is the music, and I would argue that Boe depends on sung melody to accomplish a great many of his communicative goals. Boe's music helps listeners fill the semiotic gaps in his texts, evoking but not determining the feeling and the image he presents. Basso (1996) associates this feature with good Western Apache storytelling, the ability to leave openings for your listeners to fill in for themselves out of their own lives and experiences.

As an adult, Boe told me, he is a bit embarrassed by the realization that when he was younger, he thought of these trips as fun and not hard work—that his mother would wake him and say, "Shinałil'a'é, tú nadin'aa" (get some water) and that he treated the outing as an adventure rather than as a necessity for keeping the house warm.[18] He said he never really thought about it when she was alive, but once she was gone, it struck him because "the memories are the only thing that's there. . . . What wasn't important in those days, now it *became* important." As he sings in his song about Point of Pines, "the only thing left is memories." Memories must stand in for the whole of what was once there. Boe saw now that the trip for wood wasn't just an adventure game but had to do with his mother's caring for him. "She must have done it because she loved me. She wanted me to have a warm *house*. She wanted me to have good *clothes*, wanted me to have something nice to *eat*." The song came to him as a way of reinvoking those feelings between mother and son—to say, "Hey. That wasn't really *no*thing, that we did. It was *some*thing."

The only thing left is memories. Boe wants people not to forget, and he wants to help people not forget.[19] The magic spell of his songs lies in the way he is able to blend country sensibility with San Carlos longing for place and history. At his best, Boe is able to invest intimate, personal emotions with historical significance and to weave together landscape, feeling, memory, biography, and community into moments that bind the sweep of history to the intimate details of individual experience. He evokes those feelings and memories not by contrasting past and present, but by superimposing them. At the same time, part of the affective meaning in Boe's songs lies in their double-voiced ambiguity. They evoke a San Carlos Apache sense of the past, but they neither depict nor represent that past in any direct relationship of stylistic similarity. And Boe's musical style does not iconically reference traditional Apache singing by any means. And yet it is his musical style that makes the past so overwhelming for those who are touched deeply by his songs.

On the San Carlos Reservation, the moving and poignant expression intensifies and deepens its meanings by layering and juxtaposing its

various poetic elements. Rather than presenting the relationship between past and present as a "before" and an "after," these expressions
fuse together disjunct domains, asking listeners to find meaning in un-
resolved ambiguity as well as clarity, in disjunctures as well as resonances (for example, in the punning place-names discussed in earlier
chapters).[20] Of course, people in San Carlos care about and understand
the concepts of "before" and "after." I heard numerous stories, mostly
surrounding the value of hard work, in which past and present were
directly contrasted with each other.[21] But the artistically effective utterance accomplishes this without using conjunctions that would be interpreted as "but now." The recoverability of the past in a country song,
in a Mariah Carey or Bob Marley song, doesn't depend on contrast, but
on layering and juxtaposition, on making the listener turn to the past in
her or his affective response to hearing the present performance.

This fusion of varied historical and expressive materials results in
ambiguities that are part of the affective meanings of these expressions.
Boe's songs mix the indexical signs of different cultural communities,
simultaneously pointing inside and outside the constructed boundaries
of "Apache culture." They therefore are simultaneously inside and outside various ideologies concerning what makes for a proper public presentation of identity in expressive performance. But it is precisely from
this ambiguity that they derive their evocative power for those who are
affected by them. It is iconicity of feeling, rather than of sound structure, that engenders the indexical sense of historical connection. I don't
at all dismiss the affective importance of traditional indigenous songs
or songs in a traditional indigenous style. But the emotions evoked
by George Jones, by Bob Marley, by Mariah Carey[22] aren't simply im-
portations from the outside. They are feelingful expressions of what
it means—and, more important, of how it feels—to be from the San
Carlos Reservation. Engendered by nontraditional means, these feelings stand in an imagined relationship of identity with the feelings San
Carlos Apache people had in the past.

The centrality of feeling and place is also apparent if we return, for a
moment, to Boe's conversation about how people respond to the sight
of Mount Turnbull. It's true, as he said, that in the old days "they *used*
to look at it as their great-grandfather" (emphasis added). One way of
conceptualizing this "used to" is as a change: to contend, for example,
that the loss of Western Apache kinship terminology likewise denotes a
loss of a particular kind of feelingful relationship with the landscape.[23]

But rather than speak of this situation in terms of loss, Boe immediately said, "So, in these days, *the same way*" (emphasis added). He went on to discuss what is the same in terms of feelings and emotions connected with the mountain. It gives a person who lives in the area a feeling of relief to see the tip of Mount Turnbull peeking over the horizon, a soothing feeling of being home, a sense of knowing where he or she belongs and comes from. People still talk to the mountain and still feel happy and proud when they see it in the distance when they return from a journey. And I hasten to point out that the specific people I described earlier—the woman who cried on hearing Boe's song about Mount Turnbull, the young man who drove 150 miles to pray at the foot of the mountain when he heard the song—were not responding out of a sense of loss, but out of a sense that something they *thought* was lost was actually found again: that the mountain is still powerful and that it still, as Boe sings, holds many memories for the valley. Their responses to Boe's country-western songs are very much like that of the elder who cried when his son-in-law sang Chester Buck's traditional Apache song. At the same time, I recognize that the game ranger's response to "Chiricahua Mountain" and Boe's own introduction to "Chiricahua Mountain" when he performed it at Globe centered more on a feeling of nostalgia and loss. It doesn't really concern me, though, that Boe's songs may be ambiguous enough to elicit a wide range of equally ambiguous emotional responses in his listeners or that his different songs bring out different feelings.

What I want to emphasize here is that no matter what the particular emotions associated with Boe's songs, the more we look at those songs, the more difficult it becomes to assert that their emotional or historical poignancy is necessarily linked to anything particularly "Apache" in the musical representation. Boe's magic touch is to make listeners feel what it was like to be in their shoes back then, to take the affective response to country music and make it stand for the feeling of being a San Carlos Apache anytime, anywhere. Boe's musical hybridity challenges the ability to trace indexical ties between groups of people and the sounds they make. We need to come to a fuller and more layered sense of indexicality if we are going to come to a nuanced understanding of the symbolic action that creates identities as deeply polyphonic and ambiguous as the expressive elements used in creating them. Beginning to sketch that out is part of my goal in the next chapter.

More than anything, this somehow encapsulated my sense of Minna—his impatience, his pleasure in compression, in ordinary things made more expressive, more hilarious or vivid by their conflation. He loved talk but despised explanations. An endearment was flat unless folded into an insult. An insult was better if it was also self-deprecation, and ideally should also serve as a slice of street philosophy, or as resumption of some dormant debate.—**Jonathan Lethem,** *Motherless Brooklyn*

6

Meaningful Openings and Open Meanings

In the fall of 1994, I attended the Miss St. Charles Pageant in San Carlos. "Pageants" are a gendered practice in numerous communities across Indian America—forums in which young women perform their identities through demonstrations of their skills as culture bearers. The contests in San Carlos are often sponsored by schools; St. Charles was the elementary school run by the Catholic church in the community. Pageant participants usually wear handmade traditional clothing, and the range of abilities displayed in the talent portion of the program often includes performing a traditional dance or singing a song or telling a story in Apache.

These performances are often preservationist in nature, with a heavy focus on displaying linguistic competence as opposed to other kinds of cultural competence. I say "preservationist" because the story told for the competition is generally "traditional." I put this word in quotation marks because although the story may be traditional, the story*telling* often is not. Some contestants lack the fluency to re-create a narrative. It may be the only Apache story the contestant knows in the language of her heritage. Indeed, it may be the only Apache language she knows at all. "English Only" is not just an educational agenda to be debated on the reservation; it's an adjective used to describe both yourself and others. At one Apache Jii Day in Globe, I stood with an elder woman during the performance of a story by a former winner of a pageant. The younger woman began her story in Apache but, perhaps suffering from some understandable stage fright, became flustered in her narration and with an apology completed the story in English. "See?" the older woman said to me. "She doesn't really talk Apache. She's English Only."

Yet the ability to demonstrate skill at performing in Apache is so valued that a contestant who can't drop a word of Apache into a naturally occurring conversation or comprehend others who do will learn how to recite that one story for the purposes of the contest. And so that's why I indicated the performances are centered on the display of language as opposed to other kinds of cultural skills; the proper pronunciation of words is the most important aspect of the performance. For example, the young women who learn traditional Apache songs do not seem to expend much training or effort on learning to sing them with the vocal timbre or the precise intonational contours of their grandparents. Young people often sing Apache songs tuned to a scale that one can easily pick out on the piano, rather than to the unique melodic inflections of older singers. What is most important is getting the words right.

At the same time, however, pageants are quite mixed in the means, modalities, and languages through which they represent cultural practices. Not all contestants speak Apache at the contest. Some contestants present staged vignettes of how their grandparents or ancestors lived: building a *gową*, gathering firewood, cooking on an open fire. These vignettes, which the contestants narrate in English, are often keyed on the theme of how hard people used to work as opposed to how lazy they are now. Mixing traditional and nontraditional elements can move in the other direction as well: one Miss San Carlos Pageant was won by a woman who sang the American national anthem in Apache. The status of the Apache language in various "Miss XYZ Apache" pageants reveals part of the massive problem of language shift, loss, and efforts at revitalization in the communities of San Carlos.[1] The mixed messages of contestants talking about traditional practices in English or singing nontraditional songs in Apache alert us to admit that there is no simple link between language and identity. Furthermore, a contestant with one Apache and one Tewa parent, for example, has not only less opportunity to hear Apache spoken in the home, but also less incentive to consider speaking Apache the exclusive means of honoring her heritage. Moreover, as we have seen in earlier chapters, people on the reservation hold deep and enduring affective relationships with expressive forms that are objectively "non-Apache," and these relationships are part of their identities as well.

Pageants, though, generally are taken as a context calling for some representation of "Apache tradition" for its cultural performances, however mixed or blended that representation and those performances may be. It came as something of a surprise, therefore, when the winner of the 1994 Miss St. Charles contest performed a Plains Sign Talk (PST) interpretation of the Mariah Carey hit "Hero."[2] I found out later that it was one of her favorite songs. But she didn't know what the judges would think of what she considered to be a contemporary and intertribal talent, as opposed to the more usual presentations of Apache tradition that tend to make up the talent portion of the pageants.

So when she won, she was taken completely by surprise. Being only twelve years old and nervous, she perhaps hadn't sensed that during her performance the atmosphere in the hall had been electric. People moved to the edges of their seats, and the hum of background audience murmur became sensibly lower. The response seemed to me to have as much to do with her having chosen a song that resonated with the audience as it had to do with her signed interpretation of it. In my notes from the event, I reminded myself that her performance elicited cheers and whistles at the dramatic points in the *recording*. Whatever the reason for the effectiveness of the show, however, the girl sitting beside me sang the entire song along with the performance, and at its conclusion the auditorium erupted into immense cheers.

A few days later I had the opportunity to speak with the twelve-year-old pageant winner. It turned out she was the granddaughter of one of my oldest acquaintances in San Carlos, so finding her wasn't very hard at all. With her mother's permission, we sat at a picnic table outside her house one afternoon and spoke for a while. She was soft-spoken and intelligent. She told me that she had learned how to do the PST performance of "Hero" from her aunt in Bylas.

She struck me as a thoughtful person, so at one point I asked her what she likes to think about. She told me she likes to think about "the history, my culture, the way it was, the way it *is*." And there are songs— Mariah Carey's "Hero," Guns 'N' Roses' "November Rain," the whole of *Bob Marley: Legend*—that put her in that frame of mind.[3] "Because when Indians were going through hard times," she said, "from *reading* history you get the idea that the Indians would have lost faith." The example she used was the Trail of Tears. "But," she said, "when you put that song on *top* of it, it makes it seem like they *would* have faith, if they had that *song*"—that Mariah Carey's "Hero" would have helped *them*.

Putting PST on top of a Mariah Carey song—or is it the other way around?—gives us a clearly etched example of the multiple-voiced, punning aesthetic principles that drive so much contemporary expressive culture on the San Carlos Reservation. How are we to decide which elements of the performance point toward San Carlos Apache identity and which do not? If we accept that PST reinterprets Mariah Carey, helping "Hero" to become a fitting expression of Native American feeling, we must also accept that "Hero" wasn't chosen at random; that the song was already one that allowed the young performer to imagine the history of her people; that perhaps she imagined herself in the past, giving her people faith and hope by playing "Hero" for them. I'm not sure we are meant to decide, at least not if deciding means parsing the expression into its sources. Rather, it was precisely the ambiguous layering of elements, expanding and deepening the affective meaning of the artistic expression by fusing them, that made the performance so electrifying for the audience at the Miss St. Charles Pageant. Understanding how this layered fusion works and how it contributes to the ambiguous feeling of social history and place on the San Carlos Reservation is the goal of this chapter.

This additive expressive style is a powerful aesthetic principle in San Carlos and Bylas. It cross-cuts a number of linguistic, musical, choreographic, and public ceremonial domains of expression, interaction, and interpretation. When people commented on this style in attempting to teach me, they referred to it as *bee nagodit'ah* or *ínagodit'ah*, meaning "adding on."[4] Both denote a poetic and rhetorical figure—that is, a way of putting things together in an artistically or rhetorically pleasing way. It is also a commentary on a figure. In other words, it is a concept that is applied in order to "comment on [a local] sense of . . . form and performance dynamics" (Feld [1988] 1994b:142).

Basso (1996) has discussed the concept of a cognate term, *'ínágodn'aah*, in Cibecue. He discusses it as an aesthetic of good storytelling by which the narrator leaves blank or sketchy spaces that the listener must fill in:

> According to consultants from Cibecue, the depictions offered by Western Apache speakers are invariably incomplete. Even the most gifted and proficient speakers contrive to leave things out, and small children, who have not yet learned to indulge in such contrivances, leave out many things. Consequently, Apache hearers must always "add on" (*'ínágodn'aah*) to depictions made available to them in conversation, augmenting and supplementing these spoken images with images they fashion for themselves. This process is commonly likened to adding stones to a partially finished wall, or laying bricks upon the foundation of a house, because it is understood to involve a "piling up" (*łik'iyiłih*) of new materials onto like materials already in place. It is also said to resemble the rounding up of livestock: the "bringing together" (*dalaházhį'ch'indíí[*) of cattle or horses from scattered locations to a central place where other animals have been previously gathered. These metaphors all point to the same general idea, which is that depictions provided by Apache speakers are treated by Apache hearers as bases on which to build, as projects to complete, as invitations to exercise the imagination. (1996:84–85)

Basso attaches this narrative aesthetic to locally significant representations of propriety in Cibecue: showing respect by not talking too much, speaking elliptically, not forcing your listeners to see things exactly as you do, but allowing them to let their own imaginations go to work.

In this discussion, I use the term *bee nagodit'ah* rather than *ínagodit'ah* because that was the preference of the person who first taught me about it. My experiences in San Carlos and Bylas share many similarities with Basso's in Cibecue, not the least of which is the presence of the cognate evaluative terms in the two communities. But my experience is also distinct in two broad ways. First, in San Carlos, the adding on or piling up of "like materials" often includes the mixing of disjunct forms. It is not just a process of adding more bricks to a brick wall. Producing expressive forms that feelingfully embody Apache culture in the context of the complex history of the reservation community means that judgments of what is considered to be the same or different are open to the effectiveness of the combinations proposed by individual speakers. In the linguistic domain, a number of translation practices—code-switching puns, (mis)interpretations, and (mis)translations—undermine the naturalized relationship between lexical form and semantic meaning that is at the heart of the contractualism of many theories of the linguistic sign.[5] It is in fact through the deliberate clouding of these distinctions that the additive practices of bee nagodit'ah deepen, enrich, and illuminate meaning by creating openings for meaningfulness.

Second, in San Carlos and Bylas, bee nagodit'ah isn't only a matter of what listeners add for themselves as they hear someone tell a story. Adding-on is not only a process of audition and interpretation, but a process of response, refiguration, and recontextualization. For Basso, 'ínágodn'aah in Cibecue is an active process of listening and verbal exchange, to be sure. But it also appears to be a reflective process that goes on in the interior monologue and imagination of the listener. In San Carlos and Bylas, the process is projected outward into the public space of social interaction. Participants progressively and vocally respond to previous utterances, "adding things on" to what has come before. As in the speech play of yati' nłke' discussed in chapter 2, meaning is not controlled within the imagination of any one particular person. Instead, meanings are placed in a pile between the participants for all to witness, as the imaginative process becomes a group project of adding onto what previous participants have already contributed.

That ínagodit'ah or bee nagodit'ah exists as a mark of evaluation in both San Carlos and in Cibecue leads, perhaps inevitably, to the question of the age of the practice. Is it a "traditional" Western Apache means of judging the effectiveness of expressive utterances? That it exists in multiple communities lends weight to the idea that it stems from an older substratum of cultural practice, the way that Greek pód-, Latin ped-, English pedal, French pied, Tocharian B paiyye, and Lithuanian pãdas demonstrate the plausibility of an underlying proto-Indo-European root *ped- meaning "foot." Basso locates 'ínágodn'aah in the context of historical narratives in Cibecue, whose purpose is to teach respect for traditional Apache ways, a siting that makes it easy to read Basso—or misread him—as claiming an unsullied traditionality for the practice.[6]

Whatever the historical or cultural sources of the notion of bee nagodit'ah on the San Carlos Reservation, the clash of languages and practices in the contemporary community gives it a renewed currency as a frame through which people can identify and comment on the contradictory forces at work in their everyday lives. Tempting as it is to assert the traditionality of the concept—and I am romantic enough to be sorely tempted—the strands connecting the concept of bee nagodit'ah to "traditional" practices in San Carlos and Bylas may be somewhat tenuous. At one point in my fieldwork, I tried to support a claim that ínagodit'ah explained the layered sequence of the na'í'ees, the puberty ceremony for Western Apache girls. I discussed my idea with the ceremonial practitioners I knew. Although they recognized the importance of the sequential layering of sounds and events in the ceremony that I described and suggested a number of alternative terms to describe it, none of them accepted the idea that ínagodit'ah or bee nagodit'ah had any explanatory power in the context of the ceremony. Moreover, I was first told about the powerful aesthetic force of bee nagodit'ah one night when the Pacers were on a break between sets at the bar. It was not through any traditional practice, but rather through a contemporary practice of layering translations in the confrontation of languages in the community, that bee nagodit'ah was explained to me.

Curley's Place, also known as Blake's, was sort of my home away from home. The bar was located about fifteen miles east of Bylas, on the outskirts of Fort Thomas. I knew that whenever the Pacers went to play at Blake's, the bar would be filled with people from Bylas who had known me since I was in high school—people who called me by my nickname, who would let me fool myself into believing that with just a little more practice I might actually become a good pool player. It was like a little homecoming for me. My fieldwork kept me tied up in San Carlos so much that it was hard to pull myself away to visit Bylas, much as I wanted to and knew I should. So I always welcomed the chance to go out and play there and hang out with my oldest friends, the people whom I thought of first as family.

Unlike Gino at Mark's Tavern in Globe, Curley charged a dollar cover charge to get in when the band played. And once you were inside, you couldn't leave and come back in without paying another dollar.

So when we played there, people were always hanging out outside the bar, dancing in the parking lot, calling out their song requests through the window of the bar. This was January, a New Year's party, so it was damn cold outside. The band was on a break, and after a quick round outside to see who had showed up, I was warming up back inside the bar, catching up with friends. The jukebox was blaring. Curley used to have a great old jukebox with lots of novelty songs, like "The I-95 Song" by August and the Spur of the Moment Band and "The Rodeo Song" by Gary and Showdown Lee. (The old jukebox at Mark's had a copy of Murphy Cassa and Patsy Cassadore singing a traditional Apache song called "Mescalero Trail.") But now all the bars were getting new CD jukeboxes. It cost more to play songs on them, and they also didn't have those singular local anomalous treasures. They were filled with new re-leases and old albums reissued on CDs. Most of the older novelty songs existed only on old, worn-out 45 singles. The CD jukebox had enough favorites to keep everyone happy, though—Pink Floyd, Bob Marley, the Eagles, oldies collections, Candlebox, Melissa Etheridge, country hits. So everyone was having a good time.

Jack called me over to where he was holding up the wall. I always looked forward to my conversations with Jack. It was sometimes un-clear whether or not he wanted people to know how smart he was. He had developed his own system for writing Apache and was always teaching me new words and new ways of saying things. Jack was known for being a Rasta man, a reggae disciple who was hardly ever seen with-out his shades on. And, whereas people had adopted a style of wear-ing tinted Uvex safety glasses as sunglasses, he always wore these bad-ass classic wraparounds. I bought a couple of Buds—no freebies for the band—and walked over to where Jack stood.

We caught up on old times for a while, then he said, "You know what I really like?" When I said, "no, what?" he told me he liked it when I turned the fuzz box on in the middle of a guitar solo. He said it added something to it. He called it "bee nagodit'ah," "nagodit'ah," "ínagodit'ah." I asked him what that meant, and he said it means "some-thing being put on top of something else." It's like, you're playing away at the guitar, and then you press the switch for the fuzz box, and that adds another layer to what you're doing, you put the distortion on top of it. That's bee nagodit'ah, putting something on top, adding on to it. Jack liked the way that sounded.

This was the first time I had heard this word, and because it was a word that Jack associated with musical expression, I tried to pump him for its whole meaning. He said that was its only meaning, "adding something on." In trying to teach me about the concept, though, he began by talking about translation. Melissa Etheridge's "I'm the Only One" boomed out from the jukebox. Jack told me that what the title line means is that she's saying "dasaan nashaa"—"I'm the only one going around." It's like she's alone, all by herself, walking around, singing this song, singing "I'm the only one walking around." Jack then told me why it was necessary to interpret rock song lyrics into Western Apache: "dayą́hago siłsįį"—it misses by just a little bit. As if meaning were a target at which words are directed.

Jack's sense of translational indeterminacy (Friedrich 1986) and his sense of translation as an additive process make up part of a widespread linguistic ideology in San Carlos and Bylas that holds that English and Apache are ultimately not translatable into each other. This view stands in contrast to an approach that one might term "formal linguistic," which holds that all languages are equally capable of expressing anything (though not by the same ways and means). It also stands in stark contrast to missionaries and Bible translators' sense that the Lord's Word can be transparently interpreted into any of the world's languages (see, e.g., Larson 1998). People on the reservation who make this argument about the radical difference of Western Apache sometimes appeal to certain observable grammatical distinctions between Apache and English. They say that English is "backwards" from Apache, an observation of the subject-verb-object organization of active sentences in English as opposed to the subject-object-verb order of Apache sentences. In addition, people observe that Apache lexicalizes certain aspects of communication that in English are managed through prosodic qualities such as vocal inflection and intonation contours. These qualities include, for example, the speaker's attitude toward the information being communicated, the speaker's commitment to the truth value of what she or he is saying, and so forth. People making this distinction also insist that Apache descriptions are more precise than their English counterparts. For example, Apache has—as do all Athabaskan languages—an extremely rich system of verbs for handling objects that classifies them according to size, shape, number, and animacy. This system of classificatory verbs makes it possible for listeners, simply by hearing the verb stems associated with the object at any given moment in a narrative, to follow an object as it moves, say, from a pouch to an open container to the ground. Jack's notion of English just missing, being a little off, then, is a common observation in the linguistic ideologies of the community.

The purported ill fit between the two languages makes the translation practices that people evaluate as bee nagodit'ah or ínagodit'ah important signifying expressions. Because any attempt at transparent translation is inevitably doomed to failure, the Western Apache version supplements rather than replaces the English version. This interpretive process creates a complex, multileveled linguistic object for contemplation. The two versions of "I'm the Only One" in Jack's translation stand in a tense, dialogic relationship with each other, the one no longer able to exist without the other responding at its side. This is so for a number of reasons, not the least of which is that Jack is bilingual and that Melissa Etheridge is always there—on the jukebox, on the radio, in the car, at the party on the stereo—singing in English. The version released by Island Records has a permanence and a political and economic power to it such that Melissa Etheridge will most likely never sing Jack's translation of her song. Jack's version will most likely remain a personal interpretation, perhaps one that will spread more widely in the Apache-speaking community. It can be argued that Jack's interpretation is more deeply meaningful to *him* than is the original, but that interpretation is always in opposition to a version with more presence, more market clout, and a wider distribution network. Jack can't make Melissa Etheridge disappear. Nor is it clear that he is attempting to. It doesn't necessarily follow that the meaningfulness of Jack's interpretation depends upon drowning out the English version. Indeed, his reinterpretation is powerful in part precisely because with it he enmeshes Melissa Etheridge's song in the social, political, poetic, and linguistic history of the reservation. Through his rhetorical maneuver, however, he creates a tense stand-off with an English version that cannot be expunged.

Popular music is undeniably a forceful presence in the communities of the reservation. But its force is not owing to a simple, passive absorption of songs selected and massively promoted by the international music industry. That is not to deny that selection and promotion by the music industry goes on. But as Voloshinov puts it, "Any genuine kind of understanding will be active and will constitute the germ of a response" (1973:102). If there were fifty speakers of Western Apache at Blake's that night, it may be that there were fifty personal interpretations of what "I'm the Only One" *really* means. This is how listening is done on the reservation—actively, responsively, always interpreting. If we say that Jack's reinterpretation of Melissa Etheridge's lyrics makes the song personally meaningful, the same would also be true of the others' re-interpretations. The revoicing of song texts through layered translation is one of the ways in which popular songs become personally affecting to people in San Carlos and Bylas.

Although the institutions of the culture industry certainly anticipate that listeners will make popular songs personally meaningful, I doubt that the marketing and promotion department at Polygram, Melissa Etheridge's record label, envisioned this practice. Nor are these processes part of a universal imperative to "localize" expressive culture. These translations and substitutions do not merely bring these songs home and make them about locally familiar things. Rather, they set up productive tensions and meaningful openings between the here and the out there, the local and the global. Jack's translations and others like it respond to the domination of English-language popular musical forms not by rejecting them, but by immediately and deliberately making them ambiguous. Jack does this by forcing the song to have two forms, two meanings, two worldviews—two languages. In Bakhtin's words, he places "a new semantic intention into a discourse which already has, *and which retains*, an intention of its own" (1984:189, emphasis added). These substitutions and translations can work only in the continued presence of the original, which can then be responded to, contested, commented upon, resisted, and played with through the infiltration of local practices of making meaning ambiguous and full.

A joke that went around the reservation while I was living there:

QUESTION: How do you say *ricochet* in Apache?
ANSWER: Dezht'įąǫ!

OK, I'll explain it. The punch line isn't the word for "ricochet." It's a sonic representation using Apache phonemes—an onomatopoeic icon —of how a ricochet sounds. The joke pokes fun at both translation and the widespread use of sound symbolism in Apache discourse on the reservation. The tension of translational transparency, on the one hand, and of something in experience that exceeds the bounds of reference, on the other, is played out in the attraction of sound over sense. When I went to Phillip with the riddle, he took my question seriously and provided a lexical gloss, *bee distǫǫ*, for the word *ricochet*. But that's not what the joke is asking for.

So while Jack taught me about the layerings of bee nagodit'ah by telling me about translation in the sense of a semantic clarification, this isn't the only kind of layering that goes on in Bylas and San Carlos. Practices called bee nagodit'ah aren't limited to translations of the semantic reference of words. They are also found in expressive contexts where the musical features of language are highlighted, where reference enters into a tense competition with sound, such as those of word play and punning.

During the first months of my stay in San Carlos, the Pacers played at a birthday party for Marshall's wife, which he held out at his mother's house in Soda Canyon. For this evening, Marshall asked me to make a good recording of the Pacers instead of playing with the band, so I had brought my good mike setup instead of my guitar and sat about fifteen yards away, monitoring tape levels. The band that night was Marshall, Pat, Donnie Ray, Kane on the drums, and Nawodé sitting in "unplugged" on acoustic guitar. The sun had not yet gone down when the Pacers picked up their instruments and started to jam out. After warming up on a couple of country songs, Marsh called for "Hey Joe," the Billy Roberts song that became a free-form FM radio standard in its Jimi Hendrix version. "Hey Joe" always gave Pat the chance to stretch out, and he cranked the volume on the Telecaster he had borrowed from Darryl, punched in the Boss distortion box he had borrowed from Darryl, and burned through a solo that rang the hills of Soda Canyon, giving everyone at the picnic tables around the lake something to dance to and shout "dzáłeh!"[7]

Pat tore it up for about thirty cycles of the changes on "Hey Joe." When Pat got going on a solo, it was a little like listening to a conversation, as he liked to make the guitar sing in more than one voice. He often accomplished this conversation by cutting the fuzz box in and out in a sort of call-and-response sequence. After about eight or ten choruses of "Hey Joe" with distortion, he would play clean for a chorus or two. Then when he popped the fuzz box back in, it would add something more than it had before, bringing the participants at the dance to another level of excitement and understanding.

Pat returned to the song's emblematic chromatic walking-guitar fill to signal that he had completed the exploration of his solo. He nodded to the rest of the band that he was finished, lifted the head of his guitar and brought it down to signal the final E chord of the song. The band sustained the sound as Kane whipped around the drums, rolling from tom-tom to tom-tom, Pat tearing through his last chain of riffs before the final crash of drums and cymbals signaling the end of the song. As the last note died down, the small audience yelled, and the band members laughed at their own pomposity. Then someone in the crowd of listeners called out in a cowboy's high, falsetto yodel, rising through the first syllable, then lower, hard and emphasized on the second: "Raaa-*haaa!*"

Nawodé, the Indian Cowboy, picked up on the cowboyness of the expression as well as its somewhat surprising phonological shape—the expected exclamation would have been "yaaa-haaa" or "yeeee-haaa," with the *y* rather than the *r* in the initial position. "Rawhide!" he shouted back, referring to the song (and old TV show) of the same name, in which "yahaaa!" is a recurring element of the song's chorus. A moment later Nawodé changed his response, calling out "haháái'!"—the Western Apache exclamation of delight at another's comeuppance that Donnie Ray had used when we played "Apache" at the Pacers' rehearsal. Pat approved of the joke, repeating Nawodé's "haháái'!" and laughing. A few seconds later, as Nawodé was arranging a beer delivery for the band with one of the partiers, Donnie Ray said it again—"haháái'!"—and chuckled to himself.

The entire interchange, from the first exclamation of approval from the audience to Donnie's repetition of Nawodé's second joking response, took about twelve seconds. But those few seconds of sonic juxtaposition densely packed together a wide range of potential meanings and experiences. Stephen Booth argues that a universal source of poetic pleasure is that "We seem particularly fond of things that are at once right and wrong" (1998:15). He uses the familiar rhyme, "Roses are red / Violets are blue" to introduce his point: violets are *not* blue. He argues that this fact, that violets are not blue, is part of our pleasure in the line. Although not necessarily universally applicable, Booth's insight into the pleasures of holding cognitive finality at bay does offer one possible means of understanding the tense dialogic layerings, cognitive tangents, and sonic transparencies that hold these bee nagodit'ah expressions in a relationship to each other and creates a larger whole out of the sum of the parts.

Three sonic links form this chain, and their similarities and differences can be seen in a phonological rendering of them:

1. ra: ha:
2. rɔ   haɪd
3. ha   ha:ɪ'

The three utterances are phonologically quite similar to each other. Each contains two syllables. Each emphasizes the mid-low vowel /a/. Each contains the unvoiced velar aspirant /h/ at the opening of the second syllable. And yet, despite these similarities, each conjures up a different world of experience and meaning. There are two exclamations and an English word. The first and second utterances somewhat commonly evoke a cowboy world, although the second is also more clearly attached to a mass-mediated representation of that world. The first and third utterances have in common the fact that they are both expressions of pleasure, if for different reasons. But connections between the points —the performance of a Jimi Hendrix version of "Hey Joe," a rodeo shout, a popular television show theme song, and a Western Apache interjection—must be made and added together in the participants' imaginations. The sonic similarities that seem to unify them are in fact a series of tangents. Even if the connection between each successive utterance can be "explained," to do so for the collection of utterances taken together becomes exponentially more difficult. This is the essence of "throwing words around," yati' nłke': each speaker sequentially grabs hold of something in a previous speaker's utterance and builds a new layer on it by spinning it in a new direction.

This sense of expressive adding on doesn't have to involve either the translation of an utterance or the maintenance of its sound patterns. The response from a second speaker may simply follow the tangents of cultural or personal history or social experience in a sort of stream of consciousness. On the afternoon at Beaver Spring when I learned how to say "testing" in Apache, Marshall was playing the guitar again. He finished one song and then played the opening guitar riff to Johnny Cash's "Folsom Prison Blues" as a throwaway filler. Chuck Taylor then chimed in with the first line of the song, "Hear that train a'comin'." Marshall responded with "clippity cloppity clippity clop," part of the refrain from the song "Mule Train." So the word *train* in the first line of "Folsom Prison Blues" prompted Marshall to respond with a line from a song with the word *train* in the title. On top of that, however, he performed the line by replacing the *l*s with *t*s and by palatalizing his *t*s: a joking imitative performance of a thick, rich, Apache-English accent—*ctippity ctoppity ctippity ctop.*

These reinterpretations of song texts usually occurred in the personal, private sphere, and I was exposed to them in more intimate settings— one-on-one situations, small parties, and band rehearsals. Phillip, as I have said, delighted in translating key phrases from Bob Marley songs and Neville Brothers songs. Once, on a slow cruise back from the lake, he translated the entirety of War's "Spill the Wine" as it played on the cassette player in my truck. Usually, though, and for most people, these reinterpretations were limited to one-liners—a key phrase in a song text, such as singing the Apache greeting "hant'é nnii?" instead of the English greeting "what's going on?" used by Linda Perry as the tag line to the Four Non-Blondes song "What's Up?" Or perhaps a fragment of a song lyric would create an image that was more distinct or unusually humorous if it were said in Apache.

Then again, there was the night in Navajo Point, at Bob's house, be- hind the old Boni pop stand. I had come just for a visit, but on my ar- rival Bob had walked to the back of my truck and pulled out the guitar and amplifier without a word, so I just went with the flow, and we got to playing. This was before Bob found the Lord. We switched off, each playing a few songs at a time, as people gathered for a good time. When Bob launched into AC/DC's "Hell's Bells," shouts and whoops from the people gathered there signaled that the party had officially started. We played different songs that night—"Wish You Were Here," "Hey Hey, My My," "Hotel California," "Stand Up for Your Rights." I taped some of it, but at one point I decided just to let the party go and not put people under the pressure that inevitably arose from having a live microphone there, so I turned the tape recorder off.

A few songs later, Bob began the seven-four guitar riff that announces the opening of "Money," the Pink Floyd song, and I have been kick- ing myself ever since for having turned the tape recorder off. After the requisite four cycles through the introductory riff, everyone—I mean *everyone*, and by now there were about a dozen people sitting around Bob's front porch—sang out, loudly and clearly: "zhaali!" This in itself is not so surprising. Both the English word *money* and the Western Apache word for money, *zhaali*, consist of two syllables, and both end with the high-front vowel /i/.[8] But everyone also translated the next line and the line after that and the line after that. Almost every line in the entire song had an Apache version, and everyone knew how to sing it. As the song wound around me, and as my mind raced through my options—turn the tape recorder back on? risk losing the moment? make everyone sing it again later?—my head was spinning.

Later that evening I did get Spiderman to tell me what some of the lyrics were. Not surprisingly, it turned out that this was a practice that could really be carried out only in a group. It's like when you can sing a whole Bach cantata without music when you're in the choir or sing along when a song that you like comes on the radio, but if you actually need to sing those songs on your own, without the contextual cues of group performance, it turns out you haven't actually got it committed to memory at all. As I drove Spiderman home to Southside, though, with Bob Marley playing over the truck stereo, he did his best.

SPIDERMAN: [sings] zhaali
[sings] chǫ'i nadaiłdii
DAVID: what does that mean
SPIDERMAN: "it's a crime"
DAVID: chǫ'i nadaiłdii(?)
SPIDERMAN: chǫ'i nadaiłdii
DAVID: chǫ'i nadaiłdii.
SPIDERMAN: zhaali
[laughs]
get down
money is a crime, [zhaali chǫ'i nadaiłdii
DAVID: [well
SPIDERMAN: get in trouble for money
[laughs]
it's like havin' a lot of money, you [always get in trouble
DAVID: [yeah

I hadn't known on first hearing the Apache version of the song that it had been an attempt at direct translation of the original Pink Floyd lyrics, and Spiderman and I talked about that. He told me that, as I already knew, when something is in Apache, it's backwards from when it's in English. The translation into Apache, though, also causes a reinterpretation of what a line might mean. Notice, as Spiderman taught me to say "chǫ'i nadaiłdii," he also told me that it means if people possess a lot of money, they get into trouble because of it—an interpretation tangential to that which one might expect from the original English verse, "money, it's a crime." The tangents of translation lead to further interpretive tangents that build on each other to create richer and broader meaningfulness.

These tangents form links in a chain. Successive utterances don't so much replace each other as build on each other. They successively clear away the underbrush to reveal potential new roads to be taken. At the party in Soda Canyon, it wasn't that Nawodé's "haháái" finalized some kind of meaning, but that the tension between "raaa-haaa," "rawhide," and "haháái" pried open a gap between signifier and signified, sound form and concept, and made that meaningful opening productive of an open meaningfulness. Nawodé's additions to the initial utterance of "raaa-haaa" did not clarify, correct, or explain it so much as contribute additional and equally ambiguous utterances to it. The meaningfulness of Nawodé's utterance, then, works at the level of sound. At the level of semantic content, however, his word play superimposes logically incompatible domains—but in such a way as to make it possible for listeners to consider their potential compatibilities. Recognizing the interpretive spaces that exist between speakers and hearers, words and meanings, brains and tongues, Nawodé didn't attempt to close those gaps, but instead deliberately pointed to them, in fact attempted to pry them open even further and filled them with piles of other potential signifiers and meanings. As Jack told me, and others confirmed, because everyone's attempt at creating meaning misses its target by a little bit, successive attempts must be made in order to fill those gaps.

The layering of English and Apache forms in these examples demonstrates that the realm of aesthetics and performance in San Carlos is inseparable from the realm of politics and history. The additive expressive practices of bee nagodit'ah perform the tense clash of languages and practices that marks the history of the reservation community. More than supplementing meaning, these practices create chained sets of evaluative comments that collectively critique the notion that one language or one interpretation can offer anything like a rich or complete meaning. The linguistic alternations aren't simply opposing a structured and knowable "us" to a similarly knowable "them." The consistent piling on of additional interpretation forestalls that kind of knowability precisely because it forestalls the finalization of any particular meaning of any particular sign. The additive frame of bee nagodit'ah makes the official and dominant signs of American popular culture locally and personally meaningful precisely because local and personal meaningfulness in San Carlos is intimately bound up with the desire to forestall the finalization of meaning—to keep meaning open and to create openings for further meaning.

Spiderman said, "Shit, I know this guy, man, that can sing Apache, all, every kind of music, just change it into Apache words." I asked him who that was, and he said he would introduce us.[9] As we turned across the tracks to Southside, he said, "Let's go for a ride to Home Alone 2, see who's alive."

The tension between sound and sense in speech play and translation is the most accessible way into the concept of bee nagodit'ah. Linguistic practices are exemplary for showing the ways in which people in San Carlos cooperatively disrupt and undermine clear meanings by piling up alternative interpretations in the public spaces of discourse and interaction.[10] But focusing too closely on linguistic practice in the sense of verbalizations risks overlooking the expressivity of bee nagodit'ah as an embodied and sonorous way of interacting, a cultural way of coordinating individual nonlexical practices. Bee nagodit'ah is a representation of the socially appropriate way to perform cooperatively (Feld 1988).

When I say "meaningfulness," I want to convey that meaning is richer and more complex than what can be contained in a lexical gloss of a sign. In other words, meaning is not only cognitive and verbal, but experiential and sensual as well. Although Jack quickly turned to language and translation, he introduced me to the concept bee nagodit'ah by telling me about his response to the way I added an additional musical *texture* to the ensemble sound of the Pacers in performing at Curley's. So let me now turn to the dynamics of a band performance in San Carlos to show how the expressive workings of bee nagodit'ah permeate everyday cooperative activities, adding productive richness and indeterminacies, allowing people to explore to the fullest the myriad tangents of meaningfulness.

More often than not, when the Pacers played for a party, we would set up on our hosts' front porch or in their driveway. Sometimes the hosts would have set up a small bandstand built out of plywood and two-by-sixes for us. Sometimes, if it was cold or wet outside, we would just set up inside the hosts' living room. Sometimes we would actually be on a stage. We played for a few political rallies and found ourselves on a platform about five feet off the ground. Sometimes, for a big event such as an anniversary, the people throwing the party went to the expense of renting a gym—Burdette Hall in San Carlos or Stanley Hall in Bylas—and there we played from the stage. For one political rally, the candidate rented the Knights of Columbus hall in Globe.

But usually the band set up in an intimate physical space that was very close to the audience. At Mark's Tavern, the stage—which still had a fireman's pole from when the place used to have exotic dancing on Tuesday nights—was just big enough for the drum set and some of the amplifiers. Marshall usually found a way to get a bar stool up there for himself, but Pat, Donnie Ray, and I stood down on the floor.

The physical arrangements of bodies in the performance space went hand in hand with an extremely porous "fourth wall" between performers and audience. It's not that the location of bodies determined performer-audience interaction, however; it was the other way around. People preferred band setups that encouraged a sort of interactive mingling between the band and other participants. Band members sometimes complained about the overlap between musicians, listeners, and dancers. It risked the safety of the equipment. And, in fact, things may have been changing: Darryl told me that in the old days when people had a dance at the gym, the band wouldn't set up on the stage, but on the floor at the other end of the basketball court. But the arrangement of band members and audience more generally is part of a style of expressivity in which people value a rather permeable framing of roles in the performance context. This arrangement also allowed participants other than band members to thicken and densify the soundscape of the performance (Feld [1988] 1994b; Schafer 1977) through the adding-on practices of bee nagodit'ah.

So the performance space occupied by the Pacers usually included (1) the band; (2) a number of people, usually men, standing up front between the band and the other people dancing; (3) a number of men standing around Pat, watching his every move on the guitar; and (4) a number of people standing close to the microphones to pitch in with background vocals when the opportunity arose.

This practice of "people wanting to get involved," as one of the Pacers put it to me, strikes me as a more widespread musical practice on the reservation—that is, not limited to bands playing at bars or parties. Here I might risk a comparison to traditional Western Apache participant structures. McAllester had an impression that the Apache ceremonies he attended were only somewhat loosely organized, stating that it seemed as if "anyone who knows the words can join in" (1960:469). As I mentioned earlier, the opening of the Bashas' store in 1991 was marked, at least for me, by security escorting away a second man who had joined in with the singer who had been hired to perform at the ceremony. Thus are aesthetics—in the sense of a feeling for how things ought to be done—changed by new political institutions. I was never able to find out how the first singer felt about the incident, but many people who were there or to whom I described the incident said, "They should have just let that guy sing; he wasn't doing anything."

When the Pacers played at Mark's or at a party, a couple of friends or family members would act as guards, keeping the crowd from getting too close to the band, but this was really to protect the amplifiers and speakers. It didn't stop people from standing behind us or next to us and pitching in with background vocals or from picking up a drumstick and adding cymbal crashes. The additional people around the band were almost invariably men, underscoring the gendered space in which band performances took place.

The most important elements of this additive density were rhythm and rhythm instruments. The band used to travel with a blue storage box filled with extension cords, junction boxes, guitar cables, microphones, microphone cables, drumsticks, duct tape, electrical tape, and other odds and ends that we needed in order to set up. One of the most important pieces of equipment in that box was an old, cracked, taped-over, broken-down cowbell. A number of the band members commented covetously about the beautiful, shiny new cowbell that the chicken scratch band played at the Veterans Day party. When I visited my friends and played with the band over the Fourth of July weekend in 1996, the guys had finally purchased a new cowbell.

And well they should have. The cowbell, in a sense, was the instrument and the sound that linked the band most closely to the audience.

For one thing, of course, the sound of the cowbell has associations with rodeo as well as with music. One time, after a song was over, Donnie took the drumstick and shook it inside the cowbell, which prompted a number of jokes about bullriding ("next rider! next bullrider! your bull is ready!"). More important, though, the cowbell was also the first way that the sound of the band was expanded and the first way that the personnel of the performing group was increased. Donnie Ray would often relinquish his duties as rhythm guitarist in order to pick up the cowbell and a drumstick and keep the rhythm.[11] In fact, sometimes Darryl or Marshall would call out to Donnie, "cowbell ánle'!" to let him know that he should take care of that. Or, if Darryl was tagging along with the band, taking care of the sound mix even though he wasn't playing drums, he would pick up the cowbell and play it. Still other times, someone close to the band, perhaps one of Donnie's sons or friends such as Al or J. B., would be standing off to the side of where the band was playing, pounding away at the cowbell. One night we were playing at a high school graduation party in Rainbow City in Bylas. As the band played "Born on the Bayou," I looked off to my right, where I saw someone sitting on the tailgate of Marshall's truck, cowbell tucked into his left hand, beating away at it with the drumstick in his right. Then I looked off to my left, where I saw two young boys sitting on the tailgate of my truck, pointing across the stage at the guy on the tailgate of Marshall's truck, and pantomiming to each other the gestures of playing the cowbell.

Band members consider these rhythm instruments to be a valued addition to the sound of a band. When we played "Run Through the Jungle," Marshall would sometimes say, "Now where's that gourd at?" asking after an instrument heard on the original recording. Rhythm instruments are also a way for others—including the "nonmusical"—to involve themselves in the production of a band's sound. Dominic's experience as a teenager playing the tambourine, triangle, and cowbell for Sluggo comes to mind. Joining the rhythm section is a way for "nonmusicians" to get involved in a band's performance and a way for a band to expand the range of its sound.

Closely related to the cowbell players were the air drummers and what I came to think of as "secondary drummers." Every time the Pacers played, two or three men would make their way down to the edge of the stage and just groove to the band. Clearly deep into the sound of the Pacers, they would rarely play air guitar. More likely they would play air cowbell or air drums, miming fills and cymbal crashes where they thought Kane or Darryl should put them in. At some performances, a close friend of the band, standing behind the stage, would pick up a third drumstick and add extra cymbal crashes or play the ride cymbal while Kane or Darryl played something else. The drummers rarely seemed to mind, as it gave them three hands.

Other participants not *in* the band would always be close *to* the band. Although they wouldn't actually play any instruments or sing any songs, it felt to me as if something was missing if a collection of people didn't gather to watch Kane play the drums or to watch Pat play the guitar. These participants would usually just absorb the atmosphere, sometimes more actively tuning into what Pat was up to during a solo. Sometimes, during a particularly anthemlike song—"Gloria" or "Hang On Sloopy" or "Wooly Bully," for example—they would lean into the microphones with us to sing the choruses.

This desire to add onto the textural grain of a song, to expand and thicken the participatory experience, is already anticipated in the way that rock and country songs are arranged on records. Hit records are orchestrated for an increasingly dense and expanding ensemble of musicians. Arrangers typically add musicians—strings, horns, background vocals, incidental percussion—to the basic bass-drums-guitar group. This "sweetening" usually takes place in an additive manner across the temporal performance of the song. A producer may add strings to the chorus, castanets in the second verse, horn pops on the bridge, maracas in the final verse, for example. These additions are a basic way of keeping listeners involved in the song, so that when it comes on the radio they won't change the station. The desire to pick up the cowbell and hit it is perhaps not just about how people do things together in San Carlos and Bylas, but also a call to the global from the local—what Meintjes calls a "reach and return" (2003:217–49).

When Marshall called for the cowbell in a Creedence Clearwater Revival song, or when someone picked up a drumstick and added extra cymbal crashes to what Kane was playing in the backbeat, were those layered additions "being Apache"? Or were they rather an attempt to produce a sound as full as that of mass-mediated, recorded music—an attempt to supplement the group with sidemen, background singers, additional percussionists, string and horn sections, and on and on and on? They were both, and often quite breathtakingly so. As with the translation of lyrics discussed earlier, "Apache identity" is as much about a response to the means and symbols of domination—a response to history in its broadest sense—as it is about a strict adherence to Apache traditions. After all, those traditions are also a part of the present reservation community, reproduced in the contemporary context of the community's history. Through the adding on of bee nagodit'ah, people in San Carlos reveal that shared sense of historical trajectory to each other, representing it to each other in ways that make it graspable (communicable and interpretable) and meaningful. When Marshall or Pat changes the title of a song to localize it, or when Jack translates the lyrics of a song into Apache, or when people join in to sing the background vocals for "Hang On Sloopy" or pick up the cowbell and drumstick for "Black Magic Woman," they are densifying musical and interpretive textures in order to indicate a grasping of the connections to history that make the present Apache communities of the San Carlos Reservation possible—or perhaps impossible. By adding things—by putting things on top of each other, as the girl who won the Miss St. Charles pageant put it—hidden relationships are uncovered, which allow people to understand the deeper and wider meaningfulness contained in the ambiguous spaces of those relationships.

But I have underemphasized the made and intended
production of sound—the ways in which sound is
formed for pleasurable, beautiful, and ultimately
social ends.—**Susan Stewart,** *Poetry and the Fate*
of the Senses

7

The First Intertribal Battle of the Bands in a Very Long Time

It felt as though Donnie and I had been driving back and forth through the mountains all day. The trip to Whiteriver had been long and exhausting, but worth the trouble. The message we were hoping for was waiting for us when we got back, and now we could relax. The Pacers were in.

A few weeks earlier, in June 1995, I had accompanied Donnie Ray and his family to a memorial dinner in Whiteriver. When the dinner was over, we went to spend some time with some of Donnie's relatives before returning through the Salt River Canyon to San Carlos. During a lull in the joking and conversation, they asked me to take the kids down to the store for pop and chips and whatnot. There, at the store, taped to the door, was where I saw the sign announcing a Battle of the Bands to be held at Whiteriver on the Fourth of July. Inside the store, I asked a woman at the checkout counter for more information, and she gave me a phone number to call. Back at the house, I told Donnie and Marshall what I had found out, and everyone got excited.

Back in San Carlos a few days later, I called up to Whiteriver and was put in touch with Jerry Gloshay, who said it had been a long time since they'd had a Battle of the Bands, so he was looking forward to it. He said it almost as if he were trying to revive an Apache tradition, like the kids needed to know what life was like back in the old days. Jerry Gloshay said he would fax the rules to me when he had them written up and told me there was a fifty-dollar entry fee that needed to be paid up front.

It's true, I guess, that it had been quite a long time since a Battle of the Bands had been held. Everyone relished the stories they told me about going to Burdette Hall in San Carlos or traveling up to old Alchesay Hall in Whiteriver and coming away with trophies, money, and bragging rights. Velazquez Sneezy, now a prominent political figure in the community, preferred to talk about "talent shows" rather than "battles." But he also talked about how the Statics were always coming in first. His brother Anson said, "Battle of the Bands," and told me that somewhere, in the back of someone's closet or in a shed, was the trophy that the Statics had won for coming in first. Vel remembered one talent show held soon after the Ferreira family had come back to San Carlos after living in Hawaii for some years. "They came back, and they entered the talent show, and they were playing ukulele," he said. "And they were singing in Hawaiian. And they were dressed in, like, Hawaiian style. That I remember because they just barely came back, and they entered it. See, at that time, there was no animosity toward one another. Everybody wanted to help each other." Vel also remembered when the Dominoes, with Big Bell's Aaron Neville voice, started entering shows and giving the Statics some competition. "But we still took first," he said, "because we were experienced and we knew what we were doing." I never asked Big Bell, but it wouldn't surprise me to find that he remembered things differently.

Darryl remembered going up to Whiteriver to be in Battles of the Bands with Sluggo. In fact, the first time he played with Sluggo was for a Battle of the Bands. Sluggo already knew Darryl because Darryl's brother Kenny had the Country Pacers at that time. Sluggo used to come by the house sometimes to borrow Kenny's equipment. Then, around 1971, when Darryl was a sophomore at Globe High School, Sluggo stopped by the house "because he noticed I had instruments, and he said, they said they need an extra guitar player. You know, like, 'If you don't mind, go with us to Whiteriver, Battle of the Bands.' So I said, 'Yeah, sure.'"

Even though Darryl had equipment, his uncle had even better equipment. Darryl's uncle was a manager and had what Double D called "big old stuff." So Darryl asked his uncle if they could borrow it, and he agreed. So they practiced on Darryl's uncle's "big old instruments," and then they went to Whiteriver and took second, losing out to a country band from New Mexico that Darryl recalled as the Enchanters. Darryl ended up playing lead guitar. He remembered the rest of the band as Sluggo on vocals, Kane on the drums, and the late Milton Dewey on bass. They called themselves the Trends. "I was surprised we took second that time," he said. "You know, a trophy and everything. I think what they paid was, seventy-five . . . seventy-five dollars. During that time it was pretty good, a lot of money. First place was, I think it was two hundred bucks."

The first thing Darryl thought about when he was presented with the opportunity to play for a broader audience with Sluggo was how he could get his hands on some better equipment. The sound a band makes —the particular vibrations of air that cause an audience to get up and dance—is at once a material and an imaginary thing. The live sound of a band is a highly mediated presence. Control over the constraints of that mediation allows a band to project its sound in ways that are compelling, involving, and participatory for audiences. A sound system can give a band a bass drum that audience members feel in the pit of the stomach, a hi-hat as crisp and sizzling as if people weren't out on the dance floor, but dancing between the two cymbal plates. Electronic signal processing can make a guitar whoosh between the speakers of a PA system with subtle or obvious layers of distortion, tonal or phase shift, reverberation, attack and decay characteristics. The possibilities allow band members to imagine their individual and group sounds in increasingly minute detail. In fact, they demand that musicians do this (Théberge 1997). Because these sounds are the kinds of sounds heard on recordings, being able to produce them in live performance is part of the process of transforming the "local" band into a "real" band. But of course, all of this technology costs not only thought and imagination and effort, but money as well. Access—or, more specifically, lack of access—to sophisticated equipment played out again and again in my conversations with the Pacers. Imagination and materiality played important twin roles in the ways the band members thought about themselves and the music they made.

In this chapter, I explore the material constraints that enter into the imagination and production of cultural aesthetics. If cultural aesthetics appears at times to be an endless reorganization of abstract form, an intellectually or affectively satisfying presence, it is also a material presence shaped by social as well as imaginative forces. I want to discuss that doubled question of how an artist gets from point A to point B. By exploring the Battle of the Bands in Whiteriver, I present the ways the event seeped into the band members' everyday lives, how it played in their memories and imaginations, but I also discuss what it meant that the Pacers were probably the most technologically impoverished participants in the battle. I ultimately argue that one of the social ends of sound is to produce a felt sense of locality—a locality that the Pacers were attempting to transcend.[1] What is true of sociolinguistics is also true of other expressive domains: local accents mark speakers. In musical performance, the symbolic capital of "accent reduction" may involve not only ideological decisions, but an outlay of real capital that simply may not exist. If contemporary musical practices necessitate an investment of capital in various technologies of mediation—amplifiers and microphones, PA systems and cords, electricity and junction boxes, lights, signal-processing devices and batteries—it's worth asking what effect the Pacers' inability to procure that mediating technology had on both the band's material sound and its imagination.

In his classic work *Distinction: A Social Critique of the Judgement of Taste* (1984), Pierre Bourdieu argues that taste is not simply a manifestation of monetary wealth. The distinction between high and low culture is not only a matter of real capital, but equally one of symbolic capital. The most interesting cases for Bourdieu, in that sense, are not those in which obvious price differences tie certain products (caviar, for example) to particular economic classes, but rather those "in which the same income is associated with totally different consumption patterns" (1984:177).

For Bourdieu, "most products only derive their social value from the social use that is made of them" (1984:21). Early on in *Distinction*, he presents an example in support of his thesis. Rice is the same product (and a not very expensive one) whether one chooses to make rice pudding, rice cooked in broth ("working class"), or curried rice ("bourgeois" or "intellectual"). Evocative as this example may be, however, it sidesteps the problem that a $1,500 suit costs fifteen times as much as a $99 suit.[2]

For a musician, the dilemma is analogous. Bourdieu's point might be that the same violin can be used to play Beethoven, bluegrass, or bebop. But the choices made among a range of instruments, amplifiers, signal-processing devices, and so on don't address simply questions of where to expend a financial constant, but also questions of what kind of sound you imagine yourself making. Sometimes the decisions are coordinated: a spruce-top guitar will produce a sound that is brighter than a comparably priced and equally well-made maple-top guitar, which will be mellower. But the decisions are often laid out more starkly than that. You can play on your local pawnshop specials, or you can play on handcrafted instruments through state-of-the-art signal processors and digital-emulating amplifiers. The decision is neither neutral nor inevitable. If you want the sound of a pre-CBS Fender Telecaster played through a Twin Reverb, you may just have to find those pieces of equipment and the money to pay for them. Or you can make do. The Pacers usually made do.

Decisions, decisions. For guitarists: the list price for a new Fender Stratocaster runs from around $500 to $2,900.[3] The Squier Strat clone lists for about $200, maybe $250. Should you get that classic Vox wah-wah pedal for $200? Or a cheap generic imitation for $39.95? Strings, picks, and other accessories also involve decisions that are at once stylistic and financial. Pat played with Jim Dunlop model 44R Nylon Standard picks, the white .38s, because they were the thinnest picks available. This choice was determined in part by his sense that a lighter pick gave him greater speed in his right hand, but also by his belief that a heavier pick would result in more broken strings. For the same reason, he avoided too much note bending with his left hand: by stretching the strings, he said, he risked breaking them. (I prefer a heavier pick, looking for something with the give of a fingernail.[4] All of the Pacers—and their families as well—were convinced my choice of a heavier pick was the reason that I broke so many strings.)

For drummers: a Zildjian or Sabian cymbal package that includes two fourteen-inch hi-hat cymbals, sixteen-inch crash, and twenty-inch ride cymbal, ranges in list price from around $375 to $700. A similar package made by Camber Avanti goes for around $150 or $200. If you're looking for a drum set, you can pick up a Groove Percussion five-piece set (bass drum, snare, floor tom-tom, and two mounted tom-toms), complete with hi-hat and crash cymbals, foot pedals, and stands, for around $250—in return for which you will get a serviceable, if somewhat clunky, sound. If you're looking for a name-brand set—made by, say, Tama or Pearl and constructed not of what the industry euphemistically calls "composite" woods, but of high-quality, acoustically resonant instrumental woods such as beech, maple, mahogany, or birch—you might spend many more times as much for the drums alone. And drum skins? I once went into Miami, one town west of Globe, to pick up a snare drum head at United Jewelers for Kane. The prices ranged from less than $10 to more than $30. A bass drum head can cost more than $50, so Kane would just keep holding the old one together with a lot of silver duct tape when it tore.

These decisions, then, aren't simply decisions of taste, but also of necessity, and they have strong material repercussions on the sound that a musician or a band is capable of producing. Chasing after a musical sound isn't just a matter of ideological choices about how you cook your rice. Sometimes—perhaps often—it's a question of what you do if you can afford only rice, when what you'd like to eat is caviar. Here then, in the political economy of musical sound and the sense of what the right equipment might help you accomplish, lies part of the Pacers' ideas of the discrepancy between the material and the musical resources at their command and why the Battle of the Bands held out such promise in their imaginations.

In other sections of this book, I have already written about *how* the Pacers played. I now want to give a sense of what the Pacers played on and the kinds of everyday processes that led to the sound that the band made. When I say "the band," it is quite easy to imagine that the Pacers played on instruments that you might see on CD covers and on stage at live band performances—guitars by Grover Jackson, or at least by Gibson, Ibanez, or Fender, and amplifiers by Marshall, Peavey, or Roland.

So listen to me when I tell you about the guitar that Pat owned. It was a beautiful, natural-finish Gibson SG Junior, from which Pat could produce a fantastic screaming tone and sustain. But one time at a party a number of years back, Pat leaned the Gibson against the wall, and someone tripped, fell against the wall, and sat down on the instrument, tearing the headstock away from the neck.

Pat did his best to repair the Gibson. With wood glue, four three-sixteenth-inch bolts and nuts, tightly wrapping and rewrapping the neck with strapping tape and electrical tape, he did his best to fix up the guitar and keep it in service. It was well suited to his playing style. Pat coaxed a bright, full-bodied sound out of every guitar his fingers touched, brilliant without being too sharp or piercing. But the SG Junior plugged into the Fender Super Reverb produced the definitive Pat Margo sound. He was especially proud of the humbucking pickups in that guitar and said he would put them into any other guitar he ever bought.[5]

I once took Pat's guitar to a repair shop in Mesa to find out what it would cost to have it professionally repaired. Seeing the bolts in the neck, the repairman nicknamed the guitar "Frankenstein." The monstrosity of the Gibson's headstock contrasted sharply with Pat's musical sense. He was a perfectionist, the one in the band who was most likely to call out to Kane or Darryl to play the ride cymbal rather than the hi-hat, to gesture to Donnie or me to stop fooling around and play a straight country rhythm.

Every time we played, Pat was painstaking about taking time to tune his guitar between songs, which annoyed the other band members. With the SG Junior, he had to keep retuning because of the problems of having a neck held together with electrical tape. But even when he played another guitar, he was always extremely careful with his tuning. Marshall, Kane, and Donnie joked about Pat's tuning up, usually by saying, "Don't be Pat Margo, now," when someone else took too long to get his own guitar in tune. But playing in tune was very important to Pat, I think more important than to anyone else in the band. Marshall wanted to play songs "one after the other," to keep the music coming and people dancing, but Pat always stopped to make sure his guitar was in tune. "Come on, Pat!" But Pat was meticulous and would gently urge me, as we drove home from Pacers gigs, to stop fooling around and be careful about playing in key.

Marshall was convinced that the reason Pat had so much trouble getting in tune was that he tuned by frets rather than by chords. Marsh played the bass, and when the band was tuning up, he would say "A chord" or "D chord" and tune his bass to the root. When he played the guitar, he always tuned by ear and felt this was the way to do it, whereas Pat tuned by frets.[6] Marsh couldn't understand why Pat didn't just play a G chord and get it in tune and play, why he always took so long to perfect the intonation of his guitar. When Pat and Darryl went on to play with the Sneezy Boyz, they invested in on-stage tuners.

Darryl owned some nicer equipment, one piece of which was a candy-apple red Fender Telecaster. As the SG Junior gave up the ghost, Pat sometimes borrowed Darryl's guitar, but he never bought a new ax of his own, at least not until he got hooked up with the Sneezy Boyz a couple of years later. And of course there was the summer that he bought that yellow Z-28 instead of a guitar. When the car broke down and sat lifeless in front of Pat's trailer for weeks on end, the Pacers were annoyed. But, boy, Pat could play.

Donnie Ray, in contrast, was much more lax about tuning his guitar. We might go for a few songs with the guitars out of whack, but Donnie wouldn't worry about tuning until someone told him to do it. Other band members thought it curious, to say the least, that a band member took such a casual attitude about staying in tune. But to me it never seemed that the band members became as frustrated with Donnie's nonchalance as they did with Pat's exacting care. Donnie's guitar was straight out of the pawn shop, a Peavey copy of a Fender Stratocaster that retailed new for about $200. It had cheap tuning gears, which were always loosening. Good machine heads and bridges will lock the strings on key, and you won't have to worry about them. Good machine heads might last longer than your guitar. Cheap machine heads are a pain and cost less for a reason.

Pat and Donnie were constantly pawning their instruments in the pawnshop behind Mark's Tavern. Donnie drove buses for the school district and for firefighters, but Pat was sometimes unemployed and in need of extra cash. He would pawn the Super Reverb for $40 or $50. Come the end of a month, to make ends meet Donnie might pawn in the Peavey Stratocaster or a Fender acoustic he owned. A few months after I returned to Austin, Donnie lost both guitars when he couldn't afford to buy them out of hock, and he had to go out and find a new guitar—

an anonymous Telecaster copy called an R/T 2000. And Pat eventually lost the Fender Super Reverb amplifier. But Donnie saw it for sale on another trip to the pawn shop, so he bought it for $150.

The drums we used depended on who our drummer was. Darryl owned a nice old Ludwig set, but Kane did not own any drums at all. Instead, he played an old drum set of Donnie's, which the band had nicknamed "the Silhouettes." It got that name because the drums were the same pearl gray color as the ones played by the drummer in the band of that name in the movie *La Bamba*. Darryl's drums were better, but Kane played hard enough to break the skins with his "Hawaii Five-O" style. He couldn't afford to replace the heads when they broke, though, so Darryl was understandably reticent to let Kane use his drums. So Kane pounded away instead at the taped-over skins of the Silhouettes. Whoever was playing drums, however, his bass-drum pedal was made with a leather strap that constantly broke. I can't remember how many times a rehearsal or a performance stopped so that Darryl or Kane could make repairs to his foot pedal.

The instruments and equipment the Pacers played on acted as a constant reminder of the Pacers' status. And so the Battle of the Bands presented itself as a means of overcoming this situation both artistically and materially. The prize money for the battle was $1,000 for first place, $500 for second, and $350 for third. On top of that, the highest-ranked country-western band would play at the White Mountain tribe's Independence Day Dance that night, even if that band didn't win the battle. Winning the money wasn't the most important thing, but it wouldn't hurt. The Pacers talked often about what their world would be like if they owned top-notch guitars, amplifiers, drums, and sound reinforcement. If we won, the band members said, we could use the money to buy a decent PA system.

Playing in public, especially in outdoor settings, demands a level of financial investment in the technology of sound reinforcement—instruments, amplifiers, microphones, PA systems, mixing boards, and so on—that the Pacers were unable to meet. A vital piece of this live setup was the mixing board and PA system. A good mixing board gives a band a great deal of subtle control over its public sonic representation. If you have a board with enough channels, you can run everything through the

PA system, balancing the instruments and voices for volume and tim-bre. The Pacers had a small mixing board that allowed the band to run the microphones through a speaker cabinet—not, I should point out, speakers meant for producing vocals, but a cabinet with two fifteen-inch speakers designed for a bass guitar. With no monitor speakers, the band had to keep everything behind them in order to hear each other. This arrangement resulted in the microphones being equalized so as to avoid feedback, a decision that by default dulls rather than enhances the most resonant overtones of the singing voice. A successful band, by way of distinction, will often have a superior sound-reinforcement system that allows them to control what people hear and how they hear it.

Being unable to afford such a sophisticated and powerful mediating setup, the Pacers regularly connected this lack of technological fire-power—that is, their inability to project the band's sound over long distances with both volume and clarity—to a corresponding lack of respect from the community. The band played regularly at backyard parties for birthdays, weddings, graduations, and the like. They also played regularly at Mark's and at Curley's, the Indian bars that bor-dered the reservation to the west and east, respectively. During cam-paign season, the band was often hired as the entertainment at vari-ous political rallies. But when a tribal entity was putting on a more official celebration—a Veterans Day dance, a Fourth of July dance—the Pacers were never offered the job. The sponsoring group preferred to go outside San Carlos and bring in Apache Spirit from Whiteriver or Common People from Window Rock or the Rastafarmers, the Chicano reggae band from Phoenix.

Although the need for this kind of investment and the stakes involved have multiplied more recently, they aren't new problems. Technological mediation has always been important in going after the good sound for a country band or rock band on the reservation. One of the key words in people's memories of the Band Era in San Carlos was "Silvertone." Whenever I heard the name "Silvertone" during my stay in San Carlos, it was alternately—or simultaneously—used as a term of endearment and derision. When something went wrong in a Pacers rehearsal, some-one—usually Donnie Ray—would say something like, "Come on, now! This isn't Silvertone, now!"

As noted earlier, Silvertone was a brand name for radios, home electronics, and musical instruments sold by Sears. Silvertone gui-tars were manufactured by a number of different companies and then

branded with the Sears Silvertone label. The most famous of these guitars were the Danelectro-manufactured models 1448 and 1457—the
"amp-in-case" models. The guitars came with a hard-shell case that contained its own amplifier, with the speaker mounted in the wall of the
case itself. The model 1448 was a single-pickup guitar, with a three-
watt amplifier and a six-inch speaker in the case. The 1457 featured a
two-pickup guitar, a five-watt amplifier, and an eight-inch speaker.

In the 1950s, Sears opened an outlet in the Little Hollywood section
of Globe that sold Silvertone items. When Sluggo spoke about the Cyclones rehearsals in Bylas (see chapter 3), he designated them acous-
tically by specifically mentioning that they played on Silvertone guitars and amplifiers. Vel Sneezy, telling me about his early days learning
music, also mentioned specifically that he was given, not just any electric guitar, but a Silvertone guitar. He told me he had found his first
guitar, an acoustic guitar, at the dump yard:

> And I guess my mom and dad felt sorry for me, because I loved that guitar
> so much I used to protect it with my life. And I wouldn't let anyone touch
> it, I would get mad at them. And I would even hide it underneath the bed
> so that my other brothers and sisters won't touch it. 'Cause even though it
> was a damaged guitar and it was a used guitar I still treated it like it was
> the only thing in my life. So I guess because of that my mom and dad de-
> cided to give me a Christmas gift. They bought me an electric Silvertone
> guitar, and amplifier.

So "Silvertone" denotes a brand name, a historical period, a memory,
and a sound. It isn't a sound that anybody really wants to emulate now.[7]
But it is one that is remembered with fondness and attachment. Marshall used to refer to those days as "back in the Stone Age," that time
when people were making music with the most primitive of accoutre-
ments, when you could just pull your guitar out of the case, plug it into
the case, and be ready to go.

This was the "equipment" that Sluggo used to come by Darryl's house
to borrow from his brother. When Darryl was young and starting up
his first band with Pat and Marshall, they had only acoustic, box guitars. Compared to them, Kenny had all this stuff, so they borrowed it,
too. Those Silvertone guitars sounded pretty good, and the Silvertone
amps, Darryl said, "they had a, reverb, it sounds pretty good, you know
it sounded like a . . . ," and then, searching for the right analogy, the
word that would evoke the proper level of lingering, ringing echo, he

thought of his high school days: "a *gym*." Having a little spring reverb, a little tremolo, a fuzz box, a wah-wah pedal could make all the difference between getting the sound you wanted or sounding "cheap" and "dry."

But in the 1990s it was a different story. Compared to even the deluxe, five-watt model of the Sears Silvertone, the equipment used in present-day outdoor performances is massive. Darryl estimated that Apache Spirit's PA system, with its fifteen-inch speakers and horns, probably ran around two hundred watts per channel through the stereo mixing board. And so the prospect of winning some money that would enable the Pacers to purchase some of that power had the band members excited.

But first we needed to score the $50 entry fee in order to get in. Marshall—in the first of what turned out to be a string of decisions that, in retrospect, indicated his growing nervousness about the event—commanded that I not pay the entry fee out of my research funds. Instead, Donnie Ray arranged with a friend who had had some involvement with musical groups in the past to put up the fee for us. Jerry Gloshay had the rules together by the end of the week and faxed them to me at an office-supply store in Globe, where I drove to pick them up. When I read the fax, I saw that Jerry Gloshay had written a note across the top, in big letters, saying that our entry fee hadn't arrived.

A quick trip to Donnie's house in El Taco City. He jumped into the truck, and we went over to his friend's house, where we discovered that he hadn't sent the money order yet—because, he said, he was waiting to hear if he needed to write anything special on it, like the name of the band or who the manager was. The latter question annoyed the band members. From the sound of it, they said, it was as if he wanted to say, "I'm the manager," that he didn't want to simply help us out and send the money; he wanted to "get involved." He gave Donnie the money order, and then we drove back to my trailer in Airport '79, where I called Jerry Gloshay's office and left a message on his voice mail, explaining the mixup, giving him the money-order number, and asking him to call me if he got the message.

The next morning, Saturday, I hadn't heard back from him, and down at the old house in Peridot they were resigned to the idea that we had missed the deadline. But I had a feeling we could still get in. I had sensed that Jerry Gloshay wanted a band from San Carlos and that he wanted bands who played country because of the arrangements about a country band playing at the dance no matter who won the contest. I also thought that he might be short of bands in general, so the deadline might not be as tight as it stated in the rules. At the same time, I had my own investment in the participant observation of the situation. I wanted to check out the Battle of the Bands, and because of the way it lived in my own imagination, I thought the best way to do that would be to play in it. If Jerry Gloshay talked about the Battle of the Bands with the sense of reviving a tradition, I had heard the glory-days stories for years, so I was excited about the possibility of actually taking part in such an event. I saw my opportunity slipping away in the Pacers' resignation to circumstances. And so I placed myself in the role of being the enthusiastic, never-say-never one. Besides, as we had been saying all along, I also thought the band could use the prize money.

So later that afternoon I went back to Donnie's and said, "Akú dit'aazhgo bikadit'įįgo nłt'éé shinsih" (I think the two of us should go up there and look for him). There was a Sunrise Dance going on that weekend, with people down from Whiteriver, and Donnie's wife tried to convince him to let someone at the dance take the money order up there for us. But Donnie said, "That won't be till Monday," so off we went to Whiteriver.

The drive takes a couple of hours. From Globe, you turn north and go up the switchbacks into the White Mountains and Tonto National Forest. Then you snake down thousands of feet of hairpin turns into the Salt River Canyon. You cross the canyon over a new bridge—the old bridge has been converted into a pedestrian walk. Then you lift steeply up the other side, into the Fort Apache Reservation. This highway had been built in the past fifty years, and the new bridge within the past thirty. People in the 1930s used to travel a narrower, more treacherous highway, and before that a dirt road. That back dirt road was known, at one time, as Arizona State Highway 73. Part of it, now paved, runs as a spur off U.S. 60, from Carrizo through Whiteriver and up to Show Low. The dirt road, which prompted numerous tales of woe, used to be the main route north from Globe and ran directly through the San Carlos and Fort Apache Reservations. For those willing to put up with the condition of the dirt roads it is a more direct route to Whiteriver, shaving about fifty miles from the route that Donnie and I traveled.

On the way up, Donnie was entertaining and informative. He pointed out the switchbacks of the old highway, told me stories about going up to Seneca as a boy and running down the canyon on foot to the river at the bottom, and pointed out a number of places: Itsaa Binii, Muh Bilaa, and Silver Butte.

Back up in Whiteriver, we drove to the store where I had seen the sign and asked where we might find Jerry Gloshay. A woman came out and drew a map to his house for us. I couldn't help thinking she drew the map for my benefit. We cruised down there, by the Assembly of God Church, but there was no one home. We checked at his sister's house, which someone had pointed out to us, but there was no answer there, either. We went back to his house, checked with a neighbor to be sure we had the right house, and thus assured we stuffed the money order under the door with an explanatory note. After a quick visit to Donnie's sister, who worked at the craft store, and stops to see a few other relatives, we cruised by the rodeo grounds, where a crew was setting up two sound stages for the event. They said they were looking for Jerry Gloshay, too, and if we found him, we should send him down there. Next we stopped by the tribal office on the off chance that he was there, then one more time past his house to make sure we had done our level best to locate him. Satisfied that we had done all we could, we took off back to Globe, trusting in fate. He would *have* to let us in after that kind of sincere effort, we decided. Besides, said Donnie, everything's probably on Indian time.

When we got back to Globe, we pulled into the last Circle K, where we picked up some Bud Lights. I called my answering machine from the phone booth there and found a message from Jerry Gloshay. He said he didn't live in that house anymore, but fortunately his sister had stopped in there and had brought the money order to him. So we were set. As we headed back to San Carlos, the cool of the evening was just setting in, and we were in a good mood. Donnie was saying that he wanted to take the instruments to a medicine man to get them blessed—and maybe us, too.

We let everyone know that we were on for the Battle. Back at the old house, Marshall said we should jam out and practice over the next three days, getting our set together. Saturday and Sunday, though, various people disappeared or were unavailable, so nothing happened. Finally, on Monday evening, the day before the Battle, we got together at the old house and ran through some numbers. At Marshall's request, I wrote them down as we played them, so that everyone could have a set list the next day.

The first song he called for was "Neon Moon," a slow song by Brooks and Dunn, which the band had recently learned because Marshall wanted to do some new songs. Next was "Only Daddy That'll Walk the Line," a classic made famous by Waylon Jennings and done more recently by the Kentucky Headhunters. We then played "Time," one of Marshall's originals, and followed that with "Wild Man," a song performed by Ricky Van Shelton, which suited the rough edges of Marshall's voice. Then Marshall called for "Guacamole," a conjunto-style song by the Texas Tornados that all the band members loved and that they had chosen to do because I had come to San Carlos from Austin. Because of this, I sang lead vocals on the song. We followed that with "Fast as You," a country rocker by Dwight Yoakum, and then Charlie Daniels's "Long Haired Country Boy," which was one of Marshall's signature tunes. Then Marshall wanted to do the Bob Marley song "Zion Train," also sung by yours truly; I had brought this song to the band because everyone wanted to play some reggae. Finally, Marshall ended with "Apache Girl," another of his originals.

And that was it. No discussion, no planning of what would make a winning set, no ironing out any rough spots, no question if the set was tight enough, paced properly, if it showed the Pacers in their best possible light. I was concerned about singing two songs. Hell, I was concerned about singing *any* songs. The rules said each band could have one non-Native member, but I worried about what effect my presence as lead guitarist and now lead singer for two songs might have on the band's chances. But that was it, the run-through was finished. I showed everyone the list and asked if that was the order they thought we should do them in, and everyone said, "Yeah, let's go for it." So we went home. After dropping Kane off on the way up to my trailer in Airport, I printed up the list, along with the opening chords of each song, and then went to sleep.

The next morning the band—Marshall, Kane, Donnie Ray, and I— gathered at the old house and loaded up my truck. Then we drove over to Donnie's at El Taco and loaded some extra equipment into his car and Marshall's car, gathered up the whole family, and took off for Whiteriver in a convoy of my truck and the two cars. Kane and two of Donnie's sons rode with me. On the way up, everyone was loose and in a good mood, which of course they demonstrated by teasing me without any letup. After a stop at the store at the bottom of the Salt River Canyon, we made it the rest of the way up to Whiteriver, where we spent some time with Donnie's relatives again before making our way over to the rodeo and fairgrounds.

The two stages at the center of the rodeo arena were complete. A professional local sound-reinforcement company, Mountain Sound, provided the speakers and the mixing, so all the bands would have good sound. Everything was going to go through the PA system today—drums were miked with separate channels for kick, hi-hat, snare, toms, and overheads. Amps were miked, and the bass went into the board through a direct box. Each singer had his own microphone—no bumping heads to sing harmonies. Each sound stage had massive speaker towers on either side. Having two stages meant that while one band was playing on the first stage, the next band would set up on the other so that everything would be ready to go as quickly as possible, with no lag between performances.

We drove around to the side of the fairgrounds, parked outside the gate, and waited. I pulled out my guitar and worked on the solo from "Only Daddy." Pat usually played this song, but he was not with us today. I wished that he were. By this time, whatever friction that had surfaced between Pat and the other Pacers had caused Pat to make himself unavailable to the band. When we began planning the trip to Whiteriver for the Battle, I had asked that we try to get Pat involved—in part because I thought he should share in the proceeds if we won anything, but also, again, in part because I worried about how my presence as lead guitarist would affect the band's chances. Suddenly the thing about me that apparently helped the Pacers in the local bars loomed as a detriment. I also thought Pat should be there because I respected his guitar playing. Pat could play me under the table, and I felt that our chances of winning would be improved if he came along. Kane and I had tracked Pat down at his job at the day-care center in Peridot, and Kane had tried to convince him to participate, but Pat declined. Nodding toward me, he said, "lead guitar kúgee sizįį"—there's your lead guitarist standing right there. I disagreed, but he was gently adamant in his refusal. People kept telling me it had nothing to do with me.

Standing by the truck now, Kane pulled out his drumsticks, and Donnie made sure he had extra strings in case one broke. We stood to the side where we had parked and surveyed the action. Some of the arriving bands had horse trailers with their band names painted on them;

some had nice looking vans. We had just thrown everything into the bed of my truck, then whatever was left over went into the trunks of Donnie's and Marshall's cars and onto the laps of the passengers in the back seats. Marshall called us together. Finally thinking about the Pacers' set, he said he didn't want to start with a slow song. So we moved "Wild Man" to the top of the set. It wasn't the last last-minute change he would make.

At around eleven in the morning, Jerry Gloshay picked up a microphone and called for representatives of the bands to come draw lots for performance order. Marshall sent Donnie and me to the grandstand, where Jerry Gloshay took attendance. When he called out "Country Pacers," one of the other guys there turned to us and said, " 'Country Pacers'? I played with a band called Country Pacers back in the '70s!" It was someone from San Carlos who had played with Darryl's brother back in the early days of the Country Pacers. A venerable legacy. He was living up in Whiteriver now, playing bass with a band there called Country Image. He and Donnie exchanged a few memories of people they used to jam out with down in San Carlos.

A total of eight bands were playing in the Battle—all, as it turned out, from Arizona. For the record, they were, in order of their appearance,

1. Romeo's Gospel Band, from Whiteriver
2. Common People, from Window Rock
3. Warhead, from Flagstaff
4. The Country Pacers, from San Carlos
5. Bad Company, from Ganado
6. Native Pride, from Sacaton
7. Country Image, from Whiteriver
8. Eagleheart, from Sacaton

Each band was allotted half an hour to play, and each was to be judged by a panel of four "non–tribally affiliated persons," according to the rules.[8] Drew Lacapa, who emceed the event, said, "In the rules, it says they're supposed to be 'all non-Native.' You *know* they're part Cherokee. Just ask 'em: 'I'm one hundred, three hun-, one three-thousand-two-hundred-and-five Cherokee.' Mm-hmmm? And I believe 'em, too."

Romeo's Gospel Band, also known as the Silver Butte Gospel Band, had volunteered to go first, playing while the Mountain Sound people shook out any kinks in the system. They played an easy-paced, country-gospel style. Common People, a Navajo quartet from Window Rock, featured a very tasteful and sweet-sounding country lead guitarist who played a Stratocaster through a chorus reverb and an octave box, both of which thicken the texture of the music, making it sound as though multiple guitars are playing when there's only one.

Warhead played next.

Oh.

My.

God.

A speed metal group amplified by a wall of Marshall stacks, a smoke machine, and a backdrop of an American flag with the portrait of a Plains warrior superimposed on it. We have to follow *that*? As Drew Lacapa said before Warhead played, "I don't know if they're gonna tune up or they're just gonna come out and start banging each other around." To put it bluntly, they kicked ass, and the Pacers, getting ready to go on the other sound stage, knew they would be a hard act to follow. On top of that, as soon as Warhead started playing, a bunch of young women jumped out of the crowd and rushed to the stage to dance and go wild for them. As it turned out, the guys in Warhead knew people from San Carlos, and later on, when we were hanging out backstage together, Marshall invited them to come down and play for his sister-in-law's birthday party.

Meanwhile, as Warhead thrashed around next door, we got set up and discovered that we were missing a cymbal stand, so we needed to track one down quickly from another band. Apache Spirit had been disqualified from participating because they were easily the most successful band in the area—in 1998 they took best country band honors at the first Native American Music Awards. But Midnite, the band's guitarist, was on hand with their equipment in case of emergencies, so we borrowed a cymbal stand from Apache Spirit. Then it turned out Donnie's little twenty-watt Crate amplifier didn't work, so again we borrowed Midnite's amp from Apache Spirit.

Warhead ended their set, and our adventure continued. I don't know if it was because of nerves or because our equipment troubles were so prominently on display, or what, but as soon as we were announced, Marshall called for us to open with a number that we hadn't even run through the night before—Freddie King's "Hideaway." This song was an instrumental blues number that, had I known we were going to play it at all, much less open with it, I would have practiced to get it into the tips of my fingers. All things considered, the song went all right, except that about two-thirds of the way through it the leather holding together the bass drum pedal of the Silhouettes snapped, again, and Kane had to borrow another pedal from Apache Spirit. At the same time, Mountain Sound had some difficulties of their own, so after our second song—Marshall's song "Time," at the end of which I dropped a huge brick on the guitar solo, playing some kind of weird diminished-augmented-minor thing instead of the simple G chord to D chord that I always played—they called a break. So there we stood while the sound people sorted out their difficulties over the next fifteen minutes, waiting around in the three o'clock heat of an Arizona July afternoon, watching a watermelon-eating contest with a $125 satin jacket as the prize.

After the break, we started up again, and things finally went smoothly. Later on Donnie said he thought they should have let us start over from the beginning. Then, on the last song, "Apache Girl," Donnie did something that was a fertile source of jokes for weeks after. He started singing harmonies. He had never done that before, so it confused Marshall and me. Marshall said, "I don't know what Donnie was doing, I thought it was me for a minute until I saw him standing to the microphone." Donnie said he just gave in to the temptation. "I don't know what came over me," he said. "Just, the microphone standing right there in front of me, I felt like I should do something with it." On top of never having sung harmonies on the song before, he was trying to fit in as a third voice. Two-part harmonies are easy to improvise, but each successive voice becomes exponentially more difficult to arrange—not all of his harmonies fit.

Donnie's actions highlight a distinction between local or private and more general or public performances, a distinction in which the Pacers consistently found themselves caught up. To a man, the band members wanted to extend their reach and popularity beyond the San Carlos and Bylas communities. Yet many of the things that endeared them to the local community were the things that would not translate globally—for example, Marshall's intimate knowledge of people that made it possible to drop personal references into his sung performances. At the same time, the things that would extend their reach were beyond their reach. The technological poverty of the band's sound production marked them as local. In an ironic twist of language and ideology, people referred to this problem as being "not real," as if the band right there in front of you were less "real" than the band that you heard only through the mediating channels of radio, stereo, or television.[9]

At the same time, the situation of the First Intertribal Battle of the Bands in a Long Time was somewhat ambiguous. In the world of negotiating the contextual differences between such activities as hanging out with friends just jamming on an acoustic guitars, rehearsing with the band, playing at house parties, playing at Mark's or Blake's, and other kinds of performances, varying degrees of formality contributed to creating the context and circumscribed the performance practices within it. In other words, there was a distinction between more intimate performances with peers and more formal ones in front of various publics. Playing at the bar, for example, where the owners were non-Apaches, entailed doing things in a certain way so as not to reinforce some stereotypes about people from the reservation. In the Battle of the Bands, things were not so clearly delineated. For instance, members of the Pacers were probably related to some of the people in the audience in Whiteriver—which of course doesn't mean they didn't care if the band sang on key. Even if the audience did get into the music and not notice if you were a little bit off, the judges—even those who were one-three-thousand-two-hundred-and-five Cherokee—would mark you down for it. So you didn't want to mess up.

When we finished our set, we got enthusiastic cheers and whistles from the crowd, and we broke down our equipment and loaded it back into our vehicles, which, since the bed of my truck was open, meant that we had to take turns guarding the equipment for the rest of the day. After us, Bad Company played some straight-ahead country. Then Drew Lacapa, who lives in Whiteriver, works at the hospital, and knows the people in the community, came out in a *tł'akał*, shawl, and earrings and had people rolling in the aisles with a comedy routine about the changing relationships between Apache men and women. After a sack race, Charlie Hill—an Oneida comedian who has been on *VH1 Spotlight*, the *Tonight Show with Jay Leno*, the *Late Show with David Letterman*, and *Arsenio Hall*—did a routine that never really captured the audience's attention.

After that, at about 5:30, as things began to cool down, Native Pride took the stage. A killer guitar-bass-drums trio—*their* instruments never went out of tune. They played a mix of classic rock, blues, country-western, and originals. Their lead guitarist got an incredible tone and sustain out of his Strat and never missed a note. Well, almost never. Then Vincent Craig came out with his guitar and entertained with his mixture of fish stories and folk songs. With the sun going down, we heard the local favorites, Country Image, who featured a great harmonica player; and Eagleheart finished up the evening with a mixture of folk-rock and country.

After a great Fourth of July fireworks display, the winners were announced. Native Pride won the $1,000—quite handily, I would guess. Warhead came in second, and Eagleheart was third. A jam session followed, featuring Apache Spirit and all the bands. I was hoping to join in, to meet some people and have some fun jamming out, but as soon as it was clear that the Pacers weren't in the running, Marshall sat in his car, ready to go. So we went.

When Charlie, Velazquez, Willie, and Mitch sat down to name the Statics, Willie wanted to name them the Poor Boys, and this is what I think that means. The threads of imagination and material conditions that connect mediated and live experiences of music and that also connect the experience of expressive culture to everyday life were drawn tighter for me in the Battle of the Bands. It was clear when we arrived at the fairgrounds that the Pacers were the most ill-equipped band of the day. In contrast to the bands with the huge, gleaming Pearl drum sets, Zildjian and Paiste cymbals, Kane played mightily on the Silhouettes. Instead of bright and shiny Fender Stratocasters or the polished black Gibson Les Pauls played by Warhead, Donnie played his cheap Peavey imitation Strat, and Marshall thumped away on a no-name copy of an Epiphone copy of a Gibson SG bass. Instead of the stacks and stacks of Marshall amplifiers brought on by Warhead, or the Peavey Stereo Chorus amplifiers used by the more sedate country and rock groups, our amplifiers were old and mismatched. Donnie played through a small twenty-watt amp made by Crate, which didn't work when we got to Whiteriver, anyway. Marshall played the bass through a Fender cabinet, which he bought on layaway at United Jewelers in Miami, Arizona.[10] The cabinet was connected to an old Plush bass head, which Marshall had had since no one knows when. As for me, I played on a used Japanese Fender Telecaster and used some savings to purchase a Fender amp that is now property of the band.

Don't get me wrong. We played well. I think if Pat had been there, we might have come up with $350 or $500 for the band. Even given all our difficulties, some people at the Battle of the Bands thought the Pacers should have won the whole thing—but most of them were from San Carlos. I don't think anyone could have played better than did Native Pride.

I took the next few days to ask the other band members what their feelings about the whole thing had been. They had a few thoughts about the time of day, that playing in the middle of a scorching July afternoon hurt both us and any desire on the audience's part to respond. The cloudiness in the late afternoon and the coming of night made things easier for those who played after us. And it is true that two of the three winning bands performed when the weather was gentler. Other thoughts were, of course, that stopping in the middle of our set didn't help matters, nor did changing the songs. For myself, as the only non-Native band member out of the eight bands that played, I wondered what effect that had on the judges. Nobody mentioned that we hadn't rehearsed for the week leading up to the event. But time and again the band members said that we just didn't have the equipment to get the kind of sound we needed, that we were too "dry."

"Now we know," Donnie said, when I spoke to him in the aftermath of the trip to Whiteriver. He tried to invite people to whoop and holler for the band. "We needed people to help us out," he said, "it kind of put us down [meaning made us depressed] because it would have helped us out." Even at that, Donnie said, people from San Carlos would never have rushed the stage in broad daylight, and he wondered how much the response to Warhead was staged in order to influence the judges.[11]

"This is a first experience," he said. Then, thinking about all the times he went places with Sluggo and the Valiants and came home with a trophy, he said, "Them days are gone." In the old days, when all you had to do was plug your guitar into your case and you could sound like a gym, everyone sounded dry. Or everyone sounded amazing, depending on how your imagination worked. Bands are different now, "more heavy." "But we got an experience now," he said, if we should ever find ourselves in that situation again. We need better, bigger instruments, and more sound effects. "We been running it dry," he said, "we need to get more technical." In the old days, getting a sound was just a question of running down to Sears. But now you need "more effects." In the old days, sure, people who made records had effects from the studios, "but nowadays it's on stage," he said.

The growing need for digital effects and sophisticated electronic equipment in order to create the sounds you would like to hear feeds into a vicious circle. The sound of a band marks its locality—can mark it *as* local.[12] And if you sound local, it's hard to accumulate the kind of engagements that will allow you eventually to sound less local. The Pacers' financial inability to improve the sophistication of the band's equipment contributed to the band members' sense of a lack of respect from those in the tribal administration, for example, who had the power to hire bands for various official occasions, because the band didn't sound as "real" (meaning as mediated) as it should. The Pacers' take on this sense was that the tribe, rather than supporting their own people, time after time brought in bands from the outside to provide music for dances. I would argue, though, that there was little that Apache Spirit possessed in terms of musicianship or talent that the Pacers could not also match. The repertoires of the two bands, discounting original songs, was surprisingly similar. Both Midnite and Pat were accomplished guitarists with individual styles. Whatever polish Apache Spirit had garnered over the years through the luxury afforded by their successful recordings was matched by the fact that Marshall possessed a singularly distinctive and smoky voice.

But the Pacers didn't have sophisticated sound reinforcement. More heavy. As Darryl put it to me, people these days want to hear "big old music." Now you have to have more power. You need a PA system where you can plug in the guitars, the drums, everything, and run it through the mixing board. The only thing Marshall runs through the PA system, Darryl pointed out, is vocals. You can barely hear it, Darryl said. "In the bar you can hear him pretty good, but out here, for instance down at the lake, because all the music's spaced out." Apache Spirit is one of the most successful bands in the area, with a dozen recordings to its credit. When *they* play, you can hear the bass from far off, and it thumps through you in the audience because they have good drums and amps with chorus reverb, and everything goes through the PA system. "They got a power amp," said Darryl, "then they hook [everything] up to the PA system, they got two fifteen [-inch speakers] and the horns." And that's the minimum of what it takes to get a taste of the good sound nowadays.

Without it, you don't get no respect. When we played after the Veterans Day parade, we were hired by the tribal Cattle Association. Common People were imported to perform at the official Veterans Day dance. We had enjoyed hearing each other in Whiteriver, and when they showed up early, they came by the Cattle Association event, and we hung out together. The afternoon had been a success for the Pacers. Darryl had handled sound for the band while Kane played the drums because Common People had arrived with no drummer and hired Darryl to play with them, so he wanted to save his energy. Even without the big old PA system that Darryl would have wanted (and that Common People had), the care he took in balancing the instruments and the vocals made things sound better than usual, and all afternoon people were telling us that they never knew the Pacers sounded so good, and they couldn't understand why we never got hired to play "real" things. Common People invited us to play during their breaks and to sit in and jam out with them at the end of the dance that night. But the recreation director for the tribe said, with some annoyance, that they had better not take long breaks, and his attitude and tone of voice raised the Pacers' hackles. Let Common People play, then. They're the ones getting paid! So we left and headed up the road to Pinky's, not out of any dislike for Common People, but out of dismay at the treatment the Pacers got from their own community.

This need for power and sophisticated electronics changes the relationship between mediated and live performance by demanding additional layers of mediation on stage. It thus also changes the financial stakes in the procurement of mediation necessary for successful live performances. What happens to the imagined relationship between the participatory sense of listening to the radio and the possibility of extending that participation into the realm of live performances? If the participation engendered by the radio and television today doesn't seem to inspire responsive performance on the reservation, it may not be because of anything particular to the media itself, but perhaps because it is increasingly difficult for people on the reservation to imagine themselves in that space, to imagine themselves as the voice coming through the speaker.[13] This may be one reason why—despite everyone's love of new songs, recent releases, and alternative music—the old songs, "Born on the Bayou," "Wooly Bully," "Gloria," "Hang On Sloopy," "Mathilda," are still the ones that pull people of all generations out onto the dance floor. These songs sound the way people remember hearing them. It isn't that the radio or TV makes one passive, but that a lack of capital renders one (in several senses) powerless. The availability of digital technology is presented in music trade and consumer magazines as a democratizing factor in popular-music production. Now anyone can have a sophisticated recording studio at home, says the promotional literature. But the cost of that technology—to buy an eight-track cassette recorder and digital signal-processing devices and drum machines and such—drives those who can't afford it deeper into the margins because now everyone else has that sound except you, and it is expected that live performance will have this sound from here on out. As Paul Théberge has written, "With the advent of the home multitrack studio, the idea of 'paying your dues' in the music industry fundamentally changed. . . . As the home studio became an important new market for the manufacturers of microprocessor-based technologies, there was an increasing pressure on musicians to surround themselves with an ever-expanding array of consumer goods" (1997:233–34). The game is rigged in ways it wasn't before. In my innocence, I had thought that the promise of $1,000 that could buy some of that power— or even $500 or $350—would have been enough to have inspired our performance. It wasn't. I wonder, when Marshall saw all those trailers emblazoned with band logos, the Pearl and Ludwig drum sets, those Zildjian and Paiste cymbals, those Stratocasters and Les Pauls and Precision basses and Marshall and Peavey amps, I wonder if he decided then and there that the odds were too long and resigned himself to the idea that there was no way the Pacers could come away winners. And I wonder if he was right.

On the drive home from Whiteriver, people were in good spirits despite the loss. One of Donnie's sons kept singing at the top of his lungs, "Youuuu are not alooooone, . . . ," the chorus of the recently released Michael Jackson song, and then commenting on how scary it was to think that Michael Jackson might be with you all the time.

But coming back to San Carlos without any winnings to show for our trouble galvanized an idea that the band had been toying with for a while. Since my arrival in San Carlos, the Pacers, in accepting me into the group, had insisted that part of the deal was this: we don't want you to pay us such-and-such an hour for an interview; we want you to *open doors for us*. I had no idea how to do that or even what that might mean.

But in the aftermath of the Battle of the Bands, the idea of making a tape in order to become "real" resurfaced.

Through a colleague of mine who had worked as an audio engineer in Tucson, we decided on a small studio there, called Crash Landing, and made arrangements to record. Unlike with the Battle of the Bands, the Pacers took this very seriously, rehearsing in Donnie's living room every day for five days straight before we went up.

The idea had been to make a tape, sell it, and use the proceeds to buy a good PA system for the group—one of those big old sound systems that Darryl talked about. Because it was conceived as a group project, the Pacers made every effort to involve everyone. That meant Kane and Darryl would split the drumming duties, and Pat, who hadn't played with us in quite a while, would play lead. He eventually did, but Darryl had no interest in participating, so Kane played drums on all the cuts.

The day we were to record rhythm tracks, Kane, Marshall, Donnie, and I packed all our stuff into the bed of my truck and took off to Tucson, Marshall and I up front, Donnie and Kane squeezed into the jump seats behind. Marshall had spent a great deal of time over the preceding week making sure all his lyrics were straight. He was worried about his originals. In live performance, he sometimes improvised whatever came into his head, and that sometimes meant that a verse would last an extra line or two. Marshall was concerned that he wouldn't be able to do that in the studio. In a scene in *La Bamba*, the movie from which the Silhouettes drum set got its name, Ritchie Valens (Lou Diamond Phillips) is in the studio for the first time, recording "Let's Go." He changes the words slightly with every take, until his producer tells him he can't do it that way because it has to be the same every time in order to match multiple takes. It's no secret that the recording studio can strangle the with-the-moment, unreproducible energy of live performance. *That* can't be captured on tape. Finding myself cast in the role of producer, I assured Marshall that as long as he stayed within the confines of what was laid down in the rhythm tracks, he could sing whatever he wanted.[14]

The first day of recording went well. We put down backing tracks with guide vocals for sixteen songs. The band rehearsals had paid off, as every song was done within a couple of takes. One thing I knew from my limited previous experience in recording studios was that the band needed to let the last chord of the song die out naturally, remaining silent for a much longer period of time than you would normally think.

We did that on every song—all very professional. Things went smoothly enough that we even had time to lay down some rhythm-section over-dubs, such as extra guitar parts. Phil Stevens, who ran the show at Crash Landing, gave us a dub to listen to, and we headed back down to San Carlos.[15]

We made two more trips to Tucson to overdub vocal and lead guitar parts. Marshall, Donnie, and I made the first trip, so that all the back-ground vocals could be recorded. I did lead guitar parts to songs that the band had learned since Pat had stopped playing with us, but I still held out hope that we could convince him to join in, so I left his songs alone. We started to get a little giddy with the potential that the studio afforded for signal processing. I double tracked the solo on Marshall's song "You're the One," George Harrison style—an event that Marshall noted down for himself in his lyric book. On another of Marshall's origi-nals, "Cowboy Way," I overdubbed a part using the upper register of an acoustic guitar to follow the chord changes. During the replay, I was dissatisfied.

"I wanted it to sound like bells," I said.

"Oh, you mean like this?" said Phil, doing something that made the chords ping-pong incessantly back and forth between the earpieces of my headphones. If only two of us were singing in the studio, Phil would keep the third entertained in the control room by twisting dials that made the singers sound like Mickey Mouse or by playing with some special effect or other. Ah, the infectious power of technological con-trol: on one song, I played a lead-in to the verse on dobro. I can't play dobro to save my life! We had to punch it in almost one note at a time. And ah, the eye-opening experience of realizing what you can do with a recording studio: Marshall started talking about how, if he ever made another tape, he wanted to have a song that began with traditional Apache singing and then faded into his guitar chords.

At last, Pat agreed to play on the recording, so he, Marshall, and I went back to Tucson for a final overdub session to complete lead vocals and guitar parts. The session was long and frustrating for Marshall, who had to sing all day. Plus, his worst fear was realized: on his song "Apache Girl," he sang a six-line verse where in the original rhythm sessions he had sung four lines. We stopped tape and made him do it again. "I thought you said I could sing whatever I wanted," he said to me, letting a little annoyance show through.

Marshall took a break, and we started laying in Pat's guitar parts, but for some reason whatever guitar he was playing was just a little bit out of tune with the tape. Given Pat's attention to tuning, this was more than a little ironic. We tried three or four different guitars. What might have taken an hour ended up taking several, and we decided to break for dinner.

Rejuvenated by Mexican food, we returned to put the finishing touches on the tape. Marshall still needed to cut the lead vocals for Steve Earle's "Copperhead Road," one of his signature tunes.[16] Marshall was known for singing a particular group of songs—"Long Haired Country Boy," "Copperhead Road," "Sensuous Woman"—and when we started thinking about the tape, it was an easy decision to make sure it included some of these songs. Marshall resisted including all of them, in part because it wasn't his solo recording and in part because he was afraid it would result in a tape with too many "old songs." But "Copperhead Road" easily made the cut.

One of the things Marshall had enlisted me to do in preparation for our recording sessions was to help him make sure that all the words on his lyric sheets were correct. Up until this point, there were a number of songs that I had only ever heard Marshall sing, never the originals. "Copperhead Road" was one of them. In helping Marshall double-check his transcriptions, I encountered the original Steve Earle version of the song for the first time. "Copperhead Road" is the story of three generations of bootleggers in West Virginia, sung by a character Earle named "John Lee Pettimore." In the third verse of the song, Pettimore sings about how he switched the business over from moonshine to marijuana and rigged Copperhead Road with booby traps he had learned from his time in-country fighting the Viet Cong. On hearing Steve Earle sing it, I noticed that the rhyme in the first couplet of that third verse depends quite strongly on a heavy "redneck" twang:

I done two tours of duty in Viet Nam
I came home with a brand new plan

In his recording, Steve Earle twangs the second syllable of "Viet Nam" so that it rhymes with "plan." But Marshall never twanged his voice. In fact, none of the country singers I know in either San Carlos or Bylas do, except as a joke. When Marshall sang the same lines, he always sang *Nahm* rather than *Nayum*. The words were right, but the pronunciation wasn't. Because Marshall wanted everything to be "right," and because he was treating me as the "producer" anyway, I pushed him to add a twang to the line. He eventually reached a compromise—with me? with himself?—and raised his *ah* (as in "father") to an *æ* (as in "cat"). But he was clearly uncomfortable with the idea of adding an extra twang that would mark his voice as "hillbilly" at the same time that it became more mainstream country. (A more detailed analysis of this episode is contained in Feld et al. 2004:332–40.)

Finally, Marshall was done. Pat and I overdubbed the alternating guitar parts in "High on a Mountaintop," and that was it. We were finished with the taping. All that was left was the mixing. As Pat, Marshall, and I drove back down to San Carlos, along the switchbacks through Mammoth and San Manuel, past the molten copper running off the smelter at the Christmas mine, our spirits were light, and those guys teased me mercilessly about how I had made Marshall sound like a redneck.

Marshall left the mixing to me. He didn't feel as though he had any relevant experience in the studio, and family obligations made it difficult for him to commit yet another day to going to Tucson. I suggested that he knew how he wanted it to sound, and he said he just wanted it to sound good. "Just—don't let it sound dry," he said and sent me on my way.

Again, "dry" and its opposite, "not dry." The opposite of "dry" here is not "wet." Interestingly, "not dry" has a more readily accessible sonic marker than its positive relative. It is the sound of a fraction of a second's delay, followed by large doses of slowly decaying reverb, as if you were ringing the walls of the Grand Canyon. Boe Titla once performed the sound for me using Apache phonology: a snare drum pop, vocalized as a massive, glottalized /t/ followed by a slowly fading lateral fricative: "T'ɬɬɬɬ." It's a highly manipulated sound and quite different from the natural ambience of a band playing in a room, no matter how large—which is basically what we had captured on tape. The sound Marshall imagined calls for particular miking techniques, especially on the drums. These procedures are used in order to limit the amount of natural room ambience on a recording because you're going to add ambience later on. This is all twenty-twenty hindsight. Getting that sound, not being dry, requires that you know what you're doing from the moment you walk into the studio, and none of us knew. At the same time, it involves being able to speak to engineers and to demand that they do what you want, and none of us had either the technical or the linguistic chops to do that. It takes a particular combination of technical knowledge and personality characteristics to tell the engineer that the drums sound like crap. Porcello (2002) describes a recording setup "in which the drummer played alone for well over two hours" (2002:76) while the sound engineers experimented with different miking and signal-processing techniques. So getting that sound puts demands on your budget as well. Phil was a patient and generous presence in the studio. Nobody wanted to be a jerk, nobody had the audio knowledge to perform such a rhetorical move, and nobody really knew that you're supposed to tell the engineer what you want. Engineers tack gracefully between knowing how to manipulate sound in the studio and being committed to a kind of archival naturalism, based on the authorizing endorsement of the flattest microphone responses, the least intrusive equalization, and so forth, so that what's preserved on tape is the natural and unfettered sound of the original performance. The sound that the Pacers imagined for their tape was somewhat unnatural and fettered. And of course, we didn't have the money for the kind of recording Marshall imagined: it's hard to squeeze a $10,000 recording session out of an $800 budget.

On top of that, Phil and I mixed sixteen songs in one day. The schedule was grueling and didn't leave much time for experimentation. We did some things. We gave Pat the wah-wah pedal he craved for "Apache Girl." We routed Kane's snare drum through a digital drum kit to give it a crisper pop. Phil equalized the vocals beautifully. But when I brought the finished tape back to San Carlos and played it for the band members, I couldn't help sensing a bit of disappointment behind the satisfaction of finally having something to show.

So, anyway, here's how the tape broke up the Pacers.

After some discussion, we decided to call the tape *Better Late Than Never*, based mostly on Marshall's having waited so long to record his songs. The one thing the Pacers knew was that they didn't want to do what many Indian bands do and simply call their first recording "Volume One." We toyed for a while with the idea of calling it *Home Grown* but in the end decided that the potential objection to the double entendre of local origin and marijuana use made this title more problematic than humorous and better avoided. I pointed out that with an hour of music, there was actually enough for two tapes, or one tape of only the best stuff. But, I think that in part with the sense that this might be their only chance to get something out there, the band decided to go for it all and give people their money's worth.

Completing the tape was one of the last things I did while I was living in San Carlos. In fact, Phil sent me the digital master in Austin, and it was from Austin that I ordered the three hundred cassettes from New Jersey. When they arrived, I grabbed a few of the overs for myself and shipped the rest to Marshall.

At first, all the news was good. They loved the tape. Both Bulldog and Eugene were playing it every week on their Apache-language programs on KJAA in Globe. Marshall and his wife told me that someone had driven all the way up from Phoenix to buy five copies. The money was going into a special bank account set up for the band. I heard a rumor that someone had burned the tape onto a CD so that it could be played on the jukebox at the Hon-Dah Casino near Pinetop.

Then I started to hear other rumblings. Marshall had a falling out with Donnie Ray when Donnie asked for a hundred tapes to sell on his own and Marshall said no. Pat was angry at Marshall again, or still, because Marshall was keeping all the money from selling the tapes. I never knew what Kane thought. But people started telling me that I should have sent a quarter of the tapes to each of them individually. In retrospect, they're probably right. What I heard, ultimately, was that I ended up in the middle of a dispute between the band members over what to do with the $3,000 generated by selling the tapes. The ones who wanted the proceeds divided among the members were countered by the others, who began to say, "Squirrel said we should do it this way," as if the money were mine or as if I were the band's manager—because white people understand how money works. I kept saying, "Nii dagah, it's up to you guys, it's your money. I don't care what you do with it." But that's probably not entirely true. I certainly liked the idea that I would be able to help the Pacers purchase some of the equipment they craved. It wasn't the most important thing in the world, but watching it fall apart because of the way I had mishandled the situation was extremely troubling to me and still is as I write about it now.

Nobody ever blamed me for any of it, and I convince myself that whatever was going on between the band members started many years before I knew any of them. That summer Marshall, Pat, and Darryl were going to jam out with Mono Sneezy on a float in the Fourth of July Parade on the Mescalero Apache Reservation in New Mexico, and they invited me to come along and play with them. But the Pacers were a thing of the past, and I couldn't help thinking that something I had done in trying to do the right thing, in trying to do what the band members wanted in return for putting up with me, had triggered that process of disintegration. During that same period, a few months after I returned to Austin, Marshall and Kane were involved in a serious car accident, and a few months after that Marshall was in a second wreck. That second crash made him retrospective about his life and his faith, and he came out of the experience a committed Christian. He now plays bass in a number of gospel bands and church groups.[17] People in San Carlos and Bylas sometimes lament the loss of the Pacers, remembering the good times and wondering why it couldn't be possible for Marshall to walk the straight and narrow but still fit country singing at bars and parties into his path. People assume that I feel somehow about not having the band to jam out with anymore. And I do, sort of. But I always tell them that given the choice of having Marshall and no band or the band and no Marshall, I'll take the former every time.

Pat and Darryl have joined up with the Sneezy Boyz, sons and nephews of the original Statics. Anson Sneezy, who wrote and sang the flip side of "My Little Girl" so many years ago, is also a member of the group. The group being mostly a family affair, people sometimes jokingly call Pat and Darryl "Pat Sneezy" and "Darryl Sneezy." Pat has a new guitar, and Darryl is playing bass with the band. I have sat in a couple of times with the Sneezy Boyz. They're good—Mono can sing his heart out in that upper register, and Buz is a rock-solid, in-the-pocket drummer. They sport a nice PA system, and they keep in tune using on-stage tuners that have LED lights that tell you whether you're sharp or flat.

In truth, the American colonies were as much a
dumping ground as an escape, a forgetting place . . .
a symbol of clemency, of a second chance.

—**Neil Gaiman,** *American Gods*

8

Everyday Ambiguities,
Everyday Identities

In numerous domains of culture, the problem of contemporary life emerges as the problems of homogeneity and identity. How can language be a socially shared system without prescription—if the meanings of words are indeterminate and the rules for combining them optional? How can nations be multicultural or multilinguistic? Does the concept of "nation" not imply that people will possess a shared and prescribed set of core beliefs of the national culture? Does it imply more than that—not simply national holidays or national pastimes, but national languages, religions, skin, hair, or eye color?

Conversely, what does it mean—or how does it work—when these

molds are broken? How are those instances that fall outside our expectations to be handled? San Carlos Apache expression is immersed
in this problem. Is it possible to stake a claim to identity that isn't expressed through practices that observers from the outside can recognize as qualitatively distinct from their own, coming from a different
history or tradition? Are "loss," "disintegration," and "revitalization"
the only lines along which talk about the expression of identity can run?
San Carlos Apache expression often confounds this sense of the source
materials of identity. It is not because there are no San Carlos Apache
traditions to be performed and referred to with first-person plural possessive pronouns (our language, our songs, our ceremonies). Rather, it
is because all expressions of identity, including those based in tradition,
take place within the clash of languages and practices that define the
contemporary reservation community. Because so much of the expression of identity on the reservation depends on an ironic and layered
rereading of that which is "not Apache," anthropologists are forced to
rethink the questions, What counts as culture, as cultural expression, as
identity?

The insistence that Apache identity is produced exclusively in the
performance of forms of traditional practice grows in part out of American anthropology's involvement in the dialogue around the definition
of culture. In the crafting of American anthropology's contributions to
that discussion, Native American communities have played a crucial
role. On that proving ground of culture theory, many have made persistent calls of "not traditional enough." The intertribal powwow isn't
traditional enough. Or maybe the powwow is a legitimate revitalization, but the 49s, with their Plains-style melodies and blues-inflected
English lyrics, aren't traditional enough.[1] Or the 49s are OK, but not
Indigenous's electric blues, not Robert Mirabal's or Tom Bee's or Bill
Miller's Native American pop music, not Clandestine's reggae or Lite-
foot's or Haida's rapping. For some, the work of these artists comes
too close to merely replicating the commercial expressive signs of the
mainstream, non-Native world. From that perspective, the possible redemption of these contemporary forms comes in the ability to detect
the sonic markers that index continued indigenous traditions—a flute,
a drum, a "nonsense syllable"—assuring that the colonial project of assimilation is, at best, incomplete.

At the same time, what place is to be given to the history and violence of cultural destruction in Native communities? At every turn, one

encounters the consequences of the extended, ongoing, and sometimes arduous cultural work of replacing indigenous practices by modernization. "Tradition is the enemy of progress," read one infamous sign outside a school in Navajo country in the 1950s. From this compressed mixing of messages, one senses that expressions of identity might be forged in a space in which the naturalized signs of the modernizing Bureau American state are revoiced and reinterpreted. On the San Carlos Reservation, perceiving the same signs in multiple ways is a political act, a mode of resistance no less supple or important than that of maintaining traditional practices. Indeed, this mixing was from the outset part of the very fabric of the conflicted practice of assimilation. The same fifth-grade boys who shouted "speak English!" at their Apache schoolmates in the schoolyard in Globe often approached those same Apache children at other times to ask, "How do you say our names in Apache?"

But acknowledging that a sign has a potential multiplicity of interpretations *in this particular context* maintains a faith that under other circumstances identity might be (was/is) whole and consistently reproducible, rather than contingent and constantly performed but never completely defined. Although San Carlos may be a particularly highlighted case, I want to argue in this chapter that ambiguity and indeterminacy lie at the heart of any identity production. I think the interesting question here is not, "Why are San Carlos Apache identities fluid?" but rather, "Why does the fluidity of Apache identity make people uncomfortable when the fluidity of other identities doesn't?" The ability to choose and refashion one's identity is a privilege accorded to some, but not all.

If America is the Land of Opportunity, one of these opportunities has been the opportunity to re-create yourself. For many, America symbolizes the chance for a new start, the ability to put the past behind you, to get a second chance, to pick yourself up, dust yourself off, and start all over again. This is one of the key ironies in the strict but contradictory compartmentalization of "real" identity and "real" culture on the San Carlos Reservation: America is the place where you can remake your identity.

In some instances, this rejuvenating spirit is represented as "pluck" or "gumption" and is sometimes presented as some kind of American national character—or at least personified in certain characters. In Arthur

Penn's film version of Thomas Berger's *Little Big Man* (1964), for example, Jack Crabb at one point works as a shill for Allardyce T. Merriwhether, a snake oil salesman. The two of them are eventually run out of town on a rail. Merriwhether reflects matter-of-factly: "Got caught, Jack, that's all. Life contains an element of risk." Incredulous, Jack says, "Mr. Merriwhether, you don't know when you're licked!" But his partner's reply is, "Licked? I'm not licked. I'm just tarred and feathered is all."

That game personification of the American entrepreneurial spirit is symbolically and inextricably linked with the way west, the complex image of a nation on the move. The significance of leaving the East and the past behind in the drive toward the future powers the American nationalist imagination. It is an image celebrated in the essays of Horace Greeley and the novels of Horatio Alger and satirized in the works of Nathanael West, Thomas Berger, and Ken Kesey.

A certain fluidity of identity goes hand in hand with this American sense of redemption, rebirth, and renewal. Stuart Hall touches on this re-creative possibility when he writes of America and the New World as "*Terra Incognita* . . . the beginning of diaspora, of diversity, of hybridity and difference." He explains, "The third, 'New World' presence, is not so much power, as ground, place, territory. It is the juncture-point where the many cultural tributaries meet, the 'empty' land (the European colonisers emptied it) where strangers from every other part of the globe collided. . . . It is the space where the creolizations and assimilations and syncretisms were negotiated" (1990:234).

I say that Hall "touches on" this issue because it is not entirely clear where colonial appropriations of indigenous practices fit into his model of colonialism and diaspora. Indeed, it is not entirely clear where indigenous communities themselves fit into his model of the New World, accepting as he does—albeit ironically—the "Virgin Land" thesis of American settlement. Still, Hall's call that "we should think . . . of identity as a 'production,' which is never complete, always in process, and always constituted within, not outside, representation" (1990:234) lends important insights to an exploration of the production of American identities.

For many, America has represented—and for some it has actually been—the place not only where you can be a self-made person, but also where you can acquire or invent a self-made persona (or at least a remade one).[2] Henry David Thoreau, whose *Walden* is one of the early earmarks of the American "spirit," was born David Henry Thoreau.

He reversed his given names after graduating from Harvard, perhaps as an exercise in self-creation. Rodolpho Alfonzo Rafaelo Pierre Filibert Guglielmi di Valentina d'Antonguolla came to the United States to become a farmer and ended up as Rudolph Valentino. His first wife was born Winifred Shaughnessy, but went on to fame as the renowned dancer and Hollywood set and costume designer Natacha Rambova.[3] Marion Michael Morrison and Archie Leach could become John Wayne and Cary Grant. Frank Hamilton Cushing could become Tenatsali, First War Chief and Bow Priest of Zuni (Green 1990). Sylvester Long, of mixed African American and Lumbee heritage, could reemerge as Chief Buffalo Child Long Lance, full-blood chief of the Blood tribe and eloquent spokesman for American Indian civil rights (D. Smith 1982). The publication of his autobiography, *Long Lance* (1928), made him the toast of New York, where he could be seen dancing in the Crystal Room of the Ritz Hotel with Valentino's former wife, Rambova. In the third chapter of the autobiography, Long Lance puts the matter of American identity plainly, writing, "In the civilization in which we live, a man may be one thing and appear to be another. But this is not possible in the social structure of the Indian, because an Indian's name tells the world what he is: a coward, a liar, a thief, or a brave" ([1928] 1995:41).

Long Lance, putting his finger on the pulse of modern American identity, correctly diagnosed a certain chameleon-like flexibility in its heartbeat. Think of William T. Phillips, who, as I mentioned in chapter 1, was rumored to be Butch Cassidy returned from Bolivia to settle in Globe. At one point in the history of the United States, it was possible for a notorious outlaw to become an Arizona rancher. Or at least it's thought that it was possible—that if you got into trouble in New York or Boston, you could hop on a train to Montana or Arizona, call yourself "John Smith," and people would say, "Hello, Mr. Smith," and you could start a new life. But maybe that is only a fiction. The "William T. Phillips" of Globe, Arizona, may well have been an imposter, an unsuccessful businessman from Spokane, Washington, who only pretended to be the returned Cassidy. Be that as it may, he was able to convince or bamboozle enough people to have made the issue contentious.[4] Although Cassidy may not have become Phillips, or Phillips may have had only partial success in becoming Cassidy, at some point Cassidy ceased being Robert LeRoy Parker, at least in the public imagination.

That kind of radical identity transformation is probably impossible today. Increased state surveillance in the form of Social Security cards, school and medical records, and the virtual reality worlds of banking, finance, and credit make it more difficult to escape the past and re-create your identity. Still, every so often we read or hear strange and enthralling tales: of the person who impersonated a surgeon and saved lives without ever getting a medical degree; or of big band saxophon-ist Billy Tipton, a woman who lived life as a man because, at least ini-tially, that was the only way she could secure work as a jazz musician (Middlebrook 1998).[5] Afternoon TV talk shows are filled with make-overs of every stripe and keep us titillated with the tension between new beginnings and inescapable pasts with shows about radical plas-tic surgery, gender bending, and the serial transformations of one pop star or another. Churches are filled with the born again, released from the past by their new relationship with Jesus. The medical and "beauty" professions entice us with liposuction, collagen injections, hair replace-ment, breast implants, and tinted contact lenses. Washington is filled to the brim with the reformed, the retooled, the repositioned. That was then, this is now. The promise of America is that you can change your nature.

But there's a trick. Although the hope is that redemption and re-newal are always possible, there is always a risk that they won't be. The twinned possibility and impossibility of changing persona—Can you thereby change the nature of your character?—haunts American letters. Surely this open question about escaping the past is part of the "American" subtext of Fitzgerald's *Great Gatsby*, of Malamud's baseball novel *The Natural*, of Kesey's *One Flew over the Cuckoo's Nest*, as it is of so many classic Western films *(Ride Lonesome, Man of the West, The Gun-fighter, The Naked Spur, Winchester '73)*: the tragic-dramatic problem of the person haunted by the past or of the inescapable past catching up with him. When American chickens come home to roost, they often take the form of the person who knew you in your former life. The tragic heroes of the Western—Ethan Edwards (John Wayne) in *The Searchers*, Jimmy Ringo (Gregory Peck) in *The Gunfighter*, the title character (Alan Ladd) in *Shane*, William Munny (Clint Eastwood) in *Unforgiven*—are men who come to realize that they cannot escape their pasts after all. As Shane says to young Joey Starrett, "a man has to be what he is."

The master narratives of American nationhood aren't one-sided. Be-cause progress exacts a price from tradition, they don't celebrate the victory of progress unequivocally. Because progress must measure it-self against something that stands still, these narratives often make much of rubbing together the triumph and the tragedy of Civilization's march to the Pacific. Filled with a certain imperialist nostalgia (Rosaldo 1989), they have a somewhat Darwinian tendency, proposing that for progress to occur, something must be sacrificed—the cowboy, the gunfighter, the pony express rider, the horse-drawn carriage, the open range, the family farm. It's difficult to underestimate the symbolic place of Native Americans within that play of imagery. Whether these figures recede peacefully and nobly—for part of the nobility of the "noble savages" was that they recognized the inevitability of their own demise—or with blood and violence forms another tension in the narrative of progress's progress. The Native inhabitants of America thus occupy a special place in the American nationalist imagination (Berkhofer 1978; Dippie 1982; Drinnon 1980; Goetzmann 1986; Pearce [1953] 1988; Slotkin 1973, 1985, 1992; Treuttner 1991). The tropes of history, nostalgia, and primitivism come into tension with those of rebirth, optimism, and the view to the future. This tension can be seen in the classic Currier and Ives lithographs of railroad trains passing into the burgeoning towns of America's western frontier (Buscombe 1988; Slotkin 1985). These works of art are chronological: in the movement "from" and "to," the past and the future are placed at odds with one another.

If one American nationalist dramatic trope is the desire to dissolve the past in the formation of a new identity, the tension inherent in that desire is put under greater strain in the unequal access to both the symbolic and the technological apparatuses of such transformation. To forget the past and begin anew is to claim control over your destiny, and there is differential opportunity to stake such a claim. If dominant ideologies claim the power to name, to categorize, to create the social categories, they also grant some people the freedom to ignore those categories in some circumstances. Perhaps everyone plays in the gray areas of social categories, but some people's play is more recognizable and successful than is others because these moves are contextualized, interpreted, and valued in conjunction with other discourses about race, ethnicity, history, gender, culture, and social position. The power to make the past disappear and to forge new beginnings is granted to particular groups of people, but denied to others. Who can forget the past and start over, and who can't? In the dominant mainstream American nationalist imagination, Indians can't. Or rather, they *shouldn't* if they are to remain important as an ever-present national signifier. Even if "we" all can forget who "we" are, "they" must remember who "they" are, for "us."

Because these cultural forms consider that both progress and resistant nostalgia are inevitable, the mainstream American national imaginary has readily embraced Indians who re-create themselves as more authentic. Donald B. Smith (1982) finds the most interesting facet of Chief Buffalo Child Long Lance's story the fact that he was an "impostor." More interesting, I think, is that by refashioning himself as a traditional full-blooded Indian, Sylvester Long was able to forge his acceptance by high society—and thus found his home among the other "impostors" of Broadway and Hollywood.

It's difficult to sidestep the role of early Native Americanist anthropology, and of its fascinations with language and disintegration, in accounting for this construction of what counts as a proper representation of an Indian identity. Perhaps no geographical area of the world has generated as much ethnological worry about what "they" were like before Europeans arrived as has the United States. For early American anthropology, the project of cultural preservation and reconstruction gave strong preference to the empirical evidence of continuity. And yet, as a later generation of anthropologists began to study, change was all around. Edward Sapir's elegant exposition of "genuine culture" ([1924] 1949) stands at this crossroads. On the one hand, it makes an eloquent statement about the role of creativity and adaptation as hallmarks of culture. On the other, it bemoans the loss of genuine culture among Native American communities in the loss of traditions. That is, Sapir couldn't see creativity in these changes, only disintegration.

Speaking on behalf of creativity does not paper over the massive loss, expropriation, and cultural genocide experienced by the San Carlos Apache tribe. But one of the complexities of tradition is precisely the way in which it creatively and ambiguously resists the narrative of progress. Native American tradition is not simply a Luddite insistence on backwardness that gives the entrepreneurial spirit of progress something to measure itself against. Certainly this description is one way of framing the argument: in this version, adherence to tradition is a form of resistance already co-opted by the mainstream discourse of the American national imaginary, implied in the dominant culture's ambivalence about its own dominant position. At the same time, the perplexity of traditions makes them difficult to "modernize." And the case for immutable tradition fosters irreconcilable differences with those who seem always to be there to question the authenticity of practices or beliefs: an archeologist who wants to dig, an astronomer who wants to build a telescope, a linguist who wants a verb paradigm, an anthropologist who wants to collect the text of a creation myth.

Therefore, if it's still the case that no figure is more revered or more politically powerful than the eloquent spokesperson for tradition, we can no longer avoid the compromises and complexities that are simultaneously present with that figure. Working in the late twentieth century with Bernard Second, a Mescalero Apache ceremonial practitioner, Claire Farrer recorded a version of the creation story that he told, which included the following lines:

> Their Father,
> the Sun,
> > gave Them
> > two things:
> on one hand He held
> > an object that was mysterious and it worked by itself;
> > it was deadly.
> One,
> > one Son took that.
> And in His other hand
> > He had the bow and arrow.
> > > And the other Son took that one.
> (My people's belief is that the White Man came from the One
> > that accepted the strange things that was,
> the thing that worked by itself.
> And we,
> the Apache people,
> came from the Son that took the bow and the arrow.) (1991:19–20)

We might be inclined to call Bernard Second's observation about the origins of the white man, presented as a parenthetical aside, a rationalized explanation of the contemporary world, a "not traditional" part of the narrative. But Harry Hoijer, working in the early twentieth century in the same community, was told the following:

6. The Creation [6]

(1) Now he had killed all of those different ones on earth who killed with their eyes. Now he was to create people.

(2) He made two mud [figures] just like men. He also made two just like women. He made all of them capable of speech. [7]

(3) Then, [to one] man and woman: "You two will be called Indians," he said (to them). "You others, you two will be called white men," he said to them.

(4) Then he set down [several things] for them. Child of the Water is to choose for the Indians [and] Killer of Enemies is to choose for the white men;[8] he put down a gun and a bow and arrow for them.

(5) Then Child of the Water [and] Killer of Enemies quarrelled with each other. "You choose first," they said to each other.

(6) A little later Child of the Water chose the bow and arrow for the Indians. "The making of these is understood," he said.

(7) Then Killer of Enemies picked up the gun that remained without saying anything.

(8) And then he put down two mountains for them. On one of them there was a heavy growth of vegetation. Indian food—wild growing things, deer, wild turkeys—all these were on it. The other mountain that lay there had nothing on it. Because it lay absolutely barren, Child of the Water chose [the former mountain].

(9) Then Killer of Enemies chose for the white man that mountain which [Child of the Water] had left. And that mountain which had nothing on it spread apart. From inside it, horses, the very best mules, cattle, sheep, pigs, chickens—all of these came out. In that way he gave [things] to the white man and the Indian.

(10) So the Indian lives on those wild growing things, "All varieties of deer, turkeys, [and] the things that are wild will they live on," he said.[9]

(11) "The white men, working, will live on cultivated plants," he said.

(12) Then he spoke thus to the white man: "Very far apart—on the other side of this ocean—you will live from one another. Whenever you see one another, you will fight—Indian with the white man," he said to them. (1938:13–14)

And so we must ask, for just how long have Apaches—or at least Mescalero Apaches—been telling creation narratives that include the creation of white people? For how long have Apaches been living their expressive lives in the collision of languages and practices inherent in the contact with encroaching European and American colonialism and modernity? For how many years have Apache expressions of identity been caught up in the ambiguous spaces made productively possible by those events?

By the judgment of mainstream representation and ideology, however, "they" are bound to history, place, and categorical authenticity and purity. Bound to history, not in the old sense that Apaches are inevitably disappearing and receding into the past, but rather that they remain a powerful symbolic part of the story of how America got to this point. In other words, it's not that Apaches are stuck *in* history so much as they are stuck *with* it. The binding to history is related to a further binding to place. The entrepreneurial spirit of American modernity links progress to mobility. This link is made manifest in part in the technologies of movement: trains, automobiles, airplanes, motion pictures. But unstated in that relationship of progress and movement is the notion that attachment to place hinders modernization.

The image of the westward-moving pioneer survives long after its actuality has become dust. A few days before F. Scott Fitzgerald died, he changed the name of his last novel from *Stahr — A Romance* to *The Love of the Last Tycoon: A Western*. In his notes for the novel, he paid homage to the image of the westward-pushing pioneer, writing, "I look out at it — and I think it is the most beautiful history in the world. It is the history of me and of my people. And if I came here yesterday like Sheilah I should still think so. It is the history of all aspiration — not just the American dream but the human dream and if I came at the end of it that too is a place in the line of the pioneers" (qtd. in Bruccoli 1977:vii).

This image, in its metaphorical extension, makes a virtue, albeit a problematic one, of rootlessness. As the second-generation descendant of postfrontier European immigrants, I can move from Brooklyn to Texas to Arizona to California to Massachusetts and think of each of those places as "home." Although I remain a New Yorker in some sense no matter where I go, I can go anywhere without losing a sense of myself. That is part of how I become "Americanized." The same does not appear to hold true for my friends in San Carlos and Bylas. The progress of empire makes mobility of both location and identity possible for "modern" Americans, but San Carlos Apache identity is bound up in locality, the last bit of an Apache land that used to stretch across New Mexico and into Texas and down into Mexico. Expansion and contraction: my friend Duane imagined that the space over which Geronimo and his people were pursued was "this whole reservation." Whereas it sometimes almost seems as if the original pioneers of the frontier conquered this vast continent simply so that I could be an "American" anywhere — to join F. Scott Fitzgerald at the end of that line — to leave San Carlos as an Apache brings with it a massive accumulation of ideologies about the loss of authentic tradition and genuine culture.

That people in San Carlos and Bylas may share in these dominant ideologies to one extent or another is not surprising. The locality of local ideologies resonates with the expansiveness of the mainstream. One blazing summer afternoon I stood with a woman I call "cousin," waiting to take some pictures at her family's Sunrise Dance.

"It's sure hot," she said.

"What do you expect?" I replied. "It's Arizona."

"Bylas," she said.

"Yeah: Bylas, *Arizona.*"

"No!" she insisted. "Just plain *'Bylas'*!"

There is a disjunction between her take on locality and mine. I enfold each locality into a larger imagined community, whereas she insists on locality's detachment from the national embrace that assumes localities can always be linked together in larger and larger entities within the nation-state.

What is the role of modernity in enabling these kinds of identities and identifications? As Carroll (2000) has argued, telegraph and telephone technology played a large part in helping mainstream America reimagine the ways in which various communities and regions of the country were connected. Whether the dearth of household telephones on the reservation has contributed to this difference, I don't know.[10] But it certainly fits with some popular mainstream notions about how poverty makes Apaches, or Indians in general, important to the nation. Mainstream American attitudes toward progress being as conflicted as they are (see, for instance, Almond, Chodorow, and Pearce 1977), Indians are often cast as the national repositories of rootedness, steadfastness, and authentic identity. Indeed, much American nationalist rhetoric about Indians, stretching back into the late eighteenth century, "amounts to formal public expression of American regret in the face of the tragic and triumphant meaning of the progress of civilization over savagery" (Pearce [1953] 1988:58). Those particular terms aren't used now — Pearce here was discussing the writings of Henry Knox, George Washington's secretary of war, and of President Andrew Jackson. Nevertheless, Indians continue to be imagined in terms of how their presence impacts the symbolism of stability and progress and thus of nationhood.

In this context, the Apache who speaks English, who drives a car, who puts ketchup on french fries at McDonald's, who hunts and gathers at the supermarket, who shops at Wal-Mart or Tower Records, who goes to church on Sundays, or who picks up a guitar and plays "Knockin' on Heaven's Door" presents a problematic figure. White people who shop at Wal-Mart may feel some ambivalence about it, but they're not necessarily betraying their cultural heritage when they spend money there.

San Carlos Apaches have been able to hold onto a number of traditional practices despite the massive efforts to excise them—for example, language, religious ceremonies, place-names. Although dire measures must be taken in the twenty-first century to keep the San Carlos dialect of Apache a vital and vibrant language, it has long outlasted the dozen other languages that Gustav Harders heard spoken in Globe in 1907. The survival of these practices is owing in part to the massive efforts of Apaches who have worked in the face of great institutional opposition to preserve them. It is also owing in part to the contradictory nature of the reservation itself—as either a place for the assimilation of Apaches into the American popular mainstream or as a place in which to cordon Apaches off from the American popular mainstream. The reservation has played both roles, sometimes simultaneously. Don't speak your language, but can you tell me what my name is in Apache?

But to say that San Carlos Apaches have held onto or lost certain traditions is not the same as saying that they have held onto or lost their identity. Identity is no longer tied exclusively to practices that are objectifiable as traditions, important as they are. To paraphrase Stuart Hall again, identity is not simply the expression or reproduction of something already produced, but is itself a production. Moreover, that production and expression of identity are contextualized within the contradictions of everyday life in the contemporary reservation communities.

In discussing the historical and political relationships between the local and the national, one older consultant matter-of-factly said to me regarding the way that the communities of the San Carlos Reservation have been overrun by the incursions of white people and their commerce, "What are you gonna do about progress? Progress is progress. . . ." "Progress," in all its ambivalent and ambiguous manifestations, must be included as a part of the stance toward the symbolic world in which contemporary San Carlos Apache identity is produced —for it is produced in a realm of historical imagination.

The type of statement made by this elder is often read as fatalism, the idea that there is nothing to be done. But when it comes to progress, it seems, everyone in America is fatalistic. Roy Harvey Pearce wrote of James Hall's melancholy over the removal of the Cherokees in the 1830s: "Hall's . . . hope to civilize the Indian was being dashed by the onrush of civilization itself. And no man could, in the end, regret the onrush of civilization" ([1953] 1988:73). The question isn't whether one is fatalistic, but rather what symbolic meanings are associated with one's fatalism about the inevitability of progress. How does one creatively engage with a progress that seems to take on a certain agency of its own, beyond the control of individuals, or even communities—even communities as large as the nation itself?

Rather than regarding this consultant's question as a mere expression of fatalism, then, we might more productively read it as a metadiscursive comment about social relations and histories—as a title, in a sense, for a genre of talk about everyday practices of identity. The problem of progress on the reservation is that San Carlos Apaches are presented with a stark choice: resist progress in order to maintain their identity as Other or embrace it and lose their identity. Everyone does not get to choose his or her own path of redemption and identity construction in this modern world.

But how can you know if or when you qualify to choose? One dilemma of dealing with Bureau Americans is that although they reserve the right to make the categorical rules, the rules themselves are ambiguous by definition: one of the tenets of democracy, after all, is that nothing is ever black and white, or, there are (at least) two sides to every story. And yet Indians, as a group, are consistently defined within a narrow range of categorizations. Why some people get to choose and others don't is a social, historical, linguistic, political, racial, and aesthetic problem.[11] Are there no third paths? The last time I saw Junior Dosela before he died, I drove him from his sister's house in Bylas to another sister's house in Moonbase. A graduate school colleague of mine was with me on that trip, and she asked Junior what he thought about the controversial telescopes that were proposed to be constructed on Mount Graham. "I don't know," Junior said, "I like to look at the stars, don't you?"—as if to say, "Why should white people be the only ones who get to look through telescopes?" Then Junior said, "The thing I don't understand is, How come the only thing we're allowed to say about it is that it's sacred? Why do we always have to be showing that we're more spiritual than other people? Why can't we just say that it's our land?" Here Junior showed us the horns of the dilemma: Is there really only one way out? Is there no way to play with the categories? Are they set in stone? Is there a way to insist on having the opportunity to take advantage of the (re)creative possibilities inherent in the categorizations of postmodern America?

What, then, is the meaning of an Apache like Junior picking up a guitar to sing Merle Haggard? One response (e.g., Fiske 1989; Lipsitz 1994) has been to celebrate the indigenization of the global: so long as something "really" Apache is added to the song, it's okay. And, of course, such additions are often made, as in certain songs by Apache Spirit that add the calls of the Mountain Spirits in the backing arrangements. But my point in this book is that the performance of identity need not be reduced to a question of iconic replications of practices that index tradition. It need not be something objectively "in" the expression or practice. It can be the affective response to the Merle Haggard song that people interpret as "Apache." Or, what marks the practice as part of the representation of identity may be in the ironic, distanced stance, the metacultural footing taken with regard to the practice, and the use of ambiguity and indeterminacy in the performance of it.

Drew Lacapa told a certain story both times I saw him perform, when he was master of ceremonies at the Miss San Carlos High School pageant and again when he was master of ceremonies at the Fourth of July Battle of the Bands in Whiteriver. He began it as if he were telling a myth: "Loooong time ago."

1 loooong *time* ago.
2 actually not too *long* ago
3 last *week*.
4 there was these *In*dian dogs.
5 they were *run*ning across the side of the *road*.
6 reeeeally *whack*in at the car's *tires*.
7 *"ri ri ri ri ri ri ri ri ri"*
8 you know how the kids' dogs do
9 they run out and bite the tires?
10 car drives off
11 *vhuuuuu*
12 people who own white
13 *white* people's *dogs* were on the *o*ther side.
14 car drives up.
15 dogs go
16 **"bowwow bowwow bowwow bowwow"**
17 don't *eeeeee*ven grab the *tires*
18 stay right on the *side*walk

19   get on the *grass*.
20   don't even get on the *road*.
21   **'bowwow bowwow"**
22   *wuuuuuu*
23   car drives off.
24   pretty soon the *white* dogs looked at those Indian people's *dogs* and
     said
25   "Hey!
26   "don't get up on the tire that's DANgerous.
27   "stay on the side of the road
28   "be ORganized.
29   "don't say *'ri ri ri ri ri'*
30   "gaa, wild Indian DOGS?
31   "be ORganized!
32   "say 'bowwow, bowWOW!'"
33   aaaaall *look* at each other like
34   "who's *this* guy tellin us what to do"
35   "white people's dogs."
36   you know?
37   scratchin their mange?
38   pretty soon another car comes by.
39   big pickup truck.
40   aaaaall those Indian dogs
41   start running *wild*.
42   didn't get on the *road*?
43   stayed on the *side*walk?
44   aall of em start saying **"bowwow, bowwow!"**
45   **"bowwow bowwow!"**
46   **"bowwow bowwow!"**
47   *aaaaaa*ll ways and the car took off
48   *huuuuuu*
49   pretty soon they all turned to one another looked at each other and
     said
50   "'eeeeí, 'bow wow.'"
51   and that's how the word *'eeí* came to be.

The typefaces in this transcription are meant to represent the stark shifts in vocality used by Lacapa in embodying the different characters and world-views in his story. Palatino depicts Lacapa's narrator's voice and the speaking voices of the Indian dogs. *Caflisch* denotes the "wild" barking of the Indian dogs. **Franklin Gothic Condensed** is used to depict the more staid, upright, "civilized" barking of the white dogs. I have used Tempus Sans to depict the scolding tone of voice taken by the white dogs in their instructions to the Indian dogs.

The story makes productive use of ambiguity at a number of junctures. First, it opens and closes as a "myth," thus playing with the form of storytelling, and the relationship between form and content. Second, the use of talking animals in the joke makes the points about human social relations on the reservation. Third, Lacapa has an uncanny ability to shift his body posture and movement, beyond my ability to describe it on the written page, in order to represent physically the image of a dog watching a car drive by. Finally, the joke relies on three bits of nonreferential utterance: the sound the Indian dogs make when they chase cars, the sound the white dogs make when they chase cars, and the emotive interjection that caps the punch line of the joke. The instruction that the white dogs offer demands that the Indian dogs shift their utterance from a "wild" to a "tame" version of barking (Rhodes 1994). The crux of the joke—that the white dogs act as if "bow wow" is somehow a more meaningful unit of lexical reference than "ri ri ri ri ri"—depends for its impact on certain dominant ideas about the relationship between language and meaning: the need for regularity and standardization in linguistic communication and the idea that the thing that distinguishes Bureau Americans from Indians is that the former reserve to themselves the right to tell others what to do and how they should do it.

On both occasions when I heard this story, the audience, including me, erupted in laughter. It struck me, though, on reflection, that I wasn't sure what I was laughing at. I thought I sort of got the joke, but I also thought that it must be culturally specific, a feeling that was confirmed for me when I was commandeered into telling the joke to an introductory anthropology class at the University of Texas at Austin and got no response at all. I had told the joke to about half a dozen people in San Carlos and elicited laughter every time, so I'm pretty sure it wasn't how I told it.

At the time I heard the joke, I mistakenly decided that the reason I didn't get it was that I was missing a *meaning*—that I didn't really understand what the Western Apache interjection *heí* (or, as I thought, *éí*) meant. As Drew Lacapa told the joke, the interjection *heí* is the only non-English word in the entire narrative. Interjections are a vitally important element of everyday discourse in San Carlos and Bylas. A number of Western Apache interjections have been imported, completely unmodified, into English-language discourse. Even as people fight for the survival of the Apache language in San Carlos, these interjections clearly mark the local dialect of English and thus mark one's speech as springing from this community. I decided that if I could get a better understanding of the meaning of this interjection, I would get a better understanding of the joke. As it turns out, a number of consultants told me that the interjection—not the short *heí* found in Apache, but the drawn out *'eeeeí*, spoken with a continuously rising intonation and often creaky voice—may not be Apache at all, but more intertribal in origin, perhaps more common on reservations than in nonreservation communities. In fact, Drew Lacapa later told me that he heard the joke from a Kiowa. One elder told me that people who use the drawn-out interjection are just trying to sound like the announcers on KTNN, the AM radio station in Window Rock, capital of the Navajo Nation. But this was early in my fieldwork, and the search for the meaning of this particle gave me something simple to do. As mistakes go, it turned out to be a productive one.

As a Western Apache interjection, *heí* is used when something turns out to be nothing or of no good. A number of people offered examples of how you would use the expression. When you're playing a song on the guitar and you get lost and mess up the chords, you say, "heí." When you put down ten bucks and roll the dice, and they come up snake eyes, you lose and you say, "heí." Or when your girlfriend comes to the door and says, "Don't come see me anymore because I saw you with another girl. So we're not sweethearts anymore, so good-bye," you go back inside the house and say, "heí." Still others gave me lexical glosses for the interjection. In reference to Drew Lacapa's joke, one said it means something like, "Hant'é ła' ágolzeehíí 'bow wow'?"—which he freely interpreted as, "What in the world does 'bow wow' mean, anyway?" Another explained its meaning as "'It'éégo ádishnii' niigo," which he interpreted for me as meaning, "As if they were the only ones who could say it better!" or the right way.[12] The implication of both interpretations is that *heí* was used in this circumstance to comment on the usefulness— or uselessness, rather—of the new way of doing things. "You know," said the first, "we used to chase the cars our way, and they're telling us to chase the cars their way, but what's the difference? Why not just do it our way? It's just chasing cars, anyway."

Edmund Hunter saw it differently. After telling the joke to him and his wife and relating what other people had told me—that *heí* in this case meant something like, "What does 'X' really mean?"—he said, "I don't think it's a question of defining 'bow wow.' I think it's the circumstance, that he can't argue with the white—he can't win, that's why he said, 'heí.'"

"How do you mean?" I asked.

"Whatever the Indian wanted to do, he can't argue with the white dog in order for him to do the Indian 'bow wow,' whatever it was."

"But when you say, 'They can't argue with it,' what does that mean?" I wanted him to clarify what he meant by "argue."

"Well," he replied, "what did the white man's say to the Indian dogs?"

"They said, 'Do it this way.' They said, 'You're doing it wrong, do it this way.'"

"Yeah," he said. "He would say, 'No, no, do it the Indian way.' He would say, 'Do it the Indian way, it's better.'" He laughed. "'It's better my way. If you don't want it, go do it somewhere else,' or something."

Edmund had latched onto something in the joke that I had noticed but had taken to be an anomaly, a simple plot device to move the story to the punch line: the Indian dogs do as the white dogs instruct them, even though they don't like being told what to do and think it's stupid to do things that way. And as another person said to me later on, the Indian dogs might continue to chase cars that way from that point on, even though they think it's stupid—but they would also have an ironic distance from their new practice from that point on. I now knew what Edmund meant by "argue." I also had an early inkling of why identity might depend as much on the attitude one takes toward the new as on the maintenance of the old.

"So the Indian dogs don't argue back," I said.

"In that instance he feels he can't do it," he said. "That's *our* problem," he continued. "We can't do nothing with, with the . . . ," his voice trailed off, then he exhaled, a huge sigh. "The dominant race," he concluded. Then he laughed.

Edmund began talking about the various ways in which relations between the San Carlos Apaches and the institutional representatives of the Bureau American mainstream have been predicated on domination of a coy sort, based as much on not telling as on telling, as much on setting up administrative mysteries as on offering aid. Part of the problem, Edmund said, was that "our tutors, BIA teachers, ministers from churches" want to approach everything as an individual problem and refuse to see difficulties as things that occur on a larger scale. Or rather, they recognize certain problems as "community" or "social" problems, but the only strategy they have for dealing with them is as individual cases—for each individual to solve his or her microcosm of the problems for him- or herself.

Even when assistance is offered, the supposed beneficiary may not be able to know what to expect. One time, Edmund told me, there was a man who came to the San Carlos Lutheran Church to give a guest sermon. "I forgot how many years he spent in South Africa," Edmund said. After the sermon, the church gave this pastor a dinner, and the people at the dinner were given the opportunity to ask him questions. So Edmund asked him how many diamond mines he'd seen and how the native Africans were treated there by the whites in authority, and about this pastor's stand on apartheid.

"And he didn't answer my questions," Edmund said. He continued, putting on a slippery, breathy, fast-talking, snake oil salesman's voice. "He said, 'Oh, there's a lot of diamond mines, but I never get a chance to go there, and talking about this other, African natives, whenever I leave my compound I have to sign a piece of paper, and I give it to the officials, and they give me permission to go among the natives. . . .' He never answered my question, what I was asking him. So that tells me that they don't want to tell, if they approve of that or disapprove of that." *That* being apartheid. This pastor was down in San Carlos to see if he could help the Lutheran church expand, and Edmund had been hoping to ask him some questions about helping build a bigger church. "But I stopped asking questions right there since he couldn't answer the question that I asked." More than the domination, what upset Edmund was the slipperiness that was part of how the domination works. They say "ask," then they sidestep the answers. Empty promise.

On this question of feeling the constant (if oily) pinch of the dominant race, Edmund worried that he was turning his "personal problem" into "everybody's problem," even though he said that he rejected that interpretation when it was offered by tutors, teachers, and ministers. During World War II, he was classified 1B because, he thinks, of a burn on his leg that he suffered, from which he still carries the scar. Instead of going into the armed forces, Edmund went to work. He relocated first to Phoenix, then to California, eventually staying in California for seven years, from 1942 until 1949. While he was living in Pomona, he said, "I had problems there—not with Negroes, or Mexicans, or whites"—then he reconsidered—"maybe whites, I don't know."

When he lived in California, he was reclassified 4F—he remembered receiving a classification card in the mail from Globe. So he went out and tried to get a job. In Phoenix, he had had no trouble finding employment, working in a laundry and then at Good Samaritan Hospital. But, he said, "I wasn't satisfied there," so he hitchhiked to Los Angeles and "worked around as a dishwasher, then a wood-turning shop, and then back to Riverside again I worked at Mission Inn as a dishwasher." The vegetable cook at Mission Inn was named Frank Works, Edmund remembered. "He used to tell me he was a Frenchman," he said. He told Edmund that he should go to San Pedro or Burbank and get a good job in the shipyards or in aircraft construction or maintenance. "'Why don't you go up and apply, get some good money instead of working here for seventy-five dollars a month, room and board.'"

"It sounded pretty good," Edmund said,

1   so I went down to San Pedro
2   no
3   I went to the L.A. employment office and they sent me to San Pedro.
4   and when I got to San Pedro they interviewed me and they told me that I didn't have a birth certificate.
5   so they can't hire me.
6   but they were hiring everybody right and left
7   black and white
8   and everybody else
9   turned me down for lacking a birth certificate.
10   so I went back to the employment office.
11   the guy said
12   "well
13   we'll send you to Burbank and we'll try aircraft and see what they say."
14   went to Burbank.
15   they said the same thing.
16   "well
17   we'll try to get you on a training program
18   let's try UCLA
19   you can become something over there that they're training
20   people over there
21   shipyards
22   and aircraft repairs
23   so we'll send you out there.
24   what are you interested in?"
25   so I just said
26   "well, let's try welding.
27   I can learn welding."

28 so I went off there.
29 same thing!
30 "no birth certificate
31 we can't take you."
32 so I came back.
33 this time the guy says
34 "well
35 we got an aluminum plant in Las Vegas
36 I'll send you out there and see if you can go to work there."
37 went out there
38 same thing
39 "no birth certificate."
40 came back.
41 personal problem.
42 I make it the problem of Indian people, I guess.

I have lined out Edmund's narrative in order to highlight his representation of how white people speak. As in Duane's story (told in the introduction), where the Pilgrims speak in the contemporary voice of the hippies and Vista workers who so often travel far distances to touch Indians ("hey, man, these guys are real easy to get by"), Edmund's Bureau Americans are also always saying "the same thing." Edmund references this point three times in his narrative. Twice (lines 30 and 39), the blunt phrase "no birth certificate" is uttered by white people from whom Edmund is trying to secure employment. He casts the voice of the first people who interviewed him in San Pedro as indirect speech ("they told me that I didn't have a birth certificate"), but as they were hiring "everybody, left and right" in San Pedro, and as the person at the aircraft plant in Burbank said "the same thing," by the time Edmund got to UCLA and the Las Vegas aluminum plant, his exasperation—in his life as well as in his narrative—at being told the same thing again and again comes out in the full, direct quotation (line 30–31), "no birth certificate / we can't take you." Edmund voices the Los Angeles employment office worker who sent him out to all these places in the same fast-talking manner as the Lutheran pastor who wouldn't say what he thought about apartheid. The employment worker in Edmund's telling also begins each of his utterances (lines 12, 16, and 34) with the same, Reaganesque "well . . ."

Edmund had a perfectly legitimate reason for why he had no birth certificate. He was born in 1918, and one was never filed. He had a legal and convincing substitute for a birth certificate, but the curtness with which he performs the final interviewers in the story of his quest for a job shows that these people in California weren't interested in any explanations, only in drawing the line around a category where they wanted it. Why Edmund didn't have a birth certificate and what he had in lieu of a birth certificate highlight once again the way in which white society was able to play with categorization in a way that Edmund could not and help us focus, again, on the ambiguity inherent in the production and representation of identity. "How come you need a birth certificate to get a job?" I asked him. "Did you ask them that, do you remember?"

Edmund said that he wrote the state of Arizona first, but they wrote back saying that apparently no birth certificate had ever been filed for him. So he wrote to the BIA superintendent in San Carlos, Mr. McCray, who sent him a notarized letter attesting that Edmund Hunter Jr. was a full-blooded Apache Indian born on the San Carlos Apache Reservation in Arizona. I asked again: "Why do you need a birth certificate to work?"

"It's required," he explained, "because they're at war, they have to go by what the law says."

"But it was required to prove what—that you were old enough?"

"No. They didn't know whether I was a citizen or not."

After a brief, stunned silence on my part, we laughed at the logic. "So you're telling me, what you're telling me is, you wrote back to Mr. McCray. He sent an official document that said, 'This man was a full-blooded Apache Indian born in San Carlos Arizona.'"

Edmund nodded, said, "Yeah, San Carlos."[13]

I was bewildered. "And, they still didn't know whether you were an American citizen or not?"

"That's what they said," Edmund said matter-of-factly. "There was a Romanian that tagged along with me all, everywhere I went, he was there, he also had trouble getting a job."

After that, Edmund decided to look for work through the help-wanted ads in the Los Angeles papers. He saw one asking for a worker at an orange ranch located between Ontario and Pomona, and he went out there. By this time, his wife and first-born were in California with him, but he went out to Pomona by himself, leaving them behind in Los Angeles. The owner of the grove was named "Pete—Womke. German. He told me he was a fighter pilot in the First World War." At the end of Edmund's first week on the job, "he told me, 'I'm gonna have to let you go because I can't take your family here with me.' And his mother was there, and she heard him, and she called him, and they talked about it (I don't know what they said), and so he came back and said, he told me, 'Well,' he said, 'my mother said it's OK that I take you, and you can go get your wife and bring her back, you can keep on working for me.'" So they stayed there, and Edmund worked for Womke for about six months.

Then when orange season was over, "He saw to it that I got employment before he let me go. I ended up, he got me a job in a fertilizer plant, and that's where I spent my years as a worker in a fertilizer plant, during the war. For eighty-seven and a half cents an hour. While the world war plant workers were making somewhere around four dollars, six dollars an hour, labor." He laughed. "Because of a birth certificate." The irony of the situation in which an Apache can't get a job because he can't "prove" that he is an American was hardly lost on Edmund. Nor was the idea of what it means to have worked in a fertilizer factory. "But," he said, underscoring the irony and ambiguity of his situation, "a *German* and an *Englishman* hired me, helped me that I had a job."

In the negotiation and legitimation of identities, white people set the terms of engagement. They are entitled to decide upon the categories and how to fill them. The problem, however, is that, even if you ask them, they, like the South African pastor, will not ever really tell you where they stand. Their own categories are slippery and vague, filled with an ambiguity that reinforces their control of the categories.[14] Logic dictates that a full-blooded Apache Indian must be an American, and because Native Americans were made citizens in 1924, in 1942 they must have been citizens.[15] Yet whereas one apparatus of bureaucracy recognizes "blood" as an indicator of categorical membership—itself a problematic standard (Strong and Van Winkle 1996)—another recognizes only proper paperwork. Thus is it possible to be a "full-blooded" American Indian, or Native American, yet not to be an American.

Edmund's stories and others, such as Drew Lacapa's dog story, open up narrative spaces in which people can resist the onslaught of these shifting but always dictated categories. Talk about white people is an important area in which discourse and politics meet on the reservation. These spaces close quickly, perhaps because, as Basso says, Apaches respect brevity and sketchiness in expression, but also perhaps because, as Edmund says, "We're up against something that we can't lick. We *know* we can't lick it." So the only thing left to do is to say "heí." Telling silences in the face of bald-faced dissembling is also important. Edmund says "heí," but the Lutheran church was never expanded.

Talking back to the categorizations dictated by whites insists that whites not be given the last word. With apologies to Spivak, such back talk is a form of strategic antiessentialism, claiming the agency to create and re-create ambiguous expressive identities to fit a given situation, to be represented not simply as one narrowly defined categorical *thing* to suit the dominant culture's needs. Playing with the ambiguity of cultural categories, then, is not a practice that belongs exclusively to the field either of domination or of resistance. But as assertions of power and identity—or of the power one has over the representation of one's identity—they are subject to differing constraints and emerge in different styles. One group plays with ambiguity without necessarily recognizing it; the other recognizes it without necessarily getting to play with it. At the same time, hard categorization is not exclusively non-Apache. People in San Carlos and Bylas, given the proper context, are just as likely to insist upon the hardness of cultural categories (*this* is Apache, *that* is not) as are those from off the reservation. But none of these practices can be judged independently from the contexts in which they act as responses and answers to the prevailing material conditions of identity production.

One can imagine—if one has not actually heard it, as I have—white people saying such things as, "I really don't feel like a white person," or "I really feel more Native," or even "I was (might/must/could/should have been) an Indian in a past life."[16] It is, however, rare to hear and more difficult to imagine the reverse, wherein Indians say, "I really don't feel like an Indian," or "I really feel more white," or "I'm Cherokee, but I'm proud of my one-three-thousand-two-hundred-and-five white heritage," or even "I was (might/must/could/should have been) a white person in a past life." This property of identity is not commutative. Given that Apaches at the Phoenix Indian School were instructed to dream in English, that fifth graders at Globe Elementary School would yell "Speak English!" to Apache children playing in the schoolyard, one might guess which group should have the ability to "think like" or "feel like" the other. And yet the claim is consistently made in the other direction.

This question of how it "feels" to be one thing or another is the crux of the issues addressed in this book. Ultimately, of course, it is not a question that I can answer with any authority. But it is an important issue to be explored, for if "being Apache" is a feeling, then the exploration of Apache identity must be an exploration of that feeling. And the exploration of feelingful material is an important window on that sense of identity.

It strikes me, for instance, that the incidents related in this book—Drew Lacapa's story about the Indian dogs, Edmund Hunter's story about his degrading experiences in the Los Angeles basin, Marshall's performance of the old Apache at Top of the World or his imitation of the Fenders singing "Wine"—are related in that in all these incidents the understanding of the experience is in some sense removed from a strict understanding of its rational categorizations. Drew Lacapa, Edmund Hunter, and Marshall Bylas reveal knowledge in the affective meaning of experience. They do so by highlighting the indeterminate and ambiguous nature of the characters and situations depicted—in the nonreferential, in the meter, stress, vocality, and repetition, rather than in lexical meaning. Drew Lacapa condenses the entire experience of being an Apache dog by the side of the road and taking orders from the white dogs across the street into a single, nonreferential, nonlexical, emotive interjection. Edmund Hunter depicts his incredulity at his World War II experience through his representations of the way white people speak—either talking fast or always saying the same thing. (Years later, he told me, someone came through town recruiting Apache students for UCLA. With a laugh, he said he wanted to march up there and say, "Hey, what are you doing out here for UCLA, they refused to take me one time!"). Like Marshall's performance of the nostalgic old man, told at the beginning of the book, identity is made to stand not for *something*, but for a tense symbolic *relationship*, a recognition of power relations in identity's representation of itself. These performances force ambiguity onto the expression of identity, through a punning reversal of English and Apache terms and by being presented through an ironic and joking frame.

The poetics of identity on the San Carlos Apache Reservation takes advantage of the feelingful, nonreferential aspects of linguistic and other symbolic modes of expression. The struggle over the meaning of the ambiguous signs of modernity means that identity is perhaps always performed in the space of desire (K. Stewart 1996), in the productive gaps that exist between signifier and signified, word and world, sign and referent, intention and interpretation, speaker and hearer.[17]

If, as I have argued, there is a relationship between semiological or semiotic ambiguity and affective meaning, then this relationship is where musical expression gains a particular kind of evocative power in the performance of identity. Music highlights the vagueness of all cultural experience. It cannot be reduced to an appreciation of the truth value of referential statements, to a gloss, to a paraphrase. Music highlights the nonreferential, moving along a line from sense to sensuousness, from grammatical parallelism to repetition, from reference to sound. As a communicative, expressive medium, musical understanding often occurs in the coparticipation with a performance—in tapping feet, bobbing heads, rubber necks, clapping hands, snapping fingers, dancing bodies. I once asked a woman at a party in Soda Canyon why it seemed that everyone moved out onto the dance floor for "Born on the Bayou." She looked at me as if I must be the stupidest Martian that could possibly have been sent to reconnoiter the planet Earth. "Why?!" she asked, incredulously. "Bad *music*, that's why!!"

Participatory responses embody nonverbal, felt meanings of musical expression and experience. Apache Spirit usually concluded their performances in San Carlos with a ranchera-style song that they called "Apache Mexico." Pat, who played a version of this tune with the Pacers, said that it was an adaptation of a song originally done by the Zuni Midnighters. When people heard this beat, the alternating *ng-chk, ng-chk, ng-chk* of the Tex-Mex border polka, they poured out onto the dance floor or into the backyard or the driveway and linked arms to dance a traditional Apache round-dance. Go figure. If you asked people why they did it that way—well, when *I* asked people why they did it that way—the response was a dumbfounded, "I don't know, that's just the way we do it."

This contemporary Apache response to a country band playing a Mexican-style number raises a core issue. What if musical expression—not to mention expression in general—through its ambiguous evocation of indeterminate affect opens up equally ambiguous and indeterminate cultural, political, historical, and personal spaces in which to work out the felt meaning of identity? We saw this opening in the deeply moved responses many people had to Boe Titla's songs about

Chiricahua Mountain and Mount Turnbull. We also saw it in the long-standing, feelingful relationship people on the reservation have had with the song "Mathilda" and in Big Bell's moving, embodied response to hearing it performed by the Pacers. And we saw it in the Pacers and in the other bands discussed in chapter 3, whose careers and whose music encapsulate personal, community, and cultural histories.

As I have said all along, music is not alone here, by any means. That language is a performed, embodied, interactional medium, in which expression and understanding are achieved through coparticipation, has been a key and productive insight of both discourse analysis and conversation analysis, for all the theoretical and methodological differences that divide them. Studying the social life of language is qualitatively different from studying language. The distinction opens up onto the full range of human expressive modalities. Just as other culturally achieved forms of expression are amenable to linguistic anthropologists' insights about talk, so too is talk amenable to insights from the study of other domains of meaningful cultural expression.

How does one construct an identity in modernity? Expressivity fosters a deeply, personally felt sense of imagined community (Anderson 1991), a deep personal identification that is imagined to be shared with others who experience the same expressions. But a definitive reading of the distinctive features that define the relationship between expression and culture becomes problematic in contexts of colonial domination and upheaval. Because of the ambiguity of the participatory spaces created by expressions and by the deeply and simultaneously personal and social identifications forged within that ambiguity, we can no longer predict what expressions will be indexically linked with what felt senses of cultural reality. That is to say, we can no longer predict that a feeling of Apache identity will be exclusively tied to experiencing Apache cultural expressions.[18] Rather, the poetic indeterminacy of expressivity opens up the possibility for a wide range of indexical links to be made in both aesthetic and political spheres. The participatory space of expression becomes a space of reversal, recombination, and juxtaposition.

These reversals, recombinations, and juxtapositions take on a number of forms. They may be carnivalesque, mocking and unmasking the dominant social order, in the manner of "signifyin(g)" (Gates 1988). Down at the river that flows through Jurassic Park, a drummer I knew opened a momentary interpretive window onto a stereotype by adding words to the typical Hollywood Native American drumbeat: "IN-dian, in-dian, IN-dian, in-dian." Or these reversals may take on the guise of a more formal hybridity. For example, there may be a hybridized lamination of text and tune, as when MacArthur Williams sets his Buddy Holly–influenced rockabilly melodies to Apache lyrics or as when Boe Titla composes crying, George Jones–inflected country songs to evoke in English the memories of places and pasts that hold important social memories for the people of Bylas, San Carlos, and Peridot. Recombinations may reference formal systems of cultural expression, as when Apache Spirit juxtaposes the bells and calls of the Mountain Spirit dancers onto their country songs as rhythm instruments and background vocals.[19]

The formal play of hybridity does not end there, of course. If it did, then we would be limited to a sort of art-critical discussion of how effectively people put things from column A together with things from column B, an evaluative discussion of knowingly artful hybrid expressions. Even if we take those types to be the purest statements of contemporary identity, we have not quite identified what they are a distillation of. How is identity fashioned by this means? How are people asking questions at the same time that they are making statements? How do they say "yes," "no," and "maybe" all at the same time? To reduce this issue to the combination of expressive elements of divergent origin assumes that the attribution of those divergent origins is unproblematic, that there is an unquestionable clarity in the surface representations. It also implies that identification with identifiably "Indian" elements is necessarily more primordial, more meaningful, and more powerful than identification with other elements. The elements of everyday life are messy, however, and the people in San Carlos and Bylas are full-time Indians, whereas such an attribution of the meaningful provenance of expressive forms can only be the result of a tertiary analysis, not of the lived density of everyday experience. If the relationship between expressions and cultures were so straightforward, why would people choose the ambiguous, roundabout ways and means of art to express them?

Certainly there are times and contexts in which people in San Carlos and Bylas say, "this is Apache" and "this is white," or "this is ours" and "this is yours." But to reduce these uses of possessive pronouns to statements of identity is to reduce the ambiguous flow of identity in everyday life. Marshall's pride in the light touch on the guitar that he learned from his music teacher at East Fork was something he felt distinguished him from other musicians on the reservation. To say that people in San Carlos identify with the Mountain Spirit calls and bells in Apache Spirit's songs implies that they are somehow distanced from Apache Spirit's country-western sound. This claim is clearly an oversimplification, and I would expect that many people who have represented the question of identity in terms of this kind of positive correlation would agree that people in San Carlos and Bylas identify with country-western, rock, and reggae as well as with identifiably "Indian" expressive elements. But if that is the case, then when we ask, "How do they combine 'Indian' with 'non-Indian' expressive elements?" we are asking the wrong question.

Rather, I think the ethnographic issues are: What is unique about the aesthetic experience of popular culture in this community? What is this space that people desire, and how do they get there? In its purest, most transcendent form in San Carlos and Bylas, the participatory space of expressivity becomes expansive over place and time. In those moments, the wall around the present becomes transparent, and the imagined community moves beyond the bounds of the now to incorporate people who lived and suffered and felt in the past.[20] The transformative aesthetic moment is articulated in a discourse about place, feeling, and history. "Apache culture," in this sense, is not a collection of indexically marked ideologies, values, texts, and practices. Rather, it is a deeply and feelingfully sensed identification with a shared history that flows through the present reservation communities. In that space, past and present become juxtaposed, almost interchangeable. The feelings engendered by this participatory space are available to and sharable among all Apaches in the imagined community. The space is opened up by things coming together in a sort of magical alignment. In those instances, everyday life slips easily into moments that are thick with historical significance. These layered and feelingful juxtapositions crop up in different ways. When people drive past a certain place, when they hear someone embody the voice of an ancestor, when they hear a certain song on the radio, when they think of the Pacers playing "Sail Away" in the icy December cold in Bylas, at a Christmas party on a front porch in Southside—Pat getting a tone as crisp as the night air out of his guitar, Darryl hitting the ride cymbal with his light touch, Kane crashing the snare drum on the off-beats with his whipping stroke, Marshall singing the song made famous by Sluggo. Well, it's not all of the time, of course;

a lot of the time it's just partying and dancing. But sometimes things happen.

One thing I learned from playing with the Pacers was that the people dancing to the band in Chinatown or Rainbow City or Curley's or Mark's were not waiting for the song to finish. In fact, they wanted it to go on, and one of the band's tricks was to make songs flow one into the other, like moving from "Gloria" to "Suzie Q" to "Born on the Bayou" and back to "Gloria" again, or from "Fly Like an Eagle" to "Slipping into Darkness" to "Get Up, Stand Up." The songs had similar beats and keys. People want the music to keep going, and if it can't, they want the next song to start soon. Which is why tuning up the Pat Margo way was sometimes comically annoying to the other band members. Two things I learned about musical expression from the Pacers, with all due respect to the hundreds of textualist scholars in Western musicology who have said otherwise, are that it is the continuing tension of what goes on during the temporal span of a performance that is important, and that the achievement of resolution is not what musical expression is necessarily about. Similarly, I am not sure I have a fitting resolution to this book. Bored readers may disagree, but I do not really want it to end and would like it to go on a bit longer. And so I offer a brief coda, which I hope will help tie up the key ideas of complexity, ambiguity, identity, history, and the everyday. It is a story about Ray Stevens, otherwise known as Bulldog.

Bulldog always wanted to be an artist. When I began my fieldwork in San Carlos, he was recently retired from the U.S. Forestry Service. The first time I came to San Carlos in the early 1970s, Bulldog was still working for Forestry, and he used to run a soap-box derby every summer, down the winding hill that leads to the Forestry office in Seven Mile Wash. As I mentioned in the introduction, that is how I first ended up going to Bylas: we were helping kids build their soap-box derby cars, and I was the only one who knew how to put the steering in.

Bulldog used to host a radio show called *Indian Trails* on Sundays on KJAA in Globe. Over the years, he had amassed a huge collection of Native American music in all styles—famous traditional Apache singers, country songs, gospel music, powwow songs, 49s, rock and roll, tribal songs from around the nation. And chicken scratch, the Mexican German border polkas taken up by Chicanos and Tohono O'odham alike. Ray prided himself in having been the one to introduce chicken scratch to the reservation. He often sponsored chicken-scratch bands to come up from Tohono O'odham country to play. His love for border polkas helped fuel ongoing rumors in the community that Ray was really part Mexican. Or part Chinese, or part Swedish. His family was rumored to be a mixture of just about every ethnic and national group that had made its way into Arizona at one point or another. Anyway, the one song he always wanted but could never find was "The Convict and the Rose," with Apache Spirit backing Don Hayes. Even without that song, his collection was impressive, and every Sunday he used to drive into Globe to do his radio show. When he retired from the Forestry Service, he also gave up the show—when I met him again, he wasn't doing it any longer—but he was proud of what he had been able to do. Even the born-again Christians would tune him in on Sundays, he said, "even though they're not supposed to listen to it."

When I got to San Carlos in 1994, I went over to the chuck wagon that Ray runs at lunchtime—try the stuffed frybread, if you're ever there—and reintroduced myself. He didn't remember me, but he remembered the soap-box derbies. I had figured that because he had the radio program, he would be a good person to talk to about music. He invited me to stop by his house. A few days later, late in the afternoon, I did stop by. Bulldog was outside under the shade, putting together a dish cabinet for the kitchen. He had seen something like it in a magazine and decided he could use one and was creating it from his memory of what he had seen. I helped measure and saw and nail, and then we stained the outside of the cabinet, while Bulldog played some of his tapes for me.

As it turned out, though, Ray was not really all that interested in talking to me about music. What he wanted to tell me about was all the things he had seen up in the mountains and the pine forests while working for Forestry. All the old things, like the pueblo ruins. Marshall used to say similar things about his years with the Forestry Service; he once told me about the time he was doing helicopter flyovers, taking aerial photographs with a stereo camera; they flew over an old pueblo ruin, and the ladders were still intact, but there didn't appear to be any way that you could get to it from the ground.

"I used to study about the old Pueblo ruins," Bulldog said. "They disappeared," he continued, with a note of surprise in his voice. "Like somebody just left it there. All they did is just take what they could carry, and they just left. They don't know where they went, they just left."

He told me about a rock he had seen. "Apaches used to live near a '1917' sign," he said and described the rock he had seen with what must have been the year carved into it. "A long time ago they used to live there," he said, but he couldn't figure out why someone would have carved "1917" into a rock. "Let's go up there sometime," he said, but we never did—his wife worried that his heart would not take the strain.

One time when I went by his house, Bulldog invited me in. I was unprepared for the flood of imagery that inundated my eyes when I walked through the door. Every wall of the living room was covered from floor to ceiling with his paintings and wood carvings. Landscapes, Indians on horseback, Hopi kachinas, Apache Mountain Spirits. "I always wanted to be an artist," he said, showing me around.

Another time he showed me the airbrush he had bought in Tempe with some casino winnings. He had seen people using them and had wanted one for some time. So when I went to San Francisco about a week later to visit a friend and take one of my few breaks from fieldwork, I stopped into a bookstore and picked out a book about airbrush techniques with pictures illustrating ideas that I thought maybe Bulldog could use.

I stopped by his place again when I got back and gave him the book. He offered to paint a T-shirt for me in return. He grabbed a new white T-shirt from the stack that he had bought for this purpose and asked me to plug in the airbrush. He stretched the shirt across an easel, holding it in place with clothespins. He looked at the shirt, gathering his thoughts.

"Think of something!" his wife called out from the doorway, from where she was watching.

"'Think of something,' she says," Bulldog mumbled to himself. He continued to wait for inspiration. He ran his hand over the shirt, thinking of a possible design.

"You want I should do it from my mind or from a photo?" he asked me presently. I said I didn't care. That probably wasn't too helpful.

"Do it from your head!"

"'Do it from your head,' she says," Bulldog mumbled to himself. Then he got an idea and went to work.

He attached a small jar of blue paint to the airbrush and sprayed blue swaths across the T-shirt to represent the sky, then a thin blue line to outline mountains, and another patch of blue below that to represent a lake. I noticed that Ray was left-handed.

"You see that?" he said. "It's gettin' there." He next attached a jar of yellow paint and sprayed yellow between the mountains and the water, and then more below where he had put the water. "You have to be careful," he said, "because it gets plugged up real easy." Looking over his work, he surmised, "It needs a little red, brownish color." He took out the red paint. He sprayed the red over the yellow, a long swath beneath the water, then short strokes between the water and the mountains. Next he attached a jar of white paint to the airbrush. "It comes out somehow," he said, "yellowish, greenish, bluish," whatever color had been there before.

"I'm trying to learn better," he said. "Não faz ma, não faz ma. You know what that means?" he asked me. I didn't. "It means 'it doesn't matter.'"

"Is that Apache?" I asked.

"No. It's Portuguese. During the Korean War I was stationed in the Azores for two years, picked it up a little bit." He took the green paint and sprayed to make trees at the far edge of the water and a big saguaro cactus in the dirt at the near edge.

"You like it?" he said. I said yes. "Let's see, what else is green . . . ocotillo," he said, then painted in the long spiny fingers of an ocotillo plant. He fixed one of the other cacti, then returned to the yellow paint to highlight them. "You have to be real careful with this one," he said. "Gotta have a magic touch. I'm not good enough yet, still trying to get the paint to flow free." Then he told me a little about the history of the airbrush, that it was "developed in Germany somehow, in eighteen something, for photographer work." He said that when he got good, he wanted to do a picture of the Triplets and of Stanley Butte.

Bulldog rooted around and pulled out a stencil and started spraying through the letters, which spelled out "Memories of Point of Pine."

"Why *memories* of Point of Pine?" I asked.

Ray stopped. "Oh, did you want it to say something else?"

"No," I replied. "Just, why *memories*? Why not just Point of Pine?"

"Oh!" Ray said, a little relieved. "It's a song!" He went back to airbrushing the title onto the shirt. "When I retired from Forestry, Boe Titla wrote that song for me."

The next time I saw Boe, I tried to confirm what Ray had said. At first Boe said no, he didn't write that song for Bulldog. Boe and I started talking about the song, and at one point I asked him about one of my favorite lines in the song, "excuse me my darling / there's a place I can't forget."

Boe then said, "Okay, that's the one that I refer, my mind went back to Ray. See, Ray Stevens, he grew up in Point of Pines. When he came down, I seen his wife. You know that, 'excuse me my darling,' it can be, it can be for anybody. You know, it can be for anybody but, I just picture him. That when he came down, he used to tell that, 'Kehéé, my wife tells me that, "seems like that's your home, over there."' So I kinda used that, you know, expression there."

It's possible for you to be in one place while your mind is in another. As noted earlier, Britton Goode said that in the old days some Apaches were so powerful that they could just picture a place in their minds or just speak the names, and they would be transported there physically. That probably doesn't happen so much now, but a song can transport someone back to other times and other places. "I have memories over there," Ray told me about Point of Pines. "You picture it in your mind, that the memory's still there," he said. "People look at memory as an object that's still there. So Boe wrote that song for me." Well, it does not really matter if Boe wrote the song "for" Ray in the sense that the song is dedicated to Ray or that the character singing the song could only be Ray. What matters is that when Ray hears the song, he feels himself in it, and it transports him back to other times and other places—that Boe took Ray's memories and helped make them a sharable part of contemporary identity by turning them into a song.

San Carlos Apache Pronunciation Guide

Guide adapted from Basso 1990:xix–xx

The San Carlos dialect of Western Apache contains five vowels:

a - as in *father*
e - as in *bed*
i - as in *bid*
o - as in *go*
u - as in *cool*

The last two are actually variants of a single phoneme, but speakers detect a difference and realize it in their writing of Apache. If you pronounced your *u* as *o*, you would be noticeably mispronouncing some words, so I have maintained the distinction in my own writing of Apache. I note some exceptions for the *u* sound in this guide.

All the vowels may be short or long. This is simply a matter of the duration of time taken to speak the vowel. In other words, long vowels are not diphthongs the way they are in modern English. They retain the sound quality indicated in the list of vowels but are spoken for a longer period of time. Vowel length is indicated in the text with double vowels—that is, *aa* is the long form of *a*. (The case of *u* is unique, the result being that *u* is never long.)

All of the vowels except *u* may be nasalized, which means that when speaking, you exhale air from the lungs through the nose as well as through the mouth. You can practice this by saying a word such as *gong*, an English word that ends with a nasal consonant (meaning that air is exhaled through the nose). Say the word slowly, and as you feel the back of your tongue rising to make the *ng* sound, and as you feel air begin to escape through your nose, stop your tongue before it finally closes off the airway to your mouth. You should now be pronouncing the *o* of *gong* as a nasal vowel. Nasal vowels are indicated in the text by a hook placed underneath the vowel, for example, *ą* and *ąą*, *į* and *įį*. Again, the *u* variant of *o* is an exception: *u* never appears where *o* is called for, and therefore *u* is never nasalized.

Vowels may also be pronounced with high or low tone; *u* is always high. High tone is indicated by an accent mark over the vowel (e.g., *á*, *éé*), which indicates that it is pronounced with a higher pitch than are other vowels within an utterance. In some words, the consonant *ń* is also pronounced with a high tone.

Many of the consonants in San Carlos Apache are pronounced in a similar manner as they are in English. These are: *b, d, ch, h, j, k, l, m, n, s, sh, t, w, y*, and *z*.

The consonant system of Western Apache also contains the glottal stop. This is the stoppage of air one hears in the middle of the English expression "uh oh." In the Apache text, glottal stops are indicated by an apostrophe ('). In Western Apache, the glottal stop can occur before or after any of the vowels. Certain consonants and consonant clusters are also "glottalized."

The sounds of the Western Apache language also include consonants not found in English. One of these consonants is a lateral fricative, also known as a "barred l" or "slash l," which is written in the text as *ł* (or *Ł* at the beginning of a sentence). The sound is made by moving your tongue into the position to pronounce the *l* sound as in English and then exhaling as if you were saying the sound of the letter *h*. In some orthographies, the sound is in fact written *lh*. The sound is often misheard by English speakers as *th*. It is very similar to the Welsh *ll*.

Other consonants and digraphs include:

dl - as in the middle of the word *middling*. This sound never occurs at the beginning of words in English, but it does in Apache, as in the word *dláád* (moss).

dz - as in the final sound of the word *kids*. Again, this sound can occur at the beginning of Apache words but is never in that position in English.

g - always as in *go*, never as in *gentrify*

gh - A sound not heard in English, it is the voiced version of the *ch* sound found in German words such as the name of the composer Bach, or the *j* in Spanish *bajo*.

hw - as in *where*

tł - This sound combines a *t* with the lateral fricative described earlier.

ts - as in the final sound of *pots*

zh - as in the middle consonant of *treasure*

Certain consonantal sounds in Western Apache are glottalized, which means they are combined with a glottal stop. They are written with the glottal stop after the affected consonant or cluster. One way to practice them is to begin with the airway of the glottis closed, pushing the air for the initial consonant out of the mouth only, not from the lungs. The glottalized consonantal sounds of Western Apache are *t'*, *k'*, *ch'*, *tł'*, and *ts'*.

People on the San Carlos Reservation speak a number of different dialects of Apache. The most common distinction is between the San Carlos and the Bylas dialects (the latter a variant of a dialect more commonly found on the White Mountain Reservation to the north), but there are also speakers of the Tonto Apache dialect, as well.

Transcription Guide

My principle aims in the lined-out transcriptions in this book have been to preserve visually the pace and pause structure of the discourse as it was spoken in order to guide the reader to salient instances of repetition and quoted speech. I also wanted to do so in a written form that would not be excessively uncomfortable for a general reader, which means that I have sometimes sacrificed details of intonation, stress, and breath within utterances. I have used the following guide in the lined-out transcriptions.

1. A line consists of a pause unit. This may be a word, a grammatical constituent, a complete clause, or a collection of clauses spoken by an individual.

2. Because a pause unit does not easily correspond to a "sentence," I have not always used punctuation or initial capitals to delineate speech units. Punc-

tuation is used to indicate intonation contours. A period (.) at the end of a line indicates falling intonation. A question mark (?) indicates rising intonation. In the transcripts of Apache, I have not used question marks because it is a tone language, so rising intonation at the end of a line is indicated by the diacritical mark above the affected vowel (e.g., "hant'é"; see the "San Carlos Apache Pronunciation Guide").

3. In a small number of instances, where punctuation seemed necessary to avoid confusion on the part of the reader as to the grammatical function of a word or clause, those punctuation marks appear in (parentheses).

4. Pauses within a line, shorter than that at a line break, are marked by a comma (,), period (.), or question mark (?), depending on the intonation contour of the preceding segment.

5. Stressed, emphatic speech is denoted by italics within a word (e.g., hé*la*), and/or by an exclamation point (!) at the end of a line.

6. Duration is marked by stringing letters of the affected segment together ("a loooong time ago").

7. Overlap is marked by square brackets ([) at the point of overlap, and by alignment of this bracketed text.

8. English glosses of Apache discourse are presented with standard English punctuation.

Not all of the transcribed talk in this book is lined out. In transcriptions that are either running text or block quotes, I have done my best to preserve the rhythmic patterns of the original speakers. In most cases, line endings in lined-out transcripts are replaced by commas in running transcripts. With only rare exceptions and in certain orthographic conventions (such as using *n'* for *ng* word endings), I have avoided the use of orthography to depict speakers' pronunciation.

Notes

Introduction

1. Indeed, Marshall's joke is in wider circulation than I at first realized. I related the incident at Top of the World to another friend, who jumped the gun on Marshall's punch line, saying, "nnee nshlii" (I am nnee), which echoes Marshall's utterance but without the additional code-switch that capped Marshall's performance.

2. Cultural worlds have been modeled as "fractal" (Appadurai 1990), linked to place and history as much as to practices and values (Gupta and Ferguson 1992). The global flow of people, practices, ideologies, and money has produced a cultural world of overlap, contact, and "creolization" (Hannerz 1987). On the situational negotiation and crafting of identity, see Kondo 1990, Kulick 1998,

and Rafael 1988. On the plasticity and open-endedness of tradition, see Handler and Linnekin 1984, and Hanson 1989.

3. Following Browner (2002) I use the terms *Indian, American Indian, Native,* and *Native American* somewhat interchangeably in this book.

4. For two recent and very different interpretations of the cultural power of the contemporary powwow, see Browner 2002 and Lassiter 1998. On the role of tourism and trade in the development of contemporary Navajo and Pueblo artistic production, see Howard and Pardue 1996, M'Closkey 2002, McPherson 1992, Volk 1988, Weigle and Babcock 1996, and Witherspoon 1977. On the negotiated symbols out of which contemporary Native American identities are produced, see Basso 1979, Blu 1980, Braroe 1975, Campisi 1991, Cruikshank 1998, Fowler 1987, Fried 1975, Hill and Hill 1994, Holler 1995, and Landsman 1988. This style of negotiated identity is what Gerald Vizenor (1999) has termed "survivance." Working in Australia, Jeremy Beckett (1994a, 1994b, 2000) has argued convincingly for dissolving area studies boundaries and instead examining the common threads that link the experiences of Fourth World indigenous people in European colonies of settlement.

5. These demands that identity be linked to continuity of tradition, however, are made of non–First World communities in an alarming proportion. Western Europe and the United States often trade in indexical markers of identity as suspect as any of those found in a "corrupted" community such as the San Carlos Reservation. Michael Thomas Carroll (2000) has pointed out that none of the main ingredients of the café mocha that has become the quintessential beverage of Bureau American modernity—coffee, sugar, and chocolate—are indigenous to any individuals who trace their ancestry to a European "culture." Yet questions about cultural continuity and identity are more often posed in relation to non-European people.

6. The complexities of indexicality have been a productive area of conversations in linguistic anthropology and semiotics (Hanks 1999; Ochs 1992; Silverstein 1976). Here I am alluding to a problem in the interpretation of Peirce's rich sense of indeterminacy cogently discussed by Greenlee (1973), a problem by which Peirce's ontology (the typological trichotomy of icon, index, and symbol) is sometimes conflated with Peirce's phenomenology (how people experience signs in the world). The difficulty with this conflation can be sensed in the fact that over time Peirce expanded his original model of triadic signs from 10 types of sign to the possibility of 66 types and possibly even 59,049 (Elkins 2003:148).

7. For me, one productive way of thinking through this issue has been to conceptualize a dialogue on the issue of whether the text (Urban 1996) or the context (Haring 1992) holds sway over the replicability of a discourse instance.

8. The Sophists rejected the idea that arguments should appeal ultimately to the rational faculty, proposing instead that rhetorical persuasion rather than

logical truth was the measure of oration. Aristotle countered in *De Sophisticis Elenchis* (On Sophistical Refutations) that the ambiguity of language did not preclude the idea of talking sensibly about the world and that rhetorical form should not obviate the search for truth. Aristotle's sense of ambiguity is lexical and referential and prefigures a position found in the Boasian tradition of "American structuralism" (Boas [1911] 1991; Hymes and Fought 1981)—namely, that part of linguistic ambiguity is the inevitable result of the fact that, as Aristotle wrote, "names are finite . . . while things are infinite in number." This introduction is not the forum for rehashing the history of Western linguistics. Interested readers should see Aarsleff 1982, Downing 1995, Harris 1980, Harris and Taylor 1997, and Seuren 1998.

9. The notion that language and art are phenomenally related is part of an approach that puts poetics and performance at the center of social life and identity. Bauman and Briggs (1990) codified a great deal of this approach. My own sense of the question of language and music owes much to my study at the University of Texas at Austin, and the thirty-year history of scholarship in performance and poetics that has marked the study of language and expressive culture at that institution. The legacy can be sensed in the series of authorships and coauthorships by its members: Bauman (1972, 1977, 1986); Bauman and Sherzer (1974); Nichols and Woodbury 1985; Paredes and Bauman (1972); Sherzer (1983, 1987, 1990); Sherzer and Urban (1986); Sherzer and Woodbury (1987); Urban (1991); and Woodbury (1985, 1987, 1993, 1998). Among the key moments along this arc was the publication of both Joel Sherzer's (1987) and Greg Urban's (1991) presentations of the Texas version of a "discourse-centered" approach to culture. Despite the role of Victor Turner and Richard Schechner in the development of "performance studies," I trace the notion of performance to the work of Dell Hymes (1964, 1975a, 1975b, 1981, 1985) and Dennis Tedlock (1972, 1983), as well as to the debates that ensued about their respective approaches. An approach to language and culture through performance led to a sense of the role of audiences as co-constructors of performances (Brenneis 1986, 1987; Duranti 1986; Schieffelin 1985) and to the development of new approaches to text-context relations in the production ("achievement," as some would say) of interactions.

10. From a philosophical standpoint, for example, the ambiguity of reported speech makes it a problematic linguistic tool for the production of universal logical relations. For Gottlob Frege, the existence of reported speech—of subordinate clauses in natural languages more generally—was one of the central problems to be overcome in his attempt to forge the foundations of modern analytical logic. Because logical syllogisms could not be made out of reported speech, the capacity for natural language to report speech was problematic for the clarity of logic. That is, according to Frege, one can build logical syllogisms out of premises such as the following:

a. The morning star is a body illuminated by the sun.

b. The morning star = the evening star.

c. Therefore, the evening star is a body illuminated by the sun.

However, one cannot build a logical syllogism out of a reported premise:

a. Alice believes that the morning star is a body illuminated by the sun.

b. The morning star = the evening star.

c. Therefore, Alice believes that the evening star is a body illuminated by the sun.

In other words, a reported premise does not indicate a truth value. Identity and inference cannot work unfettered in natural languages, according to Frege, in part because natural languages are not context free. See Frege 1984, Lee 1997:16–39, and Weiner 1999.

11. I am returning here to a critique of the assumptions of Western art criticism that Morse Peckham made in the mid-1960s. Peckham argued that rather than organizing a disjunct world into more beautiful forms, the purpose of art was to create ambiguity for contemplation and affect. That is, "our culture's central assumptions about art" (1965:16)—namely, the assumptions that the human mind possesses a natural drive toward order and coherence in the universe, that art is the purest manifestation of that drive, that art brings order to the chaos of the natural world, and that great art is therefore the satisfaction of that drive for order—are wrong (see Peckham 1965:3–40).

12. Anthropology's place within the academic disciplines as well as its agenda have shifted over time. At a time when it was assumed that "primitive" societies were less sensible and coherent than the developed West, it made sense that one of anthropology's goals was to demonstrate the systematic coherence of those societies. Yet we should not forget the place of coherence and sensibility in the European philosophical tradition or Boas's connections to it in the similar setting of both *aesthetik* and *kultur* as unities in diversity. Nor should we forget that a romantic sense of the "primitive" might include the idea that those cultures were *more* sensible, because less alienated, than modern European societies. For a treatment of the resonances between these concepts, see Guess 1996.

13. One went so far as to exclaim, "San Carlos! You're not gonna learn *any-thing* there!" Grenville Goodwin (1942) did a great deal of his classic work on Western Apache social organization in Bylas, but his project focused on historical reconstruction of aboriginal lifeways from his consultants' memories. By the time he arrived in Apache country, the Lutheran church had been in Peridot for forty years, Coolidge Dam had already covered over Old San Carlos, and so forth—none of which appears in Goodwin's work except as indexes of change or disintegration. It is certainly the case that San Carlos has been home

to a variety of Native people, including the Apache, Mohave, and Yavapai, who were incarcerated together at San Carlos for administrative ease. Many of those in the latter two groups relocated to their own reservations at the turn of the twentieth century, but a number remained at San Carlos as well. The first tribal constitution provided for seven council members: three from San Carlos, two from Bylas, and one each for the Mohave and Yavapai "sections" (Uplegger 1935)—a wording that may indicate that these people lived in a specific geographic area of the reservation. They are known by Apache group names— Mohave are known as *góóhn* and Yavapai as *dilzhę́'ę́*. The latter especially are known for speaking a unique dialect of the Apache language. On the political history of the Mohave and Yavapai Apaches, see Perry 1993 and Schroeder 1974. On the phonological features of the Yavapai Apache dialect, see Reuse 2002.

14. San Carlos is often found in comparative studies of various southern Athabaskan reservations. San Carlos, White Mountain, Mescalero, Jicarilla, Fort McDowell, Tonto (Payson), Camp Verde, and Navajo are all in the Southwest, all linguistically and (therefore, the argument goes) culturally related, so they make a splendid controlled environment for comparative social or statistical research. Concerning San Carlos, the recurrent question seems to be, "Why are economic and social conditions so much worse there?" See, for example, Cornell and Gil-Swedburg 1995. Compare this analysis with the presentation in Nevins forthcoming.

15. For more on the overlap of poetics and linguistics in Sapir's work, see Darnell 1990; Handler 1983, 1986, 1989; and Silverstein 1986.

16. Scholarship on the relationship between language and music has a long history, too long for me to enter into an extended discussion here. Interested readers are directed to Feld and Fox 1994, Feld et al. 2004, and the extensive bibliographies contained therein.

17. One might write it as an algebraic formula (in which L = language): $X = L - Y$.

18. See Elkins 1998 for a trenchant critique of this analogical form of art criticism.

19. Consider the lines from Shakespeare's ninety-fifth sonnet ("Marguerite"):

That tongue that tells the story of thy days
(Making lascivious comments on thy sport)
Cannot dispraise, but in a kind of praise
Naming thy name, blesses an ill report.

Empson points out that, grammatically, "the subject of *blesses* is either *tongue* or *naming*, and *but in a kind of praise* qualifies either *blesses* or *dispraise*" ([1930] 1953:51), a lack of clarity that would be unacceptable in an essay but is useful in poetic forms.

20. See, for example, Appadurai 1990; Coplan 1985; Erlmann 1991, 1996; Feld [1988] 1994b; Manuel 1993; Meintjes 1990, 2003; and Waterman 1990.

21. Many people in San Carlos and Bylas live in substandard housing. At the beginning of my stay, I had a possibility of living in a newer house in Moon-base. Ultimately the plan fell through, but when I discussed my options with one friend, she said, "You came out here to live like an Apache, didn't you?" — implying that I should live in the decrepit trailer. This question annoyed an-other friend when I told him about it: "Why should 'live like an Apache' mean that you live in shitty housing?" he wanted to know.

22. This is another reason why copies of the written work are circulating around the community.

23. Literally "big tamale." The classic tamalecho is made with deer jerky (now often substituted with ground beef), wrapped in dough and boiled like dumplings.

24. It is interesting that I (choose to) write (and think) of these relationships using terms for hardening—*forged, strengthened, toughened, hardened.* Basso (1979) writes that Apaches in Cibecue speak of long-lasting relationships in terms of softening and added pliability.

Chapter 1

1. A generation ago Dominic would have been able to utter this teasing joke in Apache—as many people did at that time—and know that the children would understand him.

2. James Haley's *Apaches, a History and Culture Portrait* (1981) may be the most complicated and problematic of these Apaches-become-less-interesting-after-1886 types of histories, as he begins with versions (whose?) of various Apache creation narratives in order to give the reader a sense of receiving a Native point of view. For more conventional histories that reproduce Apaches as warriors moving like the wind and as "eagles of the Southwest," see Roberts 1993 and Worcester 1979.

3. Narrative tensions exist between, on the one hand, ethnographic sensi-tivity to and regard for indigenous ways of representing the passage of time (historical and otherwise) and, on the other, a dependence on a straightforward, academic record in the presentation of the histories that introduce those sen-sitive ethnographic presentations. A classic case in point is Evans-Pritchard's *The Nuer* (1960), which dedicates a lengthy chapter to Nuer conceptions of time and space, yet in its introduction settles for a classification of East African cul-ture types and the probable common origin of the Nuer and the Dinka, given the similarities in their language, physical appearance, and other cultural traits.

4. This quote is from *The Apache Scout*, the Lutheran mission newsletter from Arizona. These metaphors were prominent during the 1930s and seem to have

died off with the onset of World War II, when space was dedicated to news of people associated with the Lutheran missions who were involved in the war effort.

5. Some people in Globe told me that this particular trail was a path for people working on telephone lines in the area. Others told me that it was "Stoneman's Grade," named after the general commanding the cavalry who constructed it as a route through the Pinals. Many people in San Carlos, however, think of this road and other such roads as Indian footpaths, and I have no reason to doubt that the graded trails were constructed over already existing paths.

6. Upon reflection, I asked him why he had used the third person (them) rather than the first person (us), and he told me he had momentarily slipped into the role of an outside researcher thinking about Apaches.

7. *Doo anii dá'* appears to be a contraction of *doo anii da dá'*, which would gloss more literally as "not recently" (*anii*: new, recent, young). Basso categorizes Western Apache speech into three major genres: *yat'i'* ("ordinary talk"), *'okąąhi* ("prayer"), and *nagoldi'é* ("narrative," "story"). He further categorizes the latter into four narrative genres: *godiyįhgo nagoldi'é* ("myth"), *'ágodzaahí* ("historical tale"), *nłt'éégo nagoldi'é* ("saga" [literally, "a good story"]), and *"ch'idii"* (gossip). One thing that distinguishes these genres is the time frame in which they occur. "Historical tales" take place in the time frame "long ago" (*doo'ánííná*) (1990:114–15).

8. That the Apaches "didn't know the value of gold" is a figure also found in Anglo narratives of the times as well. The sadly defunct Web site *Doc Goodman's Arizona Territorial Times* (formerly at http://www.aztt.com/pages/page-001.htm) related a tale about a group of Americans who in 1853 encountered a band of Coyotero Apaches who were willing to trade gold nuggets from a hidden mine for supplies. "In one deal, a few articles of spare clothing were traded for about $1,500 worth of gold nuggets." The American travelers traded for as much gold as they could get. "One old Apache warrior loaded his gun with bullets made of the purest gold. He used one to shoot a rabbit, which he gave to the travelers. The white men accepted the rabbit, cleaned it, pulled out and kept the golden bullet, and ate the hare for supper." Although the sense is given that the Apaches didn't know the value of gold, it is worth noting that they reportedly refused to reveal the location of the mine to the travelers. Goodman credits this story to Felix Aubrey, a Pony Express rider who apparently established the record for riding from Independence to Santa Fe in 1846.

9. It is interesting that Duane talks about Indians helping Europeans with the problem of encountering new diseases; the record of massive depopulation clearly shows that the key epidemiological problem was that of Native Americans encountering new diseases brought by the European settlers.

10. The Tribal Work Experience Program (TWEP) was a federal program that resulted in many houses being built during the 1970s.

11. I've been told that a similarly situated neighborhood in Whiteriver is called One Step Beyond.

12. The verse is Job 14:1–2: "Man that is born of a woman is of few days, and full of trouble. He cometh forth like a flower and is cut down."

13. The Phelps-Dodge Web site offers this information: http://www.phelps dodge.com/index-history.html.

14. Nitz mentions cowboys in his first sentence. Located outside the city itself, ranching and cattle punching were an important part of Globe's economic and social life. A few Globe residents told me heartfelt and harrowing family stories of how their forbears had braved hardships to bring cattle ranching to Arizona. And cattle was the mainstay of the economy of San Carlos for decades. Yet I don't think I am alone in imaging Globe as a mining town. From the standpoint of tourist promotion, it's difficult for tourists to imagine cowboys and cattle roundups as they drive through the pit mines and the tailings.

15. Inspiration Mining owned the mineral rights to the area called Little Hollywood, as best I can tell, and eventually quitclaimed the surface to Sears for the construction of a shopping center.

16. Now San Carlos finally faces the permanent loss of the Apache language as well, and many members of the community are trying to figure out how to get parents to teach it to their children and to get children to speak it. But the fact that Apache is still spoken on the reservation by most people older than fifty, when so many languages have disappeared from the off-reservation town next door, paints a puzzling picture of the assimilationist project of reservation as opposed to town.

Chapter 2

1. Although repetition may be especially salient in Athabaskan languages, its importance is certainly not unique to them. Halliday and Hasan (1976) cite repetition as a key factor in cohesion in English. Similarly, Tannen (1987, 1989) regards repetition as an important means of maintaining discourse cohesion and creating interpretable meaning. Urban (2001, esp. 159–63) relates repetition to metaculture, most prominently for this case, when he discusses the narrativization of the response to imperatives.

2. In the case of verb forms, Axelrod (2000) cites evidence that repetition accounted for up to 40 percent of all verbs in Mescalero and Chiricahua discourse and for up to 60 percent of the verb forms in the telling of Koyukon Athabaskan traditional narratives. This latter percentage excluded repetitions of the verb *say* in reported speech clauses.

3. Of course, all communities—from small family units to nation-states, institutions, corporations, and political entities—present an ideologically naturalized sense of the speaking subject. Political ideologies, ethical philosophies, and aesthetic judgments are often tied, explicitly or implicitly, to culturally

naturalized images of individual speakers involved in everyday conversations. One distinction between the San Carlos Reservation and non-Apache communities rests on the distinctions in how individual speakers are imagined. In the mold of the bourgeois Enlightenment European image of the rational subject, the seventeenth-century philosopher Baruch Spinoza wrote of political freedom, "In a free state, every man is allowed to think what he will and to say what he thinks" (the title of chapter 20 in Spinoza's *Theological-Political Treatise*; see Jaspers 1966). In his *Democracy in America*, Alexis de Tocqueville expended a large amount of ink discussing how Americans talked—not in the sounds of their regional dialects, but in the way Americans justified the naturalness of the individual right to express an opinion. Much of this ideology falls under what Deborah Schiffrin (1993) has called the "speak for yourself" rule in everyday bourgeois, Caucasian American English interactions. Looking outside the United States, Habermas (1979, 1984) has linked the rise of bourgeois modernity to shifts in public discourse and in ideas about who a legitimate speaker is, with notions of rationality and individual responsibility strongly implicated. Laura Graham (1993) has critiqued Habermas's ideal-typical sense of discourse in her discussion of the cooperative, overlapping, and citational co-construction of men's political discourse among the Xavante.

4. In fact, San Carlos Apache does not have gendered third-person pronouns. *He, she,* and *it* are covered by a single third-person pronoun (to which an animacy enclitic *ń* may be postpositioned).

5. See Declerck 1991 for a critical evaluation of these backshifting rules.

6. A related issue regarding the syntax of reported speech has to do with the assertion that direct report is the "simplest form" (Halliday 1985:251) of reporting. The lack of "simplicity" in direct report is documented in a great deal of work exploring both the roles of evidentiality and the taking up of responsibility for another's voice in direct report (e.g., Bauman 1977, Hassler 2002, Hill and Irvine 1993, Willett 1988). Still, the notion of a "simple" construction of direct report persists because direct report involves the least adjustments to the "original" reported clause. As Winfried Boeder rightly points out, this lack of shift is from the perspective of the reported clause only. "In direct speech, the reference of person, time, etc. is typically not orientated towards the speech situation of the reporting clause, and in this sense, it is not in the indirect speech that their reference 'shifts,' but rather in the direct speech, in which an 'I' is not necessarily the reporter-speaker, a present is not the speech time etc." (2002:3). See also Urban 1987.

7. I am influenced here by Urban's (1991) work on the relationship between ergativity and patient-centric narratives in Shokleng.

8. As I noted earlier, the verity of the performance is open to question. Note, for instance, that in the previous chapter Duane has his Thanksgiving Pilgrims talk like Woodstock-era hippies, saying, "Hey, wow, man." This question has led some scholars to prefer terms other than *report* to describe the phenomenon.

9. More literally, *łįį shogheeł* means "the horse was carrying me"; *łįį shił hilwoł* would be more akin to "I am riding the horse" (although still not a transparent gloss), so the sense of the former may be that the horse was just going along at its own pace.

10. *Beodzidgo* was usually glossed for me as meaning "scary," but the sense seems to encompass something like "strange" or "weird" as well. Someone dressing in a combination of stripes, plaids, and polka dots can be referred to as begodzid.

11. Linda is speaking to Hannah here. Comparing line 11 with line 9, the verb *say* is conjugated in the "fourth person" (a form used when one third person is addressing another)—*ch'inii* rather than the third person *nii*.

12. A devastating flood hit the area in August 1904. According to the *Arizona Republic* of August 21, two inches of rain fell in one hour.

13. Geronimo, his followers, and even the Chiriachua scouts who had helped the army locate him were originally sent to Florida as prisoners of war. Geronimo was later relocated to Fort Sill but was never permitted to return to the Southwest. He died in Oklahoma, and his gravesite is on the grounds of the fort.

14. In fact, as a novice speaker of Apache, I found the fact that all instances of speech are framed in the first person of the original speaker to be one of the most confusing aspects of learning how to follow a conversation in Apache.

15. Keith Basso (personal communication) has reminded me that there are, in addition to the instances I discuss here, requests for future speech. A: "What do you think he'll say when he gets here?" B: "He'll say 'We should go to White-river.' "

16. On the 2000 census, 28 percent of the households in San Carlos (241 of 874) reported no vehicle available. For the sake of comparison, in Globe 8 percent of the households (206 of 2,613) reported having no available vehicle.

17. "Green Onions" (Stax 127) spent twelve weeks on the Billboard charts, rising as high as number three. "Can't You Hear My Heartbeat" (MGM 13310) was on the charts for eleven weeks, spending two weeks at number two. "634-5789" (Atlantic 2320) topped out at number thirteen, spending eight weeks on the charts (Whitburn 1987).

18. The phrase *tah nolii* does just that and was glossed as "it might be." To help me remember it, a friend taught me a bit of speech play: "Asitiníí tah nolinii / Bini'adįhnii tah nolinii" (it might be the police / they might be crazy).

19. Among the most common Western Apache retentions in English conversations are interjections, such as the interjection denoting surprise, "kehéé!" Frequently used phrases in Apache are often calqued into English, but this has not happened to "tah nnii." An example of an interjection that has been calqued would be the intensifier *dazhǫ́*, which appears as "sure" in English utterances. For examples, see the English-language performances in Basso's *Portraits of "The Whiteman"* (1979).

20. This is something like Eco's notion of language as an open code: "A code

is not only a rule which closes but also a rule which opens. It not only says 'you must' but says also 'you may' or 'it would also be possible to do that'" (1986:187).

21. As with the features of repetition discussed earlier, it may be that the Athabaskan languages lend themselves to punning speech play. For example, a great many homophones exist among the prefixes that affect the meanings of verb stems. Young and Morgan (1992:100) list fourteen different verbal prefixes that are realized as *di* in spoken Navajo (see also McDonough 2000). On puns in Athabaskan languages, see Rushforth 1991 and Sapir 1932.

22. *Go'íí* can be interpreted as meaning something like "as you can see" (it is built on the verb stem for looking, seeing, doing something with your eyes). Speakers of Western Apache are highly aware of subtle dialect differences, even within the same town (see Goodwin 1942; Perry 1993). In the San Carlos dialect, this evidential is pronounced "wíí," and I am certain that people in Whiteriver have their own fun with that.

23. "Somehow" is a calque of the Western Apache phrase *hago shįh*, denoting an uneasy, uncomfortable feeling. One summer, a car driven by white people was speeding through Bylas and killed a man walking by the side of the road. As we sat and watched the police and an emergency medical team arrive, my friend's son turned to me and said, "Squirrel, do you think those white people feel somehow?" Similarly, *hayú shįh* means something like "somewhere," an unknown, uneasy location. Some people say that hayú shįh is the space in which dreams take place.

24. Western Apache, like all Athabaskan languages, has multiple verb stems to classify the size, shape, and number of objects being handled. For example, *-aah* refers to a medium-size roundish object, such as a large stone; *-tsos* to a thin flat flexible object such as a piece of paper; *-kaah* to an open container; and so forth. These verb stems are used both referentially and metaphorically. For instance, the singing of songs is referred to by use of the *-aah* stem, as are words. "Shi yati' nadín'aah" translates idiomatically as "take my advice," more literally as "pick up my words."

25. This point has been taken up in detail by others elsewhere (Davies 1994; Feld and Fox 1994; Feld et al. 2004; Harris 1996; Treitler 1997), so I don't wish to belabor it here.

26. Of course, with the possible exception of pure vocabulary, we may never completely escape the realm of reference, so part of the sonic play of poetic indeterminacy must almost always be embedded in the realm of sensical meaning.

Chapter 3

1. That is to say, the only band that really performed publicly at dances, parties, and other functions was the Pacers. Many other people of all ages

played guitar and sang, but mostly in more private settings. Toward the end of my stay, a punk band performed on the same bill with the Pacers for Veterans Day, and I always heard rumors of a Bylas band called Blue Cheer or the Blue Cheers but never actually saw or heard it.

2. Although many feel that winter is "out of season" for a na'í'ees, others hold the opinion that the hardships of dancing in the cold can be a productive part of the ceremony.

3. As one singer put it to me, "Translation is hard. If you're true Apache, translation is difficult" because "a small word [in Apache] means a long sentence [in English]," and as a result the English translation inevitably "leaves stuff out."

4. See, for example, Adams 1996, C. Ellis 1996, Leap 1993, Lomawaima 1994, Phillipson 1992, St. Clair and Leap 1982, Spack 2002, and Standing Bear [1928] 1975.

5. As an example, see Lassiter, Ellis, and Kotay 2002.

6. Fredrik Pacius (1809–91) was a German-born composer who moved to Scandinavia. He composed the Estonian and Finnish national anthems and the first Finnish national opera, and he is known, at least in some circles, as the father of Finnish music.

7. The depth of the conflicts between these forces can be seen in a yearbook from the St. John's Indian School from around 1968. On three successive pages of this Catholic school publication, we see a picture of the "nationally famous" St. John's Drum and Bugle Corps, decked out in what I can only describe as "pan-Indian" outfits; a photograph of four boys with electric guitars and drums ("Ray, Ron, Gabe, and Leander join forces to make music for school dances"); and a photo of a group of Apache Crown Dancers, whose ceremonial performances point "toward a meeting of the ways between the pagan heritage, and, Christianity."

8. Bell's patent for the telephone was granted in 1876, Edison's for the phonograph in 1877 and for the electric lightbulb in 1881, and Tesla's for the radio nineteen years later, in 1900. But this sequence of patents hardly reflects the order in which these inventions became common on the reservation. Many people, especially in Bylas, owned battery-operated radios long before their houses were wired for electricity, and most people on the reservation had no access to any but a public pay phone until just before the turn of the millennium. At the opening of the tribal telephone office in 2001, one speaker talked about how it would radically change political campaigns in the community. It would also have effects on face-to-face contact. One woman I know told me that she feared "the days of visiting people in their homes are over."

9. Radio KOMA is now an oldies station, so that generation can still tune into the station at night and hear their favorite songs.

10. Numerous people in the first half of the twentieth century—Adorno most

famously—worried about the links between radio announcing and fascism. I don't want to dismiss those arguments. Certainly the desire to play music just as one hears it on the radio is part of this link. But to say that this desire occurs because of an inherent passivity or patiency inculcated in radio listeners is, I think, premature.

11. Bashas' is one of the largest supermarket chains in Arizona and has apparently entered into a number of cooperative enterprises with tribal communities in the state.

12. That the speaker mentioned two music video channels rather than radio stations may be an indication that radio and video occupy different imaginative spaces or may simply be a sign of the times. Or both.

13. Brian Bunney was not a tribal member, but the son of Curtis Bunney, a pastor, first of the "Independent Church" (not an official name) in Gilson Wash (along a stretch of road known at that time as "Jerusalem Street" for the number of born-again Christians who lived in the area) and later of the Pentecostal American Indian Church in Seven Mile Wash. Curtis Bunney, though white, was one of the missionaries who went out of his way to learn Apache. He learned Western Apache literacy from my Apache teacher's father and also taught a number of other people how to read and write Apache.

14. "Slip Away" was recorded by Clarence Carter and released in 1968 (Atlantic 2508), reaching as high as number six on the Billboard Hot 100; "Sail Away" was released by Credence Clearwater Revival in 1972, on the album *Mardi Gras* (Fantasy F-9404) (if it was ever released as a single, it never made the top forty); "I'm Your Puppet," recorded by James and Bobby Purify in 1966 (Bell 648), also reached number six on the Billboard charts (Whitburn 1987).

15. In those days, according to some of my consultants, students were responsible for buying their own schoolbooks.

16. The Gila Tomahawk, which ran from Bowie to Globe, with station stops in Bowie, Safford, Thatcher, San Carlos, and Globe, ceased operation on December 31, 1953, despite a consolidated effort between the five communities to keep it running. Although the depot in San Carlos is marked now only by the black water tower that stood alongside it, the depot in Globe has been converted into a coin laundromat.

17. Duane Eddy was born in Corning, New York, in 1938, but when he was a teenager his family moved to Arizona, and he made his start as a local Phoenix phenomenon.

Chapter 4

1. When weather permitted, we practiced outdoors, under either the shade at the old house or the shade across at Darryl's house when he was playing the drums or out at Marshall's mom's place at Soda Canyon.

2. Every so often Marshall would insist on rehearsing out at the lake and would sometimes go as far as to lock the gate leading to his mother's house to keep people away while the band worked, but even this approach met with only limited success.

3. See the discussion in chapter 1 of the neighborhood called "Waco."

4. "Apache," by Jorgen Ingmann and His Guitar (Atco 6184), spent thirteen weeks on the charts in 1961, getting as high as number two. To the best of my knowledge, Apaches are the only Native American group with a rock and roll song named after them. "Cherokee," of course, has long been a standard in the jazz repertoire.

5. In four months of playing with the Pacers and five years of visiting, I had never heard them play this song.

6. The Kennelly-Heaviside layer is an atmospheric condition that makes it possible for AM signals to travel great distances at night.

7. In a sense, the form taken by this discussion, with vice on one side and liberty on the other, has changed little over the past fifty years. When Congress debated the idea of making possession of alcohol legal for Indians in the 1950s, part of the debate pitted both the constitutional rights of Indians as citizens to purchase what they saw fit without being discriminated against or patronized by the government and the wish to discourage bootlegging against the desire to contain the spread of a vice that had already corrupted too many whites.

8. One controversy over rap and hip-hop, for example, has swirled around the ideas that there is no narrative or artistic distance; that MCs aren't portraying characters, but are simply narrating reality; or that their listeners can't tell the difference.

9. Ross used to joke this way as well, sometimes getting laughs by simply strumming a G chord and singing the word *darlin'*, but swooping up to the first note from as low in his vocal register as he could reach. For more on the Appalachian dialect, see Bernstein, Nunnally, and Sabino 1997; Labov 1991; and Wolfram and Schilling-Estes 1998.

10. See also Wagner (1986), from whom Friedrich borrows the "stand for themselves" phrase.

Chapter 5

1. This conversation and most of the conversations reported in this section originally took place in Apache or code-switching interactions ("ya' lead guitar play ainł'įį bigonsįh néh"). Boe reported them to me in English during our interviews.

2. The relationship between bands and these managers is extremely complex, wavering between a relationship of generosity and communitarianism to one of extraction and exploitation. What a band member says about a former manager

may vary depending on the speaker's mood at the moment. Overall, I would say that the memories band members have of managers are more bitter than not, but the attitude is the surface level of an extremely complicated set of personal and cultural histories.

3. The confluence of these outward forms can be heard in the Apache Spirit song "Indian Cowboy" (from the recording of the same name).

4. Bylas has no high school of its own, so most students travel by bus to attend school at Fort Thomas, a non-Indian community eleven miles east of the reservation. Unlike the situation in the Globe school system, in which Apache students have been a distinct minority, the great majority of students at Fort Thomas High School are from Bylas.

5. In speaking to Boe about this help, I was never clear exactly what he thought of it. On the one hand, he seems to have appreciated their interest and their assistance in improving the lyrics of the song. On the other hand, I had the sense that he was somewhat puzzled by their taking over a project that had been his.

6. As an Apache-dominant bilingual, Boe sometimes conflates gendered third-person singular pronouns in English. Western Apache third-person singular pronouns are ungendered, being marked only for human or nonhuman referent instead.

7. More recently Boe has begun working with other musicians again.

8. I also have the sense, from what Boe said, that his relatives were impressed by the instrument's ability to "do everything for you." Boe himself, I think, also enjoyed that aspect of the Casio keyboard but would have preferred to work with live musicians if he could have done so without either compromising his feelings about alcohol or losing control of his project. For one tape, Boe did away with the keyboard and played his songs with guitar only, but he told me that the critical response to the tape was less enthusiastic because, he thought, people had gotten used to his sound with the keyboard and also wanted to hear all the instruments.

9. Boe is thus marked, in a sense, as too local. It is interesting, though, the extent to which the particular nonstandard English accent of Boe's generation is marked as "local," whereas the San Fernando Valley–influenced, nonstandard local dialect of the younger generation is somehow accepted as "standard." One afternoon, when Boe and I were rehearsing "Cowboy Rides Away," his daughter, on her way out the door, tried to correct her father's Apache-inflected English on the line "my heart is sinking like the setting sun": "Remember, Dad," she reminded him, "it's not sɛ'n, it's sɛɾiːn."

10. When I returned to Austin, Texas, from the field, it took some time for me to readjust to the everyday life of a graduate student. I was most put off by the false performances of sincerity to which one is exposed constantly when dealing with the urban bureaucracy. At one point, I mentioned during a phone con-

versation with someone in San Carlos that I was having trouble getting along with "all these white people." "Oh," she said, having a different take on the problem, "you mean how they're always telling you what to do?"

11. According to Britton Goode's notes, thunder, especially distant thunder, has the ability to make people, especially older people, cry, with an interjection meant for things fading away into the distance: "Yáálan."

12. T'ǫzhį' means "backwards." The verb stem -įį carries the meaning "look" or "see," to do something with your eyes, depending on the verbal prefixes. T'ǫzhį' dín'įį means "look back" or "look behind you." In this particular place-name, the verb is conjugated in the fourth person, which in this case carries the meaning attributed to the pronominal usage of one in English—a sort of impersonal personal pronoun. The final clitic -hé is what I call an "essentializing" enclitic, in the sense that it turns the preceding material into an essential part of the person, place, or thing being referenced.

13. Clifton-Morenci is a copper-mining town near the reservation, where many Apaches worked in the mines. The song in question is "Open Pit Mine," the lyrics of which are, "In Morenci, Arizona, where the copper mines flow, I can see Clifton in the valley below."

14. Students of oral narrative might well object that this means that Boe has never heard a great storyteller. But it strikes me as well that Boe might attribute the qualities of great storytelling to the musical features of language and narrative.

15. On seeing this passage, Boe corrected himself and told me they would sometimes walk more like three miles.

16. Ironically, shortly before Boe introduced this song, I overheard a photographer talking about taking pictures at a ceremony in San Carlos: "I was invited to take some pictures two weeks ago at a Sunrise. And even after, I shot some portraits at the end when everybody was leaving. Even then I got the parents. I tried to get them to smile . . . it looked like, you know, something from 1905."

17. An interesting exception is nonsense poetry. In that genre, syntax is always crystal clear, in part, perhaps, because the referential content of the lexicon is so open.

18. Nałil'a'é was a nickname that Boe's mother used for him. It means something like "messenger," someone who runs errands for someone, and is jokingly said to mean "servant" or "slave." Goodwin (1942) noted that husbands and wives sometimes referred to each other using this term, though never within earshot of one another.

19. The Navajo cognate of the Apache verb translated as "remember" (first-person singular binashnii, "I remember it") is based on the stem -nii, which is in actuality difficult to translate but carries an implication of "sense," "be aware," "know of," "be conscious of," "hear about." Interestingly, Young and Morgan (1992:458) raise the possibility that the verb stem that forms the word for "re-

member" is historically related to the verb stem meaning "to hurt," "to feel pain," or "to suffer."

20. See also Samuels 2001. This is similar to the way that Kapchan (1996) describes her concept of hybridity—as an expression that combines "disjunct material." Hybridity is thus distinguished from syncretism, in which expressions combine "conjunct material."

21. These stories are of the "when I was young, I used to walk fifty miles to school in my bare feet in the snow" variety. They usually take a form such as, "We are so lazy nowadays. In the old days, the people used to work hard and walk everywhere, but today we just drive in a car everywhere and say, 'I'm too tired!'" It is hard to tell how many of these comparisons were made for my benefit.

22. The list could go on, of course: Merle Haggard, ZZ Top, Pink Floyd, the Eagles, Neil Young, to name just a few.

23. I take this feeling of loss to be the attitude of the older speakers in Basso's essays on Western Apache place-names, and it is not my intention to take that attitude lightly. Kinship terminology is one of the sets of linguistic categories that are falling by the wayside in code-switching situations. It is common to hear elders refer to "shigrandkids" in conversation, and the code-switched term *shifriend* has replaced an entire range of Western Apache fictive kinship terms.

Chapter 6

1. According to the 2000 census, the three main communities of the reservation face different challenges. In San Carlos, 53 percent of the respondents reported that English was the only language spoken at home. In Bylas, 47 percent lived in English-only households, and 62 percent of Peridot residents reported English as the only home language. In addition, the English spoken in Peridot appears to be of a higher standard than in the other two communities. Only 7 percent of Peridot residents reported speaking English less than "very well" on the 2000 census. The numbers for San Carlos and Bylas were 17 percent and 28 percent, respectively.

2. "Hero" was a number one hit single from Mariah Carey's 1993 release *Music Box* (Columbia 53205).

3. "November Rain" is a nine-minute ballad appearing on Guns 'N' Roses' 1991 album *Use Your Illusion I* (Geffen GEFD-24415); *Legend* (Tuff Gong 846 210) is a posthumous release of Bob Marley's most famous songs.

4. Native speakers of Apache in San Carlos and Bylas often perceive these different terms as synonyms. Jack, who first taught me about this term, changed his mind a number of times during the preparation of this book before he settled on *bee nagodit'ah* as the one he preferred. The terms are subtly different. The high-tone *í* in *ínagodit'ah* is an object prefix that implies some form of contact

between the thing being added to and the thing being added, such as when you add paint to a wall. *Bee nagodit'ah* carries a more general sense of adding on. If in fact this distinction maps onto a distinction between the bringing together of like objects and the bringing together of unlike objects, I do not know. But if so, then that would be a distinction between the term that Jack preferred and the cognate term elucidated by Basso.

5. Punning also undermines the strict distinction between the paradigmatic and syntagmatic axes of Saussurean linguistics, at least as Jakobson (1960) has preserved the distinction in his poetics. (Because puns are in some sense motivated, they can be said to fall outside Saussurean language in its narrowest sense.) See, for example, Culler 1988, Delabastita 1997, Newfield and Lafford 1991, and Redfern 1984.

6. Basso's representation of continuity and change in contemporary Apache culture in Cibecue is extremely subtle. The elders who taught Basso about Apache traditions are often depicted wearing the souvenirs of the most mainstream of American cultural attractions. The importance of traditional knowledge to solving contemporary problems, including legal battles, is a prominent theme in Basso's work. And Basso's analysis of Western Apache intercultural joking performances is foundational not only to my own research, but also to that of numerous scholars in anthropology, folklore, and Native American studies.

7. *Dzáłeh* (more literally, "let it be right there") is an interjection interpreted for me as meaning something akin to "right on" in English. One of my friends wanted to resurrect the low-power radio station that the tribe had run in the 1970s. He thought the call letters should be KYAY, a play on a Western Apache interjection of surprise, "keyéé." He used to doodle possible bumper stickers on napkins: "KYAY: keyéé, dzáłeh!"

8. *Zhaali* is considered by linguists to be a borrowing from the Spanish *real*. Another Apache term for money, *beso*, is also borrowed from Spanish.

9. Spiderman never did introduce me to this person. He spent much of the time between then and the time I left the reservation recuperating from multiple fractures sustained in a car accident that occurred shortly after this conversation took place.

10. That is, in a sense, people cooperatively and discursively disrupt, disregard, dismantle, and otherwise defenestrate Grice's Cooperative Principles and Habermas's universal pragmatics (see Grice 1989; Habermas 1979, 1984).

11. The songs that were most likely to get the cowbell added were any chicken-scratch song or anything that sounded "Mexican"; two Santana songs, "Oye Como Va?" and "Black Magic Woman"; Creedence Clearwater Revival songs such as "Born on the Bayou"; Eric Clapton's "Cocaine"; John Cougar Mellencamp's "Cherry Bomb"; "Achy Breaky Heart"; and Marshall's song "Cry

Baby." Some of these songs had cowbells on the original recordings upon which the band based their performances. Others, though, apparently share a certain tempo or metric feel that called for the particular timbre and rhythm of the cowbell.

Chapter 7

1. For treatments of the kinds of sonic alterations involved in finding non-local audiences in the global marketplace, see Meintjes 2003; Buchanan 1996, 1997.

2. Bourdieu wrote on this subject long before the proliferation of subbrands and products that face today's shopper—before consumers could choose between a dozen varieties of Coca-Cola or fifteen brands of gourmet cat food. But now, although *rice* may not be a univocal signifier, neither is it a uniform product. There are long, medium, and short grains, as well as Arborio, jasmine, basmati, converted, and instant, to name just a few. At a recent trip to a grocery store, I counted more than a dozen brands of rice, each available in a number of varieties, ranging in price from thirty-five cents per pound (for quasi-generic store brands of long-grain white rice) to more than five dollars per pound (for Konriko Wild Pecan brand aromatic rice). Here, as in so many other areas of cultural expression, "authenticity" carries a price tag that makes the product both appeal to and available to the bourgeoisie. Arborio rice for your risotto is more expensive than other possible choices.

3. Few music retailers sell instruments at list price, but my description here seemed like a more equitable way of comparing prices.

4. I used a heavier pick because I had been given years of classical guitar lessons, thus gaining a certain amount of cultural capital, in true Bourdieuian fashion.

5. When Pat eventually joined up with the Sneezy Boyz, he did get another guitar, but he didn't replace the pickups.

6. The notes of the open strings of a guitar, from lowest to highest, are E, A, D, G, B, and E. The fifth fret of the low E string, therefore, sounds the same note as the open A string, and you can tune your instrument by matching these notes in sequence, putting your finger on the fifth fret of the low E string to get the A, on the fifth fret of the A string to get the D, on the D string to get the G, and so forth.

7. Jimmy Page sometimes plays a Silvertone guitar, but I don't think he goes on stage with the case amp. The Danelectro company has recently made a retro-inspired comeback as a manufacturer of musical instruments and signal-processing devices.

8. This is reminiscent of *iscathamiya* choir competitions in South Africa. There

a white person would be chosen at random to judge the contest. The justification was that because the person knew nothing of the music or the singers, he would be impartial. See Erlmann 1996.

9. This problem of sound production also haunted Boe Titla; his decision to use the Casio keyboard was determined in part by his economic inability to purchase something more sophisticated and advanced.

10. United Jewelry has since moved into the old Woolworth's building ("Woolsworth" in the local dialect) in Globe. Despite the official name of the store, they sell musical equipment and sporting goods in addition to jewelry.

11. A cultural and gender marking occurs here as well. Donnie's sense was that Apache women would have been too shy to have put on such a performance, and to the extent that the performance influenced the outcome, the Pacers were placed at a disadvantage.

12. A number of local sounds have obviously become marketable in the global marketplace—the Philadelphia, Seattle, Nashville, Liverpool, and Johannesburg sounds come to mind. For treatments of the ways in which those local sounds take on a global scope, see Meintjes 2003 and Jensen 1998.

13. Or to imagine yourself as the budding Hollywood hunk or ingénue on the video screen. For all their influence, Ritchie Valens and Buddy Holly, for instance, weren't all that gorgeous.

14. Why was I cast into the producer's role? I was the person with the most studio experience, limited as it was. Plus, although I thought of the money for the recording as common property, it's clear, at least in retrospect, that the other band members thought of it as mine. I had found the recording studio, although there was a second alternative and the Pacers made a group decision as to which studio to use.

15. Phil Stevens no longer runs the space as Crash Landing, but he still uses the studio to record his friends and musical colleagues.

16. For a more detailed analysis of this incident, see Feld et al. 2004.

17. In 2003, Marshall recorded a CD of gospel songs. Neither his name nor his picture appear anywhere on the package.

Chapter 8

1. Compare, for instance, Willard Rhodes's work from the 1950s (Rhodes [1952] 1967) on stability in Native American music with his later work on Native melodies with English texts (Rhodes 1963), in which he points out that the latter type of song had existed for half a century or more but flew beneath the radar of what ethnomusicologists took seriously as their topic of study.

2. On the subject of the self-made man, the gendering of the tropes of the American frontier narrative—which aspects of the "wilderness" and of "civilization" appear in masculine or feminine guises—is not to be ignored, but

neither can I do it justice here. See Namias 1993, Oatman and Oatman 1994, Rosowski 1999, and Strong 1999.

3. Rambova was acknowledged as one of Hollywood's first "geniuses," realizing a potential for set design and costume design that no one else to that time had imagined (Morris 1991).

4. The question of whether Robert LeRoy Parker and Harry Longabaugh were killed in Bolivia or returned to the United States is an ongoing subtheme of the Butch and Sundance industry. For more on the portion of this myth that brought William T. Phillips of Globe into the debate, see Dullenty 1983, 1991, 1993, 1995; Kyle 1991; Meadows and Buck 1997.

5. As I began reediting this section, *Catch Me If You Can*, the film adaptation of Frank W. Abagnale's 1980 best-seller about his life as one of the most famous imposters in the history of the FBI, was released and was one of the ten top-grossing films in the country for six consecutive weeks.

6. I have reprinted only Hoijer's English translation of the Apache text.

7. The footnotes in this text refer to Morris Opler's ethnological notes in the original publication. Here Opler notes: "The creation of human beings from mud is not a common element of Chiricahua mythology. Most informants cannot give any account of the creation of man" (Hoijer 1938:142).

8. Opler notes: "The position of Killer of Enemies in Chiricahua and Mescalero mythology is most interesting. For the Navaho, Western Apache, Lipan, and Jicarilla, Killer of Enemies is the principal culture hero and performs deeds and exploits comparable to those attributed to Child of the Water in this story. By the Chiricahua and Mescalero, however, Killer of Enemies is relegated to a subordinate position, an unenviable position, or is forgotten altogether. . . . In some versions he figures as an older but more timid brother of Child of the Water, again as a maternal uncle (brother of White Painted Woman) or as the step-father (husband of White Painted Woman) of Child of the Water. . . . Very often, as in the present version, Killer of Enemies is charged with cowardice [Opler here refers the reader to another text in the collection as means of clarification] . . . or is represented as the protector and benefactor of the white man [again Opler refers the reader to another text in the collection]. . . . Some Chiricahua informants have said that the term Killer of Enemies is synonymous with 'enemy' or 'white man' and cases have been noted where parents and grandparents will not allow children to utter the name of Killer of Enemies, giving the children the explanation that it is the name of the 'devil' or an 'evil one' [Opler gives another referral to an additional text in the collection]" (Hoijer 1938:141).

9. "The speaker here is Child of the Water" (Hoijer 1938:142).

10. As I noted earlier, for years the phone company refused to hook up any but the most accessible or necessary of locations on the reservation. Until the late 1980s, in order to call some parts of the reservation, it was still necessary to contact an "inbound operator" from Globe—a switchboard operator who

would manually connect the call. And it was not until the late 1990s, when the tribe purchased the local exchange and founded its own telecommunications company, that people generally began to have telephones in their houses.

11. The racial aspect of this process explains in part how the various ethnic groups of Globe, as discussed in chapter 1, could recast themselves as "white" in opposition to "Apaches." In his history of copper and labor activism in the Southwest, Mellinger writes of "Cornish and Irish immigrants, and the descendants of the Scotch, English, Welsh, Scotch-Irish, Dutch, and sometimes the Germans, Rhenish, Flemish, and Scandinavians" being redefined as "Americans" by their employers, in distinction to U.S.–born people of Mexican descent, who were lumped together with Mexican immigrants. Those defined as Americans held the best jobs at the mines. "Men whom the copper companies defined as Americans had a powerful inducement to accept the companies' definition" (1995:18–19).

12. "Łt'éégo ádishnii" means something along the lines of "I say it well," "I say it the right way," or "The way I say it is correct." The phrase "'Łt'éégo ádishnii' niigo" is another example of direct reported speech: "I say it correctly," s/he says.

13. Edmund was actually born in Claypool and moved to Old San Carlos as a young boy.

14. Some of the Chinese poetry carved into the walls of the Angel Island immigration center also refers to the shifting rules and categories of the American bureaucracy (see Lai, Lim, and Yung 1980).

15. Arizona effectively kept Indians from voting until 1948.

16. In speaking to one of my friends in Bylas about this past-life idea, she said, "Yeah, that sure lets them off the hook for this life, doesn't it?"

17. The existence of this "gap" and its productivity in the making of culture are long-standing aspects of materialist theoretical positions in the study of both power (Alonso 1988; Coronil and Skurski 1991; Corrigan and Sayer 1985; Hall 1981, 1982, 1986; Scott 1985; Tambiah 1989; Taussig 1987; Turton 1986) and poetics (Bakhtin 1981; Briggs and Bauman 1992; Friedrich 1986; K. Stewart 1996; S. Stewart 1991; Voloshinov 1973).

18. Mendoza-Denton (1996) has also commented on this phenomenon, writing of Chicana *cholas'* attraction to "oldies," in particular African American soul and doo-wop hits of the late 1950s and early 1960s.

19. This space of play and chiasmus will probably seem familiar to anyone who has paid attention to expressive culture in other Native American communities (see, e.g., Babcock 1978; Basso 1979; Lincoln 1993), but my focus on the communities of San Carlos made this book seem an improper forum for cross-community comparison. However, one musical example would be the "Hollywood Indian" drumbeat that powers the rhythm section in Keith Secola's song "Indian Cars," a musical celebration of the "rez ride"—hybridity paying tribute

to one of its own, in a sense. XIT's "Nothin Could Be Finer Than a Forty-Niner" goes even further: a rock song about the hybrid genre of forty-niner songs, at its conclusion a group of forty-niner singers act as the background vocalists, eventually taking over the song at the end.

20. It is important to distinguish this sense of connection to the past from a Western bourgeois notion of how expression puts one in mind of the past. Take, for example, the interest classical music lovers have with regard to the history of Western art music. The community engendered by Schubert's C minor symphony is not imagined in the same way. First of all, with the possible exception of those involved in the historical performance movement and their audiences, it is not clear that classical music listeners respond to performances by imagining what life was like "back then." The turn to the past is more likely framed as a discussion about "the test of time" that becomes part of the validation of Schubert's place in the canon. Furthermore, to the extent that the Schubert symphony prompts people to enter into a historical metadiscourse, they do it not to commune with a past society but to be puzzled by it—How could that past society have missed the beauty of Schubert? Part of the discourse about classical music that stands "the test of time" is a discussion about artists who, ahead of their times, are unappreciated in their own day and find an audience to appreciate them only years and sometimes centuries later. And it is clear that classical music lovers do not hear contemporary works and shed tears for the way people suffered in the sixteenth century.

References

Aarsleff, Hans. 1982. *From Locke to Saussure: Essays on the Study of Language and Intellectual History*. Minneapolis: University of Minnesota Press.

Adams, David Wallace. 1996. *Education for Extinction: American Indians and the Boarding School Experience, 1875–1928*. Lawrence: University Press of Kansas.

Almond, Gabriel A., Marvin Chodorow, and Roy Harvey Pearce, eds. 1977. *Progress and Its Discontents*. Berkeley: University of California Press.

Alonso, Ana Maria. 1988. "The Effects of Truth: Re-presentation of the Past and the Imagining of Community." *Journal of Historical Sociology* 1, no. 1: 33–57.

Anderson, Benedict. 1991. *Imagined Communities: Reflections on the Origin and Spread of Nationalism*. 2d ed. London: Verso.

Appadurai, Arjun. 1990. "Disjuncture and Difference in the Global Cultural Economy." *Public Culture* 2, no. 2: 1–24.

Armstrong, Robert Plant. 1971. *The Affecting Presence: An Essay in Humanistic Anthropology.* Urbana: University of Illinois Press.

Arteaga, Alfred, ed. 1994. *An Other Tongue: Nation and Ethnicity in the Linguistic Borderlands.* Durham, N.C.: Duke University Press.

Auer, Peter, ed. 1998. *Code-Switching in Conversation: Language, Interaction, and Identity.* London: Routledge.

Axelrod, Melissa. 2000. "The Semantics of Classification in Koyukon Athabaskan." In *The Athabaskan Languages: Perspectives on a Native American Language Family,* edited by Theodore B. Fernald and Paul R. Platero, 9–28. New York: Oxford University Press.

Babcock, Barbara, ed. 1978. *The Reversible World: Symbolic Inversion in Art and Society.* Ithaca: Cornell University Press.

Bakhtin, M. M. 1981. *The Dialogic Imagination: Four Essays.* Edited by Caryl Emerson and Michael Holquist. Austin: University of Texas Press.

———. 1984. *Problems of Dostoevsky's Poetics.* Edited and translated by Caryl Emerson. Minneapolis: University of Minnesota Press.

———. 1986. *Speech Genres and Other Late Essays.* Edited by Caryl Emerson and Michael Holquist. Translated by Vern McGee. Austin: University of Texas Press.

Barfield, Owen. 1973. *Poetic Diction: A Study in Meaning.* Middletown, Conn.: Wesleyan University Press.

Basso, Keith H. 1979. *Portraits of "The Whiteman": Linguistic Play and Cultural Symbols among the Western Apache.* New York: Cambridge University Press.

———. 1990. *Western Apache Language and Culture: Essays in Linguistic Anthropology.* Tucson: University of Arizona Press.

———. 1996. *Wisdom Sits in Places: Landscape and Language among the Western Apache.* Albuquerque: University of New Mexico Press.

Basso, Keith H., and Steven Feld, eds. 1997. *Senses of Place.* Albuquerque: University of New Mexico Press.

Baudrillard, Jean. 1990. *Fatal Strategies.* Translated by Philip Beitchman and W. G. J. Niesluchowski. Edited by Jim Fleming. London: Semiotexte/Pluto.

Bauman, Richard. 1972. "Differential Identity and the Social Base of Folklore." In *Toward New Perspectives in Folklore,* edited by Americo Paredes and Richard Bauman, 31–41. Austin: University of Texas Press.

———. 1977. *Verbal Art as Performance.* Prospect Heights: Waveland Press.

———. 1986. *Story, Performance, and Event: Contextual Studies of Oral Narrative.* New York: Cambridge University Press.

Bauman, Richard, and Charles Briggs. 1990. "Poetics and Performance as Critical Perspectives on Language and Social Life." *Annual Review of Anthropology* 19: 59–88.

Bauman, Richard, and Joel Sherzer, eds. 1974. *Explorations in the Ethnography of Speaking.* New York: Cambridge University Press.

Beckett, Jeremy. 1994a. "Aboriginal Histories, Aboriginal Myths: An Introduction." *Oceania* 65, no. 2: 97–115.

———. 1994b. "Walter Newton's History of the World—or Australia." *American Ethnologist* 20, no. 4: 675–96.

———. 2000. *Wherever I Go: Myles Lalor's "Oral History."* Melbourne: Melbourne University Press.

Benjamin, Walter. 1996. "On Language as Such and on the Language of Man." In *Selected Writings*, vol. 1, *1913–1926*, edited by Marcus Bullock and Michael W. Jennings, 62–74. Cambridge, Mass.: Harvard University Press.

Berger, Thomas. 1964. *Little Big Man*. New York: Dial Press.

Berkhofer, Robert F., Jr. 1978. *The White Man's Indian: Images of the American Indian from Columbus to the Present*. New York: Vintage.

Bernard, Shane K. 1996. *Swamp Pop: Cajun and Creole Rhythm and Blues*. Jackson: University Press of Mississippi.

Bernstein, Cynthia, Thomas Nunnally, and Robin Sabino, eds. 1997. *Language Variety in the South Revisited*. Tuscaloosa: University of Alabama Press.

Besnier, Niko. 1993. "Reported Speech and Affect on Nukulaelae Atoll." In *Responsibility and Evidence in Oral Discourse*, edited by Jane Hill and Judith Irvine, 161–81. New York: Cambridge University Press.

Bigando, Robert. 1990. *Globe, Arizona: The Life and Times of a Western Mining Town*. 2d ed. Globe: Mountain Spirit Press.

Blu, Karen. 1980. *The Lumbee Problem: The Making of an American Indian People*. Cambridge: Cambridge University Press.

Boas, Franz. [1911] 1991. Introduction to *Handbook of American Indian Languages*. Lincoln: University of Nebraska Press.

Boeder, Winfried. 2002. "Speech and Thought Representation in the Kartvelian (South Caucasian) Languages." In *Reported Discourse: A Meeting Ground for Different Linguistic Domains*, edited by Tom Güldemann and Manfred von Roncador, 3–48. Amsterdam: John Benjamins.

Booth, Stephen. 1998. *Precious Nonsense: The Gettysburg Address, Ben Jonson's Epitaphs on His Children, and Twelfth Night*. Berkeley: University of California Press.

Bourdieu, Pierre. 1984. *Distinction: A Social Critique of the Judgement of Taste*. Translated by Richard Nice. Cambridge, Mass.: Harvard University Press.

Braroe, Nils W. 1975. *Indian and White: Self-Image and Interaction in a Canadian Plains Community*. Stanford, Calif.: Stanford University Press.

Brenneis, Donald. 1986. "Shared Territory: Audience, Indirection, and Meaning." *Text* 6, no. 3: 339–47.

———. 1987. "Performing Passions: Aesthetics and Politics in an Occasionally Egalitarian Community." *American Ethnologist* 14, no. 2: 236–50.

Briggs, Charles L. 1992. "'Since I Am a Woman I Will Chastise My Relatives': Gender, Reported Speech, and the (Re)production of Social Relations in Warao Ritual Wailing." *American Ethnologist* 19, no. 2: 337–61.

————. 1993. "Personal Sentiments and Polyphonic Voices in Warao Women's Ritual Wailing: Music and Poetics in a Critical and Collective Discourse." *American Anthropologist* 95, no. 4: 929–57.

Briggs, Charles L., and Richard Bauman. 1992. "Genre, Intertextuality, and Social Power." *Journal of Linguistic Anthropology* 2, no. 2: 131–72.

Browner, Tara. 2002. *Heartbeat of the People: Music and Dance of the Northern Powwow.* Urbana: University of Illinois Press.

Bruccoli, Matthew J. 1977. *"The Last of the Novelists": F. Scott Fitzgerald and the Last Tycoon.* Carbondale: Southern Illinois University Press.

Buchanan, Donna A. 1996. "Dispelling the Mystery: The Commodification of Women and Musical Tradition in Le Mystère Des Voix Bulgares." *Balkanistica* 9: 193–210.

————. 1997. "Bulgaria's Magical Mystère Tour: Postmodernism, World Music Marketing, and Political Change in Eastern Europe." *Ethnomusicology* 41, no. 1: 131–57.

Buscombe, Edward, ed. 1988. *The BFI Companion to the Western.* New York: Atheneum.

Campisi, Jack. 1991. *The Mashpee Indians: Tribe on Trial.* Syracuse, N.Y.: Syracuse University Press.

Carroll, Michael Thomas. 2000. *Popular Modernity in America: Experience, Technology, Mythohistory.* Albany: State University of New York Press.

Chambers, Iain. 2000. "At the End of This Sentence a Sail Will Unfurl . . . Modernities, Musics, and the Journey of Identity." In *Without Guarantees: In Honor of Stuart Hall,* edited by Paul Gilroy, Lawrence Grossberg, and Angela McRobbie, 67–82. London: Verso.

Cheyfitz, Eric. 1997. *The Poetics of Imperialism: Translation and Colonization from the Tempest to Tarzan.* Philadelphia: University of Pennsylvania Press.

Clifford, James. 1988. "Identity in Mashpee." In *The Predicament of Culture: Twentieth-Century Ethnography, Literature, and Art,* 277–346. Cambridge, Mass.: Harvard University Press.

Coates, Jennifer. 1996. *Women Talk: Conversation Between Women Friends.* Oxford: Blackwell.

Comrie, Bernard. 1986. "Tense in Indirect Speech." *Folia Linguistica* 20: 265–96.

Coplan, David B. 1985. *In Township Tonight! South Africa's Black City Music and Theatre.* London: Longman.

Cornell, Stephen, and Marta Gil-Swedburg. 1995. "Sociohistorical Factors in Institutional Efficacy: Economic Development in Three American Indian Cases." *Economic Development and Cultural Change* 43, no. 2: 239–69.

Coronil, Fernando, and Julie Skurski. 1991. "Dismembering and Remembering the Nation: The Semantics of Political Violence in Venezuela." *Comparative Studies in Society and History* 33, no. 2: 288–337.

Corrigan, Philip, and Derek Sayer. 1985. *The Great Arch: English State Formation as Cultural Revolution.* Oxford: Basil Blackwell.

Coulmas, Florian, ed. 1986. *Direct and Indirect Speech*. New York: Mouton De Gruyter.

Craig, Vincent. 1981. *Boarding School Fish Stories: Live at Many Farms*. Independent recording.

Cruikshank, Julie. 1998. *The Social Life of Stories: Narrative and Knowledge in the Yukon Territory*. Omaha: University of Nebraska Press.

Culler, Jonathan, ed. 1988. *Puns: The Foundation of Letters*. New York: Basil Blackwell.

Darnell, Regna. 1990. *Edward Sapir: Linguist, Anthropologist, Humanist*. Berkeley: University of California Press.

———. 1991. "Ethnographic Genre and Poetic Voice." In *Anthropological Poetics*, edited by Ivan Brady, 267–82. Savage, Md.: Rowman and Littlefield.

Davies, Stephen. 1994. *Musical Meaning and Expression*. Ithaca, N.Y.: Cornell University Press.

Declerck, Renaat. 1991. *Tense in English: Its Structure and Use in Discourse*. London: Routledge.

Delabastita, Dirk, ed. 1997. *Trauductio: Essays on Punning and Translation*. Manchester: St. Jerome.

Diehl, Keila. 2002. *Echoes from Dharamsala: Music in the Life of a Tibetan Refugee Community*. Berkeley: University of California Press.

Dippie, Brian W. 1982. *The Vanishing American: White Attitudes and U.S. Indian Policy*. Lawrence: University Press of Kansas.

Downing, Thomas A. 1995. *Music and the Origins of Language: Theories from the French Enlightenment*. New York: Cambridge University Press.

Drinnon, Richard. 1980. *Facing West: The Metaphysics of Indian-Hating and Empire-Building*. Minneapolis: University of Minnesota Press.

Du Gay, Paul, Stuart Hall, Linda Janes, Hugh Mackay, and Keith Negus. 1997. *Doing Cultural Studies: The story of the Sony Walkman*. Thousand Oaks, Calif.: Sage.

Dullenty, Jim. 1983. "He Was a Stranger in Globe." *True West* (September): 13–14.

———. 1991. "Who Really Was William T. Phillips of Spokane—Outlaw or Impostor?" *Wola Journal* (fall-winter): 10.

———. 1993. "Did Regan Know Phillips *and* Cassidy? *Western Outlaw-Lawman History Association Journal* 1: 3.

———. 1995. "In Search of William T. Phillips." *Wola Journal* (winter–spring): 6.

Duranti, Alessandro. 1986. "The Audience as Co-author: An Introduction." *Text* 6, no. 3: 239–47.

———. 2003. "Language as Culture in U.S. Anthropology: Three Paradigms." *Current Anthropology* 44, no. 3: 323–47.

Eco, Umberto. 1986. *Semiotics and the Philosophy of Language*. Bloomington: Indiana University Press.

Eliade, Mircea. 1954. *The Myth of the Eternal Return*. New York: Pantheon.

Elkins, James. 1998. *On Pictures and the Words That Fail Them*. New York: Cambridge University Press.

———. 2003. "What Does Peirce's Sign System Have to Say to Art History?" *Culture, Theory, and Critique* 44, no. 1: 5–22.

Ellis, Clyde. 1996. *To Change Them Forever: Indian Education at the Rainy Mountain Boarding School, 1893–1920*. Norman: University of Oklahoma Press.

Ellis, John M. 1993. *Language, Thought, and Logic*. Evanston, Ill.: Northwestern University Press.

Empson, William. [1930] 1953. *Seven Types of Ambiguity*. 3d ed. New York: New Directions.

Erlmann, Veit. 1991. *African Stars: Studies in Black South African Performance*. Chicago: University of Chicago Press.

———. 1996. *Nightsong: Performance, Power, and Practice in South Africa*. Chicago: University of Chicago Press.

Errington, J. Joseph. 1998. *Shifting Languages: Interaction and Identity in Javanese Indonesia*. New York: Cambridge University Press.

Evans-Pritchard, E. E. 1960. *The Nuer: A Description of the Modes of Livelihood and Political Institutions of a Nilotic People*. Oxford: Clarendon Press.

Fabb, Nigel. 1997. *Linguistics and Literature: Language in the Verbal Arts of the World*. Oxford: Blackwell.

Farrer, Claire R. 1991. *Living Life's Circle: Mescalero Apache Cosmovision*. Albuquerque: University of New Mexico Press.

Feld, Steven. 1974. "Linguistic Models in Ethnomusicology." *Ethnomusicology* 18, no. 2: 197–217.

———. 1990a. *Sound and Sentiment, Birds, Weeping, Poetics, in Kaluli Expression*. Philadelphia: University of Pennsylvania Press.

———. 1990b. "Wept Thoughts: The Voices of Kaluli Memories." *Oral Tradition* 5, nos. 2–3: 241–66.

———. [1984] 1994a. "Communication, Music, and Speech about Music." Reprinted in *Music Grooves*, by Charles Keil and Steven Feld, 77–96. Chicago: University of Chicago Press.

———. [1988] 1994b. "Aesthetics as Iconicity of Style (Uptown Title); Or, (Downtown Title) 'Lift-up-over Sounding': Getting into the Kaluli Groove." Reprinted in *Music Grooves*, by Charles Keil and Steven Feld, 109–50. Chicago: University of Chicago Press.

Feld, Steven, and Aaron Fox. 1994. "Music and Language." *Annual Review of Anthropology* 23: 25–54.

Feld, Steven, Aaron Fox, Thomas Porcello, and David Samuels. 2004. "Vocal Anthropology." In *A Companion to Linguistic Anthropology*, edited by Alessandro Duranti, 321–46. New York: Blackwell.

Fernald, Theodore B., and Paul R. Platero, eds. 2000. *The Athabaskan Languages: Perspectives on a Native American Language Family*. New York: Oxford University Press.

Field, Margaret C. 2001. "Triadic Directives in Navajo Language Socialization." *Language in Society* 30: 249–63.

Fischer, Claude S. 1992. *America Calling: A Social History of the Telephone to 1940.* Berkeley: University of California Press.

Fiske, John. 1989. *Understanding Popular Culture.* Boston: Unwin Hyman.

Foster, Robert J. 1991. "Making National Cultures in the Global Ecumene." *Annual Review of Anthropology* 20: S.235–60.

Fowler, Loretta. 1987. *Shared Symbols, Contested Meanings: Gros Ventre Culture and History, 1778–1984.* Ithaca, N.Y.: Cornell University Press.

Frege, Gottlob. 1984. "On Sense and Meaning." In *Collected Papers on Mathematics, Logic, and Philosophy*, edited by Brian McGuinness, 157–81. Oxford: Basil Blackwell.

Fried, Morton. 1975. *The Notion of Tribe.* Menlo Park, Calif.: Cummings.

Friedrich, Paul. 1986. *The Language Parallax: Linguistic Relativism and Poetic Indeterminacy.* Austin: University of Texas Press.

———. 1991. "Polytropy." In *Beyond Metaphor: The Theory of Tropes in Anthropology*, edited by James W. Fernandez, 17–55. Stanford, Calif.: Stanford University Press.

Gadet, Francoise. 1989. *Saussure and Contemporary Culture.* Translated by Gregory Elliott. London: Hutchinson Radius.

Gates, Henry Louis, Jr. 1988. *The Signifying Monkey: A Theory of Afro-American Literary Criticism.* New York: Oxford University Press.

Goetzmann, William H. 1986. *The West of the Imagination.* New York: Norton.

Goffman, Erving. 1974. *Frame Analysis: An Essay on the Organization of Experience.* Cambridge, Mass.: Harvard University Press.

———. 1981. *Forms of Talk.* Philadelphia: University of Pennsylvania Press.

Goodwin, Grenville. 1942. *The Social Organization of the Western Apache.* Chicago: University of Chicago Press.

Graham, Laura. 1986. "Three Modes of Shavante Vocal Expression: Wailing, Collective Singing, and Political Oratory." In *Native South American Discourse*, edited by Joel Sherzer and Greg Urban, 83–118. Berlin: Mouton De Gruyter.

———. 1993. "A Public Sphere in Amazonia? The Depersonalized Collaborative Construction of Discourse in Xavante." *American Ethnologist* 20, no. 4: 717–42.

Gramsci, Antonio. 1971. *Selections from the Prison Notebooks.* Edited and translated by Quinton Hoare and Geoffrey Nowell Smith. New York: International.

Green, Jesse. 1990. *Cushing at Zuni: The Correspondence and Journals of Frank Hamilton Cushing, 1879–1884.* Albuquerque: University of New Mexico Press.

Greenlee, Douglas. 1973. *Peirce's Concept of Sign.* The Hague: Mouton De Gruyter.

Grice, P. 1989. *Essays in the Ways of Words.* Cambridge, Mass.: Harvard University Press.

Guenther, Edgar E. 1935. Untitled. *The Apache Scout* 13, no. 8: 421–22.

———. 1939. "A New Highway." *Apache Scout* 18, no. 8: 148–49.

Guess, Raymond. 1996. "Kultur, Bildung, Geist." *History and Theory* 35, no. 2: 151–65.

Güldemann, Tom, and Manfred von Roncador, eds. 2002. *Reported Discourse: A Meeting Ground for Different Linguistic Domains.* Amsterdam: John Benjamins.

Gupta, Akhil, and James Ferguson. 1992. "Beyond 'Culture': Space, Identity, and the Politics of Difference." *Cultural Anthropology* 7, no. 1: 6–23.

Habermas, Jürgen. 1979. *Communication and the Evolution of Society.* Boston: Beacon Press.

———. 1984. *Reason and the Rationalization of Society.* New York: Farrar, Strauss and Giroux.

Haley, James L. 1981. *Apaches, a History and Culture Portrait.* Garden City, N.Y.: Doubleday.

Hall, Stuart. 1981. "Notes on Deconstructing the Popular." In *People's History and Socialist Theory,* edited by Raphael Samuels, 277–40. London: Routledge and Kegan Paul.

———. 1982. "The Rediscovery of 'Ideology': Return of the Repressed in Media Studies." In *Culture, Society, and the Media,* edited by M. Gurevitch, 56–90. London: Methuen.

———. 1986. "Popular Culture and the State." In *Popular Culture and Social Relations,* edited by Tony Bennett, Colin Mercer, and Janet Woolacott, 22–49. Milton Keynes, United Kingdom: Open University Press.

———. 1990. "Cultural Identity and Diaspora." In *Identity: Community, Culture, Difference,* edited by Jonathan Rutherford, 222–37. London: Lawrence and Wishart.

Halliday, M. A. K. 1985. *An Introduction to Functional Grammar.* London: E. Arnold.

Halliday, M. A. K., and R. Hasan. 1976. *Cohesion in English.* London: Longmans.

Handler, Richard. 1983. "The Dainty and the Hungry Man: Literature and Anthropology in the Work of Edward Sapir." *History of Anthropology* 1: 208–31.

———. 1985. "On Dialogue and Destructive Analysis: Problems in Narrating Nationalism and Ethnicity." *Journal of Anthropological Research* 41, no. 2: 171–82.

———. 1986. "Vigorous Male and Aspiring Female: Poetry, Personality, and Culture in Edward Sapir and Ruth Benedict." *History of Anthropology* 4: 127–55.

———. 1989. "Anti Romantic Romanticism: Edward Sapir and the Critique of American Individualism." *Anthropological Quarterly* 62, no. 1: 1–13.

Handler, Richard, and Jocelyn Linnekin. 1984. "Tradition, Genuine or Spurious." *Journal of American Folklore* 97, no. 385: 273–90.

Hanks, William. 1987. "Discourse Genres in a Theory of Practice." *American Ethnologist* 14: 668–92.

————. 1996. *Language and Communicative Practices*. Boulder, Colo.: Westview Press.

————. 1999. "Indexicality." *Language Matters in Anthropology: A Lexicon for the Millenium*, special issue of *Journal of Linguistic Anthropology* 9, nos. 1–2: 124–26.

Hannerz, Ulf. 1987. "The World in Creolization." *Africa* 57, no. 4: 546–59.

Hanson, Allan. 1989. "The Making of the Maori: Culture Invention and Its Logic." *American Anthropologist* 91, no. 4: 890–903.

Harders, Gustav. 1953. *Yaalahn*. Translated by H. C. Nitz. Milwaukee: Northwestern Publishing House.

————. 1958. *Dohaschtida*. Translated by Alma Pingel Nitz. Milwaukee: Northwestern Publishing House.

Haring, Lee. 1992. "Imitation and Parody in West Indian Ocean Myths." *Journal of Folklore Research* 29, no. 3: 199–224.

Harpham, Geoffrey Galt. 2002. *Language Alone: The Critical Fetish of Modernity*. New York: Routledge.

Harris, Roy. 1980. *The Language-Makers*. Ithaca: Cornell University Press.

————. 1996. *Signs, Language, and Communication: Integrational and Segregational Approaches*. New York: Routledge.

Harris, Roy, and Talbot J. Taylor. 1997. *Landmarks in Linguistic Thought I: The Western Tradition from Socrates to Saussure*. London: Routledge.

Hassler, Gerda. 2002. "Evidentiality and Reported Speech in Romance Languages." In *Reported Discourse: A Meeting Ground for Different Linguistic Domains*, edited by Tom Güldemann and Manfred von Roncador, 143–72. Amsterdam: Johns Benjamins.

Hill, Jane. 1990. "Weeping as a Meta-signal in a Mexicano Woman's Narrative." In *Native Latin American Culture Through Their Discourse*, edited by Ellen Basso, 29–49. Bloomington, Ind.: Folklore Institute Press.

————. 1995. "The Voices of Don Gabriel: Responsibility and Self in a Modern Mexicano Narrative." In *The Dialogic Emergence of Culture*, edited by Dennis Tedlock and Bruce Mannheim, 97–147. Urbana: University of Illinois Press.

Hill, Jane, and Judith Irvine, eds. 1993. *Responsibility and Evidence in Oral Discourse*. New York: Cambridge University Press.

Hill, Tom, and Richard W. Hill Sr. 1994. *Creation's Journey: Native American Identity and Belief*. Washington, D.C.: Smithsonian Institution Press.

Hinton, Leanne. 1980. "Vocables in Havasupai Song." In *Southwestern Indian Ritual Drama*, edited by Charlotte J. Frisbie, 275–305. Albuquerque: University of New Mexico Press.

————. 1984. *Havasupai Songs: A Linguistic Perspective*. Philadelphia: John Benjamins.

————. 1994. *Flutes of Fire: Essays on California Indian Languages*. Berkeley, Calif.: Heyday.

Hoijer, Harry. 1938. *Chiricahua and Mescalero Apache Texts*. Chicago: University of Chicago Press.

Holler, Clyde. 1995. *Black Elk's Religion: The Sun Dance and Lakota Catholicism*. Syracuse, N.Y.: Syracuse University Press.

Honor the Past . . . Mold the Future. 1976. Globe, Ariz.: Gila Centennials Celebration Committee/Arizona Silver Belt.

Howard, Kathleen L., and Diana F. Pardue. 1996. *Inventing the Southwest: The Fred Harvey Company and Native American Art*. Flagstaff, Ariz.: Northland.

Hymes, Dell. 1964. "Introduction: Toward Ethnographies of Communication." *American Anthropologist*, part 2, 66, no. 6: 1–33.

———. 1975a. "Breakthrough into Performance." In *Folklore: Performance and Communication*, edited by Dan Ben-Amos and Kenneth S. Golsttein, 11–74. The Hague: Mouton De Gruyter.

———. 1975b. "Folklore's Nature and the Sun's Myth." *Journal of American Folklore* 88, no. 350: 345–69.

———. 1981. *In Vain I Tried to Tell You: Essays in Native American Poetics*. Philadelphia: University of Pennsylvania Press.

———. 1985. "Language, Memory, and Selective Performance: Cultee's 'Salmon's Myth' as Twice Told to Boas." *Journal of American Folklore* 98: 391–434.

Hymes, Dell, and John Fought. 1981. *American Structuralism*. The Hague: Mouton De Gruyter.

Irvine, Judith. 1996. "Shadow Conversations: The Indeterminacy of Participant Roles." In *Natural Histories of Discourse*, edited by Michael Silverstein and Greg Urban, 131–59. Chicago: University of Chicago Press.

Jakobson, Roman. 1960. "Closing Statement: Linguistics and Poetics." In *Style in Language*, edited by T. A. Sebeok, 350–77. Cambridge, Mass.: MIT Press.

Jaspers, Karl. 1966. *Spinoza*. Vol. 2 of *The Great Philosophers*. Edited by Hannah Arendt. Translated by Ralph Manheim. New York: Harcourt Brace Jovanovich.

Jensen, Joli. 1998. *The Nashville Sound: Authenticity, Commercialization, and Country Music*. Nashville: Vanderbilt University Press.

Jung, Dagmar. 2000. "Word Order in Apache Narratives." In *The Athabaskan Languages: Perspectives on a Native American Language Family*, edited by Theodore B. Fernald and Paul R. Platero, 92–100. New York: Oxford University Press.

Kapchan, Deborah. 1996. *Gender on the Market: Moroccan Women and the Revoicing of Tradition*. Philadelphia: University of Pennsylvania Press.

Keil, Charles, and Steven Feld. 1994. *Music Grooves*. Chicago: University of Chicago Press.

Kondo, Dorinne K. 1990. *Crafting Selves: Power, Gender, and Discourses of Identity in a Japanese Workplace*. Chicago: University of Chicago Press.

Kooij, Jan G. 1971. *Ambiguity in Natural Language: An Investigation of Certain Problems in Its Linguistic Description*. Amsterdam: North-Holland.

Kreilkamp, Ivan. 1997. "A Voice Without a Body: The Phonographic Logic of *Heart of Darkness.*" *Victorian Studies* 40, no. 2: 211–44.

Kristeva, Julia. 1980. "Word, Dialogue, and Novel." In *Desire in Language: A Semiotic Approach to Literature and Art*, edited by Leon S. Roudiez, translated by Thomas Gora, Alice Jardine, and Leon S. Roudiez, 64–91. New York: Columbia University Press.

Kulick, Don. 1998. *Travesti: Sex, Gender, and Culture among Brazilian Transgendered Prostitutes.* Chicago: University of Chicago Press.

Kyle, Thomas G. 1991. "Did Butch Cassidy Die in Spokane? Phillips Photo Fails." *Old West* (fall): 17–19.

Labov, William. 1991. "The Three Dialects of English." In *New Ways of Analyzing Sound Change*, edited by P. Eckert, 1–44. New York: Academic Press.

Lai, Him Mark, Genny Lim, and Judy Yung. 1980. *Island: Poetry and History of Chinese Immigration on Angel Island, 1910–1940.* Seattle: University of Washington Press.

Lamphere, Louise. 1977. *To Run after Them: Cultural and Social Bases of Cooperation in a Navajo Community.* Tucson: University of Arizona Press.

Landsman, Gail H. 1988. *Sovereignty and Symbol: Indian White Conflict at Ganienkeh.* Albuquerque: University of New Mexico Press.

Larson, Mildred L. 1998. *Meaning-Based Translation: A Guide to Cross-Language Equivalence.* Lanham, Md.: University Press of America.

Lassiter, Luke E. 1998. *The Power of Kiowa Song: A Collaborative Ethnography.* Tucson: University of Arizona Press.

Lassiter, Luke E., Clyde Ellis, and Ralph Kotay. 2002. *The Jesus Road: Kiowas, Christianity, and Indian Hymns.* Lincoln: University of Nebraska Press.

Leap, William. 1993. *American Indian English.* Salt Lake City: University of Utah Press.

Lecercle, Jean-Jacques. 1985. *Philosophy Through the Looking Glass: Language, Nonsense, Desire.* La Salle, Ill.: Open Court.

———. 1994. *Philosophy of Nonsense: The Intuitions of Victorian Nonsense Literature.* London: Routledge.

Lee, Benjamin. 1997. *Talking Heads: Language, Metalanguage, and the Semiotics of Subjectivity.* Durham, N.C.: Duke University Press.

Lévi-Strauss, Claude. 1966. *The Savage Mind.* Chicago: University of Chicago Press.

Li, Charles N. 1986. "Direct Speech and Indirect Speech: A Functional Study." In *Direct and Indirect Speech*, edited by Florian Coulmas, 29–45. Berlin: Mouton De Gruyter.

Lincoln, Kenneth. 1993. *Indi'n Humor: Bicultural Play in Native America.* New York: Oxford University Press.

Lipsitz, George. 1994. *Dangerous Crossroads: Popular Music, Postmodernism, and the Poetics of Place.* London: Verso.

Lockwood, Frank C. 1938. *The Apache Indians*. New York: Macmillan.

Lomawaima, K. Tsianina. 1994. *They Called It Prairie Light: The Story of Chilocco Indian School*. Lincoln: University of Nebraska Press.

Long Lance, Chief Buffalo Child (Sylvester Long). [1928] 1995. *Long Lance*. Jackson: Banner Books/University Press of Mississippi.

Lucy, John A., ed. 1993. *Reflexive Language: Reported Speech and Metapragmatics*. New York: Cambridge University Press.

Mahon, Maureen. 2000. "Black Like This: Race, Generation, and Rock in the Post–Civil Rights Era." *American Ethnologist* 27, no. 2: 283–311.

Manuel, Peter. 1993. *Cassette Culture: Popular Music and Technology in North India*. Chicago: University of Chicago Press.

McAllester, David P. 1960. "The Role of Music in Western Apache Culture." In *Men and Cultures: Selected Papers of the Fifth International Congress of Anthropological and Ethnological Sciences*, edited by Anthony F. C. Wallace, 468–72. Philadelphia: University of Pennsylvania Press.

McDonough, Joyce. 2000. "On a Bipartite Model of the Athabaskan Verb." In *The Athabaskan Languages: Perspectives on a Native American Language Family*, edited by Theodore B. Fernald and Paul R. Platero, 139–66. New York: Oxford University Press.

M'Closkey, Kathy. 2002. *Swept under the Rug: A Hidden History of Navajo Weaving*. Albuquerque: University of New Mexico Press.

McPherson, Robert S. 1992. "Naalyéhé Bá Hooghan—'House of Merchandise': The Navajo Trading Post as an Institution of Cultural Change, 1900–1930." *American Indian Culture and Research Journal* 16, no. 1: 23–43.

Meadows, Anne, and Daniel Buck. 1997. "The Last Days of Butch and Sundance." *Wild West* 9 (February): 36–42.

Meintjes, Louise. 1990. "Paul Simon's *Graceland*, South Africa, and the Mediation of Musical Meaning." *Ethnomusicology* 34, no. 1: 37–74.

———. 2003. *Sound of Africa! Making Music Zulu in a South African Recording Studio*. Durham, N.C.: Duke University Press.

Mellinger, Philip J. 1995. *Race and Labor in Western Copper: The Fight for Equality, 1896–1918*. Tucson: University of Arizona Press.

Mendoza-Denton, Norma. 1996. "'Muy Macha': Gender and Ideology in Gang-Girls' Discourse about Makeup." *Ethnos* 61, nos. 1–2: 47–63.

Merleau-Ponty, Maurice. 1964. *Signs*. Translated by Richard C. McCleary. Evanston, Ill.: Northwestern University Press.

Middlebrook, Diane Wood. 1998. *Suits Me: The Double Life of Billy Tipton*. New York: Houghton Mifflin.

Monson, Ingrid. 1996. *Saying Something: Jazz Improvization and Interaction*. Chicago: University of Chicago Press.

Morris, Michael. 1991. *Madam Valentino: The Many Lives of Natacha Rambova*. New York: Abbeville Press.

Moyer, Melissa G. 1998. "Bilingual Conversation Strategies in Gibraltar." In

Code-Switching in Conversation: Language, Interaction, and Identity, edited by Peter Auer, 215–36. London: Routledge.

Namias, June. 1993. *White Captives: Gender and Ethnicity on the American Frontier.* Chapel Hill: University of North Carolina Press.

Nevins, Eleanor. Forthcoming. "Learning to Listen: Confronting Divergent Meanings of 'Language Loss' in the Contemporary White Mountain Apache Speech Community." *Journal of Linguistic Anthopology.*

Newfield, Madelaine, and Barbara A. Lafford. 1991. "The Origin of the Specious: The Creation and Interpretation of Puns." *Language and Style* 24, no. 1: 77–89.

Nichols, Johanna, and Anthony Woodbury, eds. 1985. *Grammar Inside and Outside the Clause.* London: Cambridge University Press.

Nitz, H. C. 1939. "Pastor Harders." *The Apache Scout* 17, no. 11: 82–85.

Oatman, Lorenzo D., and Olive A. Oatman. 1994. *The Captivity of the Oatman Girls among the Apache and Mohave Indians.* Mineola, N.Y.: Dover.

Ochs, Elinor. 1992. "Indexing Gender." In *Rethinking Context: Language as an Interactive Phenomenon*, edited by Alessandro Duranti and Charles Goodwin, 335–58. Cambridge: Cambridge University Press.

Ogle, Ralph H. 1970. *Federal Control of the Western Apaches, 1848–1886.* Albuquerque: University of New Mexico Press.

"152 Years of Service." 1956. *Arizona Days and Ways*, March 18, 26–27.

Paredes, Americo, and Richard Bauman, eds. 1972. *Toward New Perspectives in Folklore.* Austin: University of Texas Press.

Pearce, Roy Harvey. [1953] 1988. *Savagism and Civilization: A Study of the Indian and the American Mind.* Baltimore: Johns Hopkins University Press.

Peckham, Morse. 1965. *Man's Rage for Chaos: Biology, Behavior, and the Arts.* New York: Schocken.

Perry, Richard J. 1993. *Apache Reservation: Indigenous Peoples and the American State.* Austin: University of Texas Press.

Phillipson, Robert. 1992. *Linguistic Imperialism.* New York: Oxford University Press.

Porcello, Thomas. 2002. "Music Mediated as Live in Austin: Sound, Technology, and Recording Practice." *City and Society* 14, no. 1: 69–86.

Pujolar, Joan. 2001. *Gender, Heteroglossia, and Power: A Sociolinguistic Study of Youth Culture.* Berlin: Mouton De Gruyter.

Rafael, Vicente. 1988. *Contracting Colonialism: Translation and Christian Conversion in Tagalog Society under Early Spanish Rule.* Ithaca, N.Y.: Cornell University Press.

Rampton, Ben. 1995. *Crossing: Language and Ethnicity among Adolescents.* London: Longman.

———. 1998. "Language Crossing and the Redefinition of Reality." In *Code-Switching in Conversation: Language, Interaction, and Identity*, edited by Peter Auer, 290–320. London: Routledge.

Redfern, Walter. 1984. *Puns*. New York: Basil Blackwell.

Reuse, Willem J. de. 2002. "Tonto Apache and Its Position within Apachean." *Proceedings of the 2002 Athabaskan Languages Conference, Fairbanks, Alaska, June 16–18*, special issue of *Alaskan Native Language Center Working Papers*, no. 2: 78–90.

Reynolds, Jno. 1896. Letter from the Acting Secretary of the Interior. House of Representatives, 54th Cong., 1st sess., document no. 320.

Rhodes, Richard. 1994. "Aural Images." In *Sound Symbolism*, edited by L. Hinton, J. Nichols, and J. J. Ohala, 276–92. New York: Cambridge University Press.

Rhodes, Willard. 1963. "North American Indian Music in Transition: A Study of Songs with English Words as an Index of Acculturation." *Journal of the International Folk Music Council* 15: 9–14.

———. [1952] 1967. "Acculturation in North American Indian Music." In *International Congress of Americanists, Proceedings of the 19th Congress*, edited by Sol Tax, 127–32. New York: Cooper Square.

Roberts, David. 1993. *Once They Moved Like the Wind: Cochise, Geronimo, and the Apache Wars*. New York: Simon and Schuster.

Rosaldo, Renato. 1989. "Imperialist Nostalgia." In *Culture and Truth: The Remaking of Social Analysis*, 68–89. Boston: Beacon Press.

Rosowski, Susan J. 1999. *Birthing a Nation: Gender, Creativity, and the West in American Literature*. Lincoln: University of Nebraska Press.

Rumsey, Alan. 1990. "Wording, Meaning, and Linguistic Ideology." *American Anthropologist* 92: 346–61.

Rushforth, Scott. 1991. "Uses of Bearlake and Mescalero (Athapaskan) Classificatory Verbs." *International Journal of American Linguistics* 57, no. 2: 251–66.

St. Clair, Robert, and William Leap, eds. 1982. *Language Renewal among American Indian Tribes: Issues, Problems, and Prospects*. Washington, D.C.: National Clearinghouse for Bilingual Education.

Samuels, David. 1999. "The Whole and the Sum of the Parts, Or, How Cookie and the Cupcakes Told the Story of Apache History in San Carlos." *Journal of American Folklore* 112, no. 445: 464–74.

———. 2001. "Indeterminacy and History in Britton Goode's Western Apache Placenames: Ambiguous Identity on the San Carlos Apache Reservation." *American Ethnologist* 28, no. 2: 277–302.

Sapir, Edward. 1921. *Language: An Introduction to the Study of Speech*. New York: Harcourt, Brace, and Jovanovich.

———. 1932. "Two Navajo Puns." *Language* 8: 217–19.

———. [1924] 1949. "Culture, Genuine and Spurious." Reprinted in *Culture, Language, and Personality: Selected Essays*, edited by David G. Mandelbaum, 308–31. Berkeley: University of California Press.

Sawyer, R. Keith. 2001. *Creating Conversations: Improvisation in Everyday Discourse*. Cresskill: Hampton Press.

Schafer, R. Murray. 1977. *The Tuning of the World*. New York: Knopf.

Schieffelin, E. L. 1985. "Performance and the Cultural Construction of Reality." *American Ethnologist* 12, no. 4: 707–24.

Schiffrin, Deborah. 1993. " 'Speaking for Another' in Sociolinguistic Interviews: Alignments, Identities, and Frames." In *Framing in Discourse*, edited by Deborah Tannen, 231–63. New York: Oxford University Press.

Schroeder, Albert H. 1974. *A Study of the Apache Indians*. New York: Garland.

Scott, James C. 1985. *Weapons of the Weak: Everyday Forms of Peasant Resistance*. New Haven, Conn.: Yale University Press.

Seremetakis, C. Nadia. 1991. *The Last Word: Women, Death, and Divination in Inner Mani*. Chicago: University of Chicago Press.

Seuren, Pieter A. M. 1998. *Western Linguistics: An Historical Introduction*. Oxford: Basil Blackwell.

Sherzer, Joel. 1983. *Kuna Ways of Speaking: An Ethnographic Perspective*. Austin: University of Texas Press.

———. 1987. "A Discourse-Centered Approach to Language and Culture." *American Anthropologist* 89: 295–309.

———. 1990. *Verbal Art in San Blas: Kuna Culture Through Its Discourse*. New York: Cambridge University Press.

Sherzer, Joel, and Greg Urban, eds. 1986. *Native South American Discourse*. New York: Mouton De Gruyter.

Sherzer, Joel, and Anthony C. Woodbury, eds. 1987. *Native American Discourse: Poetics and Rhetoric*. Cambridge: Cambridge University Press.

Silverstein, Michael. 1976. "Shifters, Verbal Categories, and Cultural Description." In *Meaning in Anthropology*, edited by Keith Basso and Henry Selby, 11–55. Albuquerque: Sar Press.

———. 1985. "The Culture of Language in Chinookan Narrative Texts: Or, On Saying That . . . in Chinook." In *Grammar Inside and Outside the Clause*, edited by Johanna Nichols and Anthony Woodbury, 132–71. London: Cambridge University Press.

———. 1986. "The Diachrony of Sapir's Linguistic Description; Or, Sapir's 'Cosmographical' Linguistics." In *New Perspectives on Edward Sapir in Language, Culture, and Personality*, edited by W. Cowan, M. K. Foster, and E. F. K. Koerner, 67–106. Amsterdam: John Benjamins.

Silverstein, Michael, and Greg Urban, eds. 1996. *Natural Histories of Discourse*. Chicago: University of Chicago Press.

Singer, Milton B. 1972. *When a Great Tradition Modernizes: An Anthropological Approach to Indian Civilization*. New York: Praeger.

Slobin, Mark. 1992. "Micromusics of the West: A Comparative Approach." *Ethnomusicology* 36, no. 1: 1–87.

Slotkin, Richard. 1973. *Regeneration Through Violence: The Mythology of the American Frontier, 1600–1860*. Middletown, Conn.: Wesleyan University Press.

————. 1985. *The Fatal Environment: The Myth of the Frontier in the Age of Indus-trialization, 1800–1890.* New York: Atheneum.

————. 1992. *Gunfighter Nation: The Myth of the Frontier in Twentieth-Century America.* New York: Atheneum.

Smith, Donald B. 1982. *Long Lance: The True Story of an Impostor.* Lincoln: University of Nebraska Press.

Sommer, Doris. 1999. *Proceed with Caution, When Engaged by Minority Writing in the Americas.* Cambridge, Mass.: Harvard University Press.

Spack, Ruth. 2002. *America's Second Tongue: American Indian Education and the Ownership of English, 1860–1900.* Lincoln: University of Nebraska Press.

Standing Bear, Luther. [1928] 1975. *My People the Sioux.* Lincoln: University of Nebraska Press.

Stanford Research Institute. 1955. *The San Carlos Apache Indian Reservation: A Resources Development Study.* Menlo Park, Calif.: Stanford Research Institute.

Starobinski, Jean. 1979. *Words upon Words: The Anagrams of Ferdinand de Saussure.* Translated by Olivia Emmett. New Haven, Conn.: Yale University Press.

Stewart, Kathleen. 1996. *A Space on the Side of the Road: Cultural Poetics in an "Other" America.* Princeton, N.J.: Princeton University Press.

Stewart, Susan. 1991. *Crimes of Writing: Problems in the Containment of Representation.* New York: Oxford University Press.

————. 2002. *Poetry and the Fate of the Senses.* Chicago: University of Chicago Press.

Stokes, Martin, ed. 1994. *Ethnicity, Identity, and Music: The Musical Construction of Place.* Oxford: Berg.

Strong, Pauline Turner. 1999. *Captive Selves, Captivating Others: The Politics and Poetics of Colonial American Captivity Narratives.* Boulder, Colo.: Westview Press.

Strong, Pauline Turner, and Barrik Van Winkle. 1996. "'Indian Blood': Reflections on the Reckoning and Refiguring of Native North American Identity." *Cultural Anthropology* 11, no. 4: 547–77.

Tambiah, Stanley. 1989. "Ethnic Conflict in the World Today." *American Ethnologist* 16, no. 2: 335–49.

Tannen, Deborah. 1987. "Repetition in Conversation: Towards a Poetics of Talk." *Language* 63, no. 3: 574–605.

————. 1989. *Talking Voices: Repetition, Dialogue, and Imagery in Conversational Discourse.* New York: Cambridge University Press.

Taussig, Michael T. 1987. *Shamanism, Colonialism, and the Wild Man: A Study in Terror and Healing.* Chicago: University of Chicago Press.

Tedlock, Dennis. 1972. *Finding the Center: Narrative Poetry of the Zuni Indians.* New York: Dial Press.

————. 1983. *The Spoken Word and the Work of Interpretation.* Philadelphia: University of Pennsylvania Press.

Terrell, John Upton. 1972. *Apache Chronicle*. New York: World.

Théberge, Paul. 1997. *Any Sound You Can Imagine: Making Music/Consuming Technology*. Middletown, Conn.: Wesleyan University Press.

Thrapp, Dan L. 1967. *The Conquest of Apacheria*. Norman: University of Oklahoma Press.

Toelken, Barre, and Tacheeni Scott. 1981. "Poetic Retranslation and the 'Pretty Languages' of Yellowman." In *Traditional Literatures of the American Indians*, edited by Karl Kroeber, 65–116. New York: Vantage Press.

Tolbert, Elizabeth. 1994. "The Voice of Lament: Female Vocality and Performative Efficacy in the Finnish-Karelian Itkuvirsi." In *Embodied Voices: Representing Female Vocality in Western Culture*, edited by L. Dunn and N. Jones, 179–94. Cambridge: Cambridge University Press.

Treitler, Leo. 1997. "Language and the Interpretation of Music." In *Music and Meaning*, edited by Jenefer Robinson, 32–56. Ithaca, N.Y.: Cornell University Press.

Truettner, William H., ed. 1991. *The West as America: Reinterpreting Images of the Frontier, 1820–1920*. Washington, D.C.: Smithsonian Institution Press.

Turton, Andrew. 1986. "Patrolling the Middle-Ground: Methodological Perspectives on 'Everyday Peasant Resistance.'" *Journal of Peasant Studies* 13, no. 2: 36–48.

Uplegger, Francis. 1935. "Constitution of the San Carlos Apache Indian Tribe." *The Apache Scout* 13, no. 1: 6.

Urban, Greg. 1987. "The 'I' of Discourse." Working Papers and Proceedings of the Center for Psychosocial Studies, no. 10. Chicago: Center for Psychosocial Studies.

———. 1988. "Ritual Wailing in Amerindian Brazil." *American Anthropologist* 90: 385–400.

———. 1991. *A Discourse-Centered Approach to Culture: Native South American Myths and Rituals*. Austin: University of Texas Press.

———. 1996. "Entextualization, Replication, and Power." In *Natural Histories of Discourse*, edited by Michael Silverstein and Greg Urban, 21–44. Chicago: University of Chicago Press.

———. 2001. *Metaculture: How Culture Moves Through the World*. Minneapolis: University of Minnesota Press.

Van Leeuwen, Theo. 1999. *Speech, Music, Sound*. New York: St. Martin's Press.

Vennum, Thomas. 1992. *The Changing Soundscape of Indian Country*. Festival of American Folklore (catalog). Washington, D.C.: Smithsonian Institution.

Vizenor, Gerald. 1999. *Manifest Manners: Narratives on Postindian Survivance*. Omaha, Neb.: Bison.

Volk, Robert W. 1988. "Barter, Blankets, and Bracelets: The Role of the Trader in the Navajo Textile and Silverwork Industries, 1868–1930." *American Indian Culture and Research Journal* 12, no. 4: 39–63.

Voloshinov, V. N. 1973. *Marxism and the Philosophy of Language*. Translated by Ladislav Matejka and I. R. Titunik. New York: Seminar Press.

Wagner, Roy. 1986. *Symbols That Stand for Themselves*. Chicago: University of Chicago Press.

Waterman, Christopher Alan. 1990. *Jùjú: A Social History and Ethnography of an African Popular Music*. Chicago: University of Chicago Press.

Weigle, Marta, and Barbara A. Babcock, eds. 1996. *The Great Southwest of the Fred Harvey Company and the Santa Fe Railway*. Phoenix: Heard Museum.

Weiner, Joan. 1999. *Frege*. New York: Oxford University Press.

Whitburn, Joel. 1987. *The Billboard Book of Top 40 Hits*. 3d ed. New York: Billboard.

White, Richard. 1983. *The Roots of Dependency: Subsistence, Environment, and Social Change among the Choctaws, Pawnees, and Navajos*. Lincoln: University of Nebraska Press.

Whorf, Benjamin Lee. 1956. *Language, Thought, and Reality: Selected Writings*. Edited by John B. Carroll. Cambridge, Mass.: Technology Press of MIT.

Wilce, James. 2002. "Genres of Memory and the Memory of Genres: 'Forgetting' Lament in Bangladesh." *Comparative Studies in Society and History* 44, no. 1: 159–85.

Willett, Thomas. 1988. "A Cross-Linguistic Survey of the Grammaticalization of Evidentiality." *Studies in Language* 12, no. 1: 51–97.

Williams, Raymond. 1977. *Marxism and Literature*. Oxford: Oxford University Press.

Witherspoon, Gary. 1977. *Language and Art in the Navajo Universe*. Ann Arbor: University of Michigan Press.

Wolfram, Walt, and Natalie Schilling-Estes. 1998. *American English: Dialects and Variation*. Malden: Blackwell.

Woodbury, Anthony C. 1985. "The Functions of Rhetorical Structure: A Study of Central Alaskan Yupik Eskimo Discourse." *Language in Society* 14: 153–90.

———. 1987. "Meaningful Phonological Processes: A Consideration of Central Alaskan Yupik Eskimo Prosody." *Language* 63, no. 4: 685–740.

———. 1993. "A Defense of the Proposition 'When a Language Dies, a Culture Dies.'" *Texas Linguistic Forum* 33: 102–30.

———. 1998. "Documenting Rhetorical, Aesthetic, and Expressive Loss in Language Shift." In *Endangered Languages*, edited by Lenore A. Grenoble and Lindsay J. Whaley, 234–58. New York: Cambridge University Press.

Worcester, Donald E. 1979. *The Apaches: Eagles of the Southwest*. Norman: University of Oklahoma Press.

Young, Robert W., and William Morgan Sr. 1992. *Analytical Lexicon of Navajo*. Albuquerque: University of New Mexico Press.

Zuckerkandl, Victor. 1956. *Sound and Symbol: Music and the External World*. Princeton, N.J.: Princeton University Press.

Credits and Permissions

Index

About the Author

David W. Samuels was born in Brooklyn, New York. He earned his Ph.D. at the University of Texas at Austin and is currently associate professor of Anthropology at the University of Massachusetts at Amherst.

For more information about Boe Titla and his music, please visit http://www.boetitla.com.